Mādhyamika and Yogācāra

SUNY Series in Buddhist Studies
Kenneth K. Inada, Editor

Mādhyamika and Yogācāra

A Study of Mahāyāna Philosophies

Collected Papers of G. M. Nagao

Edited, Collated, and Translated
by
L. S. Kawamura
in Collaboration with
G. M. Nagao

State University of New York Press

Published by
State University of New York Press, Albany

Printed in the United States of America

For information, address State University of New York Press, State University Plaza, Albany, N.Y., 12246

Library of Congress Cataloging-in-Publication Data

Nagao, Gadjin, 1907–
Mādhyamika and Yogācāra.

(SUNY series in Buddhist studies)
Rev. translation of: Chūkan to yuishiki /
G. M. Nagao.
Includes index.
1. Mādhyamika (Buddhism) 2. Yogācāra
(Buddhism) I. Kawamura, Leslie S. II. Title.
BQ7462.N3313 1991 181′.043 89-4278
ISBN 0-7914-0186-3
ISBN 0-7914-0187-1 (pbk.)
10 9 8 7 6 5 4 3 2 1

To
Toshiko
wife of Professor G. M. Nagao

Contents

Acknowledgments

When Professor G. M. Nagao's book *Chūkan to Yuishiki* appeared in 1978, the thought of translating the text into English seemed a good idea. Michele Martin, the then editor of the State University of New York Press (SUNY), approached me in the Spring of 1984. She asked whether I would be willing to undertake the task of editing and translating Professor Nagao's work. It was known to me, of course, that without Professor Nagao's approval such an undertaking would be impossible. Professor Nagao was approached and permission to commence the work of translation was obtained. The many occasions that gave me the opportunity to work closely with Professor Nagao clearly impressed upon me his arduous intent to perfect his work. It was, therefore, obvious that without his collaboration, the task of translation could not be accomplished. Fortunately, in the early part of 1985, the Social Sciences and Humanities Research Council of Canada (SSHRCC), Division of International Programs, granted me the Grant for Visiting Foreign Scholars and the University of Calgary research grants office responded positively to my application for travel to and joint research in Kyoto, Japan. The project deadline was targeted for the end of 1986, but as is evident from the publication date, the book is three years late.

The papers comprising Professor Nagao's book seemed straight forward enough. However, when the work of translating the papers began, many difficulties began to emerge. As we worked on the materials, it became evident that the newly translated papers for this volume had to be more than a simple translation. For example, the article "Logic of Convertibility" has been thoroughly reworked into the present form. The article "Buddhist Ontology," has been amended with comments that do not appear in the original Japanese text.

This work could not have reached its conclusion without the support of many people and the aid of various financial grants. I would like to thank Ms. V. Lake for typing the early draft of the manuscript. Permissions to reproduce articles are acknowledged with thanks to the following; G. M. Nagao; John Keenan; Institut Orientaliste, Université Catholique de Louvain; the University of Hawaii Press; Hozokan, Kyoto; Iwanami Shoten, Tokyo; Risōsha, Tokyo; editors of *Jimbvn*, Kyoto; editors of the *Eastern Buddhist*, Kyoto; and editors of *Journal of International Association of Buddhist Studies*, Bloomington, Indiana. For detailed information regarding the essays, please refer to "Appendix—Sources of Essays."

The financial aid given by SSHRCC and the University of Calgary is hereby acknowledged in deepest appreciation.

LESLIE S. KAWAMURA

Author's Preface

According to I-ching's report from India (A.D. 691), Mahāyāna Buddhism was divided into two schools, the Mādhyamika and the Yogācāra. The Madhyamaka (middle) philosophy, founded on Nāgārjuna's (A.D. second to third century) philosophy of absolute negation (*śūnyatā*), is really a remarkable and probably one of the greatest achievements in the history of Buddhism. It is my contention, however, that it was brought to completion by the Yogācāra, especially through the works of Asaṅga and Vasubandhu (A.D. fifth century). They complemented the *śūnyatā* philosophy with various positive theories such as the theory of consciousness-only, the three-nature theory, the theory of Buddha's body, and so on. The Yogācāra theories are said to be "positive" because by accepting the negative idea of *śūnyatā* as a whole, the Yogācāra established the positive affirmative aspect of *śūnyatā* (*abhāvasya bhāvaḥ*). During the later centuries, Indian Buddhism (as well as Tibetan Buddhism) focused its attention on only the Mādhyamika school as the main stream of Buddhism while it overlooked the Yogācāra as an independent school. In spite of that, ideas and terminologies created by the Yogācāra school continued to influence the development of Buddhism in India (also in Tibet) for a long time, and it can be said further that, without the effort and achievement of the Yogācāra, which complemented the Mādhyamika, Mahāyāna Buddhism would not have reached its present perfection.

My study has been focussed on these two schools for more than forty years. Some of the papers found in this collection were written very early in my career and consequently show certain inadequacies; however, as they contain important aspects of the development of my thought, they have been included here. The paper "Logic of Convertibility," for instance, explains the fundamental idea of "convertibility" that has been and still continues to be of great concern to me. The papers written later presuppose, more or less, this idea of convertibility and it is foundational to the ideas discussed there.

In more recent years, I discuss the two notions of "ascent and descent," and show how they apply to our interpretation of the various teachings found in Buddhism. The two notions have appeared, although only vaguely, in earlier papers from time to time, but it is only in recent days that it became evident that the two notions of ascent and descent were convenient ways for gaining a proper understanding of the various doctrinal meanings. In fact, it can be said that Mahāyāna thought is characterized as such when they are present, even though they are opposites and indicate contrary directions. That is, when these two notions are found within a certain Buddhist system, the criterion for discerning whether that system is Mahāyāna or not is established.

The Mādhyamika, more than the Yogācāra, seems to have been studied rather widely by western scholars. This is probably owing to the fact that *śūnyatā* is in sharp contrast to Western ontological ideas. However, Yogācāra thought is no less important than Mādhyamika ideas, and consequently, the readers will find that more attention has been paid to the Yogācāra in this book.

My study has been philological rather than philosophical. By the term philological, I do not mean to imply a purely linguistic investigation, but rather, I refer to the process of interpreting a text as faithful as possible. This means that I have interpreted the purport of those treatises through the ācārya's own words, and thus, I avoided the danger of being too speculative.

Many *kalyāṇamitras* helped me in preparing these papers by either translating them or improving my English. My hearty thanks go to, among others, the Reverend Yoshiaki Fujitani, Professor Norman Waddell, Professor John Keenan, Ms. Michele Martin, et al. My special gratitude is due to Professor Leslie S. Kawamura for his tireless effort in translating and editing this book. If these papers are helpful to my readers concerning their understanding of Buddhism, I shall be satisfied.

GADJIN M. NAGAO

Abbreviations

*(asterisk) in front of a title of a text indicates that the Sanskrit title has been reconstructed.

AS = *Abhidharmasamuccaya.* V. V. Gokhale, ''Fragments from the *AS* of Asaṃga.''

JA = *Journal of the Bombay Branch, Royal Asiatic Society.* 1947.

IsMeo = Instituto Italiano per il Medio ed Estremo Oriente.

La théory = S. Ruegg, *La Théorie du Tathāgatagarbha et du Gotra* (Paris: École française d'extrême-orient, 1969).

Le traité = Étienne Lamotte, *Le Traité de la Grande Vertu de Sagesse de Nāgārjuna* (*Mahāprjñāpāramitāśāstra*) (Louvain: Insitute Orientaliste, 1949. Reprint 1966). Three volumes.

MMK = Louis de la Vallée Poussin, *Mūlamadhyamakakārikās* (*mādhyamikasūtras*) *de Nāgārjuna, avec la Prasannapadā Commentaire de Candrakīrti,* Bibliotheca Buddhica IV (St.-Pétersbourg: 1903–13)

MSA = Sylvain Lévi, ed., *Mahāyāna-sūtrālaṃkāra* (Paris: Librairie Honoré Champion, Éditeur, 1907 and 1911. Kyoto: Rinsen Book Co., 1983 reprint). Two volumes.

MSg = Étienne Lamotte, *La somme du grand vehicule d'Asaṅga* (*Mahāyāna-saṃgraha*). (Louvain: Bureaux du Muséon, 1962).

MV = G. M. Nagao, ed., *Madhyāntavibhāga-bhāṣya* (Tokyo: Suzuki Research Foundation, 1964).

Mvy = R. Sakaki, ed., *Mahāvyutpatti* (Kyoto: 1917. Reprint Tokyo: Suzuki Research Foundation, 1962).

MW = Sir M. Monier-Williams. *Sanskrit-English Dictionary.*

Nirvāṇa = T. F. Stcherbatsky, *The Conception of Buddhist Nirvāṇa* (Leningrad: The Academy of Sciences of the USSR, 1927).

RGV = E. H. Johnston, ed., *Ratnagotravibhāga Mahāyānottaratantra-śāstra* (Patna: Bihar Research Society, 1950).

Siddhi = Louis de la Vallée Poussin, *Vijñaptimātratāsiddhi—La Siddhi de Hiuan-Tsang*. 2 vols. Paris: Librairie Orientaliste Paul Geuthner, 1928.

Sthiramati = Yamaguchi, S. ed., *Sthiramati: Madhyāntavibhāgaṭīkā* (Nagoya: Librairie Hajinkaku, 1934; reprinted Tokyo, 1966).

ŚrBh = *Śrāvakabhūmi*. Alex Wayman, *Analysis of the Śrāvaka-bhūmi Manuscript* (Berkeley: University of California Press, 1961). See also, Karunesha Shukla ed., *Śrāvaka-bhūmi of Ācārya Asaṅga* (Patna: K. P. Jayaswal Research Institute, 1973).

T or *Taishō* = Takakusu, J. and Watanabe, K. eds. *Taishō Shinshū Diazōkyō* (Tokyo: Taisho Issai-kyo Kanko Kai, 1905–12).

Triṃśikā = *Triṃśikāvijñaptibhāṣya*. Sylvain Lévi ed., *Vijñaptimātratā-siddhi*: Deux traités de Vasubandhu, Viṃśatikā et Triṃśikā (Paris: 1925).

Trisvabhāva = Susumu Yamaguchi, "Trisvabhāvanirdeśa of Vasubandhu, Skt. text and Japanese translation with annotation." *Journal of Religious Studies*, new series No. 8, 1931, pp. 121–130, 186–207. Reprinted in *Yamaguchi Susumu Bukkyōgaku Bunshū* (Tokyo: Shunjūsha, 1972). Louis de la Vallée Poussin, "Le petit traité de Vasubandhu-Nāgārjuna sur les trois natures," *Mélanges chinois et bouddhiques*, 2e vol., 1932–33, pp. 147, 161.

TTP = *Tibetan Tripitaka* Peking Edition (Tokyo-Kyoto: Suzuki Research Foundation, 1962).

Yaśomitra = Unrai Wogihara ed. *Sphuṭārthā Abhidharmakośavyākhyā—The Work of Yaśomitra*. Two volumes. (Tokyo: 1936 first edition. Reprint, Tokyo: Sankibo Buddhist Book Store, 1971; Shunjūsha, 1972).

Introduction

Professor Gadjin M. Nagao has devoted his life study to the investigation of the development of Mādhyamika and Yogācāra Buddhism. The articles presented in this volume have one thing in common. Each one is a step towards establishing the relational nature between Mādhyamika and Yogācāra. That is, according to Professor Nagao, the two traditions are not separate and independent but each augment the other. The Mādhyamika thought of *śūnyatā* was extended by the Yogācāra by their system of the Three-nature theory that depended upon a logic of convertibility. Throughout these papers, Professor Nagao's constant effort is to synthesize the two systems.

Professor Nagao's contributions to the academic world are many, but what becomes evident in the papers presented here is his original thought on the logic of convertibility. This manner of thinking, which results from understanding the Three-nature theory of Yogācāra Buddhism, is soteriologically the only method by which one can argue for a "systematic development" in Mahāyāna thought in India. But in what way or manner did Professor Nagao reach such an insight? The best presentation of his thoughts on this matter is found in his own "Introduction" to his book *Chūkan to Yuishiki* (Mādhyamika and Yogācāra). Therefore, I shall give an interpretation of the book's contents.

Professor Nagao begins his introduction by reflecting on his papers written during the last forty years. He humbly states that it is difficult to reach the inner alcove of Mādhyamika and Yogācāra thought. He feels somewhat pretentious in giving his book the title *Mādhyamika and Yogācāra* for that reason, but in spite of the fact that he may not have the full capacity to argue for the synthesis between Mādhyamika and Yogācāra, he still attempts to complete the task.

While he was a student, Professor Nagao was attracted to the study of the text, *The Awakening of Faith in Mahāyāna*. However, when he tried to make that study his thesis topic, he quickly realized that such a study would require competence in the elements of the Vijñānavāda school. In haste, he began to read Sthiramati's Sanskrit text, *Triṃśikā;* this was his first introduction to Vijñānavāda thought. This led to the realization that one would have to go back to Nāgārjuna's Madhyamaka system. This was natural and logical. Professor Nagao's claim is that he has wandered in and out of the two schools, and he thinks that he will probably continue to do so until he dies. Therefore he gives the title *Chūkan to Yuishiki* (Mādhyamika and Yogācāra) to his book.

In order to pursue his inquiry deeper into these schools of thought Professor Nagao knew that a knowledge of Classical Chinese alone was insufficient. He knew that he would have to go back to the Sanskrit language; also he saw the need to consult the Tibetan canon. Thus, he began his study of the *Mahāyāna-saṃgraha* in 1939 and brought it to a successful completion by publishing volume one of the work in 1982 and volume two in 1987. These two volumes will certainly become the definitive study of Asaṅga's text in the years to come. However, in the interval, from 1939, Nagao's interest was directed to a study of Lamaism in Mongolia, which ultimately led him to the study of Tibetan Buddhism. Out of these studies, he was able to acquire considerable knowledge regarding Madhyamaka philosophy. He did not anticipate much with regard to Yogācāra. He then turned to a study of the *Madhyāntavibhāga*. As a graduate student, he joined the publication workshop of Sthiramati's *Madhyāntavibhāga-ṭīkā,* an old manuscript that was deciphered and edited by Professor S. Yamaguchi. Thus, he not only had the chance to study the *Madhyāntavibhāga* extensively but he also had the opportunity to compile the index to the text, which was appended to the edition. He devoted himself for several years to the study of the *Mahāyāna-sūtrālaṃkāra.* He then began his research on Asaṅga's *Mahāyāna-saṃgraha* and on Tsong-kha-pa's *Lam-rim-chen-mo* simultaneously in 1939. The latter study resulted in a Japanese translation and analysis of the "Vipaśyana" chapter of the *Lam-rim-chen-mo* in 1954, and as mentioned above, his former study resulted in a two-volume publication of Asaṅga's work. His study of the *Mahāyāna-sūtrālaṃkāra* finally crystalized with the compilation of the *Index to the Mahāyāna-sūtrālaṃkāra,* part one, Sanskrit-Tibetan-Chinese in 1958 and part two, Tibetan-Sanskrit and Chinese-Sanskrit in 1961. He began work on deciphering and editing for the first time an old Sanskrit manuscript of Vasubandhu's *Madhyāntavibhāga-bhāṣya* brought back from Tibet by the Reverend Rahula Sankrityāyana, which was stored in the K. P. Jayaswal Research Institute in Patna, India. He completed and published his edition of the text in 1964.

When watching the moves of the players in a game of chess, it is easy to observe that the players match strength with each other at every move. Even though one of the players may seem to have an edge on the other, when a play takes place, the locus of power seems to shift. For Professor Nagao, his study of the Mādhyamika and Yogācāra schools gave him the same challenges. When he devoted himself to Madhyamaka studies, he was touched by the vast scenery of the world of Enlightenment. When he absorbed himself in the texts of the Yogācāra (i.e., Vijñānavādins), the same scenery became manifest from a different perspective. One of Professor Nagao's mentors was the late Professor S. Yamaguchi (1895–1976) who published his great work *Bukkyō ni okeru U to Mu no Tairon* (The Controversy Between Existence and Non-existence in Buddhism). Upon reading this book, Professor Nagao was agonized by the question of "existence" and "non-existence." Which was the correct view—the "non-existence" stand of the Mādhyamika or the "existence" stand of the Yogācāra? On what do they take their stand? How was it possible to synthesize the tactful and polished logic of the two schools that pressed on relentlessly. He felt that there should be a limit to incapacitation. It seemed reasonable even from a historical perspective that the Yogācāra developed and was systematized by succeeding and taking a stand on the Mādhyamika philosophy of *śūnyatā* (emptiness). If it is possible to synthesize "existence" and "non-existence," then would it not follow that such a synthesis must have been already present in its evolution and growth? However, in spite of that, there does not seem to be an end to the conflict between existence and non-existence; this held just as true for Bhāvaviveka as it did for Dharmapāla, and Candrakīrti. On the other hand, however, if there were no controversy, might that not have been the degeneration of Buddhism? In short, it seemed to Professor Nagao that the rivalry between the thoroughness of the middle path, direct perception, and religiosity of the Mādhyamika and the systematization of the cognition theory, intellect, and praxis of the Yogācāra was not only suggestive of but also disclosed the paradoxical nature of man that follows him into eternity.

In rereading some of his old manuscripts, Professor Nagao found himself feeling great pains of anxiety, especially with regard to those papers he had written prior to World War II. The realization that his thinking had not changed much since times of old and that the same thoughts occurred repeatedly in his papers made him feel that little progress had been made. Still, he reexamined his old papers, improved on their style, updated the language, modified them slightly, and collected them into his book. As inadequate as that process might have seemed, he chose to include those papers in his book because they contained the theories that were to become the basis for his later thoughts.

The reexamination disclosed further that his discussions on Mādhyamika was referenced by Yogācāra (Vijñānavāda) theories. In other words, he was unable to view the Mādhyamika school with the genuineness with which Candrakīrti and Bhāvaviveka did. Looking positively at this, he understood it as his attempt to synthesize the two systems, but he also understood that this could be a point of criticism by pure Madhyamaka scholars. Almost unawares, he began to see the *Mahāyāna-sūtrālaṃkāra,* a text attributed to Asaṅga, as a rare and towering religious and academic document seldom found in this world. For Professor Nagao, this text, unlike Vasubandhu's which demonstrated well-developed systematic theories, seemed to ooze with the flavor of concrete religious experiences. In spite of its shortcoming (it was not totally systematic), it demonstrated expressions of penetrating wisdom. If, indeed, the author of this book was Asaṅga, he would have to be one who towered high above others and one in whom practice and wisdom were in accord. Needless to say, Asaṅga made complete use of Nāgārjuna's thoughts on *śūnyatā* even though he may not have accepted it in its entirety. The text examines the Bodhisattva career, addresses questions about Buddha-body and Buddha-wisdom, deliberates on the issue of one-vehicle *versus* three-vehicles, and even gives glimpses of the Tathāgatagarbha theory that later emerged. It was no wonder that Professor Nagao's interpretation of the Mādhyamika was through Vijñānavāda eyes.

In the present collection, the article "The Silence of the Buddha and Its Madhyamic Interpretation" relates particularly to the Mādhyamika. The article "The Logic of Convertibility" examines the fundamentals of the Yogācāra (Vijñānavāda) through an understanding of the term *parāvṛtti* (conversion or turn about); papers written later are considered in the light of this logic of convertibility. "What Remains in *Śūnyatā*" argues for *śūnyatā* on the basis of Yogācāra (Vijñānavāda) tenets regarding it and therefore it is different from that of the Mādhyamika. It probably raises many questions among bona fide Madhyamaka scholars, and to that degree it is probable that something still "remains." The article "On the theory of Buddha-Body (Buddha-kāya)" resulted from a lecture given by Professor Nagao on the occasion of his retirement from Kyoto University.

These articles brought to Professor Nagao's attention that the same old issues—that is, convertibility of the three natures; the "ascent" from a world of convention and language to a world of higher principles and peace and "descent" its opposite; the revival of the conventional; and the identity between "descent" and "ascent" with *āśraya-parāvṛtti* (turn about of one's basis) as their mediator—kept storming his mind.

The outcome of the work is presented here as the sixteen articles making up the present volume. It should be pointed out, however, that many of them have appeared previously in various journals and books. Seven articles, "The Bodhisattva Returns to this World," "Usage and Meanings of Pariṇāmanā," "Tranquil Flow of Mind: An Interpretation of Upekṣā,"

"Buddhist Ontology," "From Mādhyamika to Yogācāra, An Analysis of MMK, XXIV.18 and MV, I.1–2," "Ascent and Descent: Two-Directional Activity in Buddhist Thought," and "Yogācāra—A Reappraisal" do not appear in *Chūkan to Yuishiki* (Mādhyamika and Yogācāra). Some of these were written after the book appeared and some were newly translated for this volume. Many of Professor Nagao's articles have appeared in various books and journals and many of them are now out of print; therefore, they have been edited and compiled here together with the newly translated and edited papers. The paper, "Yogācāra—A Reappraisal," has been included in this volume not only because it functions, in a sense, as a comprehensive concluding chapter for the present volume, but also as it recapitulates and reveals the ideas presented by Professor Nagao in his various essays in a very succinct and clear manner. Consequently, rather than write a concluding chapter to this volume, this last essay has been included to serve that purpose.

Chapter 1

Buddhist Subjectivity

Subjectivity—in the sense in which the term is used in existential philosophy—presents us with an important religious problem. How should the problem of subjectivity be treated specifically in a Buddhist context? It is this question that I would like to consider in this paper.

It would seem reasonable that something called ''Buddhist subjectivity'' is understood within a Buddhist context. However, it must be asked whether, in the total perspective of Buddhism, or in view of the inner relations within Buddhism as a whole, the idea of subjectivity has not been too readily affirmed. The basis for this query lies in the fact that the main tenet of Buddhism is after all ''non-self'' (*anātman*).

The idea of Buddhist subjectivity can be found, for example, in the so-called anthropology of Tsung-mi developed in *On the Original Man.* In this book, Tsung-mi discusses the moral nature of man from the viewpoint of Hua-yen school in reference to Confucianism; he comes to the conclusion that the true source of human nature is in the ''True Mind'' or Enlightenment. In contrast, in the Jōdo doctrine, the idea of human nature is centered around a ''common man'' or a most degenerate ''Sinful Man'' who acquires the self-consciousness. It is, indeed, the common man who is the ''Real Guest'' of Buddha's salvation. Through anthropological studies alone, these introspective conceptions that express the religio-existential awareness of self could not have been reached. Further, Lin-chi's ''True Man residing nowhere'' is to be regarded as an expression of human existence, because the ''True Man'' is a human being insofar as he is called the true man; but, because he has realized Buddhahood or Enlightenment, he is Buddha. For Lin-chi the ''True Man'' is a ''human being'' and a ''Buddha being'' simultaneously; therefore, the subjectivity of the True Man is not only ''human subjectivity'' but it is also ''Buddha's subjectivity.'' Thus, the problem of Buddhist subjectivity must involve an investigation into the nature of Buddhahood as well as an examination of human nature. Although such terms as bodhisattva, transformed body (*nirmāṇa-kāya*), ''True Man'', and so forth refer to "existence as human beings" within Buddhism, they are none other than a way of expressing the manifestation or the incarnation of Buddhahood.

Notwithstanding the fact that those expressions stand for a "subject," the doctrine of non-self (*anātman*) is fundamental and fixed in Buddhism; consequently, if Buddhism is to speak about an "existential subject," it cannot do so if the subject, be it in the sense of "Original Man" or "True Man," is placed within a doctrinal context of a "self." Thus Buddhism must establish religious subjectivity (i.e., an existential subject) while denying the self totally. Here lies a specifically Buddhist problem, a problem that cannot be approached in the manner of Western existentialism. If the doctrine of non-self is treated from merely its theoretical, logical aspect, without religious concerns, the result will be a mere denial of the self in which religious subjectivity tends to get lost. On the other hand, mere existentialism (i.e., existential philosophy that follows the Western thought, though religious) would deviate from Buddhistic thinking.

In addressing this problem, this short paper will allude to an instance of a Buddhist way of thinking that is based on a Sanskrit text belonging to the Vijñānavāda school.

To state the conclusion in advance, it will be argued that, in Buddhism, the "existential subject" originates interdependently, and that "dependent origination" (*pratītya-samutpāda*) is the ground or basis on which final deliverance takes place. Non-self or the denial of self is expressed by Mādhyamika teachers with the term "voidness" (śūnyatā), which implies "non-substantiveness because of dependent origination." When this idea of "dependent origination" is applied to the question of subjectivity, existence—that is religious subjectivity—is comprehended as something "dependently originating" and not as a substance or *ātman* (self). In Buddhism, therefore, the term existence is used in a different sense, and consequently is distinct in connotation from that in Western philosophy.

It goes without saying that 'ātman' was such an important concept in Indian philosophy that in its philosophical literature of old, many elaborate discussions on ātman are to be found; thus, it can be safely asserted that the awareness of self was provoked in the Indian minds from the very ancient times.[1] It must be noted, however, that the awareness of self of the ancient Indians can hardly be identified with the so-called self-consciousness considered by modern Western thinkers. The term "*ātman*" did not imply merely an individual human existence (*jīvātman*), but it implied, even stronger, the Universal Soul (*paramātman, brahmātman*). A distinguishing characteristic of Indian thought may be found here; however, it cannot be denied that the problem of an existential subject is liable to be neglected therein. The reason is that the existential subject must be purely individual, historical and temporal, and not universal and permanent. Existence is opposite to essence. The existential subject must be, by nature, anti-universal and anti-metaphysical.

It was the Buddha's doctrine of "non-self" that laid the foundation for subjectivity within Buddhism, because the theory of a Universal Soul that prevailed before the Buddha's time left no room for establishing a real, actual, individual existence due to the fact that the "self" was dissolved in the Universal. Even though the *ātman*-theory demonstrated a height in human thought, it did not have the depth of absolute subjectivity implied in the "True Man" or of existential self-consciousness implied in the "Sinful Man."

As is generally known, the self is revived in Mahāyāna literature through the expression "great self" (*māhātmya*), a term which undoubtedly had affinity to the Universal Soul of *ātman*-theory. The real awakening or the attainment of Buddhahood is explained as the annihilation of the "mean self" and the realization of "great self." However, the Mahāyāna conception of 'great self,' which once was initiated through the thought of non-self, should be distinguished from that of *brahmātman*.

There have been groping endeavors to search for an existential subject—negating the self some times, and establishing the great self at other times. Lin-chi's "True Man," for example, though having affinity with the Universal in one sense, is not a Universal that stands aloof from the world. It does not engage merely in intellectual contemplation, but it is ever active in this world, undergoing transmigration from one state to another, for it is not a substantive self. Transmigration in this world is possible only on the basis of a non-self theory. It is in this sense that one can speak about the Buddha's doctrine of non-self as the foundation for an existential subject. The "Sinful Man," who is enslaved by carnal desires also, may gain religious subjectivity only through the absolute denial of the self.

By replacing the secludedness of arhat by the bodhisattva ideal and by emphasizing the Buddhist practices of a layman instead of those of a monk, Mahāyāna Buddhism sought to establish the idea of Buddhist subjectivity, which was not so well-developed until then. In contrast to the Hīnayānic arhatship that aims at ascending and thus reaching sainthood, the Bodhisattvas and Buddhist laymen in the Mahāyāna aim at moving out and descending to the common or human level.[2]

It was in Vijñānavāda thought, more than in the Mādhyamika, that the problem of subjectivity was discussed most distinctly. Being constructed on the foundation of the *ālayavijñāna* (store-consciousness) theory, the philosophical system of the Vijñāna-vāda is deeply tinged with idealistic or spiritualistic notions regarding the view on an individual. The ideas of *manas* (mind or self-hood) or *ādāna* (seizing, appropriating) presented in this school are similar to the "I" or "ego" of Western thinkers, but the Vijñānavāda came to these ideas through a more practice oriented method; thus, this school is duly known by its other name, "Yogācāra" (Yoga practice).

The Yogācāra school's consideration on the problem of subjectivity was developed by elucidating such concepts as 'great self,' 'Buddha-body' (*Buddha-kāya*) and so forth. In the *Trisvabhāvanirdeśa* (Treatise On Three Natures),[3] a treatise of this school, there is expressed the idea of "appearer" (*khyātṛ*), which is none other than a "religiously oriented subject" at the turning point of going from defilement to enlightenment, from transmigrating existence to the great self of the Buddha.

Along with such terms as *ātman,* great self, and so forth which are related to the absolute or universal subject, we have in Sanskrit such words as "doer" (*kartṛ*), "goer" (*gantṛ*), and so forth that refer to a relative, phenomenal, daily subject. These words are formed by adding "tṛ" to the verb root, and such words are called "agent nouns" in grammar. The notions of a "doer" and so forth along with those of "doing" (*karman, kriyā*) and of the "instrument of doing" (*kāraṇa*) and so forth were utterly rejected by Nāgārjuna. Their non-substantiveness was demonstrated through his sharp dialectics, but Vasubandhu, on the contrary, used these agent nouns positively.

The second and third verses from Vasubandhu's *Trisvabhāvanirdeśa* (Treatise on Three Natures) mentioned above, reads as follows:

> That which appears (*yat khyāti*) is of the other-dependent (*paratantra*),
> And how it appears (*yathā khyāti*) is of the imaginary (*kalpita*),
> Because the former originates in dependence on conditions,
> And because the latter exists as imagination.
> The state where the "appearer" (*khyātṛ*) is devoid of "appearance"
> (*yathā khyānam*),
> Is to be comprehended as the consummated, because of its immutability.[4]

That which is of the other-dependent nature (*paratantra-svabhāva*) is herein explained as "that which appears" or is called the "appearer." That which is of the imagined nature (*parikalpita-svabhāva*) is explained as the state of "how it appears" or the "appearance"—that is, the result of the appearer's act of appearing. And when the former is absolutely devoid of the latter, the consummated nature (*pariniṣpanna-svabhāva*) is realized.

Close attention should be paid to the conception of the 'appearer,' which is foundational in the three-nature theory. As pointed out by Dr. S. Yamaguchi, the verb *khyā* means "to be known" (pass.) or "to make known" (caus.). Further, "to know" is a function of *vijñapti* (knowing), a term which, in the compound "vijñapti-mātra" (knowing only), shows the fundamental tenet of the Vijñānavāda. Thus, the appearer, that is the agent noun *khyātṛ,* stands for the agent or the subject in the act of knowing. And since, according to the Vijñānavāda, all kinds of acts are represented by knowing, the appearer is regarded as the subject of all kinds of acts. In these verses, this appearer, the subject of every act, is defined as the "other-dependent nature;" this is to say that it exists only in the manner of "dependent origination," and not as an independently existent substance to which the act of appearing is attributed. Thus, it might be said rather, that the world crystallizes itself as an appearer and that human acts are none other than the function of this appearer.

According to the three-nature theory, the world turns around with the other-dependent nature (*paratantra*) as the axis or mediator. The other-dependent nature is the ground or the basis upon which the imaginary nature (*parikalpita*) or *saṃsāra* turns about and the consummated nature (*pariniṣpanna*) or *nirvāṇa* appears. And this ground itself is the appearer, a subjective existence.[5] The "-er" (*-tṛ*), which was totally denied in the Mādhyamika treatise, was thus revived in the Vijñānavāda treatise as a "subject," an assumption without which there would be no possibilities for an existence wherein a "turning around" from defilement to *nirvāṇa* could take place.

If the above discussion be accepted, it could be said further that the subjectivity of the appearer or the "transactor of linguistic conventions" (*vyavahārtṛ*) is the foundation on which the so-called religious existence or religious subjectivity stands. Both "appearing" and "transactional linguistic conventions" are aspects of "knowing"—that is, an act of the "knower" that is of the other-dependent nature. On the one hand, this knower produces a continuous ego-consciousness through the mediation of *manas* (self-hood) and on the other, attains Buddhahood through the "turn around" from knowing to wisdom. It is a matter of course that in Buddhism defilements based upon ego-consciousness are to be removed. The aim of this removal, however, is to elucidate, as Nāgārjuna had done, the dependent nature of the "doer," "goer" and so forth all of which are wrongly assumed to have independent and absolute existence. The subject that is freed from ego-consciousness and is of the other-dependent nature can attain the perfect enlightenment. As such, the appearer is distinguished from the consummated nature. The appearer is not the universal but is the individual and at the same time, it is distinguished from the imaginary nature, because the former is the knower (*paratantra*) itself, while the latter presupposes the dichotomized realities of a subject and an object. Although distinguished from the extremes of both the imagined and the consummated natures, the appearer functions as the mediator between the two and as such includes both in itself. So far as it is captured by self-love (*ātma-sneha*) and self-attachment, the appearer must undergo transmigration and is accountable for it, because what is of the other-dependent nature is, after all, phenomenal (*saṃskṛta*) and must never be confused with what is of the consummated nature. But, when through the awakening to Buddhahood, the appearer becomes aware of the fact of being phenomenal, this is to be called the "other-dependent existence" originating in the light of the consummated.

Nāgārjuna denied *essentia,* so to say, but he did not elucidate *existentia* fully. It was the adherents of the Vijñāna-vāda who clarified the position of religous subjectivity and opened the way for existential thinking. In this paper, an instance of this was noted in the conception of the appearer, which is both individual and subjective, and which is the mediator for the "turning around" that enables one to go from the infected status of *saṃsāra* to the absolute purity of *nirvāṇa*.

Chapter 2

An Interpretation of the Term "Saṃvṛti" (Convention) in Buddhism

The theory of the so-called Twofold Truth of *paramārtha* (absolute) and *saṃvṛti* (convention) is one of the most important features of the Mādhyamika philosophy and at the same time, probably, of the whole of Mahāyāna Buddhism. Generally, *saṃvṛti* refers to being conventional, mundane, profane, worldly, and is contrasted with *paramārtha,* which means being super-worldly, super-mundane, absolute. I have already discussed these ideas elsewhere[1] together with the main tenets of Buddhism and concepts such as *pratītyasamutpāda* (dependent origination), *śūnyatā* (voidness), and *tathatā* (suchness). I wish here, however, to discuss again the concept of 'saṃvṛti,' extracting from the above mentioned article with a few revisions.

I

The word saṃvṛti corresponds to the Pāli *saṃmuti,* the root of which is √*man.*[2] *Saṃmuti* has the meanings of "consent," "permission" on the one hand, and "choice," "selection" on the other.[3] *Saṃ-* √*man* means "to consider (together)" or "to give consent to the same or common idea" as Dr. Unrai Bunshu Wogihara suggests,[4] and hence, "convention," "general (popular) acceptance," "common sense," and so forth[5] the Chinese equivalent of this word, expresses appropriately these meanings, 俗 *su* meaning "common," "ordinary," "vulgar," in contrast with 雅 *ya* which means "elegant," "noble," "refined." But ever since Pāli saṃmuti was rendered into the Sanskrit form saṃvṛti and many Mahāyāna authorities began to work out new ideas with this word, the meaning as well as the root seems to have undergone a gradual change. The development of the idea of 'saṃvṛti' will be discussed, tracing the various interpretations as they have appeared in Candrakīrti, Sthiramati, I-ching 義浄 and Tz'u-ên 慈恩.

Most Sanskrit texts of Buddhist sūtras and śāstras use the form saṃvṛti for "convention," but the form saṃvṛtti with the same meaning is encountered in Sthiramati's *Madhyānta-vibhāga-ṭīkā.*[6] This slight difference of *-vṛti* and *-vṛtti* may very well be assumed not to indicate a genuine difference of word, but to be merely a copyist's error or his individual style.[7] But both *saṃ-* √*vṛ* and *saṃ-* √*vṛt* do have "conventional" as their primary sense, and from the evidence that will appear in the following pages, I believe it is quite possible to argue the point that the early philosophers used both roots, namely, *saṃ-* √*vṛ* and *saṃ-* √*vṛt,* selecting one term or the other to circumscribe the precise meaning intended.

From the root √*vṛ, saṃvṛti* means first of all "covering," "concealing," "dissimulation," "obstruction," and so forth. However, there is another root √*vṛ* that means "to choose," and in this connection its nominal form *saṃvara* means "election" and "choice," the same meanings found in the Pāli saṃmuti. From the other root √*vṛt,* two of the earliest meanings of *saṃvartate* are "to turn or go towards," "to encounter," and then later, "to come into being," "to be produced," "to be," and "to exist." These meanings suggest an affinity between *saṃvṛtti* and *pravṛtti* (coming forth), *utpāda* (origination, production). But at the same time, it is noted that *saṃvṛtti* is "often [a] wrong reading for *saṃvṛti.*"[8]

"To cover" from *saṃ-* √*vṛ* and "to exist" or "to come forth" from *saṃ-* √ *vṛt* are evidently unrelated meanings. In Buddhist writings, however, both meanings and probable roots seem to have been employed.

First, in Candrakīrti's *Prasannapadā,* chapter XXIV, verse 8, "convention" is defined in these three ways:

1. samantād varaṇaṃ saṃvṛtiḥ.
2. paraspara-saṃbhavanaṃ vā saṃvṛtiḥ.
3. saṃvṛtiḥ saṃketo loka-vyavahāra ity arthaḥ.[9]

In the first, *saṃvṛti* or "convention" is defined as "to cover universally" and "to be concealed universally (from the truth by hindrances)." It is explained that it is *ajñāna* (not knowing), due to the very existence of fundamental *avidyā* (that is, general ignorance); *saṃvṛti* is none other than *tattvāvacchādana,* that is, "the truth concealed" for ordinary mankind, or "the truth never revealing itself." The phrase *samantād varaṇam* indicates a kind of so-called popular or doctrinal etymology, and Candrakīrti obviously adopts here the root √*vṛ* in the sense of covering or concealing. Professor Theodore Stcherbatsky, referring to *saṃvṛti* as "phenomenalism" or "phenomenal reality" in general, also gives as literal translations "covering" or "the 'surface' covering the Absolute."[10] Accordingly saṃvṛti does not refer merely to being common or ordinary, as suggested by the Pāli saṃmuti or the Chinese 俗 *su,* but means to be given to illusions and to be ignorant. This ignorance, or truthlessness, or falsehood, was placed by Candrakīrti in sharp contrast to *paramārtha,* which is the ultimate and absolute Reality. This dichotomy reminds us of Prince Shōtoku's words: "False and vain is the world; only the Buddha is real" (世間虚假、唯佛是眞).

Secondly, saṃvṛti has the meaning "causing each other to come into being," which is further explained as *anyonya-samāśrayeṇa,* that is, "with one depending upon another." Being kept from the truth, "convention" must necessarily originate and come into being in the sphere of saṃsāra[11] (birth and death). Here, however, the sense of covering has disappeared and the emphasis is put rather on an interpretation by the root *saṃ-* √*bhū* (to be or come together). Here also, if we take it as doctrinal etymology, Candrakīrti seems to adopt √*vṛt* as the root. As a whole, expressions used here suggest the idea of *pratītyasamutpāda* (origination depending upon one another), which is explained usually by the term, *paraspara-apekṣā* (depending upon one another, being relational).

Thirdly, "conventional symbols" (*saṃketa*) and "worldly designations" (*vyavahāra*) are called "saṃvṛti." To be born in this world, or to originate dependently in this world (the second definition of saṃvṛti) means to manifest oneself in some form of word, concept, idea, and so forth. Both *vyavahāra* and *saṃketa* mean nothing more than *prajñapti* (making known, notation), which has in turn the same content as that of *pratītyasamutpāda.* In this context it is stated that saṃvṛti is to fix or to determine through differentiation of *abhidhāna* and *abhidheya* (that which names and that which is named).[12]

Thus, we can briefly characterize the three interpretations of saṃvṛti by Candrakīrti as follows: (1) falsehood through ignorance, (2) contingent existence without substance, and (3) conventional terminology, manner of speaking, and name.

Of these three interpretations, saṃvṛti in the sense of "conventional symbols" appears to be the most common.[13] It is understandable why saṃvṛti in the sense of "causing each other to come into being" is also often used, for it is easily derived from "conventional symbols." That these two interpretations should represent the most widely used meaning of saṃvṛti is quite obvious: saṃvṛti, standing wholly in opposition to paramārtha, is needed if there is to be a world of creation and conditioning (*saṃskṛta*), i.e., pratītyasamutpāda or prajñapti. Paramārtha of course is something unthinkable (*acintya*), inexpressible (*anabhilāpya*), and unconditioned (*asaṃskṛta*).

The rendering of saṃvṛti in the sense of falsehood through covering or hindrance (by ignorance—definition one above), is, however, more or less unique among these three; and this particular one may prove to be the most fundamental and important in the analysis of the word saṃvṛti for Candrakīrti's Madhyamic interpretation. When Candrakīrti alludes to this term in his *Madhyamakāvatāra*, chapter VI, verse 28, he simply defines it as "delusion" (*moha* means folly), for it sets obstacles before true nature (*svabhāvāvaraṇāt*). In chapter VI, verse 23 of the same work, *saṃvṛti-satya* is explained as the object of "false view" (*mṛṣādṛś*).[14] This line of interpretation seems to have been transmitted long afterwards by Prāsaṅgika followers. For instance, Prajñākaramati, in his *Commentary on the Bodhicaryāvatāra*, chapter IX, verse 2,[15] adopts this thinking, quoting the two above-mentioned verses.

II

In the *Madhyānta-vibhāga* and the *Commentary* on it by Sthiramati,[16] we have another exposition of "convention" or saṃvṛtti. These texts, it should be noted, belong to the Vijñānavāda school, which later engaged the Mādhyamikas in constant controversy. First, saṃvṛtti is defined here generally as "vyavahāra" (verbal designation). This, in turn, is divided into three, which reflect respectively the characteristics of the *tri-svabhāva*, that is, the three natures.[17] The Vijñānavādins in this text assume tri-svabhāva to be *mūla-tattva* or "principal truth," not the twofold truth of the Mādhyamikas; these terms, namely, saṃvṛtti and paramārtha, are used here merely for the purpose of elucidating tri-svabhāva, that is, mūla-tattva.

The three aspects of saṃvṛtti mentioned here are:

1. prajñapti-saṃvṛtti.
2. pratipatti-saṃvṛtti.
3. udbhāvanā-saṃvṛtti

The first aspect, prajñapti-saṃvṛtti, is exactly the same as Candrakīrti's third definition "conventional symbols," and in this saṃvṛtti, *prajñapti* settles and determines various things (*vyavasthāna*) and confers names (*nāmābhilāpa*). This may be the very meaning of what is called "vyavahāra," verbal designations. In spite of the actual non-existence of the world (*arthābhāve*), it "makes itself known" (*prajñāpayati* → *prajñapti*) to us, but only through appellations (*abhidhāna-mātreṇa*). In this sense alone is the world saṃvṛtti, "existing." Hsüan-tsang 玄奘 translates the word *prajñapti* 假 "temporary," which suggests a concept close to that of *upacāra*, while Chên-ti 眞諦 (Paramārtha) calls it 立名 "naming."

The term pratipatti of the second aspect, pratipatti-saṃvṛtti, refers to human "action," "behavior," and "perception;" hence, as defined in the text, it is none other than vikalpa, that is, "(wrong) discrimination." This means that by this discrimination of the objective world, one adheres to the "made-known (or revealed) world" as if it were real. Sthiramati puts it thus: "pratipatti is the attachment to the outer object (*arthābhiniveśa*), in spite of its being not real." Hsüan-tsang translates pratipatti by the usual 行, "going," "action" or "practice," Chên-ti by 取行, that is, "attachment-action." On the other hand, vikalpa, which is identified here with this attachment-action, is always considered in this school to be *paratantra,* which, in turn, is a cognate term of *pratītyasamutpāda*, both meaning "dependent origination." In this context, therefore, this second aspect of saṃvṛtti is roughly similar to Candrakīrti's second definition "one depending upon another."

The third aspect, *udbhāvanā*, does not, however, correspond to the first definition "to cover universally" and "to be concealed universally" given by Candrakīrti; it rather stands opposed to it. *Udbhāvanā,* i.e., "manifestation," means to display (*saṃdarśanā*) and to point to (*saṃsūcanā*) absolute Reality, which from the beginning remains beyond vikalpa. Saṃvṛtti is thus an utterance, attempting to express the inexpressible Absolute. In this respect, saṃvṛtti is raised to a position higher than those of the other two and placed closer to paramārtha; it indeed seems to be about to replace paramārtha as the Absolute,[18] and seems to claim to have control over it. Such a state of being may be appropriately compared with the notion of *mārga* (the way), which leads to the Absolute on the one hand, and which emerges from the Absolute on the other. Thus, it is evident that Candrakīrti's definition of "covering" the truth stands almost diametrically opposite to this interpretation.[19]

As already stated above, these three distinctions are made for the purpose of the elucidating the *tri-svabhāva* (three natures), which is, unlike the *tri-niḥsvabhāva* (three non-substantialities), an explanation of the positive world of *ens.* In accordance with this, all these interpretations of saṃvṛtti have also a positive side,—saṃvṛtti being not at all negated but in fact manifesting the Absolute. Accordingly, it becomes clear that the root considered here was $\sqrt{}$*vṛt,* coming into being and manifesting or clarifying the truth. The root $\sqrt{}$*vṛ* on the other hand, covers and darkens the truth. The above-mentioned positive side was also already foreseen when saṃvṛtti was first defined as *vyavahāra*.

In this connection, Sthiramati goes on further to say that the *vikalpa* of the second aspect of saṃvṛtti, which is equated with paratantra and pratītyasamutpāda, is the only true saṃvṛtti in its essential nature, hence the most fundamental one, while the others, first and third aspects of saṃvṛtti designate uses of saṃvṛtti that have derived or secondary meanings.[20] That is to say Sthiramati does not consider *parikalpita-svabhāva* and *pariniṣpannasvabhāva* as *saṃvṛtti* in the true sense of the word.

Although Candrakīrti and Sthiramati agree on most points, there is a very marked contradiction between the former's idea of "covering" and the latter's idea of "manifestation." This difference may be properly understood, therefore, only when we conclude that they employed interchangeably the roots √*vṛ* or √*vṛt*, thereby finally deriving vastly dissimilar usages. The Mādhyamikas seem to favor the root √*vṛ*, the Vijñānavādins the root √*vṛt*. This is not to say, however, that Candrakīrti and the Mādhyamika followers did not think at all of the meanings of *saṃ-* √*vṛt*. On the contrary, they also used *vyavahāra* and other terminology in the senses shown above. Further, Sthiramati and the other Vijñānavādins, while not giving the definition "covering" as one of the meanings of *saṃvṛtti*, could not have been entirely unconscious of the existence of this particular meaning; they probably had no occasion to use it in this sense. *Vikalpa*, moreover, is always considered by them as *abhūtaparikalpa*, that is, "false imaginings," as stated throughout the first chapter of the *Madhyāntavibhāga*. Be it that *vikalpa* is the highest[21] and the most penetrating discernment of accuracy, yet, when contrasted with *paramārtha*, the Absolute,[22] it is no more than untrue and false and deceiving, so long as it remains *vikalpa*. Hence, also in the case of Sthiramati, saṃvṛtti is, from the beginning, shut out and veiled from the truth.

Saṃvṛtti then means convention by its existence, a meaning that is common to both schools of Mādhyamika and Vijñānavāda; existence is a hindrance if conceived of as covering the truth, but it is at the same time truth itself manifested. Both interpretations, although standing at opposite extremes, could have been arrived at by using either the root √*vṛ* or √*vṛt*, which, confined not merely to its etymological meaning, was extended even so far as to include an opposite meaning.

III

That both roots were employed by either or both schools, and that the meaning of convention often fluctuated over a wide range, from "covering" through "coming into existence" to "manifestation," may become more certain when we refer to Chinese sources such as I-ching's records and Tz'u-ên's writings.

I-ching (義浄 635–713) translates *saṃvṛti-satya* as 覆諦 (covered truth) or 覆俗諦 (covered conventional truth).[23] He further adds that the old translation 世俗, where no meaning of covering is included, does not express completely the original meaning. Here he presents us with a concrete example of an interpretation of the word convention as derived solely from the root √*vṛ,* "to cover."

Tz'u-ên (慈恩Honorific title 大師号 given to K'uei-chi 窺基 632–682), the eminent disciple of Hsüan-tsang, who founded the Vijñānavāda school (法相宗) in China, gives an Indian etymological analysis of the word and claims it to be the othodox meaning as taught by the ācārya Dharmapāla.[24] He describes *saṃvṛti* in the *Chapter on the Twofold Truth*[25] and again in the *Commentary on the Vijñānamātra-siddhi.*[26]

Saṃvṛti-satya is here called 隱顯諦 "covering-and-manifesting truth," and the reasons for it are given as follows:

世謂隱覆、可毀壞義。俗謂顯現、隨世流義。

The world is concealment and cover, and means that which is destructible.

The conventional is manifestation, and means that which flows with the currents of the world.

There are two definitions in this passage,[27] one defining 世 and the other defining 俗, but two subordinate meanings also play important roles in the definition of the term *saṃvṛti* 世俗.

(1) Tz'u-ên's first meaning of *saṃvṛti* is literally "concealment and cover," which is, in accordance with I-ching's interpretation, evidently derived from the root *saṃ-* √*vṛ* 隱覆, and is replaced by 覆障 in the version of the Shu-chi (述記); 障 being āvaraṇa in Sanskrit, the meaning "hindrance" is emphasized here. At any rate, in both cases the interpretation is quite close to the first definition given by Candrakīrti. It should be noted that this interpretation had its origin with Dharmapāla, who, among the Vijñānavāda scholars, was one of the most outspoken critics of the Mādhyamika tenets.

(2) Tz'u-ên's second meaning "destructible," however, does not seem to be derived directly from *saṃvṛti* or *saṃvṛtti.* At first brush it may appear to mean "to destroy (the truth)," especially if read from the first meaning of "covering (the truth)." But this does not fit the case, for the character 可 seems rather to denote the passive voice, hence "destructible."

I am inclined to believe, however, that there is little, if any, connection between Tz'u-ên's definitions, one and two. It appears that "destructibility" as a characteristic of saṃvṛti had its origin elsewhere. In the *Abhidharmakośa,* chapter VI,[28] the Twofold Truth is explained. The name *saṃvṛti* is given here to those things that are destructible, for example, a vase made of clay, which will not remain in existence when it is broken (*bheda*), and to those things which are analyzable (*anyāpoha*), for example, water, which can be reduced to more fundamental elements, such as form, color, smell and so forth. Only when these things are still whole or unanalyzed are they called "saṃvṛti." *Paramārtha,* on the other hand, is indivisible; it does not cease to exist. This type of positivistic interpretation belongs properly to pre-Mahāyānistic thinking, and it is the rule in all Abhidharma philosophy. Tz'u-ên probably referred to this concept in deriving his destructibility.

Again, in this connection, we are reminded of the word *loka,* that is, the world. The meaning "destruction" was attached to *loka* at some time in India, and its use became popular also in Chinese Buddhism. The Tibetan equivalent for it similarly means "the abode of destruction."[29] As the Chinese translation of *loka* is always 世, it is probable that this popular etymology of loka as "destruction" was applied by extension to include *saṃvṛti* also.

(3) In Tz'u-ên's third definition, 顯現 (literally "appearing" and "manifesting,") may merely indicate the meaning of *prajñapti, saṃketa* and so forth, given by Sthiramati as the first aspect of saṃvṛtti (that is, "things appear in the world"). However, from the similarity of the two Chinese words, it is probably more correct to understand it in the sense of udbhāvanā 顯了, manifestation, (that is, the third aspect of saṃvṛtti given by Sthiramati) in which case it means, as it were, that "*paramārtha* manifests itself in this world" as worldly things. It is a "coming down" or a "descent" of paramārtha into this conventional existence; the Absolute "appears" in the guise of convention, and the one becomes many.

(4) Tz'u-ên's fourth definition, "To flow with worldly currents" indicates the meaning nearest to that of the Chinese 俗, "conventional." But here also 随, "to flow with" or "to follow after," means that a higher being submits itself to a lower one. It is not that worldliness complies with worldliness, but that *paramārtha* lowers itself and follows after *loka-vyavahāra,* that is, "worldly designations." Worldliness is stronger, as it were, than paramārtha. Paramārtha abandons its sovereignty and is subject to saṃvṛti; otherwise, paramārtha would find itself entirely deprived of the means by which to manifest and express itself. Therefore, "to flow with (worldly currents)" may be distinguished from mere "worldly currents," that is, the everyday currents of birth and death[30] that are utterly unconscious of paramārtha. If this conjecture is not too far amiss, saṃvṛti here is not the mere life, but a life that indicates paramārtha and mirrors Reality. This meaning then agrees with Tz'u-ên's terms "appearing" and "manifesting" just mentioned above. In Tz'u-ên's understanding of both "appearing and manifesting" and "to flow with world currents," it is evident that the root saṃ- √vṛt was selected to designate this conventional world. Therefore in his term 隱顯, we find both Candrakīrti's "concealment" and Sthiramati's "manifestation" synthesized.

IV

These few instances of the various interpretations of the idea of saṃvṛti in India and China discussed here do not by any means exhaust the problem. There is still much to be done in tracing the development of this idea in China, Tibet, and Japan, where complex connotations have been added. However, from the foregoing discussion certain considerations are already suggested.

Briefly, 'saṃvṛti' for Candrakīrti is a negative concept, while it is a positive one for Sthiramati. These divergent views seem to have come about naturally through expansion of the germ of contradiction inherent in the term saṃvṛti; Candrakīrti developed only one aspect and Sthiramati the other. It is Tz'u-ên who finally draws the two ends together to elevate saṃvṛti to its full significance. "Covering-manifesting" is certainly a paradoxical expression, but it is only in this realm of contradiction that the Buddha and the *sattvas* have a common meeting ground. It is only in this world of paradox that the Bodhisattvas can effectively display their merits; it is indeed the basis on which the entire ideal of the *Bodhisattva-mārga* (the Way of the Bodhisattvas), the most fundamental tenet of Mahāyāna, rests.

If Candrakīrti's position is taken, saṃvṛti is destined forever to remain in the dark abyss of depravity, for paramārtha can never be seen: to look at paramārtha is not to see it at all. When paramārtha is brought into the ken of our perception, what is perceived changes in that instant into saṃvṛti or "falsehood." As such, saṃvṛti may be described as constantly moving away from paramārtha, descending forever into the bottomless chasm.

Sthiramati, on the contrary, affirms the value of saṃvṛti as the sole medium through which paramārtha can manifest itself. Or, more correctly, it is saṃvṛti alone that can reflect the image of paramārtha.[31] Thus, it becomes a thing of immeasurable worth, speeding in the direction of the Ultimate. There is then no more descent, but ascent. Sthiramati would probably say with us that after all there is but one world, the world of saṃvṛtti, in which we are born and work and die. There is no other. Without this world, that is to say, were this world negated, paramārtha would also become non-existent.

Having discussed Candrakīrti and Sthiramati, we can summarize Tz'u-ên's position as one that follows after or is based upon Dharmapāla's claim that "the covering of the truth is the manifesting of the truth." That is to say, it is by means of covering the truth and only by that means that truth can be manifested. Here there is no ascent unless there is descent; if there is no negation, there is no affirmation.

The history of the term saṃvṛti as traced briefly here gives us a faithful indication of the parallel development of Mahāyāna Buddhism, the crux of which is the Bodhisattva-mārga. Derived from the Pāli saṃmuti, saṃvṛti first began with such ordinary meanings as "common sense," "conventional," and so forth. Later, it took on the diverse meanings of "covering" and "manifesting," and finally the combined meaning of "covering-manifesting." "Covering-manifesting," which expresses the paradoxical nature of the Mahāyāna, describes precisely the world in which the Great Compassion of the Bodhisattvas must find its meaning. It is far from a perfect world, but it is the manifestation of the Perfect. It is a world of ignorance, but it enjoys the warm rays of wisdom. It is here that the Bodhisattva works, for he "abides not in Nirvāṇa" (*apratiṣṭhitanirvāṇa*). Not abiding in Nirvāṇa, he comes back to this world and dwells in the very midst of defilement. But this in itself is his enlightenment or wisdom; his joy consists in his painstaking labors in this world, not in any other.

Although this Bodhisattva world filled with contradictions is itself saṃvṛti, it should naturally be distinguished from the world of ordinary men.[32] Such a distinction is already anticipated in the Vijñānavāda's notion of paratantra, which, being the axis on which the whole concept of 'tri-svabhāva' revolves, distinguishes itself from the samsaric *parikalpita* on the one hand and from the nirvanic *pariniṣpanna* on the other.[33] Candrakīrti's saṃvṛti seems at a glance to represent merely the samsaric parikalpita aspect. But he also introduced here a new term, saṃvṛti-mātra, saṃvṛti-only,"[34] which is carefully distinguished from paramārtha-satya as well as the saṃvṛti-satya of human adherence, and corresponds to the Bodhisattva-world.[35] However, the relationship between these concepts, while very interesting, cannot be dealt with here.

Chapter 3

The Bodhisattva Returns to this World

In his celebrated book, *The Bodhisattva Doctrine in Buddhist Sanskrit Literature,* Har Dayal elucidated the fundamental differences between Hīnayāna and Mahāyāna ideas. In his work, which was written almost fifty years ago—which is still being used widely by scholars—Dayal summarized the notion of the Arhat as follows:

> An Arhat who was thus liberated, knew that he would not be reborn. He had accomplished what was to be done. He attained undefiled and final emancipation of mind and heart. He was alone, secluded, zealous, master of himself.[1]

However, as time went on, Buddhist monks began to neglect the important aspect of Arhatship and became overly self-centered. Har Dayal continues:

> They seemed to have cared only for their own liberation . . . were indifferent to the duty of teaching and helping all human beings.[2]

In short, theirs was a saintly and serene but an inactive and indolent monastic order.

In contrast to this, Dayal claimed that the Bodhisattva doctrine was promulgated as a protest against this coldness and aloofness of the Arhat. Accordingly, a Bodhisattva was one who criticized and condemned the spiritual egoism of such an Arhat.

As quoted before, "an Arhat . . . knew that he would not be reborn," but a Bodhisattva is reborn and returns to this world. Although the differences between Hīnayāna and Mahāyāna ideas can be pointed out in various ways, I will confine myself here to the idea that a Bodhisattva is one who refuses the liberation of nirvāṇa until all sentient beings are saved. In developing this theme, I shall focus my attention on two terms—*apratiṣṭhita-nirvāṇa* and *saṃcintyabhavopapatti*—because these were scarcely noticed by Har Dayal.

I

Although the Bodhisattva's way is different from that of an Arhat, the nirvāṇa, or the highest goal for an Arhat, is never neglected nor devalued by the Mahāyānists. This is because the Bodhisattva practice is in itself a way of benefiting others by helping them obtain the ultimate "nirvāṇa."

The last two chapters of Asaṅga's *Mahāyānasaṃgraha* are named "Phala-prahāṇa" and "Phala-jñāna." As fruits of the Three Learnings (*śikṣā*), the former is no other than nirvāṇa (the suppression of defilements, *phala-prahāṇa*) and the latter refers to Buddha-wisdom (*phala-jñāna*), which are none other than the three kinds of Buddha-body (*kāya*). Vasubandhu's *Triṃśikā* mentions two bodies: *vimuktikāya* and *dharmakāya*. The former is the body acquired when *kleśa-āvaraṇa* (i.e., the Śrāvaka's turbidities) are suppressed; it corresponds to the fruit of having suppressed defilements as explained in the Phala-prahāṇa chapter of the *Mahāyānasaṃgraha*. The latter is the body acquired when *jñeya-āvaraṇa* (i.e., the Bodhisattva's turbidities) are suppressed; it corresponds to the fruit of having obtained wisdom as explained in the Phala-jñāna chapter of the same text. Thus, along with the Buddha-wisdom or the Buddha-body, nirvāṇa is deemed also to be of the highest importance in the Mahāyāna.

However, in this chapter of the *Mahāyānasaṃgraha*, the word nirvāṇa is considered to be qualified by the word *apratiṣṭhita* which means "not dwelling in," "not abiding in," and so on. When this Mahāyānic nirvāṇa, that is, *apratiṣṭhita-nirvāṇa*, is considered separately from the two kinds of Hīnayānic nirvāṇa, *sopadhiśeṣa-nirvāṇa* and *nirupadhiśeṣa-nirvāṇa*, it becomes the third nirvāṇa. Or, it becomes the fourth nirvāṇa when the name 'nirvāṇa' (of the *Mahāvyutpatti*, 1725) is regarded separately from these three nirvāṇas just mentioned and is considered to be "originally pure" (*prakṛti-viśuddhi*) as stated in the *Ch'êng wei shih lun* (*Vijñapti-mātratā-siddhi* by Hsüan-tsang), chüan 10.[3] In any case, this *apratiṣṭhita-nirvāṇa* is the sole nirvāṇa to be acquired either by Bodhisattvas or by Tathāgatas.

The two words *apratiṣṭhita* and *nirvāṇa* do not always form a compound, for we can find instances in which both have case endings. For example, we find such phrases as

1. *na nirvāṇe pratiṣṭhito bhavati na saṃsāre*. [*Mahāyāna-sūtrālaṃkāra* (hereafter, *MSA*), XVII.32.]
2. *nirvāṇe 'pi mano na pratiṣṭhitaṃ*. [*MSA*, XVII.42.]
3. *apratiṣṭhito nirvāṇe*. [*Mahāvyutpatti*, 406.]
4. *apratiṣṭhitaṃ nirvāṇam*. [*Madhyāntavibhāga* (hereafter, *MV*), IV.12, V.1 (Sthiramati's *Ṭīkā*).]

In most cases, however, the two words are combined to form a compound:

1. *apratiṣṭhita-nirvāṇa.* [*MV*, II.1, IV.12cd; *MSA*, IX.45, XVIII.69, XIX.62, etc.]

In spite of the fact that we most frequently encounter this expression in compound form, we sometimes find the word "saṃsāra" added, as for example in:

2. *apratiṣṭhita-saṃsāra-nirvāṇa.* [*MSA*, XVII.32.]

There are also instances when even the word order is reversed, as for example in:

3. *nirvāṇa-apratiṣṭhita, saṃsāra-nirvāṇa-apratiṣṭhatā, -apratiṣṭhāna, -apratiṣṭhitatva,* etc. [*MV*, V.1, V.29 *MSA*. IX.14.]

Éteinne Lamotte admits that a grammatical explanation of the compound *apratiṣṭhita-nirvāṇa* would be difficult, and simply refers to J. Speyer's paraphrase: "nirvāṇaṃ yatra na pratiṣṭhīyate," even though he renders it as "le Nirvāṇa instable."[4] Theodore Stcherbatsky[5] and E. Obermiller[6] translate this term into English as "altruistic Nirvāṇa," and sometimes as "non-dialectical Nirvāṇa. The latter two translations, however, are interpretative translations, not literal ones. J. Takasaki[7] translates it as "not to stay fixedly in the Nirvāṇa," or "the Unstable Nirvāṇa."

In my opinion, F. Edgerton gives a more proper explanation in his *Buddhist Hybrid Sanskrit Dictionary* when he defines the term *apratiṣṭhita* as "not permanently fixed" and adds, "it [*apratiṣṭhita-nirvāṇa*] is the Mahāyānistic nirvāṇa in which the Tathāgata returns [in the capacity of a Bodhisattva] to worldly life to save creatures . . ."[8] From this latter definition, it becomes clear that the word *apratiṣṭhita-nirvāṇa* denotes a Bodhisattva's resolution: "I shall not enter into final nirvāṇa before all beings have been liberated."

Although *pratiṣṭhā* has the meanings of "to stay," "to dwell," "to abide" and so forth when used as a verb, and "ground," "basis" and so forth when used as a noun, the Chinese and Tibetan translators seem to have understood the term to mean "being attached to," "clinging to," "adhering to." In his *Vajracchedikā* Edward Conze always translates *pratiṣṭhita* as "support" and *apratiṣṭhitaṃ cittaṃ* as "unsupported thought." But he also admits that the meaning of *apratiṣṭhita* is ambiguous and proposes twenty-one possible translations for this term. Among those, the meanings "not attached to" and "not clinging to" are enumerated.[9] In the Chinese commentaries on the *Vajracchedikā, apratiṣṭhita* is usually interpreted as "not abiding" as well as "not clinging." *Mi gnas pa* (*apratiṣṭhita*), in the Tibetan translation *Mi gnas pa'i mya ngan las 'das pa* (*apratiṣṭhita-nirvāṇa*), is apparently considered as an adjective describing nirvāṇa. This suggests a notion of "a nirvāṇa not clung to" derived from the Skt. *apratiṣṭhita-nirvāṇa*. The use of *apratiṣṭhita* as an adjective is reinforced when *apratiṣṭhita-nirvāṇa* is aligned with *sopadhiśeṣa-nirvāṇa* and *nirupadhiśeṣa-nirvāṇa,* because the first part of the two latter compounds clearly functions as an adjective. Further in Sthiramati's commentary on the *MSA*, XVII.42,[10] *mi gnas* is replaced by *ma chags* (not clinging). Thus, *apratiṣṭhita* can be interpreted as "not clinging to." Also, in Vasubandhu's commentary on the *MSA*, IX.70 we read: *apratiṣṭhita-nirvāṇe niviṣṭaṃ,* and this can be understood to mean "[a Bodhisattva] enters into a nirvāṇa to which he does not cling."[11]

The two meanings of "not dwelling" and "not clinging" can be clearly seen in the *MSA*, XVII.42,[12] which delineates three levels of attachment and detachment that can be traced among the three types of human beings. Vasubandhu's commentary states:

> With regard to the detachedness of [a Bodhisattva's] compassion, there is a verse which reads:
>
> The mind of compassionate beings [Bodhisattvas], filled with tenderness, does not even dwell in [or cling to] the quiescence [of nirvāṇa].
>
> How much less will his loving mind dwell in [or cling to] worldly happiness or his own life?
>
> The loving minds of all worldly beings dwell in worldly happiness and their own life. Although the loving minds of Śrāvakas and Pratyekabuddhas do not dwell in such things, their minds dwell in [or cling to] nirvāṇa which is the quiescence of all pains. On the contrary, due to compassion, the minds of Bodhisattvas do not dwell even in nirvāṇa. How much less will their loving minds be attached to the two [saṃsāra and nirvāṇa]?

Here, three kinds of attitudes about love are presented. Ordinary beings covet worldly joys as well as their own life, both of which are saṃsāric. The two *yānikas,* the Śravākas and Pratyekabuddhas, though freed from saṃsāric things, are still attached to nirvāṇa. The Bodhisattvas dwell neither in saṃsāra nor in nirvāṇa and neither love nor become attached to them. By combining the meanings of "not dwelling" and "not clinging," Vasubandhu makes it clear that the ways of the Bodhisattva, the Hīnayānic saints, and the ordinary beings are different. Hence, in the case of the Bodhisattva, we find the qualification *apratiṣṭhita-saṃsāra-nirvāṇa*.

This term, *apratiṣṭhita-saṃsāra-nirvāṇatva*, is expounded in the *MSA*, XVII.32, in a very comprehensible and clear manner. The verse runs as follows:

> After realizing all saṃsāric entities as painful and substanceless, he who possesses compassion and the highest wisdom [i.e., the Bodhisattva], is neither afflicted [by saṃsāra] nor bound by the faults [of saṃsāra].

Commenting upon this verse, Vasubandhu says:

> Since he possesses compassion, a Bodhisattva does not become agitated by saṃsāra nor feels weary of saṃsāra; therefore, he does not dwell in nirvāṇa. Again, since he possesses the highest wisdom, he is not bound by the faults of saṃsāra; therefore, he does not dwell in saṃsāra.[13]

From Vasubandhu's commentary, it becomes clear that the term apratiṣṭhita-nirvāṇa means to exit from nirvāṇa and to come down into saṃsāra. A Bodhisattva does not dwell in and does not cling to nirvāṇa owing to his compassion. Moreover, a Bodhisattva's activity includes the aspect of apratiṣṭhita-saṃsāra, that is, he neither dwells in nor clings to saṃsāra owing to his great wisdom. These two activities of coming from nirvāṇa and going to nirvāṇa are to be understood to be operating simultaneously in the term "apratiṣṭhita-nirvāṇa."

The above does not exhaust all possible interpretations of the term apratiṣṭhita-nirvāṇa, for there are several others that are either separate interpretations or are derivatives of this term.

1. In the *MV,* V.29 *apratiṣṭhatā* means *avinivartana,* "not turning back." This verse expounds the ten kinds of "attainment [of fruit]" (*samudāgama*) that results from the Bodhisattva's practice, and apratiṣṭhatā is mentioned here as the eighth kind of attainment. Vasubandhu says that it means "not dwelling in both saṃsāra and nirvāṇa," and continues to explain it as follows:

> "Not dwelling in both saṃsāra and nirvāṇa" is the "attainment [of fruit]" called the "gaining of the [Buddha's] prediction at the stage of non-turning around," because he [the Bodhisattva] is now not liable to turn back from either saṃsāra or nirvāṇa.[14]

Sthiramati clarifies this further in his commentary:

> Perceiving the sentient beings, a Bodhisattva, committing himself to saṃsāra, does not turn back from the way of saṃsāra because of his compassion and also does not turn back from the way toward nirvāṇa because of his wisdom.[15]

These two commentaries make it clear that the term "not turning back," which is another name for apratiṣṭhatā, means not only not turning back from the way to nirvāṇa but also not turning back from saṃsāra.

A similar explanation can be found in *MSA*, XIX. 61–2, where, likewise in terms of ten items, the tenet of Mahāyāna is elucidated.[16] Of these ten items, the seventh and the eighth items are commented upon by Vasubandhu as follows:

> The purification of the [Buddha]-land and not dwelling in nirvāṇa are seen in the three stages of non-turning back.[17]

2. In *MSA*, IX.14, apratiṣṭhita means *advaya*, "non-duality." In this verse Asaṅga explains *āśraya-parāvṛtti*, "evolution of basis," in ten ways. Of these, the sixth is called "dvayā vṛttiḥ," "evolving of duality," because by means of this evolution the Buddha Śākyamuni has manifested the two events of Enlightenment (*abhisaṃbodhi*) at Bodhgayā and Parinirvāṇa at Kusināra.[18] These two events are also mentioned in Vasubandhu's commentary on the *MSA*, XIX.62,[19] and probably correspond respectively to the Phala-jñāna (*abhisaṃbodhi*) and Phala-prahāṇa (*parinirvāṇa*) in the *Mahāyānasaṃgraha* quoted above.

This "evolving of duality," however, is in the ultimate sense *advayā vṛttiḥ*, "evolving of non-duality," which the *MSA* explains as the seventh evolution of basis. Because the Bodhisattva dwells neither in saṃsāra nor in nirvāṇa, for him there is no duality between *saṃskṛta*, the compounded, and *asaṃskṛta*, the uncompounded. Owing to his wisdom, a Bodhisattva relinquishes the compounded and does not enter saṃsāra; and, owing to his compassion, he denies the uncompounded and does not enter nirvāṇa either.

It is this non-duality that plays a salient role in the notion of the Buddha's *samatā-jñāna*, "Equality Wisdom." The *MSA*, IX.70 explains "Equality Wisdom" with the compound: *apratiṣṭhasamāviṣṭa(-jñāna)*. The Tibetan translation, however, understands this compound as *apratiṣṭhaśamāviṣṭa(-jñāna)* (/ *mi-gnas zhi-bar zhugs-pa ni* / *mnyam-nyid ye-shes yin-par 'dod* /). *Śama* is another name for nirvāṇa, and, in his commentary, Vasubandhu makes the statement: *apratiṣṭhitanirvāṇe niviṣṭaṃ samatā-jñānaṃ*, "the Equality Wisdom is what had entered the not dwelling (or not clung to) nirvāṇa.''[20] We see here a kind of pun on the words *śama* (equivalent to nirvāṇa) and *sama* of *samatājñāna*. Sthiramati quotes in his commentary the Buddhabhūmi-sūtra and says:

> When the not dwelling nirvāṇa is realized, there is no difference between saṃsāra and nirvāṇa; they are regarded to be of one taste (*ekarasa*).[21]

Thus, at least, we can say the meaning of *apratiṣṭhita* is related to the meanings of *avinivartaṇa* and *advaya*. With these meanings in mind, it is possible to interpret *apratiṣṭhita-nirvāṇa* as ''the nirvāṇa in which the Bodhisattva does not turn back from either saṃsāra or nirvāṇa,'' and ''the nirvāṇa in which the Bodhisattva realizes equanimity and the non-duality of saṃsāra and nirvāṇa.''

II

Related to this *apratiṣṭhita-nirvāṇa*, there is a term ''*saṃcintya-bhavopapatti*.'' Saṃcintya, a gerund used as an adverb, means ''intentionally, purposely.'' Bhavopapatti means ''to be born into the world of existence.'' Thus, the term saṃcintya-bhavopapatti means ''to take birth willingly, volitionally, in the world of existence.'' Since not to dwell in nirvāṇa is to get away from nirvāṇa, by implication it means to enter into saṃsāra. Thus, a Bodhisattva voluntarily comes into the saṃsāric world.

Why does he volunteer? It is solely for the purpose of benefiting others, helping others, and making service to others that a Bodhisattva enters saṃsāric life, even though nirvāṇa is the highest bliss to which all aim and even though he is one capable of attaining it or one who does not stay in it depending upon his perspective. This he does from his unlimited compassion.

Such a birth, therefore, is a miraculous one. It does not take place in an ordinary way, but takes place in the midst of śūnyatā; it is paradoxical. For example, in the *Vimalakīrti-nirdeśa-sūtra*, one reads:

> Although there is in reality neither arising nor extinction, they [Bodhisattvas] voluntarily take on births.[22]

There is neither arising nor extinction in ultimate reality; yet a Bodhisattva intends his birth owing to his deep compassion for sentient beings and his sublime wisdom of śūnyatā. His is a paradoxical birth because it is non-existent and yet existent.

To express the idea that a Bodhisattva takes birth in the saṃsāric world, the sūtras and śāstras use a variety of different words and phrases. For example, *saṃcintya-bhavapratikāṅkṣī* and *saṃcintya-upapatti-parigraha* are phrases that appear in the Prajñāpāramitā-sūtras.[23] While one finds the phrase *saṃcintya ca bhavādānam* in the *Abhisamayālaṃkāra,* I.67,[24] the śāstras such as *MSA* (II.9, IV.25) and *Ratnagotra-vibhāga* (I.68, in its commentary)[25] repeatedly employ the expression saṃcintya-upapatti. But it is the *MSA* that deals with the idea of the Bodhisattva's birth most frequently and comprehensively. In the *MSA,* then, it seems that saṃcintya-bhavopapatti was used as the standard form of expression. In any case, the term saṃcintya, "at will," which is common to all these expressions, is the key word representing the central meaning of the idea.

Generally, the causes of birth for ordinary beings are past deeds (*karman*) and defilements (*kleśa*). But the Bodhisattva's birth is different in that it is caused purely by his will and purpose.

A typical birth of a Bodhisattva is explained in the *Bodhisattvabhūmi,* as follows:

> Wishing to benefit those lowly beings from a *caṇḍāla* up to a dog, wishing to calm their calamity, or wishing to guide them, a Bodhisattva takes any form from that of a *caṇḍāla* up to that of a dog at will.[26]

Here we see how severe and radical the Bodhisattva's rebirth is; it is almost impossible to accomplish. As his 'will' to be reborn gushes forth due to his limitless compassion, his place of rebirth ranges throughout all of the six *gatis,* even including the hells. However, as stated in the *MSA,* IV.24–5, even though his rebirth has been difficult and severe, he goes about it as if going through a joyful garden (*udyāna-yātrā*).[27] Or, again, he looks upon it like a magical creation (*nirmāṇa*) (*MSA,* XI.30),[28] in concordance with the Buddha's teaching: "Every being is like *māyā,* like *nirmāṇa,* and so on."

The *MSA,* XX–XXI.8[29] divides the cause for a Bodhisattva's birth into four kinds: (1) *karman,* (2) *praṇidhāna,* (3) *samādhi,* and (4) *vibhutva.* Of these karman is the cause for birth of a Bodhisattva who is in the stage of adhimukticaryābhūmi, that is, a Bodhisattva who has not yet entered the Bodhisattva's first *bhūmi.* This means that he is in a state similar to that of an ordinary being, and accordingly, karman is mentioned as the cause for his birth in accordance with the general rule of birth (although *kleśa* is not mentioned here). But because it is by the force of karman that his birth has been determined according to his will (*abhipreta*), his birth by karman may be understood in the sense of saṃcintya-bhavopapatti. Categories *praṇidhāna* to *vibhutva* may be seen as saṃcintya-bhavopapatti that is genuine. Of these, birth by the force of his vow (*praṇidhāna*) is related to the

Bodhisattva who is already in the first and second bhūmis. Birth by the force of samādhi, refers to the one in the third to seventh *bhūmis.* Birth by the force of superhuman power (vibhutva) or transformation, nirmāṇa, refers to the one in the other bhūmis, the eighth and so on.

A bodhisattva enters such a painful life of saṃsāra and yet does not embrace the thought of fear or disgust; he is not contaminated by the defilements of the saṃsāric world even if he has not abandoned them. Thus, for him, saṃsāra is like a joyful garden, or, it is not a place where he becomes agitated or is bound by its faults.

The *MSA*, XVIII,19–21[30] explains saṃcintya-bhavopapatti further as the *dhṛti,* "firmness" of a Bodhisattva. Firmness is first seen here in view of various ways of learning. Then, it is related to austerity *duṣkaracaryā* in which the Bodhisattva is engaged; next it is related to saṃcintya—bhavopapatti, by which a Bodhisattva is reborn at will into saṃsāra and does not abandon it (*saṃsārātyāga*); and finally it is related to *asaṃkleśa,* that is, he does not suffer from its contamination. All these activities are called the "Bodhisattva's firmness."

Or again, according to the *MSA*, XVIII.44[31] saṃcintya-bhavopapatti of a Bodhisattva can mean to be reborn as a *cakravarti-rāja* and other dignitary beings such as Indra and Brahmā. Such a rebirth naturally possesses the prosperity (*saṃpatti*) of supreme body and supreme enjoyment. And yet one so reborn is not contaminated by defilements of desire and so on.

In the *MSA*, XX–XXI.12,[32] the characteristic of each of the eleven bhūmis is explained. It is with regard to the sixth bhūmi that saṃcintya-bhavopapatti becomes an issue. In this discussion, there is a phrase, *saṃkleśasyānurakṣaṇā,* "guarding or protection of defilements." The sixth bhūmi is characterized by the fact that there is the "guarding of defilements" when a Bodhisattva is reborn at will from having stayed with the view of *pratītyasamutpāda* (dependent coorigination) for a long time. In his commentary Sthiramati says:

> A Bodhisattva is reborn, fully mindful and conscious of whatever place where he chooses to be reborn. Because he is not contaminated by the defilements owing to the fact that he has stayed with the view of *pratītyasamutpāda* for a long time, there is the "guarding of defilements."[33]

In spite of these commentaries, the last phrase, "guarding of defilements," is not clear to me. It can mean "guarding oneself against the contamination by defilements," or, perhaps more accurately, "keeping the defilement" as a course for a Bodhisattva's compassionate activity. The *Ch'êng wei shih lun (Vijñaptimātratāsiddhi), chüan* 9, reads:

留煩惱障　助願受生

[A Bodhisattva] retains the obstacle of defilement (*kleśāvaraṇa*) to sustain his vow to be reborn [into saṃsāra].[34]

In view of summarizing the discussion thus far, we have found that the term apratiṣṭhita-nirvāṇa included the two meanings of "not dwelling in saṃsāra" and "not dwelling in nirvāṇa." "Not dwelling in saṃsāra" meant not to indulge in saṃsāra, and not to be stained by saṃsāric defilements. We also saw that this was accomplished through wisdom (*prajñā*). On the other hand, we saw that "not dwelling in nirvāṇa" meant that saṃsāra was accepted as a "joyful garden" and that this was owing to the Bodhisattva's deep compassion. This latter characteristic was represented by the term "saṃcintya-bhavopapatti."

III

In both Mahāyāna and Hīnayāna, nirvāṇa has always been the ultimate aim gained by 'wisdom.' However, the Mahāyānic idea differs from that of the Hīnayānic, in that a Bodhisattva refuses even nirvāṇa so long as all sentient beings have not yet been saved. This is to say that Bodhisattvas, refusing the bliss of nirvāṇa, come down to this world because of their 'compassion.' For a Bodhisattva, the ascent of wisdom terminates at the point of nirvāṇa from whence the descent of compassion begins. The Bodhisattva is, therefore, characterized by two activities: "going up" or "ascending" and the other "coming down" or "descending."

All Buddhist learnings and practices, including *śīla, dhyāna,* and so on, belong to the "ascending" direction; they are all cultivated for the purpose of traversing the way leading to final liberation. The doctrines of the six pāramitās and the ten bhūmis belonging to the *Bodhisattvamārga* are also the same.

In contrast to these, the notions of apratiṣṭhita-nirvāṇa and saṃcintya-bhavopapatti represent the "descending" direction. The Sino-Japanese Pure Land traditions have expressed the same idea, though they used two other terms: "going-thither" (往相) and "coming-hither" (還相). These terms were originally innovated by T'an-luan (曇鸞) in the sixth century in China and were made popular by Shinran (親鸞) in the thirteenth century in Japan. According to the Pure Land Buddhist tradition, the term "going-thither" means to be reborn into Sukhāvatī, that is, to go from this world. The term "coming-hither" means to return to this world, that is, those who have been born in Sukhāvatī return immediately to this world. To go from this saṃsāric world corresponds to the ascending direction, and to return to this world corresponds to the descending direction.

Therefore, to ascend means that one negates saṃsāric reality and aspires for the nirvāṇic ideal. Hence, the motivating power of the ascent is always based upon a negation, that is, on "śūnyatā." The descent, however, begins from śūnyatā and takes place in the midst of it. It affirms saṃsāra in its true character as śūnyatā. That is to say, in Mahāyāna, more emphasis is placed on the real world of saṃsāra rather than on the ideal world of nirvāṇa.

However, it is not that these two activities of ascent and descent are opposing each other; they, in the final analysis, are one and the same.

For instance, in the *Saddharmapuṇḍarīka-sūtra,* Buddha Śākyamuni himself, who achieved Enlightenment after a long period of practice (ascending activity), declares that he had already achieved it in countless aeons past, and as a skillful means (*upāya*) appeared here on this earth (descending activity) for the purpose of benefiting others in the guise of a human being. Thus, the two directions are regarded here as identical. From the Mahāyānic point of view, even the Bodhisattvas presented in the Jātaka tales can be interpreted in this way.

We see in the *MV,* I.13[35] a theoretical basis for the identification of these two directions. According to this text, śūnyatā is defined by two terms: "non-existence" (*abhāva*) and "existence of [this] non-existence" (*abhāvasya bhāvaḥ*). Non-existence refers to the upward movement (negation of this world). Existence of [this] non-existence refers to the downward movement (affirmation of this world). Thus, the one and the same śūnyatā has these two aspects.

In a like manner, the term Bodhisattva itself is to be understood in two ways: the one is a Bodhisattva as a Buddha-to-be (ascending, from *sattva* to *Bodhi*) and the other is a Bodhisattva as a celestial being, or Bodhi-being, such as Avalokiteśvara, Mañjuśrī, and so on. The activities of such celestial beings, who come down from the state of Buddhahood, which is inactive and immovable, are seen in this world as the activities of a Bodhisattva.

Generally speaking, in every religious or philosophical thought, the ascending aspect is considered to be of central importance, while the descending direction is often obscured or neglected. In many cases, the term Bodhisattva is understood simply as the "Future Buddha" or the "Buddha-to-be." However, in the Mahāyānic ideal, this is not the case; the descending direction being clearly seen in terms of "apratiṣṭhita-nirvāṇa" and "saṃcintya-bhavopapatti." In other words, these two activities complement each other, and the Mahāyāna, or the way of a Bodhisattva, will not become a complete and total system without incorporating these two activities.

Similarly, the establishment of the Mahāyāna can be understood as the outcome of the Mādhyamika thought complemented by the Yogācāra thought. Although it is true that the idea of 'śūnyatā,' which is a negation of this world, was established through the great achievement of Nāgārjuna and the Mādhyamikas, the whole concept of śūnyatā was made explicit by Asaṅga and other Yogācāras when they interpreted it to include the 'existence of non-existence' (*MV,* I.13, above). It is in the Yogācāra interpretation that we find the possibility of establishing the descending direction. The Mādhyamika thought represents, as it were, the ascending of wisdom, and the Yogācāra idea represents the descending of compassion.

In concluding, I would like to reemphasize the fact that the two activities of ascending and descending are central to the Bodhisattva ideal. Furthermore, it seems to me that a religious system worthy of its name should include these two key philosophical concepts. It seems that they should appear also in other world religions. Could not the terms "fanā'" and "bagā'" found in Sufism be examples of the ascent and descent as understood in the Bodhisattva path?[36]

Chapter 4

The Silence of the Buddha and its Madhyamic Interpretation

Buddhism has been described on more than one occasion as a pessimistic religion, and since it declares that the world is full of pain and impermanence, this charge is not without foundation. However, as it is often pointed out, Buddhism does not aim merely at the annihilation of this world or at the escape from it: the Mahāyāna viewpoint teaches the very opposite in asserting the reality of this world. How, then, are we to resolve this dilemma posed by these apparently antithetical viewpoints. With this as the central problem, I wish here to discuss the significance of the enigmatic silence of the Buddha as seen from the Madhyamic position.

Generally speaking, the silence (*tūṣṇīmbhāva*) of the Buddha carries an important meaning in the domain of the Buddhist thought. H. Beckh says:

> Es würde immer noch einseitig sein, bei der Wirkung Buddhas auf seine Zeitgenossen nur die Macht seines Wortes ins Auge zu fassen. Man kennt Buddha nicht, solange man ihn nur nach dem beurteilt, was er geredet hat. Sondern zu der Macht der Rede gesellt sich bei ihm eine andere, die jene beinahe noch überragt, die Macht des Schweigens, und die Bedeutung dieses Schweigens richtig zu erfassen, ist für das ganze Verständnis des Buddhismus von grösster Wichtigkeit. Zu den allervortrefflichsten Eigenschaften, die im Sinne Buddhas ein Mensch haben oder sich anerziehen kann, gehört das Schweigen, und Buddha selbst ist immer Meister in dieser Kunst gewesen.[1]

In the following pages, Beckh further explains the various aspects of the Buddha's silence.

When the silence of the Buddha is discussed, the *catvāri avyākṛtavastūni,* the fourteen unanswered questions, are usually taken up. It should be noted, however, that there are different kinds of silence; the Buddha maintained silence for reasons other than that given for the catvāri avyākṛtavastūni.

There are many instances recorded in the sūtras in which the Buddha remains silent as a sign of approval of a disciple's exposition of a certain truth, or of acknowledgement for his supplication.[2] On the other hand, however, we find also an instance in which his silence means disagreement with an opponent's questions and arguments.[3]

The story, which includes the so-called noble silence is also famous.[4] Once the Buddha passed by a place where many bhikṣus were gathered, busily engaged in small talk. They were discussing the two kings of that time, debating as to which of the two was richer, or more powerful, and so forth. The Buddha immediately stopped them and on this occasion taught: "When mendicants assemble, there are two things to be done; either talk always about the Dharma, or keep the noble silence." While this instruction prohibits discussion of mundane topics it also affirms the value of silence. As may be gathered from this story and from many others, the Buddha loved the tranquil life. It is related in a sutta[5] that the disciples constantly remind each other that "our master loves tranquility." The Indian custom of retiring into a lonely place in the forest (*araṇya*) was adopted also by the Buddhist monks in practicing their yoga or dhyāna. It may be noted also that this same tendency manifested itself in Japan in the life-attitude known as "wabi" or "sabi,"[6] which developed under the influence of Zen discipline in combination with the ancient Japanese love of quietness.

Here, however, I should like to draw special attention to the Buddha's silence kept at the foot of the Bodhi tree at Gayā after his Great Enlightenment. As recorded in many biographies[7] of both the Southern tradition and the Northern, this episode tells of the Buddha's reluctance to preach the newfound Dharma to his fellow creatures. The Pāli version of this moment immediately after his Enlightenment is as follows:

> But if I were to teach the Doctrine, and others did not understand it, it would be a weariness to me, a vexation. Then also there naturally occurred to me these verses unheard before:
>
> Through painful striving have I gained it,
> Away with now proclaiming it;
> By those beset with lust and hate
> Not easily is this Doctrine learnt.
> This Doctrine, fine, against the stream,
> Subtle, profound, and hard to see,

They will not see it, lust-inflamed,
Beneath the mass of darkness veiled.[8]

The subtlety and profundity of the Doctrine makes its dissemination among the uninitiated impracticable. It surpasses human conception and expression. If cast into the mold of human language it only urges a contempt for the sacred Dharma and drives man into the sin of eradicating it. Preaching the Doctrine would be nothing but fruitless exertion. Thinking thus, the Buddha elects to remain silent and enter directly into Nirvāṇa.

According to the suttas, the god Brahmā Sahampati appears and, suspecting that the Dharma is about to vanish forever, which would straightway plunge man into eternal wretchedness, he repeatedly beseeches the Buddha to reconsider and expound the Dharma:

> May the reverend Lord teach the Doctrine, may the Happy One (*sugata*) teach the Doctrine. There are beings of little impurity that are falling away through not hearing the Doctrine.[9]

Thereupon the Buddha scans the world with his Buddha-vision and sees the misery of man and relenting, agrees to begin his merciful mission. Addressing Brahmā he says:

> Open to them are the doors of the Immortal, O Brahmā;
> Let them that have ears cast off their (old) beliefs.[10]

There remains the question to what historical fact does such a parable refer, but the solution to this problem is not within the scope of our present quest. For us, it is enough to know that since ancient times—at least since the time when the Buddha's biographies were being written—the deeper thinkers, the poets, were already looking upon the Buddha's preaching with the concept of silence playing an important role. That is to say, the Buddha was pictured not as going forth immediately to preach his Doctrine, but as hesitating, consumed with skepticism about man's ability to grasp the real essence of his teaching. And only with great misgivings did he consent to be persuaded to launch on the difficult task of preaching the Dharma. What is the significance of this hesitation, this silence of the Buddha? Indeed, the authors of the Buddha's biographies, in inserting this moment of hesitation between those of his Enlightenment and his momentous departure into the world, presented one of the stimuli for the cultivation of the subsequent forms of Buddhism.

Now, there is another silence that must be understood in a more metaphysical tone. The often discussed silence of Vimalakīrti, characterized by a typical Mahāyāna dialectic, is such a one. Evidences show that in certain instances the Buddha's silence falls within this category. It is stated in the Pāli suttas as well as in the Sanskrit sūtras, that the Buddha did not answer questions relating to metaphysical topics, such as the effect of karman, or existence after death, and so forth.[11] As mentioned at the beginning, a few scholars, in discussing the silence of the Buddha or the philosophical capacity of the Buddha, invariably introduce the fourteen *avyākṛta-vastūni* (things undetermined, or unelucidated, or unanswered).

The fourteen avyākṛta-vastūni[12] are the fourteen metaphysical questions that the Buddha refused to answer. They consist of such questions as: "Is the universe eternal?" "Is the universe infinite?" "Are the soul and the body identical?" "Does the Tathāgata exist after death?" and so forth. In a recent paper, Dr. T. W. Organ[13] gave an excellent discussion on the reasons behind the Buddha's silence regarding these questions. He concludes, however, that the most acceptable explanation for the Buddha's silence is a pragmatic one: the Buddha considered metaphysical speculation to be "not only useless but harmful, for it would sidetrack him from his main goal."[14] The selection of this single hypothesis makes his conclusion unsatisfactory, for while he recognizes the Buddha as a great religionist, Organ, in the course of his arguments, diminishes the Buddha's philosophical capabilities.

I submit that the Buddha was not only a religionist; he was also a philosopher. Certainly, at first glance the Buddha is seen as a misologist, concerned with only the salvation of humankind. But beneath that compassion is to be found a highly analytical mind. Dr. T. Watsuji, who has also made a study of the same topic, says, "That the Buddha did not answer metaphysical questions of this kind does not immediately mean that the Buddha denied the validity of philosophical or systematic thinking. On the contrary, a case can easily be defended in which such an attitude (of silence) constitutes the essential characteristic of a philosophy."[15] According to his interpretation, when the Buddha said that metaphysical speculation was "without profit (*attha*)," he substantially meant that it did not "lead to the highest knowledge (*abhiñña*), to full Enlightenment (*saṃbodhāya*) . . . ," that is, it does not inspire true knowledge. When one responds to such questions and abides on the same level as the questioner, he inevitably falls into the difficulty of antinomy, and this does not lead to the true knowledge that was the goal of the Buddha.

For instance, a monk named Vacchagotta once asked the Buddha if *ātman* existed. To this the Buddha replied with silence. The monk asked again if ātman, then, did not exist, but the reply was the same. Later, after the monk had left, the Buddha explained to Ānanda the reason for this silence. If he had made the affirmation, "ātman exists," then it would have meant that he agreed with the same doctrine of ātman held by Vacchagotta.

This is not the true doctrine of ātman, but a kind of misleading Eternalism (*śāśvata-vāda*). On the contrary, if the Buddha had merely replied, "ātman exists not," then it would have meant that he accepted a non-ātman theory, which also involved a false stand, that is, a Nihilism (*uccheda-vāda*).[16] This shows that either reply, affirmative or negative, inevitably agrees with the false assumptions that lay within the question. Facing such an antinomy, the expression by language must remain impotent.

Thus, Dr. Tetsuro Watsuji concludes that the Buddha did not avoid philosophical problems merely for religious considerations, but that "he refrained from answering them simply because they were not true philosophical problems."

Indeed, for every passage in the suttas suggesting the misological tendency of the Buddha, there is a passage showing the Buddha to be highly rational and critical.[17] For example, the Buddha says the following:

> Accept not what you hear by report, accept not tradition: do not hastily conclude that "it must be so." Do not accept a statement on the ground that it is found in our books, nor on the supposition that "this is acceptable," nor because it is the saying of your teacher.[18]

Or,

> As the wise test gold by burning, cutting and rubbing it (on a piece of
> touchstone),
> So are you to accept my words after examining them and not merely out
> of regard for me.[19]

The Buddha, of course, was not a philosopher in the narrower sense of the term of one devoted to the analysis of concepts through the use of language. Indeed, he suspected the ability of language to express Truth. This conviction of the insufficiency of language appears again and again in the Mahāyāna texts. In explaining the ādāna-vijñāna (i.e., *ālaya-vijñāna,* the store-consciousness), a gāthā in the *Saṃdhinirmocana* relates:

> Ādāna-vijñāna is highly profound and subtle;
> It is the All-seed-conscience (*sarva-bījaka*), and
> is like a violent current.
> I do not reveal it to common men,
> Lest they imagine it to be ātman.[20]

The reason the Buddha does not "reveal it to common men" is that they would, through verbal expression, be misled into the fallacy of ātmavāda. Not to reveal is here not esoterism, for the Buddha hides nothing from humankind. So long as a verbal expression is nothing but a means to communication, it serves only to alienate humans from the Truth. Not to reveal is nearer to Truth and more loyal to the dharma.

The silence of Vimalakīrti is of the same significance. At the end of the chapter "Advaya-dharma-dvāra-praveśa" (Entering the Dharma Gate of Non-duality) of the *Vimalakīrti-nirdeśanā-sūtra,* Mañjuśrī, who appears as the last in the series of Bodhisattvas attempting to describe Ultimate Reality, utters these words:

> It is in all beings wordless, speechless, shows no signs, is not possible of cognizance, and is above all questioning and answering.[21]

Finally it is Vimalakīrti's turn, and while he agreed with all that was voiced by Mañjuśrī, he expressed it by maintaining a complete silence.

The Ultimate Truth is beyond the reach of verbal designation (*prapañca*) or thought-construct (*vikalpa*). The ineffability (*anabhilāpyatva*) and inconceivability (*acintyatā*) of the Truth are descriptions frequently encountered in the Mahāyāna texts. The word is, as it were, merely a finger pointing at the moon. Just as a person would not see the moon by concentrating on the finger, he would miss Truth completely if he is engrossed in the word. No matter how minutely the word is analyzed, it will not bring about a confrontation with the Truth. *The Awakening of Faith,*[22] therefore, defines suchness (*tathatā*) as "suchness without words (離言眞如)." Yet, it is significantly supplemented with "suchness (expressed) in words (依言眞如)." Again, the Hua-yen (Kegon, 華嚴) philosophy proclaims that the realm of reward, that is, of the Buddha Vairocana, is utterly inexpressible (果分不可説), and that that which is expressible is only the realm of cause (因分可説), that is, of Bodhisattva Samanta-bhadra.[23] Thus, there is an impenetrable wall always separating the two realms. Zen thought insists that it is "transmitted outside of the doctrine" (教外別傳), and that it "does not set up letters (不立文字) that is, rely on words. This fundamental attitude of Zen expresses the same view referred to above concerning the inadequacy of language, but in the most extreme terms.

All of these Mahāyāna schools are founded upon the concept of 'śūnyatā' (emptiness) that lies at the core of Nāgārjuna's Madhyamic philosophy. Śūnyatā, furthermore, is described as inexpressible, inconceivable, devoid of designations, and so forth, which links it directly with the present problem of the silence of the Buddha. Of course, śūnyatā is not limited to the mere negation of language; it represents a much wider but consistent viewpoint that includes, besides other things, the negation of language.

Śūnyatā is originally defined as "non-substantiality" (*niḥsvabhāva-śūnya*) or as "non-perceptibility" (*anupalabdhi-śūnya*). Non-substantiality, however, does not mean the non-existence of things as it is sometimes misunderstood to mean; it means merely that beings, or things, are not really reality in themselves, that they do not possess "substantiality" and that they exist only in the manner of dependent origination (*pratītyasamutpāda*). It is in checking any attempt to give substantiality to things through conceptualization of language that śūnyatā bears the further definition of non-perceptibility. Things can not be known. If non-substantiality can be understood as an ontological term, then non-perceptibility can be understood as an epistemological one.

The inadequacy of language must be regarded as an important key in understanding the problem of the fourteen unanswered questions, and also of the Buddha's silence before his initial preaching. This same skepticism regarding the power of the word was integrated by Nāgārjuna into a clear philosophical position and explained with the concept of 'śūnyatā.' According to Dr. Watsuji, the Buddha refrained from answering the fourteen questions because he wanted to reveal these as not being conducive to true knowledge. The Buddha's silence indicates a clear philosophical position, although its crystallization into a philosophy had to await for the genius of Nāgārjuna. Indeed, the Buddha's silence was an answer; it was not merely a suspension of judgment or an utter lack of it.

Nāgārjuna, about six or seven hundred years later, recognized *prajñā*, the "highest wisdom," as constituting the crown of Buddhism with the concept of śūnyatā as its essence. He interpreted as śūnyatā (emptiness) the very subjectivity of the Buddha from which emerged the silence with respect to the fourteen questions. Furthermore, by grasping the contradictory character of words and logic, that which had been termed "knowledge (*sambodhi*)" in the early suttas was now enriched and conceived of as śūnyatā, absolute negation. Śūnyatā, however, does not end up as a mere annihilation or negation. The Madhyamic philosophy, if stated in a few words, is a logical viewpoint that sees a systematic negation of concepts, perceptions, and even logic itself. It is a logical viewpoint that proclaims logic as established only when it disappears and becomes *śūnya*.

The Mādhyamika school declares that its śūnyatā represents the very position of the Buddha, and consequently it should be termed "paramārtha" (the highest, the supra-mundane being, the absolute). Further that paramārtha is to be described as "silent." References to these points may be found in Nāgārjuna's own words:

> That which cannot be known through (the language of) others (*apara-pratyaya*),

Tranquil, cannot be designated verbally (*aprapañcita*),
Cannot be differentiated (*nirvikalpa*),
And not diverse in meaning—
Such attributes Reality (i.e., *śūnyatā*) possesses.[24]

Śūnyatā, then, transcends all conceptualization or ratiocination. It is Candrakīrti, who identifies Reality with śūnyatā in his commentary on this verse.[25] Verse 24 of chapter XXV similarly states:

Our bliss consists in the cessation of all thought,
In the quiescence of Plurality (*prapañca*).
To nobody and nowhere any doctrine (*dharma*)
By the Buddha has been preached.[26]

That all perception, all discrimination, all logic are meaningless from the supra-mundane point of view is the very nature of Buddhahood and of emptiness. Accordingly, even the Buddha's forty-five years of propagating the Doctrine is here wholly negated by the assertion that the Buddha preached not a word. Such a silence—a silence that nullifies the whole missionary life of the Buddha—is conceivable only under the name of the Absolute, the paramārtha, the emptiness. Candrakīrti also pronounces clearly: ''(About) the Absolute the Saints remain silent.''[27] Even for the Saint, for whom the knowledge of the Absolute is accessible, it remains incommunicable; it remains silent forever. No doors of verbal designation or logic leads to the paramārtha.

What, then, is the role of logic in this philosophy? On what is it established such that such propositions as ''it is silent,'' and so forth can be claimed? It is on this very same śūnyatā that logic finds its basis. While logic is negated within śūnyatā-paramārtha, through this negation itself logic will find its release.

As stated above, the śūnyatā school, in taking the stand of śūnyatā, does not end up in a mere negation. The proposition, ''the Absolute remains silent,'' does not mean either to maintain that ''the Absolute exists not,'' nor that ''the Absolute does exist.'' Just as the Buddha refrained from answering, ''ātman is'' or ''ātman is not,'' in silence there is neither affirmation nor negation. Silence is beyond such acknowledgement, which is inevitably relative in character. Besides, for one whose point of departure is śūnyatā, even the claim that all is śūnyatā is absurd, for non-assertion[28] or non-maintenance of a position is the real meaning of śūnyatā. For instance *Mūlamadhyamaka*, chapter XXII (Tathāgata), k. 11 cautions:

(The Tathāgata) should not be described as
He is void, he is non-void;
Neither should he be termed
Void and non-void simultaneously,
Nor not void and not non-void simultaneously.
But he is spoken of just for the sake of designation.[29]

Candrakīrti, with particular reference to the fourteen unanswered question, comments: "On account of that, it should not be asserted that the Tathāgata exists after death or that he does not." From this statement it is clear that the Madhyamic standpoint with regard to metaphysical questions is neither mere endless dialectical negation, nor mere temporary suspension of judgment.

Kārikā 17, chapter XXV (Nirvāṇa), of the same book also takes up the same problem of existence after death.[30] It is noted here that such a problem arises only from views adhering to the idea of substantiality (*sa-svabhāva-vāda*), not from those faithful to the idea of non-substantiality (*niḥsvabhāva-vāda*). It is because the Tathāgata is believed to exist in this world substantively that it necessarily follows that he will cease to exist after death. The Tathāgata is "śūnya," and any question regarding life after death is nonsense.

Candrakīrti then goes further and argues: as the whole world is śūnya, and being and non-being are both inconceivable, *saṃsāra* (birth and death) is not different from nirvāṇa; saṃsāra is identical with nirvāṇa. It is here, at this point, that logic, which had been negated earlier, is again affirmed.

Ordinarily, saṃsāra and nirvāṇa stand as opposite poles in a rigid dualism, but seen through the eyes of śūnyatā or paramārtha or "silence," the two become equated. Similarly, while on the one hand, language is negated and stripped of all its potency, on the other, it gains increased vitality and emerges in all its brilliant glory. Indeed, only in the recognition of the identity between nirvāṇa and saṃsāra will there be any validity in language.

Nāgārjuna explains that an activity become possible only when the world is śūnyatā. It is inconceivable that an activity takes place in a substantive being, for a substantive being is understood to be an eternal, immutable being, and, therefore, could not be active and undergo change. Only when there is no substantiality, that is, when śūnyatā is, can there be change and activity. This point is discussed thoroughly in chapter XXIV (Āryasatya) of the *Mūlamadhyamaka*. An opponent charges:

If everything is śūnya,
There can never be any appearance,
Disappearance, or transformation.
Hence there can be no Buddha-dharma,

Such as the Fourfold Truths,
(And, consequently, no emancipation or salvation).[31]

Nāgārjuna answers the charge with the very same words:

If everything is not śūnya,
There can never be any appearance,
Disappearance, or transformation.
Hence there can be no Buddha-dharma,
Such as the Fourfold Truths,
(And, consequently, no emancipation or salvation).[32]

The first verse depicts an attack by the Nihilists who take śūnyatā as mere nothingness. The second represents the Buddhist view that defends the position that "everything is dependently originated on account of its emptiness." Nihilism (*nāstika*), while claiming to represent non-substantiality (*niḥsvabhāvavāda*), shows itself to be, in fact, a kind of realism (*sasvabhāvavāda*).

A similar exchange, but now with reference to the logical capabilities of language, appears in the *Vigrahavyāvartanī* of Nāgārjuna. Here, in verse 1, the opponent charges:

If everywhere everything is devoid of svabhāva (own being)
Your words (that proclaim niḥsvabhāva) are also without svabhāva.
How, then, is it possible to negate svabhāva,
(since words do not exist)?[33]

It is not, of course, an irrelevant argument to point out that if all is śūnya, then language itself is śūnya and logical statement itself is vacuous.

Nāgārjuna's reply, in effect, would run something like this: Yes, I agree with you. As you say, my proposition, my words are altogether void without any substance. But it is for that very reason that words are able, not unable, to declare the śūnyatā of everything. Your accusations issue simply from your false assumption that everything exists substantively. You understand śūnyatā to mean nothingness, nihility, and you presuppose that the word exists substantively as a universal *agent* that possesses the power to cause something existent to vanish into something non-existent. Since you take the stand of the realist, your charge of contradiction is only natural. We, however, being exponents of śūnyatā, do not proclaim the substantiality of our words; we declare absolute non-substantiality. With words that are essentially śūnya and without substance, we can only suggest the fact that all is śūnya and non-substantial.

What Nāgārjuna does, as it were, is this: he evokes great fear by wielding a serpent-like object that is actually only a rope. That is, he uses an instrument that is in reality śūnya. Again, in relation to this idea, we are reminded of the famous phrase that appears in the *Awakening of Faith:*[34] ''words are denied by words.'' Even though tathatā (suchness) is by nature above all signs of designation, it is circumscribed unnaturally with the appellation ''tathatā.'' This is comparable to preventing others from making noises by saying in a loud voice, ''Do not utter any sound!''[35]

In any case, in such an absolute emptiness, language stands firm, logic stands firm, and the whole world stands firm for the first time. This firmness of language, and so forth, however, does not mean that language, and so forth, stand firm as substance, but that they are of the nature of *pratītyasamutpāda,* ''dependent origination.'' In his *Mūlamadhyamaka,* chapter XXIV, verse 14, Nāgārjuna says:

> When emptiness (*śūnyatā*) is established,
> The whole world will be established.
> When śūnyatā is not (realized),
> It is absurd that the whole world is (real).[36]

Also, verse 18 of the same chapter says:

> Whatever originates dependently,
> We declare it to be emptiness.
> This emptiness, further, is contingent existence.
> This, (in turn), is the middle path.[37]

The term, ''contingent existence (*upādāya-prajñapti*),'' of this verse is translated into the Chinese 假名 (literally, provisional appellation), and 假設 (literally phenomenal accommodation), and others. It means, however, the *reestablished* word, after it had been negated once by śūnyatā, and not the original, defiled, and worldly language. Therefore, it can rightly be equated with the middle path. Nāgārjuna similarly concludes his *Vigrahavyāvartanī* with this statement:

> It is only when all is *sūnya,* that all can be spoken of—,
> and this should be realized inwardly by everyone.[38]

The terms ''language,'' ''logic,'' ''words,'' ''utterances,'' and so forth, which are used in this paper, refer to the Sanskrit ''vyavahāra.'' Although vyavahāra is translated into the Chinese 言說 (literally, word and speech), it really includes both meanings of language and logic. Logic, again, is akin to such terms as "nyāya," "yukti," "pramāṇa," and especially "anumāna" (inference). The expression "Madhyamic logic" probably bears a twofold significance: (1) pure reasoning or dialectics (*nyāya, yukti*), which explains how vyavahāra will be recovered while the world is śūnya; and (2) the actual form of reasoning or syllogism (*anumāna, prayoga*), which characterizes the peculiar features of Mādhyamika treatises. The former aspect was traced roughly in the lines above, but the latter contains many problems that cannot be discussed at this time. It should be noted, incidentally, that the later split within the Mādhyamika school into the Svātantrikas and the Prāsaṅgikas, was caused chiefly by the disagreement regarding the degree to which this kind of logic should be recognized as valid.

Generally speaking, to establish a proposition "to be logical (for anyone)" means "to be deeply aware of (the meaning of) satya-dvaya-vibhāga" (discriminating between the Twofold Truth).[39] That is to say, if one wishes to be logical in one's statement or proposition, first one must recognize deeply and correctly the difference between the Twofold Truth. However, there arose a controversy between Candrakīrti and Bhāvaviveka in regard to how the term satya-dvaya-vibhāga was to be understood.[40] The Twofold Truth is composed of paramārtha (superworldly or absolute) and saṃvṛti (worldly or conventional). These two lie sharply contrasted, the former as the real truth, and the latter as the truth forever concealed by the veil of falsehood and ignorance.[41] Now, according to Nāgārjuna, although paramārtha transcends vyavahāra and is "silent," it has no other means by which to reveal itself than by worldly and conventional expressions.[42] Such is the very core of the teaching of the Twofold Truth and the "discrimination" (*vibhāga*) of it.

It may then be correct to say that the Twofold Truth opens a channel by which language recovers itself in spite of its falsehood and ignorance. As the "silence" of paramārtha is true "Wisdom" (*prajñā*), logic, which was recovered and molded into the form of language, represents "Great Compassion" (*mahā-karuṇā*) of the Buddha toward the illusory world.[43] The Madhyamic logic, which consists of the Twofold Truth, is accordingly to be named a logic of Love—a skillful device of the Great Compassion—supported by the Wisdom of śūnyatā.

When language once recovers itself, its conceptualizations, inferences, and so forth, are likewise justified. It is here, however, that the discord between the two Mādhyamika schools begins. Bhāvaviveka and other Svātantrika teachers seem to insist that there should be syllogisms and inferences that are unique to them and that are precise to the highest degree. They strive to arrange elaborate inferences, which, though expressed in conventional language, mirror paramārtha and emanate, so to speak, from it, and which, being devoid of any logical fallacies, possess their own self-sufficient arguments (*svatantra-anumāna*).

Buddhapālita, Candrakīrti, and other Prāsaṅgika teachers, on the contrary, seem to keep themselves within the limit of the thesis that language, being able to communicate the postulate of śūnyatā, is itself śūnya. According to them, the inferences and syllogisms, however accurate they may be, belong in the final analysis to the saṃvṛti (conventional) world. In contrast to the paramārtha of Buddha's silence, they remain forever false and are apt to lead man into delusion. If a syllogism is true and unique to Madhyamic philosophy, as the Svātantrikas claim, then it has already fallen into the error of aligning itself with the viewpoint of substantiality (*svabhāva*). Further, were syllogisms expressions of truth, we would miss the point behind Nāgārjuna's often said statement: "One who accepts śūnyatā does not present any *pakṣa* (thesis, proposition) as his own,"[44] or why the Buddha dared to remain in silence when confronted with the fourteen questions. Any thesis is not one's own; hence, a thesis is not a thesis. And yet the Prāsaṅgikas speak by using conventional language and reason with the logic of the mundane world for the simple reason that there is no other means by which the Great Compassion can manifest itself.

Owing to the natural thrust of Buddha's Great Compassion, inference and syllogism are used to elucidate śūnyatā by means of a language that is not of one's own (*svatantra*). Instead, Great Compassion is expressed by means of a language belonging to "some other"—that is, a language that is not paramārtha but which is saṃvṛti.

Nāgārjuna wrote his treatise, the *Mūlamadhyamaka-śāstra*[45] in the same manner. He employed the logic which was not his own; that is he used the logic of "some other." In short, he merely adopted the ordinary man's logic.[46] Logic can not be established on the absolute level; it can be established only on the conventional level. If that logic can be used (even if) only to expose the contradiction[47] that inevitably lurks in itself—if śūnyatā can be shown within the framework of the "other's" logic to be śūnyatā—then the task is completed. The Prāsaṅgika gained its name from the fact that by its logic of prasaṅga-āpatti, that is, by the statement: "You may inevitably fall into absurdity if you proclaim so and so."[48] It makes its opponents realize the self-contradictory nature of their own logic; thus, it uses the logic of its own opponent—that is, the logic of "some other." The Prāsaṅgika is like a man who, lacking his own weapons, kills his opponent with the opponent's sword.

The true nature of the Buddha's Great Compassion is exhibited in his complete dedication to the mundane world—to the world of word and speech, and in his utter negation of himself. Madhyamic philosophy and logic—if at all allowed—must be the philosophy and logic of the Great

Compassion in this sense. Mere silence, no matter how noble it may be, will not in itself activate Great Compassion. Great Compassion must necessarily express itself in the parlance of humanity. At the same time, however, such a "Logic of Love" must presuppose self-denial, that is, śūnyatā, and base itself upon it. Without presupposing this self-denial, logic, however precise it may be, can never mirror the Truth. As stated above, the *Awakening of Faith* elucidates the "tathatā (suchness) within words." But how is it possible to have "suchness (expressed) in words?" The *Awakening of Faith* does not clarify sufficiently how it is possible for "suchness (expressed) in words" to be recovered from "suchness without words." It is Nāgārjuna who must be credited with making clear that suchness (expressed) in words is recovered and established only when śūnyatā, which is "suchness without words," is presupposed.

The authors of the Buddha's biographies likewise believe that the Buddha undertook the difficult and seemingly futile task of preaching the Dharma, leaving the blissful silence of his Enlightenment, because of his Love for humanity.[49] T. W. Rhys Davids, gracefully portraying the Buddha's inner struggles, describes the Buddha's mood immediately after his Enlightenment as that of loneliness. "So did Gotama feel more and more intensely the immensity of the distance which separated him from the beliefs of those about him. . . . That feeling of utter loneliness which is often the lot of the leaders of men . . . broke upon him with such force that it seemed to him impossible to go to his fellow-countrymen with a doctrine. . . ." But at last "the religious side . . . won the victory," and his "love and pity for humanity . . . made Gautama resolve . . . to proclaim his doctrine to the world."[50]

A striking similarity becomes apparent between the Buddha's career, his inner life, and the philosophical system of the Mādhyamikas. A careful consideration of this likeness will lead, on the one hand, to a correct understanding of the Buddha's silence, and on the other, to a proper appreciation of the various philosophical systems of the Mahāyāna, all of which claim the Madhyamic philosophy as their substructure. If the Buddha had really rejected metaphysical and philosophical speculation, and kept silent merely from pragmatic considerations, then we would be at a loss to understand how, on the foundation of Nāgārjuna's śūnyatā, the superstructure of the philosophies of Asaṅga and Vasubandhu, and much later, those of T'ien-t'ai and Hua-yen, and of many others, were ever developed. The philosophical teachers of the later days, however, were by no means going counter to the Buddha's commandments. Nay, they are unequivocal in their contention not only that they did not misunderstand the Buddha's doctrine, but also that they had grasped and elucidated the very essence of his teachings.

Consequently, Nāgārjuna's śūnyatā indeed may be considered to have unveiled the real purport of the Buddha's silence and to have given it a vital significance. In both Gautama's turning of the Wheel of the Dharma and Nāgārjuna's Madhyamic philosophy, the reversion to worldly life is possible only through the negation of it once. This reaffirmation and reinstatement of life on the worldly plane is effected through Great Compassion. All philosophies of later Buddhism must also have been established on the basis of and by presupposing such a self-negation. There is never a mere naive trust in human powers of reasoning, logic, and so forth. On the contrary, all these issues must be wholly annihilated, negated, and reduced to valuelessness. Only through this negation of the world will the parlance with fellow men be recovered. From this consciousness of the utter powerlessness of man, the most profound Love towards humanity is born.

Chapter 5

"What Remains" in Śūnyatā: A Yogācāra Interpretation of Emptiness

Meditation has occupied a position of cardinal importance in Buddhism throughout its history. From the very beginning, it has been generally accepted that the higher reach of wisdom (*prajñā*) is attained either through or accompanied by meditation (*dhyāna, samādhi,* and so on). Examples of this idea can be seen in various formulas such as "the pairing of quietude and insight" (*śamatha-vipaśyanā-yuganaddha*), and in the last two of the "three disciplines" (*śīla-samādhi-prajñā*), the "five faculties" (*śraddhā-vīrya-smṛti-samādhi-prajñā*), and the "six perfections" (*dāna-śīla-kṣānti-vīrya-dhyāna-prajñā*).

Various things were adopted as objects of meditation, such as "impurity," "respiration," the "fourfold truth," and the "three dharma-marks," but later on, in Mahāyāna Buddhism, śūnyatā, or "emptiness," also came to be recognized as an object of this sort. The "three doors to enlightenment" (*trivimokṣa-mukha*), also called the "three concentrations" (*tri-samādhi*), which comprehend "the empty," "the signless," and "the wishless," as its members, were widely recommended as objects of practice. Among these three, emptiness may be regarded as the most fundamental, embodying the other two. In this way, although emptiness is usually regarded as "non-existence," it is not merely an ontological or metaphysical concept, but also a decidedly practical one. "Emptiness has far-reaching consequences for the religious life," as Richard Robinson has said.[1]

It was Nāgārjuna who established the concept of 'emptiness' with a highly philosophical shading, but to him, too, the concept seems to have been significant not only in a philosophical and logical context but also in a religio-practical sense. The Yogācāras, who, as the name suggests, were greatly concerned with yoga-praxis, inherited the Nāgārjunian notion of emptiness, and, when they elucidated features of yoga-praxis such as the six pāramitās, the ten bhūmis, and so on, emptiness, seems to have been the basis of their theories. The Yogācāra treatises enumerate "ten kinds of mental distractions" (*vikṣepavikalpa*) as obstacles to right meditation; however, many passages of the *Prajñāpāramitā-sūtra* are introduced that act as antidotes to these obstacles and that also convey the full meaning of śūnyatā.[2] Also, the "sixteen kinds of emptiness," which were originally expounded in the *Prajñāpāramitā-sūtras,* are important in the Yogācāra school, where the idea is elaborately expatiated.[3] In their interpretation of 'emptiness,' however, there are many features peculiar to their own school.

Emptiness was not the monopoly of Mahāyāna, for it appears in earlier Buddhism, too; it is not difficult to find the word "empty" in the Nikāyas and Āgamas. Among the Āgamas and Nikāyas, the *Cūḷasuññata-sutta* ("Lesser Discourse on Emptiness")[4] invites our special attention.

In this sutta, the Lord Bhagavān expounds for Ānanda the meditation on emptiness, saying: "I . . . through abiding in [the concept of] emptiness, am now abiding in the fullness thereof," and he goes on to say that, when the monks are gathered in a hall in which there is no elephant, no cow, and so on, the hall "is empty of elephants, cows, and so forth" and yet, "there is only this that is not empty, that is to say the one thing [which is not empty but] grounded on the Order of monks." Likewise, when a monk practices meditation in a forest, he perceives no village, no villager, and attends only to one thing that is not empty and grounded in the perception of the forest. His mind being pleased with and freed in the quietness of the forest, he comprehends thus: "The disturbances that might arise from the perception of a village do not exist here . . ." and yet, "there is only this degree of disturbance, that is to say, one thing grounded in the perception of a forest." That is, by practicing 'emptiness,' he acquires freedom from the disturbances (*daratha*) of villages and villagers, but the loneliness of the forest itself becomes for him a new disturbance, which should be negated through further mediation. By recourse to such mediation and negation, he travels through a number of stages, including the highest stage of trance in the "formless world," to reach, finally, "the concentration of mind that is signless" (*animittaṃ cetosamādhiṃ*). In this final stage, he is freed from every canker of "outflowing impurities" (*āsava*) and obtains Arhatship; and yet there remains the disturbance (*daratha*) of "the six sensory fields that, conditioned by life, are grounded in this body itself."[5] Thus, his corporeal being, which even the Arhat can never nullify, is his ultimate disturbance. At every stage of the progress just described, the following statement is added:

> It is perceived that when something does not exist there, the latter [the place] is empty with regard to the former. Further it is comprehended that something that remains there does exist as a real existent.[6]

The sutta repeats this sentence eight times in all. It states that emptiness is non-being on the one hand but that there is, on the other, something remaining therein which, being reality, cannot be negated. Emptiness includes both being and non-being, both negation and affirmation. This is the true definition of emptiness, as the sutta goes on to say:

> Thus, Ānanda, this comes to be for him a true, not mistaken, utterly purified and incomparably sublime realization of [the concept of] emptiness.[7]

The *Cūḷasuññata-sutta* does not seem to have attracted the attention of the Mādhyamikas, but it is given a special significance in the treatises of the Yogācāra school.

First, the *Madhyānta-vibhāga*[8] expounds the relationship between the ''unreal notion'' (*abhūtaparikalpa*) and ''emptiness'' (*śūnyatā*) in verse I.1. The actualities of daily life are here summed up as ''unreal notions,'' which are a discrimination between, and attachment to, two things—the subject grasping and the object grasped (*grāhaka, grāhya*). This two-ness, though indispensable for discrimination or conceptualization, does not have any reality at all; here, emptiness is found to belong to the ''unreal notion'' or ''imagination.'' (The adjective unreal is used to qualify the notions or imagination that singles out as existent things that are ''non-reals,'' that is, ''empty.'') At the same time, however, this ''unreal imagination,'' in spite of emptiness, is constantly operative. Hence, unreal imagination again arises in emptiness.[9]

This rather tortuous argument is repeated in the next verse, *MV* I.2, from a slightly different perspective:

> All entities, therefore, are neither exclusively empty nor exclusively non-empty. This is so because of the existence [of the ''unreal imagination''], because of the nonexistence [of the duality of the subject and object], and again because of the existence [of the emptiness of the ''unreal imagination''], as well as the existence [of the ''unreal imagination'' as the locus of emptiness]. This whole schema is named the Middle Path.[10]

When Vasubandhu comments on verse *MV* I.1, he states:

> Thus [in this verse] the characteristic of emptiness has been shown in an unperverted way as stated: ''It is perceived as it really is that, when anything does not exist in something, the latter is empty with regard to the former; and further it is understood as it really is that, when, in this place, something remains, it exists here as a real existent.''[11]

The words "as stated" suggest that the passage enclosed in quotation marks is a quotation from some scriptural authority; and, if this be the case, the quotation has to be nothing other than the idea of the *Cūḷasuññata-sutta,* the similarity between the sutta and this passage being quite clear.[12] Vasubandhu also observes that, in accordance with this sutta passage, emptiness can be "shown without perversion." And the interpretation of emptiness by the Yogācāras seems actually to be in basic agreement with the point of view of this sutta.[13]

The expression, "something remains" (*avaśiṣṭa*), however, is enigmatic indeed, for śūnyatā is generally accepted as non-being, negative in character, while something remains positively asserts the existence of something. Perhaps one should understand this as an ultimate reality that is never denied, not even at the extremity of radical negation; it is, for instance, similar to the situation in which one cannot negate the fact that one is negating. It is affirmation found in the midst of negation, and it is true existence because it is found in negation.

MV I.13, presumably in keeping with the idea stated earlier, expounds a definition of śūnyatā that says:

> Truly, the characteristic of emptiness is the nonexistence of the duality [of subject and object], and the existence of [that] nonexistence.[14]

Thus, emptiness comprehends not only the "nonexistence" but also the "existence of nonexistence," which turns out to be a special feature of the Yogācāra interpretation. The idea of adding the concept of 'existence of nonexistence' was, however, severely attacked by the later Mādhyamikas:[15] according to them, the true meaning of śūnyatā is "nonexistence," that is, nonexistence through and through; to add 'existence of nonexistence' is not only superfluous but also absurd because of the resulting internal contradiction.

In later Chinese Buddhism, however, one encounters the saying, "Truly empty [hence] unfathomable existence," (眞空妙有) which is to be understood as the identity of non-being and being, negation and affirmation, or as the recovery of existence from nonexistence. Actually, in the *Prajñāpāramitā-sūtra,* too, one reads: "Form is emptiness, the very emptiness is form."[16] The passage "the very emptiness is form" is neither redundant and superfluous, nor a repetition of the preceding passage, for it opens up a new horizon of true existence in the wake of negativism of "form is emptiness." Nāgārjuna, too, is said to have established the true significance of worldly phenomena in his *Mūla-madhyamakakārikā,* chapter XXIV.[17] Especially in verse eighteen, he equates śūnyatā, originally identical with pratītya-samutpāda ("dependent origination"), with yet another notion, namely, that of "upādaya prajñāptiḥ" ("designation having recourse to materials"), and finally with the Middle Path. The whole scheme of this verse looks like a prototype of *MV* I.1–2, given earlier; the notion of abhūtaparikalpa in the latter stands for "upādāya prajñāptiḥ"[18] here, in which all human endeavors, including religio-practical ones, are duly affirmed.

The Yogācāras, on the other hand, in their elucidation of the notions of being and non-being, often have recourse to the theory of trisvabhāva (the three natures: the imagined, the other-dependent, and the consummated). On certain occasions,[19] śūnyatā is analyzed into three: *abhāva-śūnyatā* ("emptiness as nonbeing"), *tathā-bhāva-* (or *tathā-abhāva-*) *śūnyatā* ("as thus-being" or "as not-thus-being"), and *prakṛti-śūnyatā* ("essential emptiness"), and the three are then related to the imagined nature (*parikalpita*), the other-dependent (*paratantra*), and the consummated (*pariniṣpanna*), respectively. Thus, "emptiness" synthesizes all three natures (which together represent all states of entities without exception), especially those of "non-being" and "being" in terms of parikalpita and paratantra, respectively. "Something remains," mentioned earlier, corresponds exactly to this idea of paratantra (thus-being but empty, or not-thus-being, hence empty, as seen before), which was equally a target of attack on the part of the Mādhyamikas.[20]

A statement similar to that of the *Cūḷasuññata-sutta* also appears in other Yogācāra treatises. In the *Bodhisattvabhūmi* of the *Yogācārabhūmi*, "emptiness rightly understood" (*sugṛhītā śūnyatā*) is explained.[21] Here, though there is no evidence of citation, there occurs a passage almost identical with the one quoted in the *MV*—a passage in which it is emphasized that the unperverted, true view of emptiness is taught.[22] The basic idea is further exemplified by the term "rūpa" ("form"). Rūpa, which is accepted as real in Abhidharma philosophy, is empty, insofar as it is an entity constructed by thought. But there is still something remaining, which, though itself unfathomable, has reality insofar as it provides a locus (*āśraya*) for the designation (*prajñapti-vāda*) of rūpa. The interpretation here is different from that of the *Madhyānta*, but there seems to be no essential difference between the ideas of these two treatises.

The passage in question appears also in the *Abhidharma-samuccaya* of Asaṅga, which has been preserved in its entirety in Chinese and Tibetan but only in fragments in the original Sanskrit.[23] It is here closer to the version of the *Bodhisattvabhūmi* than to that of the *Madhyānta*, perhaps indicating that the *Abhidharmasamuccaya* is quoting from the *Bodhisattvabhūmi* (?). This similarity becomes obvious when the Tibetan (as well as Chinese) versions of these treatises are compared.[24] According to the latter interpretation, what is negated is "ātma-ātmīyatva" ("self-hood and possession"), and what remains as real is "anātmakatva" ("selflessness"). Although there does not exist anything substantive (*ātmatva*) within entities such as the skandhas, dhātus, and āyatanas—the categories maintained by Abhidharma philosophy—yet therein there is the existence of non-existence—that is, [the reality of] "selflessness." The process of the argument is identical with that of the "nonexistence and existence of nonexistence" in the *Madhyānta*.

A most interesting exposition of śūnyatā, in this connection, is found in the *Hsien-yang-shêng-chiao-lun* (or **Āryadeśanā-vikhyāpana*) of Asaṅga, which survives only in Chinese, not in Sanskrit or Tibetan. At the beginning of chapter 6, "Establishment of Emptiness," there is a verse that reads:

> 若於此無有　及此余所有　随二種道理　説空相無二
>
> When [it is realized that] nothing exists here, and yet something of it remains—then the nonduality of emptiness is explained in accordance with twofold reasoning.[25]

In the prose commentary, the "twofold reasoning" (*yukti*) is explained in this way: (1) the two kinds of selfhood, that of person (*pudgala-ātman*) and that of things (*dharma-ātman*), do not exist, but (2) the two kinds of nonself (*nairātmya*) do exist. Thus, emptiness is explained as neither eternally existing nor eternally nonexisting. The wording in this reasoning is very close to that of the *Abhidharmasamuccaya,* and the process is again completely identical with the idea of 'nonexistence and existence of nonexistence' in the *Madhyānta.*

The verse was most probably composed by Asaṅga himself, and its most interesting feature is that, although in this verse "something remaining" appears in a manner very similar to that of the texts just discussed, it is stated almost as if it were a thought originating with Asaṅga himself. But it is already clear that the idea of 'something remaining' can be traced, through these Yogācāra treatises, back to the *Cūḷasuññata-sutta*. This may indicate that this particular sutta was very familiar to the Yogācāra school.

When Asaṅga wrote a commentary, the *Kārikāsaptati,*[26] to the *Vajracchedikā Prajñāpāramitā,* he employed the same idea of 'nonexistence and existence of nonexistence' in several verses.[27] In the Prajñāpāramitā-sūtras are very often seen contradictory expressions (*vyatyasta-pada*)[28] such as:

> The Buddha's own and special dharmas . . . just as not the Buddha's own and special dharmas have they been taught by the Tathāgata. Therefore they are called "the Buddha's own and special dharmas."[29]

Or:

> That which is true perception, that is indeed no true perception. Therefore the Tathāgata teaches, "true perception, true perception."[30]

In these statements, what is first negated is next affirmed; the word "therefore" is used even to connect the negation with its succeeding affirmation. The principle of 'nonexistence and existence of nonexistence' will be found to be a convenient and wholly suitable basis for interpreting these contradictory expressions.

Indeed, in all the Yogācāra treatises mentioned, the idea of 'nonexistence' *cum* 'existence of nonexistence' is given as the basic principle for the interpretation of emptiness in this school. And it may be said that the addition of existence of nonexistence, though an object of controversy, has come from "what remains" as stated in the *Cūḷasuññata*. What remains, of course, conveys the real meaning of śūnyatā in this school and never implies any "realism" whatever, substantialism being rejected by all Mahāyānists.[31]

A different application of the passage containing the expression "something remains" occurs also in the *Ratnagotra-vibhāga*. The tenets of the *Ratnagotra* are regarded as rather close to those of the Yogācāras;[32] however, to the extent that the *Ratnagotra* is a treatise expounding the theory of "tathāgatagarbha" ("matrix of the tathāgata"), its understanding of the passage concerned seems to be fairly different from that of the Yogācāras. This point shall now be discussed.

The passage under consideration appears in the prose commentary to verses I.154–155 in which "the emptiness of the tathāgatagarbha" is explained.[33] The tathāgatagarbha, which may also be called "tathāgatadhātu" ("element of the tathāgata"), "buddhatva" ("Buddhahood"), and so on, is perfectly pure in terms of its primary nature; therefore, there is no contamination to be removed from it, nor any purity to be added to it. As stated in the *Śrīmālādevī-sūtra*,[34] the tathāgatagarbha is empty in respect to contaminations, but by no means empty in respect to the virtues of Buddhahood, which are inconceivable, and far beyond the sands of the River Ganges in number. After these statements, the passage that contains "what remains" is introduced,[35] without any evidence as to whether or not it is a citation.

The differences between the *Ratnagotra*, on the one hand, and the *Madhyānta* and other Yogācāra treatises, on the other, with regard to the understanding of this passage, can be summarized in two points.

1. The theory that the tathāgatagarbha is empty as well as nonempty is established on the authority of the *Śrīmālādevī*; but here the items negated

are contaminations only, while the tathāgatagarbha itself is never negated. Contaminations or defilements are always accidental or adventitious (*āgantuka-kleśa*), not essential to the tathāgatagarbha, and therefore to be counteracted by the practice of meditation, and so on. But the essence of the tathāgatagarbha comprises the immeasurable virtues of Buddhahood, and these virtues are by no means empty.

In this case, the subject of "is not" (negation) and the subject of "is" (affirmation) are different from each other, the former being defilement and the latter virtue. In the Madhyānta, however, one and the same entity (*abhūtaparikalpa*) is the subject of both "is not" and "is," of both nonexistence and existence. The duality of subject and object, which is essential to abhūtaparikalpa, is negated; hence, śūnyatā is. And that very emptiness of what is empty is never negated, is never nonexistent. It is in this sphere of śūnyatā that abhūtaparikalpa takes its shape anew; hence, "existence of nonexistence." In such a case, one and the same thing possesses a kind of "double structure" of being and non-being. This double structure will be seen both in abhūtaparikalpa and in śūnyatā; in its aspect of 'non-being,' the abhūtaparikalpa necessarily turns out to be śūnyatā, while in that of 'being,' śūnyatā itself naturally becomes abhūtaparikalpa.

But such a double structure is not conceivable in the case of the tathāgatagarbha; there is no link between the glorious virtues of Buddhahood and mundane defilements. In the *Ratnagotra* and its authority, the *Śrīmālādevī,* the subject of "is not" is defilement, and that of "is" is Buddhahood. Buddhahood, the essence of the tathāgatagarbha, cannot be simultaneously being and non-being—it is 'being' through and through, purely, eternally, and absolutely.[36]

2. The understanding of "what remains" in the *Ratnagotra* is also quite opposite to that of the Yogācāra treatises. In the context of the *Ratnagotra,* what remains necessarily becomes something remaining after every defilement is destroyed; that is, what remains is the "tathāgatagarbha" in terms of the Buddha's virtues, which are never empty. This is just the opposite from the *Cūḷasuññata* and the *Madhyānta* and other treatises, because in the *Cūḷasuññata* what remains is ultimately the corporeal being, the strongest hindrance for human spiritual endeavors, and in the *Madhyānta* it is unreal imagination, which likewise represents the world of delusion. Both of these are mundane entities and disturbances (*daratha*), far removed from the tathāgatagarbha, which is characterized only by the highest qualities. These latter texts seem to suggest that defilement is very difficult, almost impossible, to erase—it remains even after a sort of enlightenment is obtained. In other words, enlightenment is deepened only to reveal that disturbance cannot be banished even at the final stage. In

contrast to this, the *Ratnagotra* seems rather optimistic about the possibility of annihilating defilements.

In the *Ratnagotra,* what remains is literally understood simply as an arithmetical remainder; one subtracts defilements from the tathāgatagarbha and the remaining difference is Buddhahood. This arithmetical subtraction[37] involves no error at all. But, given this simple subtraction, the fact that after the annihilation of defilements there always remains a new defilement cannot be adequately explained. In such subtraction, one cannot see the dialectical double character that is fundamentally the character of emptiness, and whose basic meaning is expressed in the concept of emptiness.

Or, one might put it in this way: although the *Ratnagotra* proposes to discuss "the emptiness of the tathāgatagarbha," it does not state explicitly that the tathāgatagarbha is empty; on the contrary, it actually emphasizes, instead, its "nonemptiness." In short, it claims that "defilement is empty," but at the same time, that the tathāgatagarbha has no qualities to be negated. When one is left with this understanding, it is natural to apply the model of arithmetical subtraction to the idea of emptiness, which was, however, originally dialectical.

Thus, one cannot but have doubts concerning the *Ratnagotra's* usage of this expression. Considering that there is no evidence that this has been quoted from some other source, could it not be said that the passage represents an independent ideal original to the author of the *Ratnagotra* commentary? If this is not the case and if its source is the *Cūḷasuññata-sutta,* is not the passage misapplied? What was the purpose behind the *Ratnagotra* introducing this passage into its scheme? If its purpose was to prove "the emptiness of the tathāgatagarbha," why, instead of stating the emptiness of the tathāgatagarbha, did it maintain its 'being' in the final analysis?

Generally speaking, what remains is encountered by a practitioner when one is awakened. When consciousness is converted (i.e., in the *āśraya-parāvṛtti*) through training and truly becomes pure faith, the truth of tathāgatagarbha will be realized as "what remains." According to the tathāgatagarbha doctrine, however, it is accepted generally that the tathāgatagarbha has always existed so that it is actually not what remains, but rather "what has existed from the beginning." In the śūnyatā doctrine, the situation is quite the reverse. After śūnyatā has been realized through the medium of abhūta-parikalpa, abhūtaparikalpa itself is re-realized as having always existed in emptiness and again as remaining forever in that same emptiness. Only when such a realization and the re-realization of disturbance are combined will Buddhahood become manifest, the "consummated" (*pariniṣpanna*) be achieved, or the "Middle Path," be traversed.

Owing only to its double character of being and non-being, emptiness can be the principle underlying those old Mahāyānic sayings such as ''Defilement is identical with bodhi,'' ''Birth and death are equal to nirvāṇa,'' ''Without destroying defilements one enters into the nirvāṇa,'' and so on. The double structure found in the relationship between abhūtaparikalpa and śūnyatā represents the identity or the nonduality between saṃsāra and nirvāṇa. Unless the double structure of the world, which is characterized as ''empty,'' is apprehended, these Mahāyānic sayings remain meaningless paradoxes.

If, in the doctrine of the tathāgatagarbha too, these sayings are held to be true,[38] then it must follow that the tathāgata-garbha, which is often regarded as a supreme Being, is ''empty as well as nonempty,'' and also that ''defilement is the tathāgatagarbha'' in the manner that ''saṃsāra is identical with nirvāṇa.'' But such is not the case with the tathāgatagarbha doctrine. While in the *Ratnagotra* the ''mind,'' is discussed only in its ''essentially pure'' aspect (*citta-viśuddhi, citta-prakṛti*), and so equated with the tathāgatagarbha, in the *Awakening of Faith* (a treatise that appeared later and extant only in the Chinese version by Paramārtha), the tathāgatagarbha is found within the ''ordinary human mind.'' This mind is defined as having two aspects: ''the mind of suchness'' and ''the mind in saṃsāra,'' but the text seems to put more emphasis on ''the mind of suchness'' and thereby equating the human mind with the tathāgatagarbha. In contrast, in the *Madhyānta,* ''unreal imagination,'' which in a sense is more debased than the ordinary human mind, is taken up and defined as ''empty as well as non-empty'' as stated above. It is also characterized as being ''essentially lucid.''[39] However, this lucidity is realized only when the unreal imagination is negated as empty and is itself re-realized or recovered through this emptiness. This view of the *Madhyānta* does not advocate a higher being such as the *Tathāgata,* a view that was reached by means of envisaging the *Cuḷasuññata-sutta* as its standpoint. The double character of abhūtaparikalpa and śūnyatā elucidated in the *Madhyānta* is hardly conceivable in the doctrine of the tathāgatagarbha.

Chapter 6

The Buddhist World View as Elucidated in the Three-Nature Theory and Its Similes

Magic shows, performed on roadsides, stages, and elsewhere, have been popular in India since ancient times. The magician, by using some material such as wood, stone, or grass, by casting magic spells, or by other devices, produces his illusions and conjures up fierce animals such as tigers or elephants, which appear to the audience and frighten them by pretending to attack.

The magic show appears in Buddhist texts as an illustration for the view that holds that worldly things are not real but only appear to be so. It is also used to elucidate the so-called "three-nature theory" (*trisvabhāva*)[1] that was expounded and elaborated by the Yogācāra school of Mahāyāna Buddhism. The magic show is cited to illustrate that a magically created form, while devoid of substance, still appears clearly to the eyes of the audience. The three-nature theory was systematized by the Yogācāra school to illustrate what it believed to be a similar feature in the world at large: the apparent reality of what is actually non-existent and empty (*śūnya*).

In this essay, I would like to discuss briefly the main features of the three-nature theory, and to examine several of the similes (*upamā*) that have been used to illustrate it. I hope to clarify the characteristics of the general theory, the characteristics of each of the individual natures, and the relationship between the three. This should help to elucidate the Yogācāra view of the world as it is explicated by this theory, a Weltanschauung of a sort peculiar to Buddhist philosophy.

I

According to the Yogācāras, all beings, whether psychical or physical, can be comprehended within these three states of existence, which in this context are called ''natures,'' *svabhāva* in Sanskrit. Everything in the world possesses these three natures. The three are: (1) ''parikalpita-svabhāva'' or the imagined nature, (2) ''paratantra-svabhāva'' or the other-dependent nature, and (3) ''parinispanna-svabhāva'' or the consummated nature.

The names given to these categories seem to have been selected not from a single consistent viewpoint but rather from several different viewpoints—epistemological, ontological, soteriological, and so on. Therefore, it may be better to explain first the general meanings and usages the three terms have.

The word parikalpa means in Buddhist usage ''imagination'' with a common implication of falsity; hence its cognate word, parikalpita, ''imagined.'' The past participle form, parikalpita, even suggests attachment (Hsüan tsang's Chinese translation of the term by 遍計所執 conveys this). When one (falsely) imagines something and becomes attached to it, the reality and existence of the thing imagined are negated. The ''imagined'' nature, therefore, is characterized by ''unreality'' and ''total nonexistence.''

In contrast to this, parinispanna or ''consummated'' means perfect, real, and existent and connotes ''reality,'' ''truth,'' ''real existence,'' or ''the absolute.'' It does not mean that this reality exists in an ontological sense or that it is to be perceived epistemologically. It is a reality completely perfected or consummated by a practitioner through arduous practice. This implies that the world of reality and truth should not be imagined to exist independently in a transcendental manner outside this ordinary world; the ordinary everyday world becomes real and true only when it has been consummated. Hence, a translation such as ''consummated,'' which conveys this fact, seems preferable to a more direct interpretive rendering such as ''truth'' or ''absolute.''

The imagined nature on the one hand, which is nonexistent, and the consummated on the other, which is real and existent, stand as direct opposites. Between them is the third nature, called ''paratantra,'' the ''other-dependent.'' It exists, but only by depending on some other entity. Paratantra stands opposed to the idea of 'svatantra,' which means self-dependent, independent, and hence absolute. It is relative and characterized by relativity.

The three-nature theory holds that the world is constituted of these three natures. This does not mean that the world is divided into three divisions or parts, and that these three components make up the world. Neither does it mean that there are three separate and different worlds. According to the three-nature theory, the world remains at all times one and the same, appearing on different occasions to possess one of the three natures. While various different worlds exist, the world of human beings, the world of animals, or the heavens, the hells, and so on, according to the three-nature theory are understood and explained as the one unchanging world being converted into these various other worlds; those various other worlds do not exist from the first.

It must be emphasized that the world remains one and the same at all times. This is the world that is dearest to us, the world into which we are born, in which we are to die, and in which we are now living. It is always this world with which we are concerned, not some other world outside and beyond it, though we might believe otherwise.

Now let me explain the three natures one by one in more detail. This one unchanging world is originally neither contaminated nor purified, but rather neutral, just like the world with which a scientist deals as the object of his research. However, insofar as our interaction with this world occurs directly or instinctively, like an animal, without reflection or self-consciousness—that is, insofar as we are not yet enlightened to its reality but remain in a deluded state—we speak of this world as a world of the imagined nature; it is an imagined world. Through our cognitions, or discriminations, or intellect, we are always projecting some kind of imagination (which is always false imagination from the Buddhist point of view) onto the world that is originally neutral. This projection of false imagination changes or contaminates the world. People become attached to this contaminated or imagined world, thinking that it is the real world. This attachment gives rise to all forms of human suffering, discontent, conflict, defilement, and so on. In short, this contaminated world to which people become attached is the world of saṃsāra, which the Buddha declared to be full of suffering. The imagined world, then, appears upon the change, conversion, or turnabout of the world from a neutral, pure, uncontaminated state to an impure, imagined, contaminated state.

The sages and enlightened ones also live in this one, unchanged world. But, because they are enlightened and are free of all false imagination and attachment, for them, the world is no longer imagined and contaminated; it is pure and consummated. The world in which they live their lives differs in no way from our world. For them, too, summer is hot and winter is cold; willows are green and flowers are red.[2] Due to their deep insight and detachment, however, only the pure and real world is manifested to them; the imagined world does not appear. It is in this sense that the one, unchanging world is referred to as possessing a "consummated" nature. It is consummated in the sense that it has assumed a nature of perfection owing to the long, assiduous training of the enlightened sages. In other words, the consummated world is established anew by them. It is not established independently outside of this world; it is the very same world, thoroughly transformed and purified. Although the *sahālokadhātu,* the world system in which we are born, is the Buddha-land of Buddha Śākyamuni, it appears to us to be contaminated, with good and bad, wisdom and folly, and so on; this world system is now manifested as the Buddha's "Pure Land" in which all these differentiations disappear, a land whose purity is visible only to those with the eyes of a Buddha. This consummated world is the world of nirvāṇa.

But what is the constituent nature of such a world, which, although neutral itself, can be transformed into the imagined world of the ordinary being or consummated by the enlightened being as the world of purity? It is the "other-dependent" nature as the constituent of this one unchanging world that makes both the transformation and the consummation possible.

The term paratantra (other-dependent) is very closely related to and conveys almost the same meaning as the term "pratītyasamutpāda" (dependent co-origination). According to tradition, the Buddha Śākyamuni acquired his Great Enlightenment by realizing the principle of dependent co-origination under the Bodhi-tree, and later taught this principle on various occasions. Many scholars regard it as the basic principle of Buddhism. It connotes the idea of the "relativity" of all things, and denies all absolutes, either ātman, brahman, prakṛti, and so forth, as permanent entities, or Īśvara as an absolute god. This characteristic of pratītyasamutpāda is to be found in the notion of the other-dependent nature. It is owing to this relativity that the world, as Nāgārjuna revealed, is śūnya (empty), devoid of the absolute. (Thus, the one unchanging world mentioned above is relative and śūnya, and the principle underlying its existence is "śūnyatā" itself.)

A world constituted of the other-dependent nature, the world of dependent co-origination, however, is beyond the scope of ordinary reasoning,[3] and thus a world not easily realized. It is realized only by a Buddha, and only as the result of his assiduous effort. Nevertheless, it often happens that an ordinary person, living in the world of the imagined nature, believes that he has grasped the paratantra world by the ordinary means of his human reasoning, which, being far from perfect, leads him to become attached to the absolute that he has grasped. He believes his imaginary creation to be true. His belief has great conviction for him. His attachment to his belief, as well as the belief to which he has become attached, are nothing other than the figments of the false imagination referred to above. The other-dependent world (the one unchanging world) is thus transformed into the imagined world. Only when attachment and false imagination are removed is the one unchanging world thoroughly purified and consummated as the pure world; that is to say, the imagined nature has become changed or converted into the consummated nature.

From the discussion above, the other-dependent nature can be understood to be the "basis" (*āśraya*)[4] for the other two natures; it is the basis in its capacity as the essential relativity. On this basis of the other-dependent, the imagined nature presents itself on the one hand as false imagination, which the ordinary person believes and becomes attached to as an absolute. On the other hand, the consummated nature is realized, on the same basis, by the enlightened. Thus, the other-dependent nature is the basis upon which the imagined nature and consummated nature both become possible. Therefore, there is neither an independent world of delusion of ordinary unenlightened people, nor an independent world of purification of enlightened sages; the worlds of the imagined and the consummated natures are both relative and interrelated, being based upon and encompassed by the other-dependent nature.

This notion of the basis of the other-dependent nature leads us to an idea of "convertibility,"[5] which describes the relationship between the three natures. The other-dependent world converts itself into the imagined world, or into the consummated world, and vice versa. The principle of convertibility (expressed by words such as "change," "transformation," or "conversion" in the previous discussion) is a remarkable and important feature of the three-nature theory. It prevails in all the three natures and enables them to constitute one and the same world. Through convertibility, it is possible for the world to be one and at the same time to possess the three natures. These changes, conversions, or transformations are possible only on the basis of the other-dependent nature.

The other-dependent nature functions as a "medium" or "mediator"[6] also in its capacity as the basis. It mediates the relationship between the imagined world and the consummated world and thus it makes possible the leap from the former to the latter, the crossing over from this shore to the other shore. It is because both the imagined and consummated natures are essentially transformations of the other-dependent nature that the imagined world can become the consummated world through the medium of the other-dependent.

A Buddhist's ultimate concern is enlightenment, or reaching the world of nirvāṇa by ridding oneself of the world of saṃsāra. Salvation, liberation, and enlightenment refer to a "crossing over" from this shore to the other shore. From the viewpoint of the three-nature theory, it is a crossing over from this imagined world to the consummated world yonder. To this extent, only the imagined and consummated natures would seem to be the ultimate concern. Actually, the dualistic view—the dualism of the deluded world and the purified world—plays a great role in most religions.

However, a bridge that will link the two worlds, a boat that will carry one across the ocean from this shore to the other, often remains as a problem. It is sometimes even said that such a link is entirely lacking in our world, because the gap between the two worlds is so despairingly deep that no conceivable human effort would be sufficient to enable one to leap over the gap or to build a bridge across it. Although most religions believe or operate under the assumption that such a bridge exists, they have rarely substantiated their claims upon a firm logical basis. It goes without saying that, insofar as it is the Buddhist's concern to get to the other shore, a bridge must exist. Actually, in the history of Buddhism, such a bridge has been postulated in various ways; one such instance is the Mahāyāna understanding of ''pāramitā'' (perfection) as ''pāram-ita'' (reached to the other shore). But what is the fundamental principle that enables the bridge to be postulated? The three-nature theory, especially through the other-dependent nature that functions as the basis of and the mediator between the imagined and the consummated, supplies an answer to this question.

Crossing over is possible only in the world of the other-dependent nature; it is not possible either in the imagined world, wherein everything is false, or in the consummated world, where the problem of crossing over, having already been overcome, no longer exists. The jump from the imagined world to the consummated world, at least from a purely theoretical point of view, cannot take place in a direct way. The abyssal gap that yawns between them is too deep and too wide. The jump must be made indirectly via the other-dependent world.

There are in Buddhism some well-known old sayings such as, ''saṃsāra is identical with nirvāṇa'' or ''defilements are themselves enlightenment.'' In the ordinary sense, saṃsāra can never be nirvāṇa; defilements (*kleśa*) are the very opposite of enlightenment (*bodhi*). They should never be confused or identified. And yet those enigmatic sayings flow out from the very fact of enlightenment; they represent directly the deep insight and profound intuition of the enlightenment experience; they are enlightenment itself. In these sayings two contradictory, opposing situations are identified directly, without being mediated by something else.

From a theoretical point of view, however, the crossing over to the consummated world occurs indirectly via the other-dependent nature. That is to say, through the elimination of the imagined world, the other-dependent world is recovered in its original purity; whereupon this recovery[7] of ''pure relativity'' itself turns out to be the consummated world. It is in this way that the other-dependent nature functions as a mediator. In this manner, the other-dependent nature is proposed by the Yogācāras as the logical basis not only for the other two natures but also for the identification postulated in the sayings mentioned above.

The Yogācāras devoted much attention to the investigation of ''cognition'' (*vijñāna*). They are also known as the ''Vijñāna-vāda'' or Cognition (-only) school, as the theory of ''cognition-only'' (see notes 16, 18) is one of the major themes. According to the Yogācāras, although cognition is essentially the other-dependent, it is in ordinary life always defiled and always appears in the guise of the imagined nature. Hence, they regard it as the "discrimination of the unreal" or "unreal imagination" (*abhūta-parikalpa*). At the same time, however, they maintain that "this cognition is turned about to constitute the Buddha's wisdom" (転識得智). This turnabout, the "transmutation of the basis" (*āśraya-parāvṛtti*) as they call it, is the final goal of the school. In this case, again, the other-dependent nature (of the cognition) functions as the basis for the turnabout or transmutation.

II

Now, let us examine several similes that appear in the Yogācāra texts as illustration of the three-nature theory. The quoting of similes to exemplify abstract theories is a characteristic feature of Indian and Buddhist texts. Similes or examples (*dṛṣṭānta, upamā*) are regarded as indispensable even for logical syllogisms (*pramāṇa, prayoga*). We must be aware, however, that a simile is nothing more than that. Even though it may be helpful for our understanding, it does not necessarily convey the full meaning that the theory intends to clarify.

In the following, I shall examine the "snake-rope-hemp," "gold-ore," and "magic show" similes.

In the first of these, snake-rope-hemp simile,[8] a man encounters a snake lying on a road at twilight, and becomes frightened. He starts to run away but then decides to examine it more closely. A close inspection of the snake reveals that it is not a snake after all but a rope. He realizes that the snake is illusory and does not exist; what really exists is the rope. He is enlightened to the fact that his situation of seeing a snake was illusory, and imaginary. But he then perceives that the rope is also illusory and less than the final reality. It can be analyzed into strands of hemp, or further into elements such as earth, water, fire, and wind, or even further. Thus, what exists in reality is hemp or elements or atoms, not rope.

In this simile, the snake is, of course, to be equated with the imagined nature, the rope with the other-dependent nature, and the hemp with the consummated nature. Both snake and rope are negated to reach the final, substantial reality, hemp. The simile illustrates well the progressive steps from the imagined snake to the rope, and from the rope to hemp, which is assumed to be the final form of existence. This simile has also been very popular in Sino-Japanese Buddhism, in which, for the sake of convenience, it is called simply the snake-rope-hemp simile; there is no mention of elements or atoms. Its significance seems to be somewhat different from the Indian usage discussed above. But I shall return to that later.

In the "lump of clay containing gold" simile[9] (*kāñcana-garbhā-mṛttikā,*) literally, "clay as an embryo of gold" (called the "gold-ore" simile here for convenience), the gold-bearing ore appears simply as clay, for no gold is visible. When the clay is burned, it disappears and gold becomes manifest.

In this simile, three things are mentioned: the gold-ore, the clay, and the pure gold. The gold-ore represents the "earth-element" (*pṛthivī-dhātu)*, which is characterized by "hardness" and which contains the "seed" of gold. It is equated with the other-dependent nature. The clay, which is transformed state of gold-ore (i.e., other-dependent nature), represents the imagined nature. The gold, another transformed state of gold-ore, is the consummated nature.

Just as it was the case in the gold-ore simile, insofar as the other-dependent world has not yet been burned away by the fire of "non-discriminative wisdom"[10] (*nirvikalpajñāna;* the highest wisdom, free of discrimination), the whole world remains as the imagined world of ordinary beings. But when burned away by the fire of non-discriminative wisdom, the one world is transformed into the consummated world of the enlightened ones, and the consummated nature is fully manifested.

The manner in which the other-dependent nature functions as a basis is illustrated well by this simile, because gold-ore is the basis for both the clay and the obtaining of the gold. From the same train of reasoning, the characteristic of the other-dependent nature as the mediator becomes evident. The simile illustrates clearly also the convertibility of the three natures, that is to say, the conversion from gold-ore (other-dependent) to clay (imagined), from gold-ore (other-dependent) to gold (consummated), or from clay (imagined) to gold (consummated).

What becomes evident in this connection, however, is that the factor that actuates the conversion from clay to gold—that is, the non-discriminative wisdom that converts the world from the defiled state to the purified state—seems to stand apart from the three-nature theory. Of course, non-discriminative wisdom is designated as belonging to consummated nature, but it is cultivated and achieved through assiduous training pursued on an established path, the logic of which seems to be somewhat different from that of the three-nature theory.

Usually, in ordinary condition, the two factors of subject and object are assumed to be indispensable. Non-discriminative wisdom, however, materializes where both subject and object are abolished. How is this possible? When the two epistemological factors, subject and object, are examined in the context of the three-nature theory, a path leading toward this non-discriminative wisdom will be found to open up naturally. That is to say, even when subject and object are held to be originally of the other-dependent nature, and discernment that makes that discrimination, being the cause of false imagination, will perforce be regarded as belonging to the imagined nature. If the cognition becomes free of this discrimination (and hence of the imagined nature) and recovers its other-dependent nature, then non-discriminative wisdom will establish itself with the consummated nature.

Thus, the three-nature theory becomes the basis not only for the conversion of the world through non-discriminative wisdom, but also for the cultivation and perfection of this wisdom.

The final simile is the one I referred to at the beginning of this paper. It is called the "magic show" (*māyā*) simile.[11] The word māyā, on its primary level of meaning, connotes "deception," "trick," "phantom," or "apparition"; secondarily, it connotes "illusion," "magic," "unreality." Māyā, as the "unreality" or "illusory image" of the universe, is a term used widely in almost a technical sense in several Indian philosophical systems. In Buddhism, however, the term māyā usually denotes "illusion" and, more specifically, "magic show." In a metaphorical sense, it is used especially as a simile for the three-nature theory, and for the other-dependent nature in particular.

As I stated before, the magician in a magic show takes pieces of wood or other materials, and by employing chemical compounds, incantations, and so forth, creates an elephant, tiger, or some other illusion. The audience is astonished, even frightened, by the magically created form. But once the magic show is over, what remains on the stage is not an elephant, but the wood or other material that was hidden from the audience throughout the performance. Although the audience is frightened by the magically created elephant, the magician is not. He remains calm and unmoved throughout, because he knows the truth about the magic and the skillful deception he is performing.

The purport of this simile can be summarized as follows. An elephant form appears; but this magically created elephant is not real; what really exists is the wood or other material. It is not difficult to see which of the three natures these three elements are intended to represent. The words "an elephant form appears" stand for the other-dependent nature; "magically created elephant" stands for the imagined nature which is "not real"; and "what really exists is the wood or other material" stands for the other-dependent nature as well as the consummated nature.

The audience is frightened on seeing the magically created elephant, because they believe that the elephant they are seeing really exists. They believe and become attached to what they see on the stage. This belief, attachment, or imagination is called the "imagined nature." Because the audience believes that what is not real is real, their belief is called "imagination."

However, no one would deny that an elephant form has appeared on the stage and that this elephant is seen by all. This undeniable fact, which would be acceptable to ordinary people and enlightened people alike, belongs to the other-dependent nature. The wood and other materials the magician employs, and the whole process of making the elephant form appear from these materials, can also be understood to pertain to the other-dependent nature. The form of the elephant is magically created with these materials as its basis, in the manner of dependent co-origination (*pratītyasamutpāda*), and this means that the creative process at work has a nature of other-depending.

Thus, the appearance of the magically created elephant and the process by which it was made to appear on the basis of certain materials (both of the other-dependent nature) are events that occur to both unenlightened and enlightened onlookers alike. Yet there is a difference. For the unenlightened ones, the events that occur serve only to expand their imagined world, because they are the causes of their attachment to the world that is originally of the other-dependent nature. For the enlightened ones, such is not the case. The unenlightened ones look at the other-dependent world through colored glasses, as it were, the original other-dependent world appearing to them not as-it-is, but tinged by the colored glass of imagination. Removing the colored glasses, like burning away the clay from the gold-ore by means of the non-discriminative wisdom, is no easy task, but once it is achieved, the other-dependent world recovers its original nature. This recovery of the other-dependent nature is none other than the realization of the consummated nature, as stated before.

The consummated world thus becomes manifested by the recovery of the other-dependent nature. Explaining the notion of the consummated nature, Vasubandhu states in his *Triṃśikā:*

> When the other-dependent nature obtains a state absolutely free of the imagined nature, it is then the consummated nature.[12]

"A state absolutely free," equated here with the consummated nature, is the "recovery" I mentioned above. In the magic show simile, the magically created elephant, which is not real, illustrates the imagined nature, while the fact that what really exists is wood or other material refers to both the other-dependent nature and the consummated nature. The recovery of the other-dependent nature, the wood and so on, thus means that what really exists is manifested. It also implies that the consummated nature is to be realized indirectly via the other-dependent nature.

In the magic show simile, the consummated nature is understood also to be the knowledge by which one becomes aware of the totality of events constituting the magic show—in other words, of the whole ongoing process of the world. It is the knowledge through which the world is seen simply as a magic show and through which it is understood that there is no elephant, except as an apparition whose nature is other-dependent. The Buddha, who is accomplished in this knowledge of the consummated nature, is compared in the simile to the magician (*māyākāra*), because the magician, like the Buddha, differs from his audience in that he is well aware of the magic show's hidden secrets.

The *Triṃśikā*, however, goes on to state:

> When this is not seen, that is not seen.[13]

Here "this" refers to the consummated nature and "that" to the other-dependent nature. The verse is in effect saying that so long as the consummated nature is not realized, the other-dependent nature cannot be realized either. This is very important in that it reveals that a direct intuitive knowledge of the truth—Enlightenment—precedes everything. As quoted above, through the state of "being free of" attachment, the other-dependent nature is recovered in its original state, and through this recovery becomes equated with the consummated nature. This indicates a direction from the other-dependent to the consummated. In the verse above the direction is opposite,[14] from the consummated to the other-dependent. Unless the consummated nature is realized, the other-dependent nature cannot be realized truly either, though the latter can be apprehended theoretically by human intellect. It is clear from this that the realization of these two natures is simultaneous. Theoretically speaking, or from a logical approach, the consummated nature may be accomplished indirectly, through the mediation of the other-dependent nature. But the basic fact of the religious experience itself is an essentially direct realization of the truth.

Therefore, the three natures are spoken of in Yogācāra texts as being "neither different from each other, nor identical to each other."[15] It should be clear from the magic show simile that the difference between the other-dependent nature and the imagined nature is very subtle and delicate; the former is compared to an elephant form and the latter to an attachment to that form. The difference is established on the basis of whether "attachment" is operative or not. The difference between the other-dependent and consummated natures is likewise very subtle. When the other-dependent nature ceases to be the cause for the delusory imagination to appear, it is identified with the consummated nature, the difference being whether such a cause is operative or not. The three natures, then, are neither different from each other nor identical to each other; or, rather, they are both different and identical at one and the same time.

Another significant feature of the magic show simile is that it can be used to illustrate the thought of "cognition—only"[16] that is fundamental to the Yogācāra school. In the Yogācāra school, the term "to appear" (*pratibhāsate, khyāti,* etc.) a word generally suggestive of the world of magic, is often used to elucidate the term "cognition" or "to know." The *MV.*, for instance, states:

> When cognition (*vijñāna*) functions, it appears as the outer world, individuality, the self, and [various other] presentations.[17]

Here, the term "cognition" signifies simply that something appears and is seen by us; in this verse, four things, "the outer world," and so forth, appear and are seen. In the case of the magic show, the form of the magically conjured elephant appears and is seen by the audience, though the real cause for its appearance is unknown to them. What exists in the magic show is the "appearance-only," not an elephant. An understanding of appearance-only can lead to an understanding of cognition-only, though it may belong to a lower level.[18] The magic show simile differs from the other two similes in that it combines thus the three-nature theory with the notion of cognition-only.

Apart from the three similes explained above, there are several others used also to illustrate the three-nature theory. The "crystal simile" (*sphaṭika*), for instance, is found in the *Saṃdhinirmocana-sūtra.*[19] When a crystal, transparent and colorless, is placed together with things of various colors, it takes on their colors. If placed with something yellow, it appears as a precious golden stone; people seeing this are deceived and become attached to what they assume to be gold. Here, the appearance and the attachment to the appearance correspond to the imagined nature, the crystal itself to the other-dependent nature, and non-existence of the gold to the consummated nature. I will not, however, explain these other similes in detail; they are, I think, represented sufficiently by the magic show and gold-ore similes elucidated above.

III

Now, we notice that each of three similes discussed above possess certain implications of its own that may influence somewhat the way in which we understand the characteristics of the three natures.

The gold-ore and magic show similes illustrate well the convertibility of the three natures. In the simile of the magic show, the very principle of magic—the fact that there is appearance-only with no real existence—is applied, equally and consistently, to all three natures. Elimination of attachment to this appearance (the imagined nature) reveals directly both the other-dependent nature and the consummated nature. The fact that the one principle remains valid for all three natures indicates most clearly the convertibility of the three natures. Convertibility is also evident in the gold-ore simile, but there the other-dependent nature is more cogently exemplified as the basis or mediator for the other two natures. Thus, although the gold-ore and magic show similes may differ in emphasis, as aids to understanding the world in terms of the three-nature theory, they both enable us to grasp the structure underlying the conversion of the one world into three and the conversion of the three into one.

In the snake-rope-hemp simile, the principle of convertibility hardly appears at all. It is perhaps possible to say that the relation between the rope and snake is a case of conversion similar to that found in the magic show, but the relation between the rope and hemp is entirely different. Hemp introduced to illustrate the consummated nature, is in fact a third element totally unrelated to the snake; it has no relation either to the snake delusion or to the elimination of that delusion. The understanding of rope as hemp results not from conversion but from an analysis that concludes that the rope is hemp, and further, elements and atoms. The analytical knowledge of hemp as the consummated nature is far removed from the Buddha's non-discriminative and yet all-embracing wisdom.

The process of understanding, which takes place in the realization that the rope is a snake, is "conversion." The process of understanding which occurs in the realization that rope is hemp, is "analysis." In the snake-rope-hemp simile, then, the two wholly different principles of conversion and analysis are merely fused together. The simile thus fails to convey the sense of a world supported and encompassed by one dynamic principle. The world it illustrates is not one world but a world of two or three separate parts fused together. The world view of a practitioner, who relied solely on this simile, would possess no sense of conversion, and consequently, any absolute world he postulated would have to exist somewhere entirely apart from this world of delusion.

The merit of the snake-rope-hemp simile is, however, that it illustrates "phases of spiritual advancement" or "stages" through which a practitioner advances in the course of his training. First, the illusion of the snake is eliminated by the perception of the rope; then, the rope is analyzed into hemp and negated. These stages of negation and analysis help a practitioner proceed, step by step, to the final stage of śūnyatā, absolute negation, which corresponds to the consummated nature.

In this case, however, the other-dependent nature remains simply a stage or a step that connects the imagined nature to the consummated nature. The rope is analyzed into hemp, the hemp into elements, the elements into atoms, and so on. The number of steps is indefinite, the analysis virtually endless. As a result, the world comes to be conceived as being not of three but of many natures. The other-dependent nature can still be assumed to be a step mediating between other steps or stages, but it loses its role as a "basis" from which to construe the steps above and below it.

It may be said that the highest merit of the three-nature theory lies in its having established a systematic and well organized world view, one which provides a doctrinal foundation for yogic practice. As a simile for exemplifying this world view, the magic show is perhaps the most appropriate. The snake-rope-hemp simile, while illustrating the path towards final liberation in terms of the three natures, fails to clarify the organic working of this world view. To explicate the three-nature theory, the Chinese Fa-hsiang school employed almost exclusively the snake-rope-hemp simile. Since most Sino-Japanese interpretations of this theory follow the Fa-hsiang, the world views they expound lack mostly the organic wholeness depicted in the magic show simile; particularly rare are interpretations that demonstrate the convertibility of the three natures, and the other-dependent nature's role as basis.

To recapitulate, in the three-nature theory a world view peculiar to Buddhism was developed. The ancient notion of "dependent co-origination" was integrated into the theory. It was called the "other-dependent nature," and was taken as the basis of the world. The other-dependent nature thus occupies the central position in the theory, the consummated nature does not, though sometimes it may be conceived to do so. From this basis, the convertibility of the world, a characteristic of this world view, is derived. This convertibility explains the world of delusion as a product of the neutral and pure world of the other-dependent nature; it is also the principle that enables the practitioner to make the leap from this shore to the other shore.

Other topics remain to be discussed, in particular the relationship between this theory and fundamental Mahāyāna standpoints such as śūnyatā and the Middle Way. In this paper, however, my intention was simply to discuss the three-nature theory by way of its similes. It is hoped that, through the discussions above, a general idea has been given of the Buddhist world view revealed in this theory.

Chapter 7

Connotations of the Word Āśraya (Basis) in the Mahāyāna-Sūtrālaṃkara

The term *āśraya,* which may be rendered roughly into English as "basis," "support," "substratum," and so forth is one of the most important terms in the Yogācāra Vijñāna-vāda School of Mahāyāna Buddhism. The reason for its importance lies in the close relationship it has with the terms "ālaya-vijñāna" and "paratantra-svabhāva," both of which are ideas fundamental to this school. Moreover, it appears in the compound *āśraya-parāvṛtti* (turning about of the basis), which is identified with "final deliverance." These ideas will be dealt with later in this paper. The importance of this word may be deduced from the fact that the *Mahāyāna-sūtrālaṃkāra*[1] (hereafter, *MSA.*) employs it in more than forty passages, a frequency almost unmatched among terms of a purely technical nature.[2] In the present paper, I will examine briefly the use made of this term in the *MSA*.

Dictionaries give various meanings for the term āśraya, some of which occur in the *MSA;* but they do not cover all the meanings found in this work. Unrai Wogihara[3] mentions "body" (*i-shen* in Chinese), a meaning which appears also in Edgerton's *Buddhist Hybrid Sanskrit Dictionary*)[4] where the meanings of "ālaya-vijñāna," "six organs," and so forth are also mentioned. In general, the basic meanings of the word, especially in the Buddhist texts, are probably "support," "body," and "recipient of states of consciousness," as put by A. Bareau.[5] I wish, however, to analyze in the following the meanings that appear in the *MSA.*, namely: (1) substratum, support, (2) basis, (3) seeking shelter, (4) origin, source, (5) agent or subject, in the grammatical sense, (6) physical body, sometimes the six sense organs, (7) the total of (human) existence, (8) *dharma-dhātu* (sphere of dharma), (9) basis of existence (*āśraya*) which is to be turned around (*āśraya-parāvṛtti*). Of course, these meanings overlap each other and are closely related to one another. The first six meanings (from substratum to physical body) may be found also in general dictionaries, but the rest are more or less peculiar to this text.

The meanings substratum, basis, and origin (the first, second and fourth definitions of *MSA*) express the most fundamental sense of the word. Sir M. Monier-Williams[6] defines āśraya as "that to which anything is annexed or closely connected or on which anything depends or rests." This definition is derived from Pāṇini and others. We cannot imagine a rider moving along without an āśraya (support, viz., that of the horse, *MSA*. XVIII, 84, 86):[7] water tastes differently in accordance with the difference of the rivers from which it is taken (substratum, *MSA*. IX 82–85). The notion "basis," which is placed by Edgerton at the top of his entry, sounds adequate. The Cosmical Body of the Buddha, (the *dharmakāya*) for instance, is the basis of the other two Bodies of the Buddha (the *saṃbhoga* and *nirmāṇa kāyas*, *MSA*. IX. 60, 65).

I should like, in this connection, to mention a peculiar example that appears in *MSA*. XI.3. Among the four reasons why a text is called "sūtra" the first is that a sūtra is "related to an āśraya." This āśraya is explained as threefold, namely, the place where (*yatra deśe*), the expounder by whom (*yena deśitam*), and the audience to whom (*yasmai deśitam*). According to Sthiramati a sūtra is a sūtra when it reads:

> Thus have I heard. The Blessed One once stayed at Rājagṛha together with many bhikṣus and bodhisattvas.[8]

In this passage the Blessed One (the expounder), Rājagṛha (the place), and the assemblage of bhikṣus and bodhisattvas (the audience) are all equally the āśraya. Such an explanation seems to fit the various meanings which will be analyzed later.

That which is a basis for something else, can, for that reason, be regarded also as the last refuge or shelter of that other being (third definition of *MSA*). The last refuge, in our case, might be the Buddha or merely a good friend. When it is said that a Bodhisattva should have recourse to a sat-puruṣa or "true-man" (*MSA*. XIII.10), or that he relies upon the kalyāṇa-mitras for support (MSA. XX.29), then āśraya means "dependence" or "help" as well as "refuge" or "shelter".

However, the meaning "basic element" is easily associated with the ideas of "origin" and "source" (fourth definition of *MSA*). A passage in *MSA*. (XVIII. 77–78) states that the pañcopādāna skandha or the five aggregates are the "basis" for the twofold misconception that a subjective person (*pudgala*) and an objective being (*dharma*) exist in reality. The basis is, in this case, nothing else than the genetic foundation of these misconceptions. When the "mind creative of Enlightenment" (*bodhicittotpāda*) is said to be the basis of the Buddhist practice (V.1), this also means that the creative mind is the cause and the origin that must necessarily precede all true efforts (*vīrya*).[9] This signification of "basis" or "origin" seems to be the widest and the most fundamental one, shading off into all the other meanings.

Let us examine the meaning of āśraya as the agent or "the subject to which the predicate is annexed" (the fifth definition of *MSA*). It is said that a bodhisattva is the āśraya of charity (and of the remaining five pāramitās, *MSA*. XVI.52–56). Here he is meant not to be the object of almsgiving but to be the subject, that is, the doer of the act of liberality. In his commentary on this passage, Vasubandhu explains āśraya as "one who offers" (*yaś ca dadāti*). And of the eight terms[10] of the verse—āśraya, vastu, nimitta, pariṇāmana, hetu, jñāna, kṣetra, and niśraya—the first seven are interpreted by him to indicate the eight syntactic cases, with āśraya corresponding to the nominative case.[11]

In connection with the meanings discussed above, the notion of āśraya as "body" (the sixth definition of *MSA*), will naturally arise; many examples of this occur in the *MSA*. The statement that one defends his āśraya against poisons and weapons (*MSA*. XV.4), and the fact that the twelve actions of Śākyamuni Buddha's *nirmāṇa-kāya* (Transformation Body), beginning with his residence in the Tuṣita-heaveṇ, are called "āśraya-nidarśana" or "manifestations of the Body" (*MSA* XX–XXI.16) are likewise examples of this usage where āśraya is meant to be the physical body (translated into Tibetan as *lus*). Āśraya, in the sentence "the āśraya possessing the ability of understanding" (*MSA* VIII.8), is translated in Sthiramati's commentary as *lus* (body);[12] a similar expression, "the āśraya competent to undertake the right effort (*vīrya*)" (VIII.10), is commented upon by Sthiramati[13] as "the body devoid of any disease."[14]

While āśraya has the meaning of the "six sense organs" in most dictionaries, it is also quite usual that the body (*deha*) is equated to the six sense organs, or that it is called the "body accompanied by the organs of the sense."[15] There is an example belonging to this category in XI.4, where the changing of a sexual organ (*vyañjana*) into that of the opposite sex is called "āśraya-parāvṛtti" (the turning about of the āśraya).[16] In these cases, āśraya means, on the whole, the body.

The ordinary body is physical and, in contrast to the invisible mind, visible. But there may be another kind of body, which abides without any discrimination between mental and physical elements. In this case āśraya could properly be translated as "the total of (human) existence" (the seventh definition of *MSA*). For instance, the differences of *vīrya* (the energy of right practice) are directly related to the differences in the āśraya of practitioners of the three *yānas* (*MSA* XVI.69). Here āśraya may mean "personality'' rather than the physical ''body''; it is rendered in the Chinese translation by *jen* (man), which corresponds to the *jana-āśraya* or *prayukta-jana* in the text. In any case, it means neither the body nor the mind, but the total existence of the sentient being. Another example of this kind can be seen in *MSA* XI.8, where the āśraya is twofold: the first āśraya leads a family life and is associated with hindrances; the other āśraya leads a homeless life and is without any hindrances. In this example, the āśraya actually means a way of life attitude, so to speak, which is to be understood as a basis or cause for the attainment of final deliverance, and which is twofold by reason of the existence or non-existence of hindrances to this goal.

The ''recipient'' mentioned in the dictionaries is close to this meaning, but it should not be misunderstood merely as a passive ''receptacle'' of the objects perceived. The āśraya as the total of existence is, however, also a storehouse being the receptacle of all products of actions in the past by which all future actions, religious or secular, good or bad, are conditioned.

Another kind of meaning, seemingly peculiar, is shown in the equating of āśraya to dharma-dhātu—''sphere of essences,'' or ''elements of mental objects'' (the eighth definition of *MSA*). In IX.66 it is stated that all the three Buddha-Bodies are in reality homogeneous, because the āśraya—the dharma-dhātu in the commentary—is one and the same.[17] Now, among the various meanings of dhātu, the most predominant are ''sphere'' or ''plane'' on the one hand, and ''element'' or ''cause'' (*hetu*) on the other. And both of these implications approach the central meaning of āśraya in the sense of basis or origin.

But, of what is the dharmadhātu a basis? A term ''sarva-traga-āśraya'' (universal āśraya) appears in another passage (*MSA* XI.44). According to the commentaries on it, the dharmadhātu, undefiled and synonymous with emancipation, is called ''*sarvatraga-āśraya,*'' because it is a basis common to the three kinds of men, śrāvaka, pratyekabuddha, and bodhisattva. That the dharmadhātu, the sphere of the Buddha's Enlightenment, is referred to as the common basis or the common ground of the three kinds of men seems to be due to the consideration that ultimately all three kinds of men aspire to attain Enlightenment, even though their actual ways of practice (and hence the preconceived Enlightenment for which they aim) may be different.[18]

However, the most important usage of āśraya in this text is probably that of *āśraya-parāvṛtti,* (the ninth definition of *MSA*) which occurs more than twelve times with the variations of ''°parivṛtti,'' ''°parivartana,'' or ''parāvṛtta°.''[19] The āśraya-parāvṛtti may be translated literally as ''turning about of the support.'' It implies various meanings such as emancipation (*mokṣa*) and absolute independence (*sva-tantra*) (*MSA* XIX.54), perfection (*parinișpanna) (MSA* XI.17–18), the first bhūmi or stage of the bodhisattva's career, which usually is called the "darśana-mārga-prāpti" or "the entering into the way of illumination in truth" (*MSA* XIV.29), and, at the same time, the buddhabhūmi (*MSA* XIV.45) that culminates in the "bhāvanā-mārga" or "the way of cultivation." Hence, it implies also the attainment of the dharma-kāya or the Cosmical Body (*MSA* IX.60) and the Highest Wisdom (*MSA* VI.9). All these interpretations convey something that stands for the highest and final aim of Buddhism. However, we cannot determine what the word āśraya actually meant in these passages. What was it that revolved to make the attainment of Supreme Enlightenment possible? The object of such a revolution could be neither the mere physical body as opposed to the mind, nor the mere material basis, and of course it could not be the grammatical subject.

The most appropriate interpretation of āśraya in this case appears to be the total of (human) existence (the seventh definition of *MSA*),[20] which comprises all other meanings mentioned above.

Definitions of āśraya and āśraya-parāvṛtti are, however, found in other treatises also. In the *Mahāyānasaṃgraha,*[21] for instance, āśraya is explained as an "appellation of paratantra-svabhāva" (other-dependent nature), which is akin to "pratītyasamutpāda" (dependent origination). It is the field or plane where the state of contaminated existence has "revolved" to that of purity; the result of this turning about is called "emancipation" and "mastership" (*vibhutva*), and indicates the "refined aspect" of paratantra-svabhāva.[22] Such an explanation of āśraya, however, remains abstract because it indicates or describes a form of existence, but not the thing in itself.

It is stated in the *Triṃśikā* that āśraya is "ālaya-vijñāna" (the store-consciousness) that has the characteristics of *vipāka* (maturation) and *sarvabījaka* (universality of seeds). The word ālaya here has meanings quite similar to those of āśraya; that is to say, the ālaya is, on the one hand, the "receptacle" or the storehouse where all impressions (*vāsanā*) of past influences are deposited and preserved, and, on the other, it is the "source" of all future phenomena, because, according to the doctrine of this school, the impression itself acts also as *bīja* or seed of future activities. Thus, ālaya is a "basis" where the effects (*vipāka*) of all the past are stored and from which the future originates. Accordingly, ālaya is āśraya. However, the mere corporeal body has no sense of ālaya; it is perishable and lifeless and not fitted to constitute the true basis for mental processes which, when accepted, leads one to the conclusion that the impressions and the seeds, the past and the future, are one and the same. A true ālaya, or a true āśraya, must be a vijñāna, or "consciousness"; hence, the texts refer to the ālaya-vijñāna. The physical body is able to function as āśraya only when it is conceived as a vijñāna[23] and thus endowed with life.

The vijñāna or the ālayavijñāna, which is also called "abhūtaparikalpa,"[24] and so forth is usually defined as "paratantra-svabhāva"; thus the interpretation of ālaya-vijñāna in the *Triṃśikā* is closely associated with that of paratantra in the *Mahāyānasaṃgraha*.

Returning to the *MSA*, we find, however, a series of compounds of which the latter half is parāvṛtti and the former comprises various terms other than āśraya. In *MSA* IX.38–48 eight parāvṛttis are enumerated as follows: (1) pañcendriya-parāvṛtti (turning about of five sense organs), (2) manasaḥ-p. (—of minding), (3) artha-p. (—of the object), (4) udgraha-p. (—of taking up), (5) vikalpa-p. (—of discrimination), (6) pratiṣṭha-p. (—of the resting place), (7) maithuna-p. (—of carnal enjoyment), and (8) ākāśa-saṃjñā-p. (—of space-conception). As confirmed by verse *MSA*. IX.48, all these types of "turning about" possess the meaning of āśraya-parāvṛtti because they all result equally in the "state of power" (*vibhutva*). Thus, it will be quite proper to assume that these eight terms, beginning with pañcendriya, are integral parts of āśraya, although, as I have said earlier, we cannot find in this text a definition that refers directly to āśraya-parāvṛtti. Another similar series of parāvṛttis can be seen in *MSA* XI.44–45. When *bīja-parāvṛtti* (turning about of seeds), which is none other than *ālayavijñāna-parāvṛtti* (turning about of the store-consciousness according to Vasubandhu) takes place, other cognitions (*vijñāna*) of pada (abode), artha (object), and deha (body)[25] become manifest (*nirbhāsa*). These three "turning abouts" denote *anāsravadhātu* (sphere of purity) or *vimukti* (emancipation). The other three "turning abouts," *manasaḥ-p, udgraha-p.* and *vikalpa-p.*,[26] which have been mentioned above, appear once more in the text and are described as the "states of power" (*vaśitā*). In any case, all of these terms convey the meaning of āśraya-parāvṛtti. As the things to be turned about are endless (*MSA* IX.48), the integral meanings of āśraya seem to grow richer and richer.

Now, the turning about of this āśraya, or the conversion from contamination into purity, takes place solely on the plane of the ālaya-vijñāna or on that of the paratantra, when, the old basis having become extinct, a new basis (though actually it should not be called a basis) emerges. The turning about of the basis is really the annihilation of the basis itself, and therefore it is called a "great conversion." Or, as in certain cases,[27] the *ālaya-vijñāna* converts itself into the so-called Undefiled Consciousness (*amala-vijñāna*).

The āśraya of āśraya-parāvṛtti is thus a basis that is neither merely the body nor merely the mind. Containing both of these, the translation, "the total of (human) existence," (seventh definition of *MSA*) mentioned above seems to be the most appropriate meaning for āśraya in this instance. But the expression, "the total of (human) existence" should be taken to have deep logical and metaphysical meanings. In short, āśraya is to be understood as the ultimate basis of all existences, whether of the inner world or of the outer, and as lying in the deepest, "unconscious" level of every consciousness. Whenever this basis is overturned, the world of ordinary life changes into the dharma-dhātu or sphere of dharma (the eighth definition of *MSA*) and vijñāna converts into the amala-vijñāna.

The various meanings for the term āśraya given in the dictionaries are often correlated with each other and offer definitions that apply to the various and sundry uses of this Sanskrit word. However, I should like to suggest in conclusion that, of the various meanings given for the term āśraya, the root meaning is "basis" in its widest sense. Especially when āśraya is used by the masters of the Yogācāra-Vijñānavāda School, this notion of "basis" reflects the fundamental reality of the world, the substructure of reality. Such a basis covers a wide range of notions, from human body and mind up to the dharma-dhātu or the sphere of the Buddha himself.

Chapter 8

Usages and Meanings of Pariṇāmanā

Pariṇāmanā is a very important idea not only in Pure Land Buddhism, especially Jodo Shin Shu (True Pure Land) Buddhism, but also in Mahāyāna Buddhism. The term, often translated "merit-transference," is found in the sūtras and śāstras in various Sanskrit forms. The standard noun form is Pariṇāmana or °nā, but pariṇamana or °nā and pariṇati, nati, and so forth also appear. Sometimes pariṇāma and its adjective form pariṇāmika are used. Concerning its verbal form, the form pariṇamati is yet to be seen, but the forms pariṇāma-yati, together with its derivatives pariṇāmayet, pariṇāmayi-tavya, pariṇāmita, pariṇāyamāna, and so forth are widely used. The verbal form pariṇāmayati, which is the causative formed from pariṇamati, is regarded by scholars to be the denominative form derived from pariṇāma. The root pari √ṇam means "to bend," "to change," "to develop," "to become ripe," and so forth when used in an intransitive sense; and the Buddhist Hybrid Sanskrit form pariṇāmayati has the same sense. However, when pariṇamayati is understood as a causative formed from pariṇamati, it can function as a transitive verb as well and means "to transfer."

These words are sometimes translated *pien* (変), *chüan pien* (転変), and so forth in Chinese translations, because the meanings "to change," "to transform," are predominant in the root pari √ṇam. Likewise, the Tibetan equivalents are 'gyur ba, gyur, bsgyur ba, which mean "to change." But in its special doctrinal meaning, pariṇāmanā is invariably translated by the Chinese characters *hui hsiang* (廻向) or *e-kō* in Japanese and *sngo ba, bsngo ba, yongs su bsngo ba,* in Tibetan. Hui hsiang or ekō literally means "to turn around and direct towards" and the Tibetan bsngo ba, probably means "to intend," "to desire," as this root is interpreted "yid kyis mos pa byed pa," or "smon 'dun byed pa."

In translating pariṇāmanā into English, scholars usually do not follow the fundamental meanings that are given in dictionaries. Instead, they translate the term: ''transfer [merit, virtue, etc.],'' ''to turn [merit] towards or for,'' ''to turn over [merit] to,'' ''to direct,'' ''to dedicate,'' ''to apply,'' and use the word in its transitive sense with ''merit'' or ''virtue'' as its object. These translations are close to what the Chinese term hui hsiang intends to convey. Probably, the translators were influenced by the Chinese translation and thus diverged from the fundamental meanings that are given in dictionaries.

Although not rejecting them explicitly, Edgerton, however, does not adopt these translations and defines pariṇāmanā ''(fig.) development, causing to grow, ripening, maturation,'' and regards pariṇāmayati as an intransitive verb. He apparently was not aware of the Chinese translation hui-hsiang. He also claims that the Tibetan translation is ''somewhat confused,'' because it uses ''sometimes yongs su (b)sngo ba.'' I disagree with him but more about this later.

In Sino-Japanese Buddhism, the term pariṇāmanā, in its meaning of hui-hsiang or ekō, is very popular and is understood to mean that one's own merit is transferred or turned toward others for the sake of fulfilling one's ultimate aim. Thus, pariṇāmanā is used in a transitive sense and means a practice to be accomplished by a practitioner or a sage or a bodhisattva. A bodhisattva engages in such difficult practices as the six pāramitās on the ten bhūmis and thus accumulates enormous merits. But he does not accumulate these merits for his own benefit but for the sake of fulfilling his ultimate aim. That is, the merits are accumulated for the benefit of others and thus are directed toward others.

Although it is universally understood that one cannot reap what one has not sown, the idea of pariṇāmanā goes beyond this, because a bodhisattva finds his delight in having others enjoy what he has contributed. The use of the term pariṇāmanā in this sense of ''benefiting others'' probably occurs for the first time in the Mahāyāna texts, but prior to this, it appears in a Pāli Vināya text (vin., iv. 157), in a wholly different sense. There it is used in the sense of a monk taking possession of property donated to the saṃgha. This latter use of the term also involved a ''transference'' or a ''change'' of ownership, but this meaning is far removed from the sense of pariṇāmanā as a bodhisattva's practice. For a monk to take possession of property, of course, is prohibited. Pariṇāmanā, therefore, can be said to represent the main purport of the Mahāyāna or the bodhisattva-mārga, and it appears together with such notions as bodhicitta, praṇidhāna, śūnyatā, and dharmatā.

Some examples of the term pariṇāmanā that appear in Mahāyāna texts are the following. The *Aṣṭasāhasrikāprajñāpāramitā* states:

> Having thus rejoiced, he utters the remark: "I turn over into full enlightenment the meritorious work founded on jubilation. May it feed the full enlightenment [of myself and of all beings]!"[1]

The *Daśabhūmika-sūtra* states:

> A bodhisattva turns over (or transfers) the roots of merit to the highest perfect enlightenment.[2]

The *Madhyāntavibhāga* also states:

> All the roots of merit should be transferred (or turned over) to the perfect enlightenment by a bodhisattva [who is desirous of obtaining enlightenment and who is freed from obstacles].[3]

Of these, the sentence, found for example in the *Daśabhūmika* quoted above, is constituted of four elements that appear in the following order:

> Nominative—accusative—locative—verb.
> (In English, Nom.—verb—acc.—loc.)

From this scheme, it is clear that the verb is transitive, because the action (i.e., the verb) of the agent (nominative) is directed towards its object (accusative). Whether it be a denominative of pariṇāma or whether it be a causative of pariṇati, the form pariṇāmayati is used in a transitive sense. The agent of this verb is expressed by the word "bodhisattva," which, in other examples, is replaced by the word "sattva" (sentient being), "kulaputra" (a son of a noble family), or even "śrāvaka" (*aniyatagotra-śrāvaka*, see later). The direct object of the verb pariṇāmayati is in most cases kuśalamūla, puṇya, that is, one's merits and virtues. When the word *citta* (mind) appears in the position of the accusative and becomes the direct object of "to direct towards," pariṇāmanā has almost the same meaning as *cittotpāda,* (awakening the thought of enlightenment), *praṇidhāna* (vow), and so forth. The indirect object, *samyaksaṃbodhi* (perfect enlightenment), is the aim of or the point to be reached by pariṇāmanā, and it is expressed in the locative case; however, it can also be expressed in the dative case, as for example, *anuttarāyai samyaksaṃbodhaye,* in *Aṣṭasāhasrikā,* 337. The dative case expresses the degree of sincerity of the desire (*prārthanā, ākāṃkṣā*) of pariṇāmanā more strongly. The compound bodhi-pariṇāmanā occurs several times in the *Śikṣāsamuccaya* (pp. 33, 158) and in such cases, the term bodhi, the former part of the compound, should be understood as being in the locative or dative case.

In this context, Edgerton, maintaining his definition of pariṇāmanā as "development" or "ripening," (intransitive) translates the *Daśabhūmika* passage (p. 58.18–19) in the following way:

> all depravities and impurities foreign to the Bodhisattva-course are to be recognized, through mastering the development (ripening) of enlightenment.[4]

But I would recommend the following interpretation:

> all bodhisattva-courses should be recognized as freed from depravities and impurities, owing to the force of merit-transference (or directing one's merit) toward the enlightenment.

which is attested by the Tibetan translation.[5]

This passage, which explains the seventh bhūmi of the bodhi-sattva-mārga, indicates that all bhūmis beginning from the first up to the seventh are "freed from depravities and impurities" simply because a bodhisattva directs all of his merits towards enlightenment. Edgerton's interpretation results also from reading the passage "sarvāḥ . . . kleśakalmāṣāḥ . . . pratyetavyāḥ" when he should have read it "sarvā bodhisattvacaryā . . . pratyetavyā."[6]

A milestone in the history of Buddhism occurred when T'an-luan (476–542) divided pariṇāmanā into two kinds: (1) pariṇāmanā in the aspect of going forth (往相迴向) and (2) pariṇāmanā in the aspect of coming back (還相迴向). The former means that one transfers one's merit to go forth from this world and to be born in the Pure Land. The latter means that the same merit is transferred to return to this world from the Pure Land. Both are a bodhisattva's practice, because the former is for the sake of acquiring *mahābodhi* (great enlightenment) and not a śrāvaka's parinirvāṇa, by being born in the Pure Land, and the latter is for the sake of engaging in the work of benefiting others by returning to this world of sentient beings.

In the above examples, the term pariṇāmanā connotes an action directed towards full enlightenment (*samyaksaṃbodhi*) or *mahābodhi*, that is, it connotes action in the direction or aspect of going forth, not in the direction or aspect of coming back. In the *Sukhāvatīvyūha-sūtra*, the word pariṇāmanā appears in several places (5, 8, 27), but in all these cases, it connotes an aspiration to be born in Sukhāvatī; that is, it refers to the aspect of going forth, not to the aspect of coming back. In his *Ta-ch'êng i-chang* (chüan 9), about a half century after T'an-luan, Hui-yüan of Ching-ying-ssu (523–592) divided *hui hsiang* into three kinds: pariṇāmanā directed (1) towards *p'u-t'i,* that is bodhi, (2) towards *chung shêng,* or sentient beings, and (3) towards *chih chi,* or *bhūtakoṭi,* the "extremity of reality." Among them, the first (p'u-t'i) and the third (chih chi) refer more or less to the aspect of going forth. The second one (chung shêng), pariṇāmanā directed towards sentient beings is an example of using the term in the sense of aiming at a lower world with an intention of benefiting others. Still it does not cover directly the meaning of "returning" to this world. Do we have, then, an example in the Indian Mahāyāna texts wherein the term pariṇāmanā connotes the "aspect of returning?"

To date, I have encountered only two instances of this kind in the Sanskrit texts. The first instance is found in *Mahāyāna-sūtrālaṃkāra,* XX–XXI verse 11, where the characteristic of the fourth stage (*bhūmi*) of the bodhisattva-mārga is explained. In his *Vyākhyā,* Vasubandhu comments on this verse as follows:

> On the 4th stage, although [a *bodhisattva*] dwells frequently in the [37] aids to enlightenment, he transfers the [37] aids to enlightenment to saṃsāra.[7]

And Sthiramati's commentary on this reads as follows:

> Question: If the 37 aids to enlightenment become the cause for liberation from *saṃsāra,* how can they be transferred to *saṃsāra* and become the cause for [being born into] *saṃsāra*? Answer: For example, poison which is not properly administered (lit. taken over by *upāya*) is the cause for death, but poison which is properly administered (lit. taken over by *upāya*) becomes medicine. In the same way, the practice of the 37 aids to enlightenment which is not embraced (*parigṛhīta*) by the *upāya* of compassion is a cause for liberation, but the practice of the 37 aids to enlightenment which is embraced by great compassion becomes the cause for being born once again in *saṃsāra.* When a *bodhisattva,* through compassion, practices such 37 aids to enlightenment that are contrary and adverse (*vimukha*) to *saṃsāra,* because he practices them for the sake of benefitting sentient beings by virtue of his compassion, those 37 aids to enlightenment become non-contrary to *saṃsāra* and become the cause for coming face to face (*abhimukha*) with *saṃsāra;* thus, it is stated that he transfers [the 37 aids to enlightenment] to *saṃsāra.*

From this commentary by Sthiramati, it becomes clear that what was originally the cause for nirvāṇa is transformed and becomes the cause for saṃsāra. By means of pariṇāmanā, a bodhisattva can voluntarily choose to be reborn into this world and to engage in the work of benefiting others. This is bodhisattva's upāya, or skillful means, which is constituted of compassion.

The second instance is found in *Mahāyānasūtrālaṃkāra,* XI.56. This verse number fifty six is one of seven verses that explicates the doctrine of *ekayāna,* "one vehicle," and that explains how a śrāvaka turns his mind from Hīnayāna to Mahāyāna and becomes a bodhisattva. The verse reads:

> Those two [who have realized the truth] will be endowed with a birth inconceivably transformed (or incarnated), because they transfer the holy path that they have obtained to [the world of] existence.[8]

One of the reasons that the Buddha established the doctrine of *ekayāna* was to attract and to convert to Mahāyāna those śrāvakas who were not yet fully settled as śrāvakas (*aniyatagotra*). When they become converted, they will enjoy the Mahāyāna teachings just as the bodhisattvas. To become a bodhisattva, however, means that a śrāvaka must be reborn in the world again and pursue the bodhisattva-practice, that is, the practice of benefiting others. Now, a śrāvaka who has trained himself in accordance with the śrāvakayāna, has already eliminated *kleśas,* the cause for rebirth in this world. A bodhisattva, however, does not eliminate kleśas for the purpose of remaining in saṃsāra, that is, not entering into nirvāṇa (*apratiṣṭhita-nirvāṇa*), and his compassion is nothing but a sort of kleśa retained by him. Therefore, for the śrāvakas who have been trained to always aspire for nirvāṇa, there is no way to be reborn in this world, except by means of *pariṇāmanā*. This means that they must "transfer the holy path . . . to existence," as the verse states.

The words "those two" in the verse refers to "śrāvakas." "The holy path" obtained by them is, like the previously mentioned 37 aids to enlightenment that are adverse and opposed to the world of existence (*bhava*), but when it is transformed or transferred, it becomes the cause for existence.

The compound *acintyapariṇāmikī-upapatti* in this verse is a problematic phrase that appears also in texts such as the *Śrīmālādevī-sūtra* and *Ratnagotra-vibhāga*. How this phrase is to be understood is problematic, and it raises other issues that require further investigation. The word pariṇāmikī here is usually translated "transformation" (変易 pien-i); therefore, I provisionally translated the phrase "a birth inconceivably transformed (or incarnated)." Differing from the ordinary birth of sentient beings into this world, this birth is a birth into a realm outside of this world by a mighty bodhisattva who is endowed with a supreme and subtle body. Engaged in the work of benefiting others with this body, he is able to transform at will his body, the length of his life, and so on; hence, this birth is said to be "a birth inconceivably transformed."

However, within the context of this verse, the word pariṇāmikī can be understood also to mean "transference"; thus, the phrase can be interpreted to mean "a birth constituted by inconceivable transference." In his translation Prabhākaramitra, the translator of this text into Chinese, used the word *hui-hsiang* (迴向) instead of pien-i (変易). The term hui-hsiang means "a birth [acquired] by transference," not "a birth by transformation." Commenting on the term acintya, "inconceivableness," Vasubandhu's *Vyākhyā* reads:

> It is inconceivable, indeed, that their holy path is transferred (or dedicated) to a birth; hence [the birth is] *acintyapariṇāmikī*, i.e., what is transferred inconceivably.[9]

In the two instances discussed above, the indirect object of pariṇāmanā is either "saṃsāra" or "existence" (*bhava*) instead of the usual "supreme enlightenment," and so forth. To have either saṃsāra or existence as the indirect object clearly indicates that pariṇāmanā in these two cases refers to "the aspect of returning to this world."

To summarize, we have seen that the word pariṇāmanā had several meanings. First, we saw that, with respect to this word, the meaning "transformation" predominated in both its transitive and intransitive senses and that the meaning "transformation" was used to indicate that what was originally not a cause is transformed into a cause, or what was originally the cause for one's own benefit is transformed into a cause for the benefit of others. In this context, *kuśalamūla* or the root of virtue and other human efforts, which are declared to be nothing but śūnya in the *Prajñāpāramitāsūtra*, are dedicated to and are transformed into the cause for the ultimate enlightenment.

Secondly, pariṇāmanā was used in the sense of "to direct toward," a sense that seemed to have been the focus when the term was translated into Chinese. Used in this sense, it meant that something of one's own was directed towards or given to others, or that the mundane was directed toward the supra-mundane and vice versa. In this context, we saw that the aids to enlightenment or the holy path (both supra-mundane) were directed towards saṃsāric existence.

Of course, the two meanings mentioned above are seen in most cases mixed and conjoined. If the two meanings of "transformation" and "to direct toward" can be represented by the Chinese characters *hui*, (迴) and *hsiang* (向), then the Chinese translation would seem to be a good one. Further, it was mentioned that pariṇāmanā was closely related to other notions such as "wish" and "desire" (*prārthanā, pratikāṃkṣati*) and that it was almost equal to even ideas such as "aspirating for enlightenment" or "awakening to the thought [of enlightenment]" (*cittotpāda*) and "vow" (*praṇidhāna*).

Now, the explanations given above convey the general meanings of pariṇāmanā. But, in Jodo Shin Shu (True Pure Land) Buddhism, pariṇāmanā is said to be wholly an attribute of the power of Amida's Vow; in other words, there can be no pariṇāmanā on the part of ordinary sentient beings. Whether Amida's activity of pariṇāmanā should be understood in the meanings mentioned above; whether it should be understood in a totally different way; or whether a bodhisattva's practice in general, including the work of Dharmākara, should originate from the power of Amida's Vow—all of these, including the doctrinal interpretations of Amida's pariṇāmanā "in the aspect of returning to this world," are questions worthy of further investigation. I shall leave that investigation up to specialists of Jodo Shin Shu Buddhism.

Chapter 9

Tranquil Flow of Mind: An Interpretation of Upekṣā

We find in Buddhism a religious term called "*upekṣā*" often translated as "indifference." It is one of the mental factors (*caitasika*) found in human beings and is classified as morally good (*kuśala*), not as defiled or neutral. Upekṣā is an object of religious practice and also a virtue that can even be attributed to Bodhisattvas and Buddhas. For a religion, the ultimate concern is usually considered the attainment of a state of highest bliss or salvation from all sufferings. In Buddhism, too, liberation (*vimukti*) or enlightenment (*bodhi*) is often assumed to be such a state. In contrast to this, however, "indifference," getting rid of both love and hatred, means to be interested neither in happiness nor in suffering, neither in pleasure nor in sorrow. It seems to be rather particular to Buddhism that such a mental state is applauded as "good" and as a higher virtue.

The original Sanskrit for indifference is upekṣā (*upekkhā* in Pāli). According to dictionaries, its root √īkṣ means primarily "to look at, to perceive" and then "to overlook, disregard, neglect, abandon," and so on. Thus upekṣā as a Buddhist term is usually rendered into English by such words as "abandonment, indifference, apathy." The Chinese equivalent is always given as *shê* 捨 (to abandon, to spurn), and the Tibetan equivalent as *btang snyoms* (to abandon and equalize). The word indifference, however, will be used throughout this paper as the English equivalent.

The term upekṣā appears in various Buddhist texts with different connotations. It is used for example in a secular or literal meaning: "It is unreasonable to think that the Buddha remains indifferent to a future calamity of his Doctrine" (*MSA*, I.8). The Tibetan translation for upekṣā changes from the usual *btang snyoms* to *yal bar 'dor ba* (to diminish and abandon), when used in such passages as: "to abandon living beings," that is, to be indifferent to the happiness of other beings (*MSA*, IV.17; IV.27; XVIII.13) or "to abandon moral precepts" (*MSA*, XVIII.4), and so forth. This kind of upekṣā is, of course, to be negated or prohibited.

A sensation neither painful nor pleasing is also called "upekṣā." But this is a subdivision of the category "sensation" (*vedanā*), which is one of the mental factors (*caitasika*), and is distinguished from this separate mental factor called upekṣā that we are discussing here.

A very famous upekṣā is one of the four "infinitudes" (*apramāṇa*), also called "brahmic states" (*brahma-vihāra*). The other three infinitudes are that of friendliness (*maitrī*), compassion (*karuṇā*), and rejoicing (*muditā*), with indifference (*upekṣā*) as the fourth. These four are all regarded as the highest virtues. Upekṣā, however, is unique in that it means infinite indifference, being free from both love and hate towards living beings. Or we can say the first three virtues are ethical ones more applicable to the social realm, while upekṣā is a more religious one concerned with the realm of meditation.

There are still other categories in which upekṣā is included as a member. The *Visuddhimagga*, for example, mentions ten kinds,[1] and the "seven members of enlightenment" (*bodhyaṅga*) is one of them. The upekṣā belonging to the category of the four infinitudes stated above is regarded in some cases[2] as different from the upekṣā that I will discuss in this paper.

Here, I shall confine myself to an examination of the upekṣā that is classified as one of the morally good mental factors. Also it will be noticed here that a mental factor (*caitasika*) means a mentality, a possibility common to every living being. Although various teachers have given definitions of upekṣā, the Yogācāra definition by Sthiramati in his *Triṃśikā*[3] may be the most advanced one. His definition reads as follows:

> Upekṣā is equilibrium (*samatā*) of the mind, tranquil flow (*praśaṭhatā*) of the mind, and effortlessness (*anābhogatā*) of the mind. By three words, the stages of indifference at the beginning, middle, and end are respectively illustrated. Here, inequality of the mind is either mental depression (*laya*) or mental exaltation (*auddhatya*). Upon extinction of this inequality, one first attains equilibrium of the mind. Then, [as for *praśaṭhatā*,] without volitional effort and without special exertion, the concentrated and even mind takes place in due order, and this is the tranquil flow of the mind. However, in this stage, the mind is still followed by the anxiety of mental depression and exaltation, because it has not been cultivated for a long period of time. After that, [as for *anābhogatā*,] since the meditational exercise reaches higher and higher degrees and its adversaries [such as diversity of the mind] become farther and farther away, this anxiety is nullified. Then, the stage of effortlessness of the mind is reached by one for whom there is no need to make any effort to obtain remedies for mental depression and mental exaltation.
>
> And this has the function of giving a foundation for not allowing the space where all principal and secondary defilements arise.[4]

In this definition of upekṣā, there are three key terms that I shall examine in particular: (1) samatā, (2) praśaṭhatā, and (3) anābhogatā. Anticipating this definition, and probably its prototype, are other definitions in the *Śrāvakabhūmi* (ŚrBh) of the *Yogācārabhūmi* and in Asaṅga's *Abhidharmasamuccaya* (*AS*) accompanied by Jinaputra's *Bhāṣya*. As far as I know, these texts are the first incidences of the three key terms appearing together with more or less similar wordings.

In the above definition by Sthiramati, the first paragraph gives the general characteristic of upekṣā, described by the three key terms: equilibrium, tranquil flow, and effortlessness. The second paragraph explains the function of upekṣā.

Of these three key terms, *samatā* is philosophically a very important term with varied connotations. In the case of upekṣā we are using the translation "equilibrium" for samatā, but it has also been used with the meaning of "equality." In the Madhyamic or metaphysical approach, equality of existence and non-existence is stated as the fundamental standpoint. In the Yogācāra or epistemological approach, equality of perceiving and nonperceiving represents another fundamental standpoint. Numerous sūtras expound the equality of various aspects of reality such as self and other, saṃsāra and nirvāṇa, or the equality of all dharmas, or of all sentient beings. The *Daśabhūmikasūtra* mentions ten kinds of equality that were quoted by Candrakīrti in his *Madhyamakāvatāra*, chapter 6, where he discusses the equality or śūnyatā of all entities in order to demonstrate the character of universal nonproduction (*dharma-anutpāda-samatā*).

In our discussion of the samatā aspect of upekṣā, equality or equilibrium of the mind is an extinction of the inequality that is called "mental depression" (*laya*) on the one hand and "mental exaltation" (*auddhatya*) on the other. In most lists of the mental factors, the word *laya* is replaced by *styāna* (Pāli *thīna*, sluggishness); styāna and laya seem to be one and the same thing since the Chinese translation *hun-ch'ên* 惛沈 is common to both. Outside these lists, as far as I know, we always encounter laya alone, which is sometimes defined by using a term such as *līnaṃ cittam* (despirited mind). Auddhatya and styāna or laya are serious hindrances on the course of a monk's yogic practice, both being classified as secondary defilements in the list of mental factors.

Of these, laya means "mental inactivity" (*MW*). In the definition of styāna, a similar meaning is stated: "it (styāna) means the mind lacking in readiness or workability (*akarmaṇyatā*); it is a part of delusion" (*AS*, p. 17.29). The word karmaṇyatā, which appears in this definition with a negative prefix, has important connotations of "workability, capability, alertness, or agility." It is a mental state able to respond quickly at any critical moment. It is a free action without hesitation or doubt, not an instinctive one, but an action of the illuminated mind freed from all concern. Laya is the absence of this enlightened responsiveness or karmaṇyatā. Sthiramati adds another explanation to that of *AS,* saying (*Triṃśikā,* p. 31.23): ''styāna is a motionless state (*staimitya*); . . . being united with this, the mind becomes dull, insensitive, and cannot perceive the object [of meditation].'' Styāna is languor or torpor, and the Chinese equivalent *hun ch'ên* 惛沈 means ''dark and depressed (sunken).'' ''Because all human beings are to attain enlightenment (i.e., all beings have Buddha-nature), because they are all continually attaining it, and because an infinite number of them attain it, you need not be depressed (laya),''—speaking thus, the *MSA,* X.11 brings to life the depressed mind.

On the other hand, *auddhatya* ''mental exaltation'' is the opposite of laya and is defined as the mind ''restless'' or ''not stilled'' (*avyupaśama*) (*AS,* p.17.30). To this Sthiramati adds the explanation (*Triṃśikā,* p. 31.27): ''Śamatha is the remedy for it. One remembers, in conformity with one's desire, what was formerly laughed at, loved, and enjoyed, and consequently one's mind is not stilled. . . .'' The Chinese equivalent *tiao chü* 掉擧 means the mind ''unsettled and uplifted,'' that is, the state in which the mind is proud, unsteady, and lacking seriousness. It is a state in which the mind becomes ambitious, buoyant, excited, and ebullient.

Auddhatya and laya, thus, stand in opposition: the former moves in an upward direction and the latter moves downward. (These two terms may resemble in some ways the modern psychologist's definition of manic depression). Both auddhatya and laya are classified as secondary defilements, as negative values. Upekṣā ''indifference,'' however, transcends these two and constitutes their negation. The former two must be rejected and thereby upekṣā is realized. Thus, auddhatya, laya, and upekṣā correspond to a set of notions combined in a dynamic process where the first two members are contradictory to each other, and by negating them a third, upekṣā, is attained. As a result of the negation of the two extremes of laya and auddhatya, upekṣā can be seen as the middle.

√ Related to these three terms is another set called the ''three marks'' (*nimitta*) which include: (1) the mark of calming (*śamatha*), (2) the mark of uplifting (*pragraha*), and (3) the mark of indifference (*upekṣā*). To begin with, the *Saṃdhinirmocana,* chapter VIII, reads as follows:

> What are *śamatha-nimitta, pragraha-nimitta,* and *upekṣā-nimitta*? [Answer:] When the mind is exalted (*auddhatya*) or feared to be exalted, one concentrates uninterruptedly on things which call forth disgust (*udvega*) [at the saṃsāric existence] or on similar things—this is the mark of calming (*śamatha-nimitta*). When the mind is depressed (*laya*) or feared to be depressed, one concentrates on things that call forth delight (*abhirāma*)

> and one reflects on one's delighted mind—this is the mark of uplifting (*pragraha-nimitta*). Whether practicing only the path of calming (*śamatha*), or only the path of intuitive discernment (*vipaśyanā*), or the pair combined together (*yuganaddha*), one's mind is not defiled by the two defilements mentioned above; the mind occurs spontaneously and concentrates effortlessly—this is called the mark of indifference (*upekṣā-nimitta*).[5]

When the *Bodhisattvabhūmi* expounds meditational exercise (*bhāvanā*) and vigor (*vīrya*),[6] it uses these three terms as one set. In the *Śrāvakabhūmi* (Wayman, p. 116–7; Shukla, p. 391–94),[7] however, we see four terms, instead of three, *vipaśyana-nimitta* (mark of intuitive discernment) being added as the second mark. The glosses explaining these four terms are much richer in the *ŚrBh* than in other texts. But, as *pragraha* in this context is synonymous with *vipaśyanā*, no difference in principle seems to exist between the system of the three marks and that of the four.

The three marks are also adopted by Vasubandhu in his *Bhāṣya* on the *Mahāyāna-sūtrālaṃkāra*, XIV. 7–10, XVIII.49, XVIII.53, and XVIII.65. Sthiramati's subcommentary in these places can be roughly summed up in the following way:

> When the mind is depressed, one should meditate on the activities and other virtues of the Buddha. The mind being elevated (or uplifted) thereby, mental depression will be removed. This is the mark of *pragraha* (uplifting). When the mind is exalted, on the other hand, one should meditate on the faults of saṃsāra such as birth, age, and death. The mind being calmed thereby, mental exaltation will be removed. This is the mark of *śamatha* (tranquility). When the depressed mind is thus eliminated by means of intuitive discernment (*vipaśyanā*) and the exalted mind eliminated by means of making it tranquil (*śamatha*), a practitioner attains equilibrium (*samatā*) of the mind and dwells immovably in indifference (*upekṣā*); he now concentrates neither on the mark of *śamatha* nor on the mark of *vipaśyanā;* because any concentration on them will mean a failure of the equilibrium of the mind. This is the mark of *upekṣā*.[8]

This is a clear exposition concerning the relationship between the three marks. Also it is obvious that pragraha is synonymous with vipaśyanā. Usually translated into Chinese by *chü* (擧 to lift up), the word pragraha (its verbal form is pragṛhṇāti) literally means "to hold, seize," and I put it as "uplifting." But it is now clear that in the present context it means "to activate, stimulate, incite, encourage, cheer up," and so on.

In Sthiramati's exposition, it is also remarkable that, in the state of upekṣā, one should not concentrate even on the mark of śamatha or on the mark of vipaśyanā, which are used in traditional forms of practice. Of course, śamatha and vipaśyanā, and their synthesis *yuganaddha,* are the highest means of training. But the sense given by the text is: śamatha, if applied wrongly, is equal to depression (*laya*); only when it works correctly, is it a remedy for exaltation (*auddhatya*). Likewise, vipaśyanā (or *pragraha*), if applied wrongly, is nothing other than auddhatya, and only right vipaśyanā (or pragraha) is a remedy for laya. If wrongly applied, both śamatha and vipaśyanā become obstacles for attaining the equilibrium of upekṣā. We can easily understand that śamatha and vipaśyanā tend to become hindrances if people cling to them. From the above discussion, we can see a certain relationship between upekṣā and yuganaddha. Yuganaddha is a synthesis of śamatha and vipaśyanā, as is upekśā, with the difference that upekṣā originally arose from negation of laya and auddhatya and, therefore, in transcending śamatha and vipaśyanā, it maintains a stronger sense of negation than yuganaddha, which remains closer to its original sense of a combination of śamatha and vipaśyanā.

Thus, the first definition of upekṣā is "equilibrium." It is a balanced state of the mind and originates from the negation of laya and auddhatya. Upekṣā can also be interpreted as a dialectical synthesis of śamatha and vipaśyanā and, consequently, a sublation of the two. These relationships may be represented in the following way:

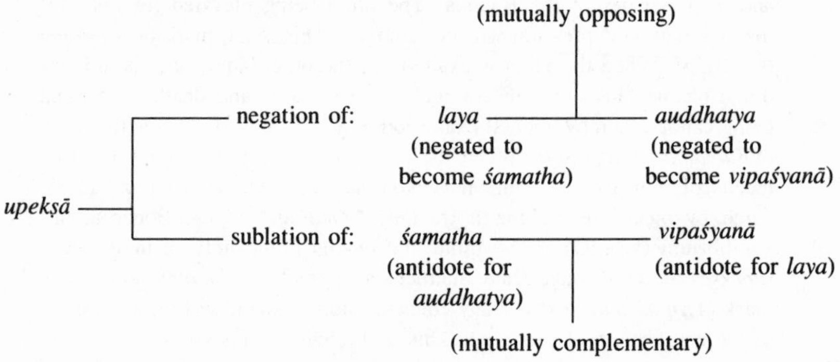

The second definition of upekṣā given by Sthiramati in the *Triṃśikā* is "tranquil flow" (*praśaṭhatā*) of the mind. This word is accompanied by the phrases "without volitional effort" (*anabhisaṃskāreṇa*) and "without special exertion" (*aprayatnena*) and is synonymous with "the concentrated and even mind." Among these various terms, praśaṭhatā is a difficult and curious word.

According to dictionaries, praśaṭha means "sehr falsch, boshaft" (*Sanskrit-wörterbuch in Kürzerer Fassung,* von Otto Böhtlingk, letzte

Nachträge, S. 362), or "very false or wicked" (*MW*). Actually we have a cognate word *śāṭhya* as one of the defiled mental factors and it means "guile, deceit." These meanings, however, obviously cannot be applied to the present case.

Praśaṭha is listed in the *Mvy* as No. 2101, which Sylvain Lévi refers to in his French translation of *Triṃśikā.*[9] He translates its Tibetan equivalents: *rnal du 'bab pa* or *rnal du 'dug pa* (elsewhere, *rnal du 'jug pa* also appears) as "être en repos, en quasi-somnolence" and its Chinese equivalent *hsiang chü hsiang* 降諸相 as "abaisser les caractêres." Based upon these, his translation of praśaṭha is "rémission" (remission, forgiving). He also suggests that praśaṭha may be a Prakrit form of the Sanskrit praśratha (from root √*śranth*) "relâchement" (or relaxation). Although Edgerton refers to *Mvy* in his dictionary and translates the Tibetan equivalent as "entrance into tranquillity," he does not refer to Lévi's etymological theory nor propose one of his own. In his edition of the *ŚrBh,* p. 117 n., Wayman refers to Lévi's note and Edgerton's dictionary and then translates praśaṭha as "repose." Herman Jacobi translates it "Regsamkeit" (agility, activity).[10] Walpola Rahula translates the word as "la passivité" and its root śaṭh as "être paresseux" in his translation of *AS.*[11] I would like, however, to propose "tranquil flow" as a translation for praśaṭha, the reason for which will follow presently.

Although its etymology in Sanskrit seems to be problematic,[12] the Tibetan translations and some of Chinese translations can be helpful in understanding the most relevant meaning of the word. Here in this paper, I shall examine mainly the Chinese translations of *praśaṭha.*

The Chinese translation found in the *Mvy* is not a good one; it is not clear as can be seen in Lévi's translation above. Apart from the *Triṃśikā,* of which we have no Chinese translation, there are at least three texts, preserved in Sanskrit and in Chinese translations, where the word *praśaṭha* appears: *Śrāvaka-bhūmi, Madhyāntavibhāga* (including its *bhāṣya*) and *Abhidharma-samuccaya*. (We do not find the word *praśaṭha* in the *Mahāyāna-sūtrālaṃkāra* and *Abhidharmakośa*). All three texts are translated by Hsüan-tsang and the *MV* is also available in Paramārtha's translation. Hsüan-tsang's translation of *praśaṭha,* however, is found in two or three versions, which vary according to the texts.

To begin with, upekṣā is defined in the *AS* by the same word "citta-praśaṭhatā" as in Sthiramati's *Triṃśikā*. Hsüan-tsang translates it as "correctness and straightness of the mind" (*hsin chêng chih hsing,* 心正直性) (*Taishō,* hereafter *T,* XXXI, p. 664b). Such a translation is understandable since upekṣā means the attainment of a mental state that is correct or undeviating and not curved or uneven, because the inequalities of laya and auddhatya have been eliminated. This translation is also adopted in texts such as: *Hsien-yang-shêng-chiao-lun* by Asaṅga (*T* 1602, XXXI, p. 481c), *Pañcaskandha-prakaraṇa* by Vasubandhu (*T* 1612, XXXI, p. 849a), and *Ch'êng-wei-shih-lun* (*T* 1585, XXXI, p. 30b). These are all Yogācāra treatises and may be assumed to be somewhat Abhidharmic in their way of defining upekṣā. In Hīnayānic Abhidharma treatises such as *Abhidharmakośa, Abhidharmāvatāra* (*T* 1554), and so forth, the word praśaṭha does not appear in the definitions of upekṣā. Therefore, Yogācāras most probably introduced *praśaṭha* into the understanding of *upekṣā*.

In the *Śrāvakabhūmi* (Wayman, p. 117; Shukla, p. 394), *praśaṭha-svarasa-vāhitā* is the word used to define upekṣā. In this case Hsüan-tsang translates praśaṭha as "balanced, flexible, correct, and straight" (*t'iao jou chêng chih,* 調柔正直), and *svarasa-vāhitā* (which in Sanskrit means "being conveyed, flowing, or coursing in one's own path") as "spontaneously occurring" (*jên yün chuan hsing,* 任運轉性) (*T* 1579, XXX, p. 456b). Thus, Hsüan-tsang includes the four characters for praśaṭha in the eight that he selects to represent clearly the nature of upekṣā.

The *Madhyāntavibhāga,* IV.5 explicates the fourfold supernatural power (*ṛddhi-pāda*) and mentions as its basis the mental factor "agility" (*karmaṇyatā*), a very important notion to which I referred to above. Agility is explained here as a result of the "eightfold relinquishing activity" (*prahāṇa-saṃskāra*) that relinquishes the five faults (*doṣa*) (i.e., sloth, inattentiveness, depression-exaltation, overexertion, and inexertion). Upekṣā is the eighth of this relinquishing activity. Commenting on this type of upekṣā, Vasubandhu states: ". . . when laya and auddhatya are made tranquil, there is upekṣā of the mind, that is, *praśaṭha-vāhitā*."[13] Hsüan-tsang in this case translates praśaṭha-vāhitā as "flowing in equilibrium" *p'ing têng êrh liu,* 平等而流 and its abbreviated form in the verse as *têng liu* 等流 (*T* 1600, XXXI, p. 471b). Paramārtha's translations corresponding to these are *fang shê* 放捨 (in verse) and *fang liu hsiang hsü* 放流相續 (in prose) (*T* 1599, XXXI, p. 458c). I am not quite sure how to understand these phrases, but provisionally I shall translate them respectively as "freely abandoned" and "freely flowing in succession." In any case, *liu* "flowing" is used in common with Hsüan-tsang; *shê* "abandoned" or "spurned," directly suggesting the nature of upekṣā, must have the same context as the prose and mean "to let go, to let flow"; *fang* may mean either "to let . . ." or "to make free"; and *hsiang hsü* seems to correspond to the Sanskrit *vāhitā* or *vahana* (flowing, conveying) that form a compound where praśaṭha is the first member.

Based upon all these meanings and also considering the Tibetan *rnal du 'jug pa,* I have translated praśaṭha as "tranquil flow." It is "tranquil," not depressed nor exalted, but relaxed and in repose. Further, it is not static, but calmly "flowing"; while accumulating deep inner energy, it is ready to move. Praśaṭha, translated as "tranquil flow," is more positive than the supposed Skt. etymology praśratha which means "relaxation."

Praśaṭha appears again in the *Madhyāntavibhāga,* V.28. This time, however, Hsüan-tsang translates it as *yün* 運 (an abbreviated form in the verse) and *têng yün* 等運 (in the prose), *T* XXXI, p. 477a), which may mean respectively "to convey" and "to convey in equilibrium." "To convey" probably alludes to the same meaning as "flowing" in the phrase above, "flowing in equilibrium." Paramārtha translates it a little differently as *shêng* 生 "to bear, to bring forth" (*T* XXXI, p. 463b).

The subject of *MV,* V.28 is the various objects of learning in Mahāyāna practice or the Bodhisattva Path (*bodhisattva-mārga*). These objects are arranged in twelve categories. The first two, the fundamental objects of learning, are: (1) *dharma,* the teachings as established in the scriptures, and (2) *dharmadhātu,* Dharma-realm; the former includes the six perfections (*pāramitās*), the fourfold noble truth (*āryasatya*), and others, and the latter is equated with suchness (*tathatā*). Next, the objects of the three kinds of wisdom, those of the ten stages, and so on, are enumerated. "Tranquil flow" (*praśaṭhatva*) is mentioned as the eleventh object and is said to be studied on the eighth stage (*bhūmi*) of the Bodhisattvamārga. The twelfth object, the highest one, is called "supreme object" (*prakarṣa-ālambana*) and is studied on the ninth, tenth, and eleventh Buddha stage. Although the term upekṣā does not appear in the explanations involved here, we may assume that it is upekṣā that is indicated by praśaṭhatva since we find this term only in conjunction with upekṣā. Thus, upekṣā or the "tranquil flow"(of the mind) is a fairly high object, the last but one, in the course of the Bodhisattva's path.

It is also explained by Vasubandhu that only the first two items, *dharma* and *dharmadhātu,* are the real objects to be studied throughout the whole path under different names according to the different kinds of wisdom acquired or the different stages of advancement. Thus the same dharma and dharmadhātu are studied from a special angle, that is, that of upekṣā, on the eighth bhūmi that is characterized as "effortlessness."

The third definition of upekṣā in the *Triṃśikā* is "effortlessness" (*anābhogatā*) of the mind. This effortlessness, of course, does not mean a negation of effort; it is a state that one has reached after a long assiduous effort, but at this point effort is no longer needed. In the previous discussion on praśaṭhatā, we read the phrase: "without volitional effort (*anabhisaṃskāreṇa*) and without special exertion (*aprayatnena*)." The text goes on to say: ". . . there is no need to make any effort for the purpose of obtaining remedies for mental depression and exaltation."

We often encounter in the sūtras and śāstras a statement that effortlessness (*anābhoga*) is the characteristic of the eighth stage (*bhūmi*) of the ten stages on the Bodhisattva Path.

First, when a Bodhisattva realizes the universality of the Dharma-realm (*dharmadhātu-sarvatragārtha*) (*MV,* II.14) or the ultimate śūnyatā (*MSA,* XX-XXI.10), this realization is called the "entrance into the first bhūmi" or the "path of insight" (*darśana-mārga*). The "path of cultivation" (*bhāvanā-mārga*) starts immediately after the moment of this insight. In this path, from the first to the sixth bhūmi, a Bodhisattva will understand the insight he attained by means of the marks (*nimitta*) (of the teachings) and exercise every effort in deepening that insight. The seventh bhūmi, however, is characterized by the word "marklessness" (*nirnimittatā, nirnimittavihāra,* etc., *MV,* II.14; *MSA,* XX–XXI.15, etc.); that is, these marks are abolished at this stage and the practitioner realizes that reality has no mark, that it is markless or formless (*ānimitta*), and in truth *śūnya.* Further, in the next step of the eighth bhūmi, not only marklessness but also "effortlessness" (*anābhoga, anabhisaṃskāra*) is to be realized. This means that reality is beyond [human] effort, or that what is attained by effort is not yet the ultimate reality. [There is a situation where reality manifests itself only when every effort has been abandoned.] Thus, while the seventh bhūmi is defined as "without mark, but with volitional effort" (*animitta-sasaṃskāra*), the eighth bhūmi is defined as "without mark and without volitional effort" (*animitta-anabhisaṃskāra*) (*MSA,* XX–XXI.19–20). The words *saṃskāra* and *abhisaṃskāra* [both can be translated as volitional effort] here convey almost the same meaning as *ābhoga* (effort).

Upekṣā is such effortlessness. One who is interested in and is clinging to something will naturally endeavor to attain it. But, in the situation where attainment needs no more effort, one is indifferent, clinging to nothing. Detachment, and consequently freedom of the mind, is an effect of the effortlessness of upekṣā. Thus, the Bodhisattva on attaining the eighth bhūmi is called "one who is indifferent" (*upekṣaka*) (*MSA,* XX–XXI.15), one who shares the virtue of upekṣā with the Buddha, although the virtues of the Buddha are not limited to upekṣā only.

To give an example from everyday life, when one is learning how to drive a car, one must devote total attention to following exactly what the instructor taught. But, after receiving training and practicing repeatedly, when one has fully mastered the technique, one will be able to drive a car correctly and safely without any effort or special attention on one's part, even forgetting the "marks" of instruction. The *Visuddhimagga* states that it is like a well-trained thoroughbred that a skilled rider allows to follow its own course.[14] We can compare this situation with the effortlessness of upekṣā; effort of "volitional effort" (*abhisaṃskāra*) is important, but effortlessness in the end is more important, because in so far as effort is needed the truth cannot manifest itself.

The same idea is also expressed by Takuan, a seventeenth century Zen master, in a letter to his student, Yagyū Tajima no Kami, who was a swordmaster serving the Shogun, Iyemitsu. Daisetz T. Suzuki has paraphrased it in the following manner:

> [*Prajñā* is possessed by all Buddhas and also by all sentient beings. It is transcendental wisdom flowing through the relativity of things] and it remains immovable, though this does not mean the immovability or insensibility of such objects as a piece of wood or rock. It is the mind itself endowed with infinite motilities: it moves forward and backward, to the left and to the right, to every one of the ten quarters, and knows no hindrances in any direction. Prajñā Immovable is this mind capable of infinite movements.[15]

Or, again:

> The thing is not to try to localize the mind anywhere but to let it fill up the whole body, let it flow throughout the totality of your being. When this happens you use the hands when they are needed, you use the legs or the eyes when they are needed, and no time or no extra energy will be wasted.[16]

In these words of Takuan we can find the ancient idea of upekṣā. To instruct Yagyū Tajima in the art and way of swordsmanship, Takuan used Prajñā, which is the Buddha's nondiscriminative knowledge, to convey the subtle aspect of upekṣā.

To recapitulate what has been stated above, we can see that upekṣā constitutes the elimination of mental depression and exaltation; it is an equilibrium, calm and balanced, a state of "tranquil flow" in which every effort, interest, or attachment disappears, and yet at any critical moment, a quick and apt response arises freely and spontaneously.

As a final instance of upekṣā, we turn to the "seven members of enlightenment" (*bodhyaṅga*), which are elucidated in *MSA*, XVIII.57–63. Upekṣā, the last member of the seven, is explained in the XVIII.61 which reads:

> Through *upekṣā*, he [a Bodhisattva] dwells anywhere he wishes as a supreme being, because of abiding in [the twofold wisdom of] nondiscrimination and its sequels.[17]

Vasubandhu comments on this verse saying that "upekṣā is nondiscriminative wisdom," and that, having this upekṣā, a Bodhisattva can dwell or stay anywhere he wishes. He goes on to say: "Because of abiding in subsequent [wisdom] (*tat-pṛṣṭha-labdhena vihāreṇa*), he obtains other [virtues and *bhūmis*] and [faults] vanish. Because of abiding in nondiscriminative [wisdom] (*nirvikalpena vihāreṇa*), he sets up his dwelling without effort." It is remarkable that, in referring to the Buddha's highest wisdom, upekṣā is expounded and equated with nondiscriminative knowledge.

In the system of the seven members of enlightenment, the last three members—*praśrabdhi* (alleviated-ness), *samādhi* (concentration), and *upekṣā* (indifference)—are regarded as the highest attainment in which all defilements are nullified. Praśrabdhi is the condition of this nullification, samādhi, the foundation, and upekṣā, the nullification itself.

In conclusion, we can assume that upekṣā represents a rather high mental state. As we have seen, it is mentioned as one of the eleven mental factors (not a large number) characterized as morally good, and it is also regarded as the characteristic of an advanced stage such as the eighth bhūmi. Further, upekṣā is associated with a high mental factor such as *praśrabdhi* (alleviated-ness), which in its turn is equated with *karmaṇyatā* (agility). Upekṣā comes last as the fourth member in the four infinitudes, transcending, as it were, the positive, ethical three members—friendliness, compassion, and rejoicing. And finally, when upekṣā appears in the same way as the last member of the seven members of enlightenment, it is equated with nondiscriminative knowledge. All these facts indicate the delicate and profound quality of upekṣā. Ancient Indian teachers were aware of this subtle faculty and, delving into this subtle state of mind, Takuan called it "the mind that is no-mind, the mind that knows no-stopping, or the mind abandoned and yet not abandoned. . . .[18] Although in *Ch'êng-wei-shih-lun*,[19] upekṣā is explained as a nominal, provisional entity, I believe upekṣā is such a high virtue that it should not escape our attention.[20]

Chapter 10

On the Theory of Buddha-Body (Buddha-kāya)

I

How to conceive the true significance of the concept Buddha has been one of the most important themes discussed among Buddhist disciples and followers ever since the religion originated in India. Theories concerning the Buddha-body (*buddha-kāya*) underwent various developments during the course of a history ranging from India to Japan and from Ceylon to Mongolia. They may present interesting problems in comparison with the concept of deities in Brahmanism and Hinduism of India, or with the theological concepts in Christianity and other religions, or with the concept of god, godhead, the absolute, and so forth, in religious studies in general. Here, however, I would like to confine myself to reviewing some aspects of the theory of Buddha-body formulated in Indian Mahāyānism, viewing them from within Buddhism.

It is needless to say that the word Buddha, which means "an awakened one" or "an enlightened one," is an epithet of respect for Gautama Śākyamuni, the founder of Buddhism. Different from a so-called deity, a transcendent being, the Buddha is, above all, none other than a way a human being should be. The attributes and virtues attached to the Buddha came to be variously readjusted in later years. Of these, wisdom (*prajñā*) and benevolence (*karuṇā*), the intellect that penetrates human life and the love for all living beings, are said to be the two principal pillars. From the name Buddha (an awakened one), and a word such as bodhi (enlightenment), it may be easily discerned that a greater emphasis is put on wisdom. Gautama Buddha's (the historical Buddha, Śākyamuni) breaking the bonds of transmigration and entering nirvāṇa signifies the perfection of this wisdom.

All his disciples, of course, showed infinite respect for Gautama Buddha. But this was not the awe-inspiring reverence such as for a deity, but respect for a great elder and forerunner. They did not place much importance in a transcendental god, an omniscient and omnipotent god as the creator of the universe, or a god that governed and punished human beings, even though they did not necessarily repudiate such concepts. To them the Buddha was a great elder and teacher, but neither a prophet nor even an authority, such as the leader of a religious order. This can be understood from the following words of the Buddha uttered on his deathbed in answer to the Venerable Ānanda, who, overcome with grief, had asked whom he should revere as teacher when the Buddha had passed away: "Let the self be a lamp, let the self be a refuge; let the dharma (truth) be a lamp, let the dharma be a refuge." And also: "After I am gone the dharma (teaching) and the vinaya (discipline) which I have expounded will be your teacher."[1]

But later this Buddha came to be super-humanized and was made divine, until, as will be described, the theories of the twofold and threefold body of the Buddha were gradually systematized, and even a highly theistic conception finally materialized.

The theory of the twofold body of the Buddha advocates that the Buddha had two bodies, (1) the Dharma-body (*dharma-kāya*) and (2) the Physical-body (*rūpa-kāya*). This theory became stabilized in a variety of earlier sūtras, and in early Mahāyāna sūtras, the *Prajñāpāramitā,* the *Saddharmapuṇḍarīka,* and so forth. The rūpa-kāya is the Buddha seen in a human body, while the dharma-kāya is the Buddha's personality seen in the dharma or dharma-nature. The disciples, quite bewildered at the loss of their teacher, decided first of all to confirm in themselves the Buddha's teachings and then to compile them in order to transmit them to future generations. To the disciples, the sayings which the teacher had left behind—the expounded dharma—were now their only lamp, just as the Buddha had instructed on his deathbed. Though the Buddha's body had perished, the dharma he had left behind was imperishable. The teacher to whom they should address their questions lived in the dharma; the dharma itself was the teacher. The Buddha once said: "Those who see 'dependent origination' (*pratītya-samutpāda*) will see the dharma; those who see the dharma will see 'dependent origination.' "[2] He also said: "Those who see the dharma will see me; those who see me will see the dharma."[3]

In this way the concept of 'dharma-kāya' occurred. The Buddha as dharma-kāya in eternal aspect, which could not be seen with the naked eye, was conceived in addition to the Buddha's earthly form which the disciples still vividly remembered. The word dharma has many meanings. Not only does it signify the "teachings" that the Buddha expounded, but it has as its original meaning the idea of "essence" that makes a thing what it is. In this sense, it is also the "law" that lies at the basis of things, and is also "existences" that are formed by the laws and that shoulder the laws. Beside these meanings, dharma designates "religious rites" as well, and also "religion" itself. When the dharma-kāya as the dharma itself was discussed in relation to the Buddha, people seem to have understood it with these different meanings in mind. The word thus included religious and ethical as well as philosophical and metaphysical meanings.[4]

Later in the advanced stages of Mahāyāna Buddhism, the word *dharmatā* (*dharma-nature*) came to be also used to represent the essence itself of this dharma. Therefore, the dharma-kāya is the body of the dharma-nature as well. Again, when the universe is conceived in the dimension of such dharma, the universe is none other than the "dharma-dhātu" (*dharma-realm*). Being the true way of the universe, the dharma-dhātu is identified with dharmatā or tathatā (suchness) and even with śūnyatā (emptiness). Dharma-dhātu extends over the two realms of enlightenment and of deluded human beings, but when it manifests itself as the dharma-dhātu, which is purified of all human delusions, it is then called the "Buddha." In this way, the Buddha was made to be more and more superhuman and finally culminated in becoming absolute. Such is a rough sketch of the Mahāyāna development of the doctrine of Buddha-body.

In Mahāyāna Buddhism, however, together with these metaphysical views of the universe, to which the doctrine of the Buddha's body is closely related, there is, on the other hand, a well-established concept of the 'bodhisattva,' which may be said to constitute the core of Mahāyānism. The concept of a bodhisattva as a seeker after enlightenment, a seeker after truth, came into existence quite early. It may be said to have developed from investigations that were made concerning Buddha (-hood), or independently and in parallel with them. The fact that Gautama realized the highest enlightenment in human flesh, that is, with the defilements of joy and sorrow, was regarded by his disciples as an extremely marvelous event, unheard of in the history of humankind. Furthermore, they found it inconceivable that this great event had been brought about through the discipline of one short lifespan. As a seeker of truth, Gautama must have accumulated from time without beginning a great stock of merit in innumerable past lives, and finally, in this life, this must have born fruit in the marvelous event of his enlightenment. Such beliefs gave rise to the many narratives of Gautama Buddha's former lives, the *Jātaka* tales. In former lives, Gautama accumulated merits by performing good deeds as a rabbit, a monkey, a deer, or as a wealthy man, a minister of state, a king, and so forth. The rabbit, the monkey, and others were all Gautama himself, the seeker of truth. His long career as a seeker of truth (*bodhisattva*) finally perfected the "human Buddha."

The seeker of truth, however, is not to be limited to Gautama alone. There were and will be innumerable seekers of truth in the past and in the future, as there are also at the present time. In some sense, all living beings essentially have the potentiality of becoming seekers of truth. The dharmadhātu may be regarded as being filled with such bodhisattvas.

Inquiry into the essential meaning of the one called a bodhisattva or seeker of truth brings forth the subject of the bodhisattva's vow and discipline. His vow (*praṇidhāna*) is a pledge intrinsic to a bodhisattva; his discipline (*pratipatti*) designates all the practices he performs to fulfill this vow. There are different vows and disciplines in accordance with the way of each individual bodhisattva. The vow and disciplines of Gautama, too, being restricted by historical circumstances, were accordingly various and individual. But generally speaking, the vows of a bodhisattva, which arise from profound love and benevolence, aim at the deliverance and emancipation of all living beings. Pure wisdom and indefatigable practice are required for the realization of this aim. An innumerable number of such bodhisattvas have been conceived in Mahāyāna: benevolence was especially emphasized and personified in the Bodhisattva Avalokiteśvara; discipline was represented by the Bodhisattva Samantabhadra; and wisdom was concretized in the Bodhisattva Mañjuśrī.

It is probably in Mahāyāna sūtras such as the *Avataṃsaka* and, especially, the Pure Land sūtras, such as the *Sukhāvatīvyūha,* that the abovementioned careers of bodhisattvas are most typically expounded. According to the *Larger Sukhāvatīvyūha,* the Bodhisattva Dharmākara made forty-eight primal vows, which he fulfilled in a long period of discipline, until he became Amida Buddha. Amida Buddha signifies both unlimited wisdom (*Amitābha*) and unlimited benevolence (*Amitāyus*).

The way such as that of Amida Buddha came to be understood by the name Reward-body (probably *saṃbhoga-kāya* in Sanskrit; see footnote 11) of the Buddha.[5] Here appeared the third concept, the 'Reward-body,' apart from the Dharma-body and Physical-body, mentioned above. The Reward-body is the body of the Buddha in which the fulfillment of his above-described vows and disciplines has been rewarded. Therefore, the Reward-body is not limited to Amida Buddha. If it were the case that the fulfilling of one's vows and disciplines was the reason and principle for becoming a Buddha, then all Buddhas, in so far as they have fulfilled their vows and disciplines, must be Reward Buddhas. The bodhisattva ideal necessarily indicates the way of the Buddha as Reward-body which is in accord with his vows and disciplines.

It may be said that in this way all the materials (or the elements) for the later theory of the Buddha's threefold body had made their appearance: the elements of the Dharma-body and the Physical-body plus the elements of the Reward-body.[6] Until the time of the Prajñāpāramitā Sūtra and the time of Nāgārjuna who developed the Mādhyamika philosophy based on the sūtra, only the twofold body of Dharma-body and Physical-body[7] was conceived as a theory of the Buddha's body. It was in the philosophy of the Yogācāra school (or the Vijñāna-vāda school) represented by Asaṅga and Vasubandhu that the two-body theory developed until it was consummated into a three-body theory. The ideas and faiths that became the materials for the three-body theory must have been established in various forms before that time. There was already a tendency toward the universalization of the concept of Buddha. It was thought that Gautama Buddha was not the only Buddha; that there had been many Buddhas in the past, and there would be many Buddhas in the future; and that actually there existed innumerable Buddhas in the innumerable Buddha-lands in the ten directions. Thus, names of Buddhas, such as Vairocana, Akṣobhya, Amitābha, Amitāyus, Bhaiṣajya-guru, and countless others had already been conceived. It was the Yogācāra-vijñāna school that organized the three-body (*tri-kāya*) theory by synthesizing these conceptions of the Buddha.

II

In the tri-kāya theory of the Buddha brought to perfection by the Yogācāra-vijñāna school, the three Buddha-bodies were called, successively, "svābhāvika-kāya," "sāṃbhogika-kāya," and "nairmāṇika-kāya," which can be said to be more theoretic names[8] than those mentioned in the last section.

The *svābhāvika-kāya* (Essence-body), the first of the three bodies, corresponds to the dharma-kāya (Dharma-body) described above.[9] Each of the three bodies is an effusion of the dharma-dhātu and can be taken as a "arising" (*vṛtti*) of the dharma-dhātu[10] [in this sense they are all Dharma-bodies]; however, the *svābhāvika-kāya,* in particular, is called the Essence-body in view of the fact that *dharmatā* (dharma-nature), *dharma-dhātu* (dharma-realm), *tathatā* (suchness), or *śūnyatā* (emptiness) is itself the Buddha's real essence. The word *svabhāva* (own being), which Nāgārjuna once rejected, is used here to mean the Buddha's enlightenment which is one with the absolute, free from the agonies of life and death of the world of relativity. It exists all over the world with the *dharma-dhātu* as its own being; it is an immovable wisdom, an eternal body of the Enlightened One. Being absolute, it transcends human understanding and speculation; it is incognizable, invisible, inconceivable, without color or form. Moreover, as it makes the dharma-dhātu its own being, it can be the foundation and basis for the two other bodies, the *sāṃbhogika-kāya* (Enjoyment-body) and the *nairmāṇika-kāya* (Transformation-body). In contrast to the fact that the svābhāvika-kāya is immovable, invisible, and is the basis, the sāṃbhogika-kāya and the nairmāṇika-kāya are movable, changeable, visible, and are dependent on the svābhāvika-kāya.

The *sāṃbhogika-kāya,* the second Buddha-body, is the same as the Reward-body described above.[11] *Saṃbhoga* means "enjoyment." It is understood that one can enjoy the Pure Land and the dharma as a result of the fulfillment of one's vow and discipline. From this enjoyment of the Pure Land, we see that the Reward-body is closely connected with the Pure Land teaching. But to the *sāṃbhogika-kāya,* the enjoyment of the *dharma* is of prime importance. The Buddha's biography tells us that after he attained his enlightenment under the bodhi-tree, the Buddha spent, with appreciation, several weeks pondering over the dharma that he himself had realized. This is called "the Buddha's own enjoyment of the dharma-delight" (自受用法楽). Having finally attained his enlightenment, the Buddha, standing on the top of the mountain, as it were, might have looked back, with serene delight, at the winding road of suffering he had just climbed. But this "for one's own enjoyment" (自受用) later developed into "for the enjoyment of others" (他受用). This is the sharing of one's own dharma-delight with others, that is, the preaching of the dharma to others. Therefore, the sāṃbhogika-kāya is said to be the "Buddha-body seen at an assembly for sermons"—a gathering of people who wish to hear the Buddha's preaching. This is none other than a Buddha-body that is visible, in the sense that human beings can understand it intellectually (and emotionally, as well).

The third Buddha-body, *nairmāṇika-kāya* (Transformation-body), is not only equally visible but is truly a physical body of a corporal human being. The Buddha Śākyamuni is its best example: he was a being born from the womb of his mother, Queen Māyā and one who possessed human sufferings and who conformed to the physical law of life and death. This was none other than a Buddha-body that appeared temporarily as an actual historic being. The reason that this is called a Transformation-body is that the dharma-dhātu, limiting itself, transforms itself to appear temporarily in the form of a physical human body. As regards the Transformation-body, there is the view that it is not limited only to the case of Gautama Buddha but extends to also the cases of the rabbit, the monkey, and so forth of the *Jātaka* tales, or to other beings such as *nirmita* (transformed) and *upapāduka* (self-produced). In the former case of Gautama, it is clear to everyone that the Transformation-body is the Buddha; but in the latter cases of the rabbit and other beings, it cannot immediately be known whether it is a bodhisattva or a Buddha in his former lives.

Now, among the three Buddha-bodies, the *svābhāvika-kāya* is the foundation of the other two Buddha-bodies, while it remains as a principle, abstract and invisible. In contrast to this, the *sāṃbhogika-kāya* and the *nairmāṇika-kāya* are concrete and visible—they are Physical-bodies belonging to the phenomenal world. Various differences, however, are found between the sāṃbhogika-kāya and the nairmāṇika-kāya.

In the first place, nairmāṇika-kāya was the Buddha from whom, face to face, his disciples were able to hear the teachings. In contrast, the *sāṃbhogika-kāya* is the Buddha-body that can be seen only by bodhisattvas in the Buddha-land and not by ordinary unenlightened men. The sāṃbhogika-kāya is, above all, one that enjoys the dharma; it is said to be the Buddha who preaches to the assembly of bodhisattvas. However, if this point is carried through to its logical end, it follows that, according to the trikāya theory of Mahāyāna, Śākyamuni's teaching of the dharma occurred in the context of the *sāṃbhogika-kāya*.[12]

It is well known that the Buddha-body has thirty-two physical marks characteristic of a great man. They are, to mention some of them, a fleshy protuberance on the crown of the head, a white hair between the eyebrows emitting light, webbed fingers, and so forth. Although sculptors of Buddhist images have made efforts to represent these marks, there are some among them that are conceptual and impossible to visualize, and some that are abstract and almost impossible to represent in sculpture and painting. The trikāya theories of later ages tell about these marks of the Buddha only in relation to the sāṃbhogika-kāya, and do not recognize them in the nairmaṇika-kāya. In view of this fact, it can be said that in the story of Asita, the seer,[13] who shed tears when he saw the newborn Gautama and foretold of his fortune, what he saw was not a physical body but, in reality, the *sāṃbhogika-kāya*.

Furthermore, as for the Buddha's acts, those of the sāṃbhogika-kāya are said to be steady and indestructible, while those of the nairmaṇika-kāya are temporary and unsteady.[14]

Putting these points together, we know that all the superhuman elements found in Gautama Buddha became the elements which constituted the *sāṃbhogika-kāya*. That is to say, compared with the *nairmāṇika-kāya*, a higher universality and divine nature are attributed to the sāṃbhogika-kāya. In this sense, the sāṃbhogika-kāya is transcendental to human beings. Again, this sāṃbhogika-kāya is connected with the way of the Reward-body. An accumulation of innumerable virtues in the past lives of Gautama Buddha, transcending the eighty years of his human life, was conceived and this concept served as a model for the idea of the Reward-body as fulfillment of a vow and discipline. This body is, therefore, the universal Buddha, transcending history and the Buddha as a human being.

But the trikāya theory's peculiarity can be seen in the point that such transcendency of the Reward-body cannot immediately be regarded in the same light with the dharma-kāya or the svābhāvika-kāya. In contrast to the svābhāvika-kāya, which is entirely abstract, theoretic, and absolutely immovable, the sāṃbhogika-kāya is, above all, one that enjoys the dharma. Although the svābhāvika-kāya is dharma-kāya, which has the dharma as its essence, nothing is said here about the enjoyment of the dharma. It is improbable that stirring of "enjoyment" should be found in the svābhāvika-kāya, which is immovable. In order to enjoy the dharma, the *svābhāvika-kāya* must become concrete and relative by descending a step from the seat of the absolute. It must come down from the seat of immutable *śūnyatā* or *dharma-dhātu,* and enter into the realm of mutability—where the Buddha-land is to be established through the act of purification, or where the Reward-body will be realized as a result of the cause, the bodhisattva's vow and discipline. Therefore, Sthiramati even said, "the *kāya,* abiding in which the *svābhāvika* would attain enlightenment . . . is the *sāṃbhogika-kāya.*"[15] That there is no such thing as the svābhāvika-kāya attaining enlightenment or enjoying the dharma is probably because it was originally the enlightenment itself, the so-called original enlightenment (本覚). In contrast to this, the sāṃbhogika-kāya, is as it were, "initial awakening" (始覚).[16] Human deliverance can be established in such Buddha-body as the sāṃbhogika-kāya, not in the svābhāvika-kāya. The sāṃbhogika-kāya as the concretization of the svābhāvika-kāya is also called "niṣyanda-kāya" (等流身). *Niṣyanda* means outflow, that is, the outflowing of the Buddha-body from the dharma-dhātu, urged by the Great Compassion.[17] The Great Compassion crystallizes itself into the preaching—a form in which the dharma-dhātu manifests itself.

Thus, we know that the sāṃbhogika-kāya is composed of a twofold character. While, on the one hand, there is the aspect of transcending the human Buddha, the *nairmāṇika-kāya,* there is, on the other hand, the concretization of the absolute, the *svābhāvika-kāya.* Therefore, the sāṃbhogika-kāya has the two aspects of being at once transcendental and phenomenal, and at once historic and super-historic.[18] When the historical Buddha is contrasted with the super-historic Buddha, it is commonly done in the light of the two-body theory, signifying the Physical-body and the Dharma-body. Contrary to this, the sāṃbhogika-kāya, while modelling itself after the historical Buddha, is a temporal and spatial presentation of the absolute dharma-nature. The story of Amida Buddha as the Reward-body is not something like a myth of a stage before history; even if we might call it "a myth," it was produced by the association of history with super-history. It is owing to this character of sāṃbhogika-kāya that such things as the thirty-two physical marks of the Buddha are attributed to the sāṃbhogika-kāya and that the Buddha-land is expressed as a Pure Land in the context of sāṃbhogika-kāya.

The same double nature of the sāṃbhogika-kāya also has been described from the aspect of "benefit for oneself" and "benefit for others." Gautama Buddha's acts, whether in his past or present lives, were all altruistic [i.e., benefit for others]. In comparison with this, sāṃbhogika-kāya is rather egocentric in that it is a body that has been accomplished by virtue of "self-perfection," that is, by virtue of perfecting each one of the Buddha's own merits (*buddhadharma-paripāka*). On the other hand, however, the svābhāvika-kāya is "indifferent," transcending both ego-centeredness and altruism. Compared with this, the enjoyment or the preaching of the dharma by the sāṃbhogika-kāya is explained to be a perfectly altruistic deed.

The sāṃbhogika-kāya, through this double character, lies between the svābhāvika-kāya and the nairmāṇika-kāya, and serves as a link between the two. But that's not all! Sāṃbhogika-kāya occupies the central position in the triple-body doctrine, and in particular, the soteriology in Buddhism revolves around the axis of this double character of the sāṃbhogika-kāya. In this sense, the sāṃbhogika-kāya can be called the "Buddha par excellence." But, if this were the case one might think that both svābhāvika-kāya and nairmāṇika-kāya are superfluous and unnecessary and that the one Buddha-body of sāṃbhogika-kāya is sufficient. Such a claim is possible, and it might have been supported especially from the standpoint of religious monotheistic demands. But the special characteristic of the Mahāyānic doctrine of Buddha-body lies in the persistent maintenance of the triangular position of the three Buddha-bodies. For in that respect there is something fundamentally different from either the one-body or the two-body theory.

In the simple one-body theory, Gautama was the only Buddha. But later with the discovery of the *dharma-kāya* concept, the two-body theory was formed. The dharma-kāya in this stage, however, was the dharma-kāya of Gautama himself, without any universal meaning. The historical Buddha then existed with the physical-body, and his Dharma-body was something abstract, with less reality than his corporal body. Later on, to the contrary, this abstract dharma-kāya must have gained universal reality—the reality that claimed equal realness with the corporal body. At this stage, however, there was nothing that could reconcile the two realities of dharma-kāya and rūpa-kāya. The sāṃbhogika-kāya was discovered here as something that would fill the gap. In the trikāya theory, the dharma-kāya alone, under the name of *svābhāvika-kāya,* is regarded really to exist, and to be the sole basis and principle of all Buddha-bodies. Therefore, here the Physical-body, which had been a reality in the sphere of historical time, became shadowy and was slighted as a transient existence under the name of "*nairmāṇika-kāya.*" Historicity came to be regarded as illusionary, so to speak. Against this, the *sāṃbhogika-kāya* shouldered a temporary meaning while being a true reality, and regained its historic nature while transcending history. It can be said that with the birth of this *sāṃbhogika-kāya*, the doctrine of 'Buddha-kāya' reached a stage of perfection in the *trikāya* theory.

All the attributes and virtues of the Buddha were also clarified in the system of the *trikāya*. As it is impossible to describe them here one by one, I shall give only a few examples: the Buddha's wisdom was regarded as an attribute belonging especially to *svābhāvika-kāya;* his will (*āśaya*, vow) was treated especially in regard to *sāṃbhogika-kāya;* and his acts (*buddha-karman*) especially in regard to *nairmāṇika-kāya*. But at the same time, since the three Buddha-bodies are not independent of each other but are related in the manner of a basis and a thing based on it, these virtues are also considered transferable to each other. Similarly, the elucidation of such questions as whether there is only one Buddha or other Buddhas numerous in number, or for what reason the Buddha is said to be everlasting and always abiding, and so forth, has been attempted through the system of the trikāya. I will not go into these problems here, but I would say that, in short, these problems would not likely be answered thoroughly without the trikāya theory. The theoretic perfection of the doctrine of Buddha-body lies in the triangular concept of the three Buddha-bodies;[19] the two-body theory would be insufficient, and a four-body and other many-body theories would be plethoric in principle.

III

It may be possible to say that the structure of the *tri-kāya*, as described in the last chapter, is akin to the concept of the Trinity in Christianity. For example, A. K. Coomaraswamy says that the *svābhāvika-kāya, sāṃbhogika-kāya*, and *nairmāṇika-kāya* correspond respectively to the Father, the figure of Christ in Glory, and the visible Jesus.[20] But the Reward-body in which one's vow and discipline have been rewarded as described above is especially Buddhistic and seems to be quite removed from the Christian idea. We find rather something more familiar than Christianity in the same author when he compares the view of the Hindu deities with the *tri-kāya*. According to him, "the Dharma-kāya is the Brahman, timeless and unconditioned; the Saṃbhoga-kāya is realized in the forms of Īśvara; the Nirmāṇakāya in every avatār." When Brahmā (the creator god) is regarded as a personification of the Brahman (the Absolute), he is the first of the triad (*trimūrti*) of Hindu gods, and other two beings Īśvara (Śiva, the destroyer) and Viṣṇu (the preserver).

A. K. Chatterjee also observes that among the trikāya, the sāṃbhogika-kāya represents "the concept of God par excellence." But at the same time he explains important differences between the Buddha and Vedāntic Īśvara. Namely, unlike the Brahman as the principle, "Īśvara, though phenomenal, yet acts always from above." The Buddha, on the other hand, "actually takes birth as man," as historic human being, his training for realizing the truth being conducted from below; in him the truth was concretized and personified. The ultimate object here was the attainment of Buddhahood by all humankind as an ideal of the phenomenal world. Chatterjee further continues: "To Īśvara are ascribed the cosmic functions as well; He is the creator and the sustainer of the world. . . . Indeed in all Buddhism, this notion of a god is vehemently opposed. . . . The Tathāgata is merely a spiritual preceptor. He cannot, or rather does not, interfere with other cosmic functions."[21]

Chatterjee's opinion mentioned above can be accepted overall, but some additional comments may be acceptable. If an expression such as "a personal God" were to be applied within Buddhism, the closest equivalent would be *sāṃbhogika-kāya* or the Reward-body, as Chatterjee states. The word "body" of Buddha-body may correspond to "personality," but there is no implication of a theistic personality in the *svābhāvika-kāya* or *dharma-kāya,* although this may depend on one's interpretation. The reason is that within the context of *svābhāvika-kāya,* dharma or dharmatā itself is considered as the Buddha-body or Buddha's being. Furthermore, when this dharmatā or dharmatā-dhātu is thought about within the context of śūnyatā or absolute emptiness the peculiar Buddhistic doctrine of Buddha-body can be seen. The Buddha, together with the svābhāvika-kāya and dharma-dhātu, do not "exist" in an absolute sense, but transcending "existent" and "non-existent," are *śūnyatā.*

Mahāyāna Buddhism expounds a specific idea called "non-abiding in nirvāṇa" (side by side with non-abiding in saṃsāra), in addition to the usual ideas of nirvāṇa. Nirvāṇa is the ultimate aim of practitioners and the śrāvakas (disciples). Translated as or equated with "annihilation" (滅 *nirodha*) in Chinese, it is related also to śūnyatā mentioned above; it is a realm of absolute calmness and quietness on "the other shore." But in Mahāyāna Buddhism one does not care to remain on the absolute and transcendental "other shore," but persistently puts oneself in the world of transmigration, without entering nirvāṇa—this is the ideal of non-abiding in nirvāṇa (*apratiṣṭhita-nirvāṇa*). It may be said that the structure of the trikāya doctrine also follows this idea. The svābhāvika-kāya, because of its being wisdom, is not abiding in saṃsāra, and is equal to the "Emancipated Body" (*vimukti-kāya*), freed from every obstacle of defilement; it corresponds to absolute nirvāṇa. But, on the other hand, insofar as its function never ceases, the dharma-kāya is "non-interruption" or "eternalness," it does not remain in nirvāṇa but positively returns to this shore of the phenomenal world as sāṃbhogika-kāya and nairmāṇika-kāya on account of its benevolence.[22]

In parallel with this, there is the term, "intentional birth" (*saṃcintya-bhavopapatti*), which means that a bodhisattva volunteers to be born into a life of suffering.[23] A Bodhisattva appears in this world of transmigration; this is, however, not an ordinary physical result of his former karman, but it is due to his own "delusion" that he has purposely left unextinguished with the intention of entering into *saṃsāric* existence. Such a power to be reborn "at will" may be said to originate by nature from śūnyatā, which is characteristic of svābhāvika-kāya; but, at the same time, to take birth "in saṃsāra" is solely due to his great compassion (which is attachment, hence delusion, in a bodhisattva) for the living beings that are afflicted in the whirl of saṃsāra. It is understood that Jesus Christ, too, was born on the horizon of history as a child of man by emptying (*kenosis*) divine attributes. In Buddhism a similar idea has been universalized as a way of the bodhisattva, without being confined to the life of Gautama Buddha.

The trikāya doctrine developed as a system with a background of these Mahāyāna concepts, which in their turn became ever more firmly solidified by having recourse to the trikāya doctrine. Therefore, we must say that the trikāya doctrine is fairly different from the Trinity of Christianity or the trimūrti of Hinduism.

Later on the Buddha-body theory made a further development, giving rise to four-body and other theories. For example, Hui-yüan of Ching-ying-ssu temple says that the *Laṅkāvatāra Sūtra* enumerates the following four Buddhas: 如如仏 (Suchness-Buddha), 智慧仏 (Wisdom Buddha), 功徳仏 (Merit Buddha), 報化佛 (Incarnation Buddha).[24] Again, it is well-known that the *Buddha-bhūmi-śāstra* and the *Ch'êng-wei-shih-lun* expound a theory of four Buddha-bodies by dividing the Enjoyment Body into the Own-enjoyment Body and Other's-enjoyment Body.[25] Furthermore, in the *Abhisamaya-ālaṃkārāloka,* in addition to the three Buddha-bodies, the Buddha-body called "jñāna-dharma-kāya" (Wisdom-dharma Body) is given, placed in the second place among them, forming the four Buddha-bodies.[26] Many other theories of Buddha-bodies were formed by introducing various concepts, such as the Emancipation Body (*vimukti-kāya*), Outflowing Body (*niṣyanda-kāya*), Result-maturation Body (*vipāka-kāya*), and so forth. They may present characteristic developments both in doctrine and in spiritual history, but I shall not treat each of them here. For, as stated above, the trikāya theory may be regarded as a consummated theory, establishing the fundamental principle of the doctrine insofar as the ways of Buddha-body are concerned.

However, it does not mean that because of this, every problem has been completely solved. It is true that by this trikāya theory the nature of the Buddha and all his virtues and functions has been delineated. But as for how Gautama, a human being, was able to become a Buddha possessing virtues equal to those of a divine being, almost nothing has been said in these theories. How can a leap from the relative world to the absolute world be made? Since Gautama was an exceptional person, as his disciples thought, it might have been possible for him to become a Buddha owing to his innumerable virtuous deeds accumulated in the past. But if it were owing only to that, Gautama would have been a divine existence from the beginning, and not a human being. Moreover, that would be a unique case involving Gautama alone, it would not explain anything about the existence of all the Buddhas in the ten directions. In Mahāyāna Buddhism, it is specifically said that all living things are expected to attain Buddhahood, but then, it must be asked: In what way is it possible for a common living being to become a Buddha?

IV

The possibility of all living beings attaining Buddhahood is a problem that seems to have been answered from two sides. One is the idea that all living beings possess Buddha-nature—the idea that is mainly advocated by the tathāgata-garbha (*tathāgata-matrix*) theory. The other is the introduction of the concept of 'āśraya-parāvṛtti' (the revolving of the basis). Let me take up the latter first.

The concept of āśraya-parāvṛtti is frequently used by the Yogācāra-vijñāna school that consummated the trikāya doctrine. Āśraya-parāvṛtti means, as the word indicates, the basis on which one relies, revolves, and turns into a different basis (or non-basis); the ground itself on which one stands, overturns, revealing a new world, illuminated by a new light. There is the anxiety of one's foothold being fundamentally challenged—the anxiety that it might collapse and disappear, meaning death. But through this death, there is the possibility of the same basic structure coming to life again by being illuminated with a new light. This is not simply the renovation of the mind, which is a part of oneself, or that of the body, or simply the one's disappearance and becoming non-existent; it is the conversion and the transmutation of one's whole existence. For example, if we were to imagine a magnetic field flowing through man's being, then the *āśraya-parāvṛtti* would be the flow of this magnetic field in the opposite direction from its usual flow. One's acts are based upon and determined by such a magnetic flow. Also the matter of purification in human beings is not the removal of something filthy, but is none other than the backward flow of man's mechanism or magnetic field, with its structure unchanged. A negative film may look like a positive picture when the light shines on it from different angles; in the same way, when the light permeates into one's whole system, it receives light in a new scene, whereby the same existence that has been in darkness begins to shine brilliantly.

In the Yogācāra-vijñāna school, the idea of āśraya-parāvṛtti had already been prepared in the school's unique theory of the "Threefold nature" (*trisvabhāva*). This theory explains the system of the world by means of the true way of the world or by its three aspects or natures, namely: (1) the relative nature (*paratantra-svabhāva* or other-dependent nature), (2) the imagined nature (*parikalpita-svabhāva*), and (3) the consummated nature (*pariniṣpanna-svabhāva*). On the basis of the relative nature of the world (*paratantra-svabhāva*), the world appears in its imagined, unreal, and polluted character (*parikalpita-svabhāva*) to the ordinary man on the one hand, and, on the other, it appears as the consummated and purified nature (*pariniṣpanna-svabhāva*), to the saints. The magnetic field spoken about above may be conceived as related to the other-dependent nature. A detailed explanation of these three natures is not possible in the space allotted here. In short, the revolving of one's own foundation means that on the field of relative nature, the state of being polluted with delusions (i.e. the world of imagined nature) revolves its basis to become a state of purity, a world of consummated nature. The principle that makes this revolution possible can be found in the fact that the world is essentially of the nature of relativity or of "dependent origination" (*pratītyasamutpāda*), and this world of relative nature has been turned around into a polluted condition to form the world of imagined nature; it has been turned around, and is like a positive picture that appears on the negative itself under certain light conditions. One's foothold, hitherto believed to be firm and unshakable, is now realized to be something unreal and polluted, being covered with fundamental ignorance (*avidyā*)—with something called "original sin or radical evil," in religious terms. Through this self-realization one's foothold revolves and becomes purified.

The Buddha-body is described as a result of this "revolving of the basis," which can be explained in various ways. For one thing, the eight *vijñānas* (cognition or consciousness, originally "dependent-on-other" in character), including the *ālaya-vijñāna* (store-cognition), by revolving their own foundations, become four kinds of Buddha's wisdom. "Cognition is revolved and Wisdom is acquired" (轉識得智), it is said, and this wisdom is none other than the essence of the threefold body of Buddha.[27] Thus, the doctrine of 'āśraya-parāvṛtti' is an attempt to clarify that the human way of being, along with its basis, revolves itself and becomes the

Buddha's way of being, or realizes the Buddha's body, his basis. And the direction of this revolution, therefore, can be said to be ascendent.

Contrary to this, what is descendent is the concept of 'tathāgata-garbha,' the idea that all beings have Buddha-nature. According to the tathāgata-garbha theory, it is strongly advocated that the human mind is essentially identical with the tathāgata, or the dharma-dhātu or the dharma-body. It is true that human beings are steeped in the world of suffering, and are far removed from the world of the Buddha. But viewed from the ultimate standpoint, the essence of the human mind is transparently luminous; it has lost its light only because of its being covered with adventitious defilement (*āgantuka-kleśa*). When the adventitious defilement has been removed, the true mind or Buddha-nature becomes apparent—this is the "āśraya-parāvṛtti." No living being can exist outside the world of the absolute called "tathatā" or "śūnyatā"; one cannot escape from the dharma-dhātu. Just as the birds fly freely in the air, all sentient beings breathe in the Buddha-nature. Just as all things are filled with air, all living beings are filled with the Buddha-nature. It is because all living beings store such Buddha-nature concealed within themselves that they are regarded as the germ that produces the Buddha. Therefore, every living being is said to be a "tathāgata-garbha" (tathāgata-matrix). As for the term tathāgata-garbha, various interpretations appeared in later ages, but its original meaning seems to have been that it was the embryo that conceived the tathāgata, nurtured it, and gave birth to it. To say that a sentient being is a tathāgata-garbha means that one possesses Buddha-lineage and is a member of the Buddha family (*gotra*) and that one possesses Buddha-essence or Buddha-nature by birth.

It is believed that this idea of Buddha-nature or tathāgata-garbha appeared fairly early in Indian Buddhism, in parallel with the philosophy of "cognition-only" or "mind-only." Buddhism made great advancement with this discovery of Buddha-nature within ordinary living beings. The relative importance of this concept within Buddhism gradually increased as time advanced, especially in Chinese and Japanese Buddhism, where it became the central, basic concept. As this was almost the same with Tibetan Buddhism as well, it can be inferred that this concept had probably become the core of Buddhist thought in the last stages of Indian Buddhism.

As for the problem of the possibility of attaining Buddhahood by common beings, it can be said that an answer has been tentatively given by means of the idea that all beings possess Buddha-nature. But at the same time, many new difficulties have arisen. For example, if common beings already possess Buddha-nature equal to the dharma-body, why is it that they are still sunk in the depths of transmigration? Why is it that the essentially undefiled minds of the common beings are still roots of delusions?

The declaration that all beings are tathāgata-garbha is sure to encourage them greatly, and their efforts toward enlightenment will not be fruitless. But at the same time, if they already possess the dharma-body, or at least possess it in its potential form, efforts to attain it will be, in effect, unnecessary.

The characteristic of the doctrine of tathāgata-garbha lies not so much in theory as in its religious poignancy and literary beauty, which must have been products of mystical experience. In Japan this literary mystery was further enhanced by advocating that not only sentient beings but also insentient beings, such as mountains and rivers, trees and grasses, all possessed Buddha-nature and the possibility of attaining Buddhahood. This religious, mystical, intuitive attitude can be seen in many sūtras. But the descriptions in sūtras can be said to be derived from the standpoint of the Buddha who has already attained enlightenment; they are the descriptions of the tathāgata-garbha or Buddha-nature when seen from the Buddha's viewpoint and not from the viewpoint of ordinary beings. The reason is that if something is to be declared by ordinary beings when they envisage truth, it must be always a confession of sin or of delusion and impurity, not of possessing Buddha-nature. Therefore, it is probably natural that Indian Buddhist philosophers were not able to fully theorize and systematize the idea of the tathāgata-garbha, the substance of this religious intuition, for it was something whose nature could not apply to human logic and logical categories. The book, *Ratnagotra-vibhāga,* seems almost the only treatise extant that has attempted a systematization of the theory of tathāgata-garbha. It is a "śāstra" that one expects to be theoretical in nature, but rather than being a theoretic, philosophical book, the *Ratnagotra-vibhāga* is a literary work, revealing religious faith, and it is filled with beautiful expressions and figures of speech of praise to the Buddha. The theory of the threefold body of the Buddha is also adopted in this book and more pages are devoted to it than even the treatises belonging to the Yogācāra-vijñāna school. The theoretic structure between the three bodies, however, is not necessarily clarified. This book seems rather to focus on the idea of twofold body rather than on the theory of the threefold body[28]—a fact that might indicate that this book is more religious than philosophical.

Contrary to the theories of 'trikāya' and 'āśraya-parāvṛtti' of the Yogācāra-vijñāna school that can be described as an ascent, the fact that the theory of tathāgata-garbha is descendent, as I have already said, can also be surmised from the tendency of this theory of tathāgata-garbha. Above all, the ordinary mind of living beings is called the "tathāgata-garbha" on the basis that the ordinary mind is presupposed to be the dharma-body or dharma-realm, that is, the dharma-body or dharma-realm is first set up, and then flowing out from the dharma-body, which is regarded as the real basis, the world of ordinary beings manifests itself. In such a way, the theory of tathāgata-garbha also treats the human being and human mind, but since the mind is first grasped[29]as something sublime that flows out from above, the actual problem of the ugly minds of human beings cannot but be left behind, forgotten. While the mind is believed here to be pure and luminous in its original nature, the delusions (*kleśa*), which bring forth every human ugliness, are apt to be regarded simply as something accidental, foreign, and nonessential. And it seems that the delusions are believed not to be serious but rather to be easily dispelled, because of their characteristics of being adventitious and nonessential.

The "Buddha's lineage" (*gotra*) mentioned above has been discussed also by the Yogācāra-vijñāna school in the *Mahāyāna-sūtrālaṃkāra* and other treatises. A bodhisattva is a bodhisattva because he belongs to the Buddha's lineage and is endowed with the Buddha-nature. But at the same time a bodhisattva is here described as an existence that is tortured with excessive delusions in spite of its lineage. Some bodhisattvas, being king's vassals, are forced even to commit murder, and some do the same when confronted with robbers and rascals.[30] To these bodhisattvas, the delusion, not the lineage, is their grave concern in the actual world. Reflections are further extended even to beings who are completely devoid of any "possibilities of getting into nirvāṇa," the so-called beings without any (Buddha) lineage (*agotra*).[31] We see here the forerunner of the theory of the 'five distinct gotras' (including *agotra*), which later met with severe criticisms from the advocates of the doctrine of the tathāgata-garbha.

Such essentially negative aspects of inherited nature can hardly be seen in the *Ratnagotra-vibhāga*, where only beautiful words of praise to Buddha's virtues can be seen. This is so probably because the *Ratnagotra-vibhāga* discusses only the ratnagotra (gem-lineage) or Buddha-nature and takes no account of human nature (*gotra*) in general; but if this ratnagotra is the source of all beings' deliverances, it is insufficient to simply neglect and discard the faults. Instead, one should reflect deeply on human passions (*kleśa*), investigate them, and thereby pave the way for the turning around (*parāvṛtti*) of passion into enlightenment. An excellent study on this treatise has recently been introduced to the academic world.[32] According to it, the idea of 'āśraya-parāvṛtti' (or *-parivṛtti*) in the tathāgata-garbha theory is likewise not a rotation upward from below, but is a self-manifestation of the dharmadhātu existing above, or its realization into the human world below. This, in truth, is the exact opposite to the āśraya-parāvṛtti of the Yogācāra-vijñāna school. It can be said that such unfolding from above is the basic point of view of the theory of tathāgata-garbha. However, because of it, the unrestricted and independent human existence, the existence that might revolt against its god and become the subject of evil, has been ignored, and what is optimistically emphasized is only the fact that common human beings are endowed with the tathāgata-garbha.

In contrast to this, the āśraya-parāvṛtti of the Yogācāra-vijñāna school is functional within saṃsāra through and through, as already described, and the whole of one's existence, whose basis is always the basis for transmigration, revolves itself and realizes the Buddha-body. As the whole of one's existence is none other than an existence of paratantra nature, the aforesaid revolving means the revolving of the paratantra; the *Mahāyāna-saṃgraha*[33] expounds that the paratantra converts itself sometimes into the parikalpita and at other times into the pariniṣpanna. We may say, in accordance with this, that when the imagined, polluted world revolves itself into the consummated world, this revolving takes place on the plane of paratantra, the paratantra being the basis for everything that exists. These ways of revolving should all be sought thoroughly within the sphere of human existence, that is to say, within the structure of human cognition, vijñānas. This is the reason that, in the Yogācāra-vijñāna school, the problem of the eight vijñānas became the focus of its extensive investigation and analysis. Thus, the logical meaning of the āśraya-parāvṛtti is also sought in the structure of vijñānas—that is, in the way they recognize, judge, discriminate, imagine, and so on, and the structure of the vijñānas is reflected in the āśraya-parāvṛtti. Contrary to the case of the theory of tathāgata-garbha discussed above, in the case of āśraya-parāvṛtti, the Buddha-body is understood in an ascent direction. Whereas with respect to the theory of tathāgata-garbha, the understanding of the Buddha-body is religious and intuitive, with respect to āśraya-parāvṛtti, the understanding of its structure is more philosophical and theoretical.

The term "tathāgata-garbha" is also familiar in a treatise of the Yogācāra-vijñāna school[34] and yet another text explains that the mind is essentially pure and luminous[35] in accord with the tathāgata-garbha theory. In the latter case, however, the mind can be so explained because śūnyatā (absolute negativity) is found right in the midst of discrimination (*abhūta-parikalpa*) itself, not outside it—the mind being śūnya, negated, and not affirmed as in the case of the tathāgata-garbha theory. Now, *śūnyatā* is none other than another name for the dharma-realm or dharma-nature, which should be realized later in the āśraya-parāvṛtti, that is, when every human *āśraya* (basis equals cognitions) is negated, turned over, and revolved. It is at this moment and only at this moment that the mind can be pure and luminous.

It is a fact that the mind is essentially pure and luminous; but, contrary to this, it is also a fact that the human mind actually gives rise to evil acts. From where do human evils come? They cannot, at any rate, be products of the dharma-dhātu, nor of any divine beings; it is not from above, from the pure dharma-realm, that evil flows down. Therefore, the origin of human evil should not be sought outside of human existence, but only within the structure of cognitions, through whose contradiction and self-negation the evil can be elevated to the level of the dharma-nature. The analysis of the cognitions thus becomes a clue to the research of the Buddha-body, which is the goal of the āśraya-parāvṛtti.

In the discussion of the Buddha-body following the theory of 'trikāya,' the dharma-realm and the Essence-body are described as a "basis." But it is the basis for the other Buddha-bodies such as the Enjoyment-body and Transformation-body, or the basis from which the true and pure dharma-preaching flows out; it is never the basis for human transmigration, saṃsāra. Again, the fact that the Essence-body is the basis for the other two Buddha-bodies can be interpreted as reflecting or corresponding to the structure of the eight vijñānas. Among these eight vijñānas, the *ālaya-vijñāna* (store-cognition) becomes the basis for the other seven working cognitions, which include *ātma*-cogitation (*manas*), mind-consciousness (*mano-vijñāna*), and five other vijñānas. When these eight cognitions revolve, the four wisdoms of the Buddha— the mirror (*ādarśa-jñāna*) and the other three wisdoms—manifest themselves (see note 27). With this mirror-wisdom—the wisdom that reflects the reality of everything like a transparent mirror—as their basis, the other three wisdoms—the samatā-jñāna, and so on—arise on the mirror. The mirror-wisdom itself is called "non-differentiated wisdom" (*nirvikalpa-jñāna*), which is like a mirror that reflects everything without discrimination. With this wisdom as the basis, the Buddha is said further to have a wisdom called "the wisdom acquired succeedingly" (*pṛṣṭhalabdha-jñāna*), which agrees with the mundane actuality. That the mirror-wisdom (or the non-differentiated wisdom) becomes the basis for all other wisdoms parallels the fact that in the Buddha-body theory the Essence-body becomes the basis for the other Buddha-bodies. Accordingly, the fact that the Essence-body becomes the basis for the other Buddha bodies seems to correspond, albeit conversely, to the fact that the system of the eight vijñānas, which are paratantra in nature and have the ālaya-vijñāna at their foundation, are the basis for the mundane world. I have said "to correspond, albeit conversely," because the system of the vijñānas is regarded as having been brought into and reflected in the understanding of the Buddha-world, although the direction is "converse," because the former is in an ascending direction, while the latter is in a descending direction.

Probably, such issues as the manner of Buddha's existence, as it was the case with nirvāṇa, were originally beyond human thought and beyond speech. In this sense, even the Yogācāra-vijñāna school that consummated the trikāya theory of the Buddha could not directly make it an object of theoretic consideration. They could at most represent it only in a negative or paradoxical way. In radical terms, any attribute that transcended and was invisible to human beings might be ascribed to the Buddha. But these attributes are not merely transcendental and do not exist high above as isolated existences. They are what correspond, albeit conversely, to the structure of the vijñānas by virtue of the revolving of the structure of vijñānas. If the Buddha-body were not thus conceived as that which has been turned over from below, the Buddha would simply be a transcendental, isolated existence, something unrelated to human beings. If it were so, the search for enlightenment by common beings or their deliverance by the Buddha would become impossible or meaningless. But if it is correct to conceive of a "correspondence, albeit conversely" in connection with the Buddha-body, then a path from the relative to the absolute and from the absolute to the relative would be opened naturally.

I have merely introduced the theories of Buddha-body in India and touched upon several questions relating to them. The Buddha-body theory made complicated and variegated development later on in the various Buddhist sects in China and Japan. The triad concept of the trikāya theory has been generally accepted, studied, and developed by most of these sects. In a case of a strong religious demand, however, the triad system, which is highly theoretic in character, might not have been felt as necessarily exigent; rather, the two-body system, in which a strong contrast between the relative and the absolute was predominant, might have sufficed. It seems that there also developed a tendency toward a one-body theory that treated the absolute dharma-body solely. It is impossible to refer to each of these Buddha-body theories now. Generally speaking, however, Gautama the historic Buddha has been expelled in many cases from the most important position, and the so-called celestial Buddhas or Dhyāni-buddhas have come to the fore. Furthermore, the relation between the Buddha-body theory and the concept of god or the absolute in religions other than Buddhism would be another interesting area of investigation, but it is one which is, however, beyond my present capacity.

Chapter 11

Logic of Convertibility

It is a well known fact that the logic behind the Yogācāra School is different from that of the Madhyamaka School. Although they can be summed up as Buddhist logic, there is some difference between them. The Mādhyamika logic expounded in the Prajñā-pāramitā literature and systematized by Nāgārjuna and Āryadeva is believed to be accepted in full by Asaṅga and Vasubandhu, the founders of the Yogācāra school, but also it must be admitted that the Yogācāras who focused their discussion on vijñāna (cognition) were to that extent different from the Mādhyamikas. It should be pointed out, however, that the difference that existed was not one of mutual contradiction and separation, but one which indicated a development in the Mahāyāna. The fact that Asaṅga and Vasubandhu demonstrated a specific Vijñānavāda standpoint does not mean that they took a stand opposite from that of Nāgārjuna.[1] The speculative thinking of the Mādhyamika and the logic of the Yogācāra are both linked to Mahāyānic thought movements that must include the bodhisattva doctrine whose final goal lies in liberation and nirvāṇa and in the path of practice that leads to the goal. We should surmise that differences in direction and in depth reflected by different authors become naturally manifested as historical developments with the transition of eras. In short, this means that, on the ground of Mādhyamika śūnyatā, the Yogācāras newly established the truth concerning internal and mental activities of human beings. That is to say, to the universal there was added the particular, the individual, and thereby the concrete seen in yogic practices emerged on the stage on śūnyatā, the abstract.

In so far as the Mādhyamika logic is concerned, its salient feature can be summed up in two principles: śūnyatā and the twofold truth.[2] Śūnyatā principle, states, "dependent origination is itself emptiness," while in the twofold truth, "the ultimate truth always transcends the conventional truth." Śūnyatā reflects a principle of unity and continuity; the twofold truth a principle of disunity and non-continuity.

Dr. D. T. Suzuki expressed these two principles in the one expression: "identity-difference," which can be interpreted in various ways such as, "identical as well as different," "identity of difference," "identity in difference," "identity is difference," and so forth. This can be said to represent the essence of the Mādhyamika, hence that of the Mahāyāna. However, the expression "identity-difference" does not mean that difference is perceived immediately in identity, for the joining together of identity with difference is itself another form of identity and thus cannot subsume difference that is absolutely non-continuous. The joining together of identity with difference is nothing more than a mystical intuition. A mystical intuition is of course admitted in the Yogācāra school in terms of *nirvikalpa-jñāna* (non-discriminative wisdom), but the school goes further and tries to theorize such mystical elements. To say that "dependent origination is itself emptiness" means that non-existence is originally included in existence: it does not mean that through identity, or through mystical intuition, they become one. Identity cannot in itself be difference or non-continuity. Absolute non-continuity becomes manifest only through another principle—the ultimate truth is never the conventional truth and always transcends the latter. Thus, the Madhyamaka standpoint always establishes itself on the basis of these two principles that compliment each other. This theory will be discussed here from the viewpoint of the logic of "convertibility," because "convertibility" represents the most remarkable feature of the three-nature theory of the school.

Some may claim that the systematization of vijñāna (cognition) or the theory of vijñapti-mātra (representation only) are more appropriate expressions of this school, the Vijñāna-vāda. Others may claim yoga practices as the unassailable, salient feature of this school (the Yogācāra). Although these express the standpoint of this school well, that the theory of 'vijñāna' or of 'vijñapti-mātra' is founded on the three-nature theory and is meaningless without its backing will be shown later. To systematize the vijñānas and to clarify the processes of mental functions are not the only concerns of this school. Unless the theory of cognition goes hand in hand with the theory of practice in which there is the clarification of how "the vijñānas are converted and jñāna (wisdom) is acquired," it would have no Buddhistic significance. To be significant as a Buddhist theory, it needs to be founded on the three-nature theory. With regard to the yogic practice, the situation is similar with the above. Yoga, which Buddhism shares with other non-Buddhist schools, includes various contemplations and meditations. In the Mahāyāna, the six pāramitās and the ten bodhisattva stages are the main target of practice. Only when these practices are penetrated by the realization of śūnyatā, however, do they become really Buddhistic, and this is accomplished in the Yogācāra school through the three-nature theory.

The various treatises of Yogācāra-vijñānavāda, usually begin with a discussion on vijñāna, then discuss the three natures, and thereafter, explain the practices and their fruits.[3] If, in contrast to such a "sequence of exposition," the issue is addressed from the view of "logical sequence," the three-nature theory with its logic of convertibility should come first, on the basis of which the theory of vijñānas will be properly developed and yogic practices also will be established. The three-nature theory has within itself the intermediary "place" where the catalytic function occurs and takes one from the theory of vijñānas to the yogic practice and attainment of its fruit; not only does it give quality of convertibility to all the "dharmas," but it is also the driving force that functions in the consummation of the fruit through converting cognition (*vijñāna*) into wisdom (*jñāna*).

We shall now begin our examination of the logic of convertibility in accordance with the "sequence of exposition," by beginning our investigation from the theory of 'vijñānas.'

I

Convertibility will be examined first in view of the phrase "evolving of cognition" (*vijñāna-pariṇāma*).

The term "evolving" means to convert into something other by undergoing a change in form. Sthiramati has commented upon this term by using the terms "becoming different" (*anyathātva*) and "to be different from the previous state" (*pūrvāvasthāto 'nyathābhāvaḥ*).[4] The term "pariṇāma" is an important term that has been used by many different philosophical schools in India. It is well-known that the term appears within the Sāṃkhya system; however, unlike the Sāṃkhya that talks about pariṇāma as the evolution of substantial existence (*avasthita-dravya*), the Vijñāna-vāda rejects such an idea and explains pariṇāma as an evolution of cognition (*vijñāna-pariṇāma*).[5] Within the Buddhist tradition, the idea of evolution is often understood in relation to "karma." The so-called dependent origination as fruition of karma (業成縁起), the theory of dependent origination (*pratītya-samutpāda*) as interpreted by the earlier sectarian Buddhism, seems to be established on the basis of an idea that everything evolves and is differentiated by means of karma. Karmic action is an accepted principle within the way of thinking of the people of India; it is believed that on the basis of the past karmic actions, the present world is determined and established. In a similar way, in Buddhism too, it is stated that the continuity of existence (i.e., corporeal, material existence of sentient beings) evolves and is differentiated by means of karma. Yogācāras, however, claim that what evolves and is differentiated by karma should be the internal mental functions instead of outer material substances (see Vasubandhu's *Viṃśatikā*, k.6); hence, the term evolution of cognition.

Now then, how is the idea of 'vijñāna-pariṇāma' to be understood? The *Ch'êng-wei-shih-lun* explains it with the statement, "evolving means that cognition evolves and appears as two divisions." The two divisions refers to the seeing division (*darśana-bhāga*) and the form division (*nimitta-bhāga*); thus, the statement shows the dichotomizing process of cognition into subject (*grāhaka*) and object (*grāhya*). However, the explanation given here cannot be considered to be a satisfactory understanding of evolution. As stated above, Sthiramati explained evolution as "becoming different" (*anyathātva*) and having done so, he goes on to state:

> "Evolving" means the acquisition of the totality of effect (*kāryasya ātma-lābhaḥ*), which takes place in the same moment with that of the extinction of its cause (*kāraṇakṣana-nirodha-samakāla*), and is different in nature from [the status of] the cause at the moment [of change] (*kāraṇa-kṣaṇa vilakṣaṇa*).[6]

The essential points of this very short explanation are as follows:

1. evolving means evolution of cause to an effect, that is, becoming different and
2. evolving is simultaneous.

Cognition (*vijñāna*) refers to the process of discriminating a perceptual object and thus is spatial but not temporal. On the other hand, however, when cognition is said to transform or evolve from the cause to the effect, its temporal aspect must be considered.

In this context, it is significant that the "evolution of cognition" is said to be "simultaneous." By this simultaneity, the category of time found in cognition is negated, but, at the same time, this does not mean that only the category of space is affirmed. Consequently, here, the instantaneous evolution of cognition should be considered as that which constitutes the basis for time and space. That is, it should be considered in view of timelessness that precedes time. The evolution of cognition does not depend on the categories of time and space. However, the reverse holds true that is, time and space are produced on the basis of the evolving cognition (viz., on the basis of the evolution of the *ālaya-vijñāna*). In other words, all existences appear with the limitation of time and space on the basis of that evolving cognition.

The consideration that the "evolving cognition" is at the basis for time and space lies in the fact that evolution means conversion from cause to effect. In this case, however, the Sanskrit terms for cause and effect are kāraṇa and kārya respectively and not the usual hetu and phala. Kāraṇa means the act of doing or making and has an active sense; kārya is the made or what is to be acted upon and has a passive sense. As Sthiramati stated, this means that, with regard to a certain activity (seeing, hearing, etc.), an activity is realized simultaneously with its outcome (what is seen, heard, etc.), although, owing to its having a different form, the outcome (*kārya*) is understood as different from activity (*kāraṇa*) itself. This is the basic idea of 'evolving.'

Such an evolving is probably possible only in the evolving of cognition. An action that is expressed outwardly is without a doubt a kind of karmic action, but it does not subsume its own outcome within itself. For an action to possess the responsibilities of its own doing within itself, that karmic action would also have to have mentalistic or conscious qualities. This was the theory put forth by Vasubandhu in his *Viṃśatikā*. It is also in accordance with the chain in the Sino-Japanese Buddhist tradition that "dependent origination as the fruition of karma," referred to above, was given greater significance in the Mahāyāna tradition when it was understood as the "dependent origination as the function of ālaya-vijñāna (阿頼耶縁起)." This is also the reason for defining the evolving of cognition as "different in form," and at the same time, as "the simultaneity" of kāraṇa and kārya.

While hetu and phala are fixed notions as far as they denote cause and effect respectively, kāraṇa and kārya can be used in a reverse way, that is, kāraṇa is "cause" and kārya is "effect" but in the next moment kārya can be the cause to produce another kāraṇa as effect. However, there is no occurrence in which phala can be understood as a cause and hetu as an effect. Hetu always precedes phala and the reverse never holds true of them. Whenever there is hetu, there is phala, but there can never be phala without hetu. When the evolution of cognition is considered to be the basis for all dharmas, the cognition, specifically the ālaya-cognition, as the hetu for all phenomenal appearances, becomes the seed (*bīja*) and phenomenal appearances occur as the phala of the seed. This point can be understood most clearly when it is seen in the context of a theory in which the "evolution" is divided into two kinds, that of hetu and that of phala.

In his *Triṃśikā-bhāṣya,* Sthiramati alludes to the theory of a "twofold evolving" of cognition—hetu-evolution (*hetu-pariṇāma*) and phala-evolution (*phala-pariṇāma*). His explanation of them can be summarized roughly as follows.[7] The hetu-evolution means that cognition evolves and becomes hetu or seed and the phala-evolution means that cognition evolves and becomes phala or phenomenal appearances. In the former evolution, hetu-evolution, the phenomenal appearances (which are originally phala) are the kāraṇa, and the seed (which is always the hetu) is the kārya; conversely, in the latter evolution, the phala-evolution, the seed is kāraṇa, and the phenomenal appearances are kārya. In these evolutions, kāraṇa and kārya are convertible and have the characteristics that they are simultaneous but different in form, as defined above. Through this convertibility between kāraṇa and kārya, the twofold evolution elucidates that all the entities in the triple world are cognitions—cognitions, including ālaya-cognition, in their capacity either as seed or phenomenal appearances.

If causality is taken simply as moving from hetu to phala, or from seed to phenomena, then it would be unidirectional; this interpretation can be classified as a kind of emanation theory. If cognition [equals seed equals hetu] is established as "cognizer" and the object of cognition [equals phenomena equals *phala*] is the "cognizable" [what is cognized] and these two are contrasted in opposition as subject and as object and if it were the case that the evolution of cognitions is understood as a unidirectional flow from such a subject (equals hetu) to such an object (equals phala),[8] then in that case there would be no sense of "mutual dependence" as expressed in pratītya-samutpāda; cognition, specifically ālaya-cognition, would become the first primordial cause for everything, just like prakṛti or pradhāna of the Sāṃkhya or brahma-ātman in the Upanishads. But the phrase "the triple world is nothing but [evolving of] cognition" probably does not acknowledge such an idea. Contrarily, the evolving of cognition puts emphasis on the mutual simultaneity of kāraṇa (as seed and as phenomena) and kārya (as phenomena and as seed).

When kāraṇa is the seed (deposited in the ālaya-cognition) as hetu and kārya is phenomena as its phala, such an evolving is called "producing" (phenomena being produced from the seed). In contrast, when kāraṇa is phenomena as phala that constitutes the seven functioning cognitions (*pravṛtti-vijñāna*) and kārya is the seed or impression (*vāsanā*—impression impressed on the ālaya-cognition by the phenomena), such an evolving is called "perfuming" (the seed or the impression being perfumed in the ālaya-cognition). When the world is understood to be constituted through the mutual simultaneity of producing and perfuming, then it is said that the three world systems are nothing but "mind." The significance of the producing and the impressing or perfuming—that is, kāraṇa and kārya evolving simultaneously as stated above—is important and can be found not only in Sthiramati's commentary but also in the Fa-hsiang school. In that school, there is the saying: Three dharmas are simultaneous, mutually being cause and effect (三法展転因果同時). In this passage, "three dharmas" refer to seed, phenomenon, and seed,—the three events that arise from the two dynamics, of "seed produces phenomena," that is, "producing," and of "phenomena impress seeds," that is, "impressing." In these two dynamics, the cause (either seed or phenomena) and the effect (either phenomena or seed) are simultaneous. Consequently, the cause and the effect in the expression above must be kāraṇa and kārya, not hetu and phala, respectively.

Producing and impressing should constitute the real contents of the "evolving of cognition"; however, in the *Ch'êng-wei-shih-lun,* there is a tendency to separate evolving of cognition from producing and impressing, for in it, the evolving of cognition is explained by the phrase "cognition evolves and appears as the two divisions" of seeing and of form (or subject and object) as discussed earlier (p. 126). Such a definition of evolving connotes at best the producing, that is the producing of phenomena, and does not include the meaning of impressing. It represents nearly the "one-way" of producing and does not represent the "reverse-way" of impressing. Further, Hsüan-tsang always translates the Sanskrit pariṇāma (evolving) as *neng-pien* (能変) "what evolves," of which neng yields the meaning of an "agent." Neng-pien (evolving agent, evolver or transformer) stands in contrast to *so-pien* (所変what is evolved, transformed). When the evolving of cognition is defined in terms of "cognition as the evolver, the agent," then the movement is naturally toward "what is evolved," that is, phenomena, and there is no reversing of direction.[9] Therefore, in spite of its saying, the reason for the Fa-hsiang school mentioning the three dharmas and for its inclusion of the reverse direction therein is not necessarily clear. However, the above saying must signify the movement of the three dharmas from seed to phenomena and from phenomena to seed, the two movements in opposite directions, and this always within the context of the simultaneity of kāraṇa and kārya. The two movements in opposite directions are synthesized into one single evolving of cognition. It is on such an evolving that the whole world is based and established.

When evolving is understood to be simultaneity and when that simultaneity is understood as the three dharmas evolving simultaneously as kāraṇa and kārya, one might think that time has been compressed into a single time moment and thus time is completely nonexistent. Accordingly, one may think that all phenomena would appear in a single moment. But that is not the case, because as stated earlier, it is the simultaneity of the evolving of cognition that becomes the source of time and space; time and space originate on the basis of the evolving of cognition. Being born with that evolving as their basis, time and space are not nonexistent; phenomena duly appear in time and space.

Further, simultaneity is contextually related to the Buddhist idea of "momentariness" (*kṣaṇikatva*). Everything comes into being momentarily and perishes momentarily in that instant. Things cannot go beyond the moment and become eternal; everything is evanescent and impermanent (*anitya*). To be more than momentary means to be still, without any movement or function or action. But in such stillness the world cannot exist. This means, the world is established when there is the evolving and convertibility of kāraṇa and kārya instantaneously. The world is born every moment and dies every moment. Momentariness does not mean total extinction of the world; on the contrary, it is the way by which the world establishes itself as full of life and spirit.

The idea of 'saṃtāna' (相続) or continuity-series refers to such a state. Saṃtāna is closely related to momentariness; consequently, everything that is is momentary, hence a continuity-series. Nothing exists substantively but whatever is is a continuous flow. On the one hand, all beings are not eternal because of their momentariness, but, on the other hand, they are not merely instantaneous because they are comprised of continuity-series. The idea of saṃtāna is applicable to various concepts such as saṃsāra, karman, and others; however, it is more commonly used in reference to citta-saṃtāna or vijñāna-saṃtāna (continuity-series of mind or of cognition), and this is to say that all cognitions, the functional ones as well as the ālaya, evolve in continuity-series. The fact that the world is transient yet continues as an uninterrupted flow parallels the fact that all cognitions always evolve as continuity-series on the basis of the simultaneity of kāraṇa and kārya.

II

The evolving of cognition discussed above affords us with a basic and necessary component in the logic of convertibility. But this convertibility is thought of and developed solely in the realm of 'being,' because cognition affirms something being cognized. It cannot be denied, however, that convertibility to be real must carry the meaning of conversion from being to non-being, and vice versa.

It is the three-nature (*tri-svabhāva*) theory that responds to that idea. Three natures are:

1. the imagined nature (*parikalpita-svabhāva*),
2. the other-dependent nature (*paratantra-svabhāva*), and
3. the consummated nature (*parinispanna-svabhāva*).

By making these three concepts into a system, the theory elucidates the structure of the world. And, insofar as the theory is concerned with 'being,' it can be said not to differ much from the cognition theory. However, there is a great difference between them. The three-nature theory holds or suggests that 'being' itself always and directly points to 'non-being,' because, not only does the three-nature theory explicate 'being' in terms of real existence or nonexistence, but it also involves in it the "three-non-nature theory" (*tri-niḥsvabhāva*) and gives birth to it.

Moreover, it serves as the bridge that links one to one's religious practice. In this respect, it differs greatly from the cognition theory that is rather theoretical. Although the three-nature theory is also a theory, it is a theory that upholds the principle or prepares the ground for Buddhistic practice.

Thus, it can be said that the cognition theory together with its logic of convertibility constituted in the evolving of cognition in the simultaneity of kāraṇa and kārya is perfected on the basis of the three-nature theory which was, consciously or unconsciously, anticipated by the cognition theory.

The world is considered to be constituted of these three natures that are also called three "characteristics" (*lakṣaṇa*). The world, however, must remain at all times one and the same; therefore, the fact that the world is constituted of three natures does not mean that there are three worlds or three different realities side by side; it means that there is a world that is convertible from one nature to another.

Our world remains one and the same all of the time; there is no hell and no heaven separate from this world. Of course, the three natures are wholly different from each other; the "imagined" nature (*parikalpita*) that characterizes our worldly existence is totally opposite to the "consummated" nature (*pariniṣpanna*) that denotes the world of enlightened ones. In this sense, it may be said there are the two worlds of confusion and illumination, entirely different from each other. Still it is not that the world of the enlightened ones exists at a place entirely different from the world of ordinary people. There needs to be a conversion of the imagined nature of the world into the consummated nature, and it is in such a conversion that there is the possibility for the ordinary, unenlightened people to get enlightened. But, where can this possibility of enlightenment be conceived?

It is again in this one and the same world that is characterized as "other-dependent" (*paratantra*), the third nature. The other-dependent nature connotes the idea of "dependent origination" (*pratītya-samutpāda*). It is in this world of dependent origination that we make our continual rounds of birth and death and it is therein that we become liberated from saṃsāra. Hell, and likewise the heaven, too, are to be found in this world, not elsewhere. It is the world itself that converts. Thus, the three-nature theory accounts for the structure of this world and sets forth the ground on which these conversions occur.

The three-nature theory has been widely discussed in various texts from various angles. It has been discussed in view of its material contents, its linguistic meanings, its oneness and otherness, its similes, its meaning in view of practice, and so forth. One of its standard exposition reads:

> What is the "imagined nature" of what does not exist in reality refers to discrimination through dichotomy of subject and object; when this discrimination occurs in accordance with various conditions, it is defined as the "other-dependent" nature; and the "consummated" nature refers to the very same "other-dependent" nature, completely devoid of the discriminations of the "imagined" nature.[10]

Now, in order to clarify the meaning of "convertibility" found in the three-nature system, we shall turn to a discussion on the word *paryāya* (synonym)—a term that is very useful and convenient for the purpose of showing the structure of convertibility[11] found in the three-nature system. The term paryāya is found in the dictionary under the verb root $\sqrt{i}$ (to go) and is defined as "going or winding round," "lapse of time," "revolving," "repetition," "succession," and so on. In its instrumental form *paryāyeṇa,* it has the meanings "successively" and "alternately." The word is also defined as "a convertible term" or "synonym." Hsüan-tsang's translation of this term into Chinese as *i-men, i-ming, pieh-ming* (異門，異名，別名), are all in accord with the meaning synonym, a meaning which is most frequently encountered in the Buddhist texts. To elucidate a certain idea through the use of many synonyms is a very effective way of explanation. Sthiramati defines paryāya as "different name" (*nāmântara*) and he says: "paryāya makes known that a thing (*artha*) has different appellations (*śabda*)."[12] Aside from these usages, the compound *dharma-paryāya* (or simply paryāya) has been translated into Chinese as "dharma-gate" (*fa-men* 法門). Dharma-gate means that the doctrine or teaching is introduced through many gates; it is said that the Buddha taught his doctrine through 84,000 dharma-gates. The reason that the teaching is so varied and many is that the Buddha taught in accordance with the variety of the listener's understanding, language, logic and so on. This also shows that one reality can be understood differently or that one reality can be taught "alternately" in various ways, through various gates. Thus, the manner in which paryāya is used here is not different in use from that of synonym.

The five or six "superknowledges" (*abhijñā*) of the Buddhas and bodhisattvas include the "superknowledge of another's mind."[13] This means that through his Buddha-eye a Buddha has the superknowledge about various states of mind of other people, such as the state of passionate attachment or that of being emancipated, and so on. The various states of mind is "cetaḥ-paryāya" in Sanskrit, and R. Sakaki (in his edition of *Mahāvyutpatti*) interprets this paryāya as "the mind's functions in succession."[14]

Several other usages of the term paryāya are found in Böhtlingk's *Sanskrit Wörterbuch*. There, we find, together with their Sanskrit equivalents, additional meanings of paryāya explained as follows:

> "Art und Weise, prakāra" (sort, mode, manner): "Gelegenheit, avasara" (occasion); "Bildung, Schöpfung, nirmāṇa" (forming, transformation).

It is not difficult to see that these meanings are derived and developed from the fundamental meanings mentioned above and are associated more or less to each other with the meaning "synonym" in their centre.[15] At any rate, it should be clear now that the term paryāya is closely aligned with the meaning "convertibility," which will be discussed presently.

In the *Mahāyāna-saṃgraha*, II.17 (Lamotte's edition), the three-nature theory is structured around the word paryāya, synonym. In a discussion on whether the three natures are one or different, we find the following passage:

> ngo bo nyid gsum po 'di dag gi tshul ci tha dad pa zhig gam / 'on te tha dad pa ma yin zhe na / tha dad pa ma yin pa / tha dad pa ma yin pa yang ma yin par brjod par bya'o / / gzhan gyi dbang gi ngo bo nyid ni rnam grangs kyis na gzhan gyi dbang ngo / / rnam grangs kyis na de nyid kun brtags pa'o / / rnam grangs kyis na de nyid yongs su grub pa'o
>
> Are the manners in which these three natures exist different from each other or not different? It should be said, they are neither different nor not different. The other-dependent nature (*paratantra*) is other-dependent from one perspective (*paryāyeṇa*). From another perspective (*paryāyeṇa*), the same [other-dependent] is the imagined (*parikalpita*). From still another perspective (*paryāyeṇa*), the same [other-dependent] is the consummated (*pariniṣpanna*).[16]

What becomes obvious from the above passage is the fact that if the term paryāya were limited to meanings such as "synonym" or "gate" explained above, such meanings would limit and be very unsatisfactory in the context of the above passage. In fact, within the above context, the term encompasses a wide range of meanings including such meanings as "mode," "kind," "occasion," and so forth. Having the complex of these meanings in mind, paryāyeṇa has been translated as "from one aspect," a translation that intends the meaning "convertibility." While the one reality is convertible to be of the other-dependent nature on a certain "occasion," or "from a perspective," or "alternately," the same other-dependent similarly becomes the imagined or the consummated.

Another point we noticed in this statement is that there are three conversions that relate the four terms:

other-dependent = the other-dependent,
other-dependent = the imagined, and
other-dependent = the consummated.

Other-dependent is mentioned first and occupies the central and prominent position (a prominent position always occupied by the other-dependent throughout the *Mahāyāna-saṃgraha*). It is well-known that the *Mahāyāna-saṃgraha* expounds the other-dependent nature as having "two-divisions" (二分依他)—the two divisions of impurity and purity. The impure division of the other-dependent is seen as the imagined and the pure division as the consummated. Here, the convertibility of the other-dependent is encountered already. The term "division" does not simply mean "part" such that the other-dependent is constituted by the coming together of the two parts; it is better understood as "aspect" that reveals itself in the conversion(s) of the other-dependent. In contrast to the two divisions or two aspects, however, the three divisions or the three conversions of the other-dependent seems to have been advocated in the statement above that begins with the phrase, "other-dependent is the other-dependent. . . ." However, how is one to differentiate between the two "other-dependents?"

In the phrase, "other-dependent is the other-dependent . . . ," the two are identified, although, or rather, because a difference is seen between them. Of the two, the first other-dependent represents ultimate reality, the total and single reality, which transcends all expressions and cannot even be called other-dependent. Still it is called other-dependent, because "dependent origination" (*pratītya-samutpāda*), which was originally taught by the Buddha, is considered to represent the ultimate reality and the other-dependent is none other than this pratītya-samutpāda. In contrast to this, the second other-dependent is conceived in a more concrete sense. The ultimate reality limits itself and reveals itself as the reality of this world, hence, it is the other-dependent or the dependently originated. The relationship between these two other-dependents may be regarded to be similar to the two interpretations of pratītya-samutpāda, that is, the interpretation on the one hand, by the formula: "this existing, this exists . . ." and so on, and, on the other, through the more concrete interpretation manifested in the so-called twelvefold causation, beginning with ignorance and ending with birth, age, and death.

When it is said that "the other-dependent from one perspective is the other-dependent," the expression *paryāyeṇa* "from one perspective" or "in a certain aspect" can be understood to express a "limitation." That is to say, the first other-dependent limits itself to become the second other-dependent. In such a manner the two other-dependents will be distinguished, but, insofar as both of them are, in some sense or another, dependently originating, they are not different. Or, we may understand the relationship between the two other-dependents in the following manner. The first other-dependent functions as the subject of the sentence (*dharmin*) and is regarded as the real (*dharmatā*), while the second other-dependent functions as the predicate (*dharma*) of the subject and is regarded to limit the subject; hence, the statement: "dharmatā is dharma" (Reality is actuality). Thus, it is natural that the two other-dependent are combined with a copula.

In any event, these two other-dependents are considered to be in the relationship of being both different and not different at the same time. This relationship of not one and not different is the logic introduced by the word paryāya and here we are attempting to understand it as convertibility.

The other-dependent world so far discussed becomes or converts to the imagined (*parikalpita*) from one perspective and becomes or converts to the consummated (*pariniṣpanna*) from another perspective. In these cases also the convertibility is indicated by the same expression paryāyeṇa. Just as the other-dependent was a total and single world, so too in the case of the imagined world, the world is completely the imagined, and therein, there is no other-dependent or no consummated. Similarly, when the world is the consummated, then it is completely perfected, and therein there is neither the other-dependent nor the imagined. Convertibility is not in reference to only one part of the whole.

The three natures are thus not lateral in their relationship but are convertible realities. The convertibility of paryāya—that is, the meaning that reality is one and different at the same time—has been clearly explained as follows in the *Mahāyāna-saṃgraha,* II.23:

> [Question:] If the other-dependent nature, from one perspective, can be the three natures, then how can the three natures be differentiated? [Answer:] When from the one perspective [something is defined] as the other dependent, from that perspective it is neither the imagined nor the consummated. When from the one perspective [something is defined] as the imagined, from that perspective it is neither the other-dependent nor the consummated. When from the one perspective [something is defined] as the consummated, from that perspective it is neither the imagined nor the other-dependent.[17]

This means that the world that is one and the same as the original other-dependent converts into other modes of the world, that is, into the world of defilement and confusion or into the world of purity and enlightenment.

So far, the relationship between the three natures has been explained in terms of convertibility through a discussion on the term *paryāya*. However, problems still remain. What is the motive behind paryāya? In other words, what is the contents that comprise these various perspectives? Here, the question of how and why the other-dependent converts in its entirety to the imagined world will be discussed.

Hsüan-tsang translated parikalpita with the compound *pien-chi-so-chih* (遍計所執universally calculated with attachment). Different from parikalpa (*pien-chi* 遍計 , calculation, discrimination), the word for the imagined is *parikalpita,* a past passive participle of the former, and this past passive sense is expressed by *so-chih* (with attachment); by this the meaning of the word is fully expressed, though the past passive form does not necessarily have the sense of attachment. When one clings to calculation or discrimination as true, this constitutes the imagined nature. Consequently, to translate parikalpita simply by the term "discrimination" (*fen-pieh* 分別), as Paramārtha has done, falls short of the mark as there is no sense of the past passive or of attachment therein. Moreover, in Chinese translations (in those of Paramārtha as well), the word "discrimination" usually stands for the Sanskrit *vikalpa, parikalpa,* and so forth, which are the functions of "cognition" (*vijñāna*), and all of them belong to the other-dependent nature, not to the imagined nature. Sthiramati states:

> It should be admitted that cognition (*vijñāna*) exists in reality because of its nature of dependently originating. And a cognition that dependently originates is known by the term "transformation."[18]

From this statement, it is clear that cognition, discrimination, and the like are to be understood as dependently originating, hence they are of the other-dependent nature.

It is needless to say, however, that to be dependently originating and thus to be the other-dependent does not mean to be the consummated nature. In the first chapter of the *Madhyānta-vibhāga,* cognition is discussed in the context of "unreal discrimination" (*abhūta-parikalpa*). Unreal discrimination is so called because it is a discrimination (*parikalpa*) but it always results in unreality (*abhūta*)—that is, it is not true, not tranquil, and not pure. It refers to the world of error.[19]

Here, discrimination or cognition in general is modified as the "unreal." It is not that a specific discrimination is singled out from the many and labelled unreal. Therefore, to say unreal does not mean to say that there is a mistake that occurred in a judgment of our conventional life. Even if a discrimination or a judgment is correct and without mistake, that is, even if no error is involved therein, in contrast to the consummated nature, it is still said to be unreal. This corresponds to the conventional truth (*saṃvṛti-satya*) of the Mādhyamikas in that the conventional, though a truth, conceals and covers (*saṃvṛti*) the ultimate truth (*paramārtha-satya*). Insofar as discrimination is other-dependent, it is real; still it is unreal from the perspective of the ultimate truth. That is, although discrimination arises depending-on-others, it arises as the unreal so long as the darkness of the basic ignorance (*avidyā*) is not removed. A judgment that has its basis in this ignorance is, owing to that very ignorance, one colored by the attachment to its own judgment as true (or false) and this means that one clings to the fruit of one's judgment as true (or false).

The saṃsāric world, or the imagined world, has its beginning here. The other-dependent world always and instantly becomes the imagined world at this point. In the fact that the other-dependent is at once real and unreal, we can see the momentum by which the other-dependent converts to the imagined nature. Of course, from the same fact, we can see the possibility of the other-dependent converting into the consummated nature that exists in the other-dependent; however, in this case, one will require arduous practice and effort to have the conversion take place. In contrast, the inclination for one's life to fall and convert to the imagined nature is primal in our ordinary mundane existence. In this case, the world converts to the imagined nature without any effort on our part. This may be indeed the characteristic of cognition, discrimination and the like, insofar as such circumstances are examples of the other-dependent nature that has not yet converted to the consummated. Thus, it is quite normal for the other-dependent world to always and instantly convert in its entirety to the imagined world that is permeated by basic ignorance and clinging. Further, these two worlds are not two worlds having different material ingredients; they simply reflect the conversion of the basic ignorance and clinging. To use Sanskrit words, one could say that *abhūtaparikalpa* (which is other-dependent) undergoes conversion to become the past passive *parikalpita* (the imagined).

There is an interpretation among scholars that the imagined (*parikalpita*) refers to what is perceived (*viṣaya*), or the object of cognition, while the other-dependent (*paratantra*) refers to the cognizer (cognition as an agent). Actually we encounter expressions in the treatises that seem to support such an interpretation. In the *Mahāyāna-saṃgraha,* for example, the imagined is explained as "what appears as object (*artha*)" (II.3), or as "what is imagined by discrimination" (II.17). Further, in the *Triṃśikā,* kk.20–21, we find that the imagined is referred to as "the thing which is discriminated'' (*yad vastu vikalpyate*) and the other-dependent as ''that which discriminates'' (*vikalpa*).

However, so long as two things—cognizer and cognized, or cognition and its object—are thought to formulate a pair, this procedure is in itself of the other-dependent nature. Therefore, if it were firmly fixed that the cognizer was the other-dependent and the cognized was the imagined, then the relationship between the other-dependent and the imagined would be of the other-dependent, and this would make no sense. To distinguish between (i.e., to perceive from different perspectives) the other-dependent and the imagined is quite a different matter than to contrast the ideas of the active (cognizer) and the passive (object cognized). In the former case, we have an example of convertibility, but in the latter, we don't; the cognizer stands in opposition to the cognized and the former never converts into the latter. (The identification of subject and object can take place only on a level quite apart from that of the mundane world.) Both the active (cognizer) and the passive (object cognized) can be understood as ''the other-dependent'' from one perspective and also as ''the imagined'' from another. When the subject and the object are confronting each other in their pure and genuine form, such a confrontation signifies the other-dependent, hence, both of them are the other-dependent, and neither is the consummated nor the imagined. But, when the same confrontation is viewed and clung to with the idea of substance or of ''I-ness'' and ''mine-ness,'' the world becomes the imagined, the defiled, and both the subject and object are of the imagined nature.

Then, why is the imagined nature expressed by the words ''the thing which is discriminated'' (*vikalpya-vastu*)? This is self-evident if we take into account the structure, that is, the convertibility, of the three natures; if we do not, it will be difficult to comprehend. The reason is as follows. So long as one assumes that the cognizer or subject is the other-dependent and the cognized or object is the imagined and thus fixes them and adheres to them as substantive existences, then it follows that one does not see the possibility of converting the other-dependent into the imagined but see them, instead, as two separate worlds side by side, because when the other-dependent and the imagined are fixed, the other-dependent cannot convert into the imagined, just as the subject can never convert into the object. However, it has already been pointed out (see notes 18 and 19 above) that the other-dependent refers to the evolving of cognition or of unreal discrimination, and that the evolving refers to the mutual relationship between kāraṇa and kārya (p. 127 above) in the function of which cognition appears with the two divisions of subject and object (p. 126 above). Accordingly, both subject and object belong to the evolving of cognition, that is, to the other-dependent. When subject and object are fixed, stabilized, and adhered to as substantive existences, the same subject and object of the other-dependent nature convert themselves into the imagined nature. This procedure of conversion is referred to in the *Triṃśikā* by the phrase, "a thing . . . is discriminated." That is, "a thing" in this context refers to both the subject and object which, through being discriminated, become fixed and are adhered to. Although reality or unreality of things or objects of cognition are discussed in various ways in the history of this school, the point here is to clarify that when the evolving of cognition, a flow of the other-dependent, becomes suspended and stabilized, every "thing" thus suspended and stabilized comes to the fore as the object of discrimination and that owing to this process, the world of the imagined nature is established. Therefore, it is probably more accurate to say that it is not that the imagined is the object of cognition, but that all objects turn out to be the imagined.

So far, through a discussion on the convertibility of the other-dependent to the imagined, we have discussed and criticized the claim that the imagined is the object of cognition. Further, even a view contrary to that claim can be seen in the *Mahāyāna-saṃgraha,* II.16. The text enumerates three notions:

> parikalpa, what discriminates,
> parikalpya, what is to be discriminated, and
> parikalpita, what is discriminated and is attached to, that is, the imagined.

How are these to be understood? The text goes on to explain the three notions one by one and the gist of the discussion can be summed up as follows:

> The minding-cognition (*mano-vijñāna,* consciousness) refers to "what discriminates." The other-dependent refers to "what is to be discriminated." When what discriminates (*parikalpa*) is confronted with what is to be discriminated (*parikalpya*), there arises what one discriminates and what one becomes attached to, viz., the imagined nature (*parikalpita*).[20]

How the imagined nature (*parikalpita*) arises is thus clearly explicated. It is also clear by this summary that the other-dependent becomes the object of cognition (*parikalpya*). In the former discussion, "what is discriminated" was the imagined, but now it is referred to as the other-dependent; the other-dependent was previously (p. 138) thought to be "that which discriminates," but here it is explained as "what is to be discriminated." This is not a contradiction. It is understandable when the three natures are seen as convertible, and not parallel to each other. Convertibility means that discrimination that sets off the subject from the object converts from its other-dependent existence to its imagined existence. Just after the last sentence of this explanation, a passage follows that explains well the feature of convertibility. That is, when what discriminates equals minding-cognition and what is to be discriminated equals the other-dependent,

> . . . the other-dependent is conceived and is attached to with some specific form and this specific form is of the imagined nature.

The Tibetan version of this passage and my restoration of its Sanskrit equivalents, read:

> rnam pa gang du gzhan gyi dbang gi ngo bo nyid la kun tu brtag pa de ni de la kun brtags pa'i ngo bo nyid do / yenâkāreṇa paratantra-svabhāve parikalpitaḥ sa tatra parikalpita-svabhāvaḥ /

The text goes on to explain:

> The words "with some specific form" means "in some such form." / rnam pa gang du zhes bya ba ni ji ltar na zhes bya ba'i tha tshig go / yenâkāreṇeti yathety arthaḥ /

When the mind-cognition takes the world of other-dependence, the pure and genuine world, as its object, and conceives and discriminates it, the "form" thus conceived and discriminated is of the imagined nature. No matter how the other-dependent is conceived by the minding-cognition, the "specific form" thus created is no other than the imagined, as is elucidated by the text in its latter passage. Even though both the object of judgment and judgment itself are the other-dependent, and are accordingly pure and not defiled, what is already judged and discriminated is of the imagined nature. It is needless to repeat that the expressions, "some specific form" and "some such form" are directly related contextually to the word *paryāyeṇa* (from one perspective) explained earlier.[21]

III

The conversion of the other-dependent into the consummated is properly called "the turning around of the basis" (*āśraya-parāvṛtti*). It is directly opposite to the conversion of the other-dependent to the imagined.

But both conversions are based on the same idea of paryāya, the same convertibility of the other-dependent.

Now, the consummated nature is referred to by a variety of names such as "non-changing" (*avikāra, ananyathā-bhāva*), "the highest being" (*agrārtha*), "perfected" (*parinispatti*), and so forth. Among such descriptions, the consummated is most appropriately expressed by the word "rahitatā," which means "separated-ness," that is, "to get rid of," or "to be free of," hence, "devoidness." It seems to suggest well the essential logical process of how the consummated is to be acquired. In accord with descriptions of the imagined and the other-dependent, Vasubandhu states in *Triṃśikā,* k.21:

> When it [the other-dependent] is always devoid of (or separated from) the former [the imagined], this is the consummated.[22]

Sthiramati comments on this verse as follows:

> When the other-dependent is at all times absolutely free of the subject / object dichotomy, this is the consummated.[23]

He further adds:

> "Separated-ness" (*rahitatā*) is no other than dharmatā, the reality, (of the other-dependent).

Mahāyāna-saṃgraha II.4 defines the consummated "the other-dependent that is absolutely free of (*atyantābhāvatva*) the form of sense-object." In II.17, when asked, "What is the paryāya concerning the consummated?" the text explains: "It is that things are absolutely non-existent in a manner they are conceived and imagined." The fact that these notions of separated-ness, dharmatā, non-existence (*atyantābhāvatva*), and so forth are referred to as the consummated hints at the theory of "non-substantiality in the ultimate sense" (*paramārtha-niḥsvabhāva*) that is another name that denotes the essence of the consummated.

When the consummated is of concern, what is nonexistent is the imagined. The imagined, however, is in some way "existent" because, as explained above, it refers to things discriminated, or it means that a thing appears as if a real object while there is no object at all.

According to Vasubandhu's *Trisvabhāva-nirdeśa,* in contrast to the other-dependent that is defined as "what appears" (*yat khyāti*) or "the agent who appears" (*khyātṛ*), the imagined is defined as "the way how something appears" (*yathā khyāti*) or simply "the appearance" (*khyāna*) itself. However, such an appearance is merely an appearance and is not true and real "existence." It is simply an imagined existence to which one is attached as real. We exist and our world really exists here and now, but such an appearance produced by the imagined is far removed from this real existence, and is neither the consummated nor the other-dependent. In this appearance, that is, in the imagined, the object of cognition, though extensive and variegated, is made up by constructing and grasping what does not really exist, or what does not exist as it appears, as really "existent." Through this grasping or clinging, a world of existence is built up, but the building, the structure thus built up, must be negated in its entirety. It is "nothing." Therefore, the *Triṃśikā* (k.20) states explicitly that whatever is discriminated and clung to "does not exist" (*na . . . vidyate*). Again, in response to the question: "In what manner is the imagined nature referred to in the various Mahāyāna sūtras?" the *Mahāyāna-saṃgraha* (II.26) states: "It is taught by various synonyms (*paryāya*) of non-existence."[24] This means that sūtra passages that explicate non-existence are passages that actually refer to the imagined nature. In fine, what appears as existent in the case of the imagined is in reality nonexistent.

When the consummated nature is explained as "being got rid of" (*rahitatā*) or the non-existence of something, what is meant is the nonexistence of the imagined nature that is absolutely nonexistent. This means that the world of the consummated is not established positively at some remote place apart from the world of the imagined, but that the nonexistence of the imagined is itself synonymous (*paryāya*) with the existence of the consummated. Although from one perspective (*paryāyeṇa*) the other-dependent converts to the imagined, when the other-dependent is rid of the subject / object dichotomy (which is of the imagined nature), then it is, from another perspective, the consummated.[25]

The nonexistence of the imagined is itself the consummated, but this does not mean that the imagined becomes directly the consummated, as a saying such as "kleśa (affliction) is itself bodhi (enlightenment)" might suggest. This simply returns us to a mystic intuition of nonexistence or mystic "unification" or "identification" of two contradictory components. Not only that, if that were the case, we would be unable to fully understand why the other-dependent nature would be necessary as the third member of the three-nature theory. When the other-dependent nature is regarded as the basis for the convertibility of the three natures, one may claim that, admitting it as the third member of the three natures, it degenerates to form a world of the imagined, and in negating this, the consummated world is acquired. Indeed, when one speaks of "from the perspective of nonexistence," such a meaning is included. But, if the other-dependent were thought to be nothing more than the starting point in the process of one's realization, it could not function as the basic intermediary existence, that is, as the mediator from the imagined to the consummated, for in this case, realization would not necessarily have to involve the meaning of the other-dependent. However, the conversion from the imagined to the consummated is itself the conversion of the other-dependent to the consummated; the conversion is only pursued on the basis of and as the function of the other-dependent. This is the meaning of the statement: "From still another perspective, the other-dependent is the consummated" referred to above (p. 133). In the manner "the body / mind drops down" (as put by Dōgen), the other-dependent drops down and becomes the consummated. (The term "drop down" reminds us of *rahitatā*—referred to above, p. 141). Such a conversion is called the "turning around of the basis" (*āśraya-parāvṛtti*).

The turning around of the basis is explained as the "acquisition of liberation (*vimokṣa*), dharma-body, almighty (*vibhutva*), omniscience (*sarvajñatva*), non-abiding in the nirvāṇa (*apratiṣṭhita-nirvāṇa*) of the bodhisattva," and so on. As all of these point to the apex of the Buddhist path, the "turning around" indicates the ultimate meaning. It normally refers to the "moment that a bodhisattva penetrates the path of insight" (*darśana-mārga*), but it has a wider meaning than just that. It takes place even when one is still on the path preceding the path of insight; it also refers to the "final attainment of dharma-body," which is possible only through the "diamond-like samādhi" (*vajropama-samādhi*). In short, throughout one's personal career of spiritual development, "turning around of the basis" plays various roles at such times as when one enters into the faith, when one attains realization, and so forth.

Now in this turning around of the basis, what is the basis that turns around? As a matter of common sense, in our everyday life, both the mind and the body constitute the basis that undergoes the turning around. In the Buddhist texts, the human body is given the name "body with its organs" (*sendriya-kāya*) and is often referred to as the "basis" (*āśraya*). The world as a container (*bhājana-loka*), which is the foundation and circumstance for sentient beings, can be also a basis. However, both sentient beings and the world as a container are found, ultimately and truly, only in the *ālaya-vijñāna*. Consequently, when a cognition (*vijñāna*) is regarded as ālaya (store, depository) and when this is said to have been dhātu (cause) from time immemorial,[26] it is so named in the sense that it is the "basis" from which everything in the three world systems arise. In his commentary to the *Triṃśikā*, Sthiramati states:

> The basis [for the turning around] is the *ālayavijñāna* which is the seed for everything.

The *Mahāyāna-saṃgraha* (IX.1) states:

> The basis refers to the other-dependent which has two divisions [of the defiled (imagined) and the pure (consummated)].[27]

Further, the meaning that the other-dependent is the basis is also found in an explanation in the *Mahāyāna-saṃgraha* (at the end of II.2) as follows:

> The other-dependent is the basis for the confusion which is non-existent to appear.[28]

We find a similar expression as this in *Sūtrālaṃkāra,* XI.13:

> It is the basis for confusion (*bhrānteḥ saṃniśrayaḥ*).

Then, how is the term "turning around" (*parāvṛtti*) explained? The *Mahāyāna-saṃgraha* (IX.1) explains it as follows:

> The turning around [of the basis] means that, when the antidote for it arises, the impure division of the other-dependent becomes annihilated and the pure division comes to the fore.[29]

Hsüan-tsang has translated into Chinese the term "becomes annihilated" with the word *chüan-she* (転捨turn and reject) and the term "comes to the fore" with the word *chüan-te* (転得turn and acquire), thus conveying well the meaning of turning around. Sthiramati amplified the meaning further and gives in detail an interpretation of the word in his *Triṃśikā-bhāṣya* as follows:

> In overcoming the gross turbidities of the two kinds of hindrances, intellectual and afflictional, the turning around of the basis is attained. The "gross turbidity" (*dauṣṭhulya*) means that the basis (i.e., the personal mind / body existence) lacks the power to function freely (i.e., lacks the power of agility or dexterity *karmaṇyatā*). When there occurs the turning around of the basis, the gross turbidity changes into agility; the maturation of body which comes about as the fruit of past *karma* ripens into the dharma-body; and knowledge which comprises the subject / object dichotomy transforms into non-discriminating wisdom. In short, the contaminated impurity is eliminated and a state of purity, freed of contaminations, is attained.[30]

In such a "turning around of the basis," the ālaya-cognition, or the other-dependent nature, is its basis. The "basis" (*āśraya*) is mediator, however, from the perspective of two meanings: foundation and cause.

First, it is foundation, root substratum, and so on. Based on this foundation, the other-dependent or the *pratītya-samutpāda*, both saṃsāra and nirvāṇa can be considered. However, the turning around of the basis does not mean that the imagined converts directly into the consummated on this foundation of the other-dependent. If this were the case, the consummated would never be consummated, as it would be on the dimension of the other-dependent and would be limited by the latter in the same way as the imagined is. On the other hand, the other-dependent, too, could never be really an intermediary foundation, as it always would fall into the level of the imagined. To be dependent on others, that is, to be originating depending on others, means not to stand still even for an instant but to evolve or turn around itself continuously. If the world of other-dependent, as such, would become stabilized as a foundation, it cannot become the consummated. Therefore, the turning around of the basis must refer to the fact that the very foundation of the other-dependent itself turns around.

Second, the basis means cause (*hetu*). As stated above (n.26), the *dhātu* (which means cause, hetu) is understood as the basis for both saṃsāra and nirvāṇa.[31] The statement: "From one perspective (*paryāyeṇa*), the other-dependent becomes the consummated" may indicate the same meaning that the other-dependent is the cause (*hetu, nimitta*) for the consummated. Later developments, such as the Buddha-nature theory and the tathāgata-garbha (tathāgata-womb) theory should be reconsidered in this light of the other-dependent. That is, the Buddha-nature to be found in all sentient beings, too, should be of the other-dependent nature and not of the consummated. The same holds true for the un-afflicted seeds (*anāsrava-bīja*).

However, it is also true that there is no cause directly for the consummated; it is "baseless," in this sense. Cause and effect belong to the world of the other-dependent, not to that of the consummated which is characterized as "unconditioned" (*asaṃskṛta*), because the unconditioned always transcends the conditioned world. When the other-dependent is spoken about as comprising causes and conditions, it always encompasses a tendency of falling into the error of the imagined. This is because the evolving from cause to effect does not stand still even momentarily, but flows continuously, owing to its instantaneous nature (*kṣaṇikatva*), and this refers to the convertibility of the other-dependent, while the minding-cognition (*mano-vijñāna*, the sixth cognition) brings this flow to a halt, stabilizes it in time and space, and thereby constructs a "self" (*ātman*), the origin of all errors.

As stated before (see, n.28), the other-dependent is said to be the "basis for confusion"; it is not a cause directly for the consummated. Only when such a basis, the basis for confusion, turns around, the consummated is realized. It means that the other-dependent simply stops to be the basis for confusion, or bewilderment, the tendency to fall into the imagined. It means that the two kinds of attachments to subject and object are wiped out and purity reigns. The contamination possessed impurity is eliminated and there occurs purity.

When we say that the basis that is other-dependent in nature turns around and the consummated is realized, such a turning around does not take place in a manner that a chrysalis becomes a butterfly. I mean that it is not that the other-dependent is first stabilized as something real (chrysalis of the metaphor), and then it turns about into the consummated (butterfly). Such a stabilization represents nothing but the imagined nature, not the other-dependent. The other-dependent nature is represented by cognition that is always moving and flowing. As we saw earlier, the cognition (*vijñāna*) evolves from cause to effect and from effect to cause, simultaneously and instantaneously. Consequently the chrysalis would be the imagined, not the other-dependent, and the butterfly would be the consummated. The turning around or conversion thus takes place from the imagined to the consummated. This leads us to consider the popular saying, "Affliction is itself enlightenment," which conveys a similar meaning.

In this saying, affliction and enlightenment are intuitionally and directly identified. In the three nature theory, however, the imagined and the consummated cannot be identified in that manner, nor does the turning around or change take place directly between them, for these two are transcendentally separated. Instead, apart from the imagined and the consummated, there is the other-dependent, the third principle, the principle of convertibility, which provides the "place" for the turning around of the two. Therefore, when "body / mind drops down" (p. 143) in terms of the other-dependent, what drops down is no other than the affliction of the imagined nature; accordingly, when it drops down and the consummated world presents itself, the status of the other-dependent does not become extinguished, because purity simply means that the other-dependent has been purified.

As stated before, the consummated is the "dharmatā" (real reality) of the other-dependent; consequently the other-dependent is the "dharma" of the consummated world and represents actual existences. The fact that the other-dependent (*dharma*) and the consummated (*dharmatā*) are neither one nor different has been discussed in the *Triṃśikā,* k.22. Also the fact that the "representation-only" (*vijñaptimātratā*) is, in the final analysis, equated with the consummated suggests the same existential relationship. In this case, although both terms are other-dependent and are translated as "cognition" or consciousness (*shih* 識) in Chinese, the term *vijñapti* should be distinguished from vijñāna that always has a tendency to fall into the imagined nature.

The idea of the so-called means for entering into non-existence (*asallakṣaṇa-anupraveśa-upāya-lakṣaṇa*)[32] is related to this discussion. It clarifies the orderly sequence of the turning around of the basis, schematically and in steps as follows. What exists is cognition only and the object of cognition (the outer world) does not exist; but if the cognized does not exist, the cognition as its cognizer also does not exist; in spite of that, finally, the world is realized as "representation-only" (*vijiñaptimātratā*). The steps involved here go in a zigzag fashion and thus a zigzag logic must intervene. I cannot discuss in detail the logic involved here, but it is likely that this logic is not simply a product of the cognition theory; the logic of the three nature theory, the logic of convertibility, must exist and operate therein.

From the viewpoint of 'being,' the cognition theory may afford us with the categorization of mental factors (*caitta*) and various characteristics of things (*dharma-lakṣaṇa*; hence, the name Fa-hsiang in China for this school), and thereby it may clarify the theory of 'cognition-only' while rejecting the existence of the outer world. However, the same cognition theory could not account for the abnegation of the cognition itself and could not make the claim, "the cognition also does not exist." In order for the cognition system to incorporate this abnegation, it would have to have the logic of convertibility operating from its inception. If it is claimed that the representation-only (equals the consummated nature) is consummated[33] solely by means of the cognition theory, in such a claim there is no need for the abnegation of cognition itself. What is negated in this case is vijñāna while what is affirmed as the final representation-only is vijñapti. When the logic of convertibility, which is centered around the other-dependent and which is the logic for the practice of turning around of the basis, is applied to and actualized on the realm of cognition, which is taken as other-dependent, only then is there established the scheme of the "means for entering non-existence."

IV

Statements such as "Affliction is itself enlightenment" or "birth-and-death (*saṃsāra*) is at once nirvāṇa" are accepted generally in Mahāyāna Buddhism as its universal axioms that well describe the scenery of ultimate emancipation, the result of the turning around of the basis. The idea of complete "identity," "interpenetration," and so forth expressed therein is regarded as the Mahāyāna principle. However, as for the problems of how and why two contradictory events like affliction and enlightenment, or saṃsāra and nirvāṇa, could possibly be united or identified, there are many discussions from various perspectives in the history of Buddhism. Because one confronts many difficulties in such an investigation, there is a tendency to explain the idea of "identity" or of "at once" or "is itself" in these sayings, as mystical or intuitive. This tendency seemed to increase in later times and, especially, in the Buddhism of China and Japan. But a mysticism or any form of intuition can hardly be accepted as a logical investigation. A logic, such as the "logic of identity," that underlies and explicates as well such an axiom, must be of the kind that we have called the "logic of convertibility." It is the logic that was the undercurrent of Śākyamuni's insight known as *pratītya-samutpāda* and that continued until the development of the three nature theory, especially of the idea of the other-dependent nature, of the Yogācāra school.

In the *Mahāyāna-saṃgraha,* for instance, the phrase "birth-and-death is at once nirvāṇa" is explained, in several places throughout the text (VIII.21; IX.3; X.28, k.12, etc.), as indicative of the profound meaning of the *dharma-kāya,* or as suggestive of non-discriminative wisdom. Especially, commenting on a passage from the *Brahma-paripṛcchā-sūtra*, which reads, "the tathāgata does not see saṃsāra, does not see nirvāṇa," the same text (II.28) elucidates the "non-distinction between saṃsāra and nirvāṇa" (*saṃsāra-nirvāṇa-nirviśeṣa*) by employing the import of the three-nature theory. This clearly shows that the axiom stated above is assumed to have the logic of convertibility as its framework. In a similar vein, we even find an exposition that saṃsāra, nirvāṇa, and the identity of the two should be understood in the light of the three natures—the imagined, the consummated, and the other-dependent, respectively (II.30). Thus, affliction, that is absolutely separated from nirvāṇa, converts into and becomes the seed (*bīja,* cause) for the attainment of nirvāṇa or for the release from saṃsāra. Such convertibility can be logically understood only on the basis of pratītya-samutpāda or of the other-dependent.

So far we have discussed this convertibility in the light of evolving (*pariṇāma*), synonym or "from one perspective" (*paryāya*), and the turning around of the basis (*āśraya-parāvṛtti*). Therein, the synonyms applicable to the three natures were the logical foundation for establishing the idea of the "turning around of the basis" on the one hand and, on the other hand, its actual structure was understood in view of the dynamics of "evolving of cognition." In relation to the idea of this evolving or convertibility, however, I would now like to add a few more points.

In the later development of Buddhism, the term *hui-hsiang* (迴向), usually translated "merit-transference," began to play an important role in texts such as T'an-luan's *Ch'ing-t'u-lun-chu* (淨土論註). The term hui-hsiang is actually the same word as "evolving" discussed above, because its Sanskrit equivalent is "pariṇāmanā," "pariṇati," and other words that are cognates of "pariṇāma." According to the Chinese tradition, *hui* is explained as meaning "to turn around," and *hsiang* as "to direct toward." This means that the good roots and virtues of one's own religious practices are turned around and directed to where one wishes. Accordingly, it is in the idiom, "hui-hsiang toward bodhi" (merit-transference toward enlightenment), that the term appears most frequently, but it is explained further as "to re-direct" one's merit from oneself to another, from cause to effect, from phenomenon (*shih* 事) to principle (*li* 理), and so forth. In the Sanskrit dictionaries, we can find only the sense of "evolve" for the term pariṇāma and its cognate words; it is difficult to encounter the meaning of "to re-direct." But the meaning to re-direct can be observed in the usage of this term throughout the Buddhist texts; it is given in the Tibetan translation, too, in this meaning.[34] In the Sanskrit tradition, Sthiramati[35] has interpreted this term (*pariṇati*) as follows:

> [By the function of pariṇati] the good roots are yoked to *mahābodhi.*

or

> *pariṇati* means that one intends to have the good roots, fixed (determined) on to Buddhahood.

These interpretations are closely aligned to the idea of redirecting.

Thus, the merits accumulated by sentient being are transferred toward the bodhi, or from oneself to other beings.[36] Or conversely, the Buddha's merits accumulated by his vows and practices are transferred and directed toward sentient beings. However, how is it possible "to transfer" or "to re-direct" one's merit?

It is natural that wherein there is a cause, therein there is an effect, and thus wherein goodness has been accumulated, therein there will be fruits of that goodness, not elsewhere. That being the case, how is it possible that one's merits can be transferred or directed to others? The question is a perennial one that concerns the relationship between karma and its fruits or between cause and effect in general. One can grant such a possibility only on the explicit claim that, when considered from the idea of śūnyatā, "self and others are not two, but are equal." But such a response may be considered to be an insufficient explanation, even though it is only on such a claim that one can grant such a possibility. In this connection, it can be pointed out that, actually, the term "pariṇāma," evolving, that plays such an important role in Yogācāra philosophy, is scarcely mentioned in connection with śūnyatā by the Mādhymikas.

In any case, when seen from the soteriological point of view, both on the part of the sentient beings and on the part of the Buddha, the merit-transference must be a fact, without which neither emancipation nor salvation would be possible. And for the term pariṇāmanā to have the meanings, "transference" and "redirecting," it must be submerged in the background of the logic of convertibility clarified in the light of the three-nature theory developed in the Yogācāra philosophy. Merit-transference, together with its possibility, can be interpreted properly only within the structure of convertibility. In such a transference (evolving), affliction can be, at once, *bodhi,* because while the Buddha may direct his virtues toward sentient beings, ordinary people have nothing but afflictions that can be directed towards enlightenment.

Apart from the fact that terms "evolving" and "merit-transference" share the same Sanskrit *pariṇāma,* I would like to draw your attention to another usage of it in the phrase, *acintya-pariṇāmikī-upapatti.*[37] In most cases, the phrase is translated into Chinese pu-ssû-i-pien-i-shêng-ssû (不思議変易生死) which means "birth-and-death through inconceivable transformation," and here, *pariṇāmikī* corresponds to *pien-i* (変易) "transformation." When the *Ch'êng-wei-shih-lun* (chüan 8) interprets this phrase, *pien-i* is explained by the statement, "a former bodily existence is turned over to a better life of later time." I feel dubious, however, about the fact that pariṇāmikī has been translated as *pien-i* and interpreted as "transformation."

There are two kinds of birth-and-death. The first is known as "birth-and-death with limitations and divisions" and the second is known as "birth-and-death through transformation (*pariṇāmikī*)," the one that is of concern here. Of these the first one refers to the ordinary birth and death, samsaric and corporal, which is constituted in various divisions and is limited in many ways. In contrast to this, the second one refers to the birth and death that are "inconceivable," and that are of the śrāvakas, the pratyeka-buddhas, and the powerful bodhisattvas. It is also named "manomayakāya," "body produced by mind."[38] The second one is called "inconceivable" because, as explained in the *Ch'êng-wei-shih-lun,* it is a birth that "resulted from the un-contaminated and resolute vow and has magnificent powers beyond measure." In most cases, parinākimī in this phrase is understood as "transformation" (*pien-i*), but as it is a cognate word of pariṇāmanā, it can be interpreted in the meaning of "merit-transference" and I believe this is preferable. The following example will support this argument.

The phrase *acintya-pariṇāmikī-upapatti* appears also in the *Mahāyāna-sūtrālaṃkāra,* XI.56. There the phrase is discussed in relation to the idea that those śrāvakas and pratyeka-buddhas, who are not finally determined as members of the two vehicles, can attain the enlightenment in the Mahāyāna by means of the single vehicle (*ekayāna*). The Chinese translation of the phrase here reads:

> the persons of the two vehicles take "the birth of inconceivable merit-transference."

It does not interpret pariṇāmikī as "transformation," but as "merit-transference." This refers to the so called doctrine of the "conversion to the Mahāyāna" of the persons of the two vehicles. That is to say, having been converted to the Mahāyāna, even those of the two vehicles can transfer their merits—that is, the path of sages acquired by them—toward the world of beings, that is, to the samsaric world, and thereby they take birth among the sentient beings and exert themselves in the practices of benefiting others. The entrance into or conversion to the Mahāyāna is accomplished on their behalf only by being born into saṃsāra and thereby conferring benefits to others. The reason why such a birth is called "inconceivable" is that, differing from the ordinary birth that is a result of past karma and afflictions, in such a birth, the path of the sages itself can become the cause of saṃsāra and one takes birth on account of great compassion. In his commentary to this phrase (*MSA,* XI.56), Vasubandhu states:

> Because the two persons [śrāvaka and pratyekabuddha], who have already penetrated into truth, transfer the path of sages they have acquired toward all existences, they are said to possess "birth which is the inconceivable merit-transference." Truly, this transference of the path of sages toward their birth is inconceivable. Therefore, it is called, "birth which is inconceivable merit-transference."[39]

In their subcommentaries on this portion, both Sthiramati and Asvabhāva emphasize the point, "on account of great compassion they take birth in saṃsāra."[40] This also supports the interpretation merit-transference for pariṇāmikī. The *Ch'êng-wei-shih-lun* does not overlook this point either as it explains that "one transforms one's bodily existence through the power of compassion and the vow."

The sage who should have already attained emancipation from birth-and-death also takes birth in saṃsāra through "transformation" (actually through merit-transference) and puts great compassion into practice. Only when such practices are actualized, can it be said that the vehicle is one (*eka-yāna*), not the three (of *śrāvaka, pratyeka-buddha,* and bodhisattva). Moreover, the practices are spurred on by the attitude of great compassion of benefiting others. This shows that this merit-transference is in some sense or other the one in a descending direction that comes down to the samsaric world, although it is needless to say that for the sages of the two-vehicle path, it is the merit-transference in an ascending direction. Consequently, this "descending" merit-transference is closely linked to the bodhisattva's attitude of "non-abiding in nirvāṇa" (*apratiṣṭhita-nirvāṇa*).

As a matter of fact, also in the *Śrīmālādevī-sūtra* and in the *Ratnagotra-vibhāga,* it is stated that the one who takes the inconceivably transformed birth is not only the sage of two-vehicle path but also the great powerful bodhisattva. Non-abiding in nirvāṇa and taking birth in saṃsāra, a bodhisattva can be said to abide in a "state of merit-transference," as it were, though it is far from the perfected and immovable state of the Buddha. It is a state in which a bodhisattva transfers his merits toward fellow beings unceasingly and untiringly forever.

The Chinese term *pien-i* (transformation) can also encompass the logic of convertibility. However, if pien-i referred simply to a matter of transformation, exchange, or conversion from birth to death and from death to birth, then such a "transformation" could not refer to the birth and death of the powerful bodhisattva or of the sage who has entered the one vehicle of Buddha-yāna. Therefore, pien-i must bear the meaning of "merit-transference," without which meaning it would be difficult, in the final analysis, to understand why it is called "inconceivable."

It can be seen that the "logic of convertibility" includes the two aspects or the two directions of "ascending" and "descending." To summarize, the logic of convertibility was first examined in terms of the "evolving of cognition," and its real features were found in the theory of three natures, centering around the other-dependent nature. We then examined it in view of the "turning around of the basis." In its ascending direction we saw that cognition turned around and became wisdom and in its descending direction we discussed it in terms of "merit-transference," which was closely related to the bodhisattva's "not abiding in nirvāṇa" and "taking birth in this world willingly" (*saṃcintya-bhava-upapatti*).[41]

Postscript.

Being written about 35 years ago, in 1952, this paper contains many shortcomings. In spite of that, I chose to include it in this volume as the idea of "convertibility" influences my understanding of Buddhism to this date and because most of my papers that have appeared hence are, more or less, based upon that idea. For a fuller exposition on the doctrinal system of the three-nature theory, consult in particular my essay, "The Buddhist World-View as Elucidated in the Three-Nature Theory and Its Similes" included in this volume.

Chapter 12

Ontology in Mahāyāna Buddhism

I Buddhism and Ontology

Ontology within a Buddhism context is naturally related directly to the most fundamental tenet of Buddhism; therefore, it should be discussed in reference to all of Buddhist thought and doctrines. However, in what follows, I shall discuss it specifically, and mainly, from the perspective of Mahāyāna ideas.

Now, what does ontology signify? It goes without saying that the terms "ontology" and "metaphysics" are technical terms developed in Western scholarship and philosophy, but one must question whether these terms can be applied to or even found in Buddhist thinking in the same manner.

Ontology represents a theoretical principle by which one investigates existence as 'existence' itself, and it is understood as having the same meaning as metaphysics or, what has been known from ancient times, as "*philosophia prima.*" In these cases, existence, especially substantial or intrinsic existence, has been the object of discussion, and it was investigated in view of questions such as: "What is the fundamental principal underlying existence?" or "What is the first cause of existence?" or "What is true reality?" and so on. Ontology is, on the one hand, closely related to cosmology that investigates the origin and make up of the universe and to the philosophy of nature that investigates the laws of nature, their dynamics, the atomic principles, and so on. On the other hand, ontology has concerned itself with question of the existence of God, that is, the question of God's existence as the highest existence, and thus, it developed along theological lines insofar as it attempts to prove God's existence. Therefore, ontology has a very strong tendency towards the logic of metaphysics and is to that degree different from philosophies based upon empiricism or psychology.

Seen from the perspective of ontology, there seems to be a positive evaluation for existence and a negative value for nonexistence. For example, in the question above on the proof of God's existence, a thing that is the absolute and perfect cannot be a thing that has something lacking, and it is in this respect that the absolute and perfect God is said to be truly existent and a real reality, because God does not lack the quality of existence. Of course, mere existence does not imply absolute reality right offhand, but when from the perspective of ontology, the quest for real reality is pursued it seems that existence is accepted as if it were one of God's virtues. In contrast, what does not exist is considered to be something lacking perfection, something flawed, or, at times, even the source of evil.

But in Eastern thought, it is more often the case that nonexistence or nihility becomes the principle underlying ontology. Non-being (*wu*) of the Taoists and emptiness (*śūnyatā*) of the Buddhists are examples. In the *Upanishads,* one can find the philosophy of the philosopher sage, Uddālaka Āruṇi Gautama (c. 700 B.C.), who pursued existence or 'being' (*sat*) as the source for the cosmos, but one also finds older ideas which take "non-being" as the principle behind the creation of the world. Also, the Creation Hymn (*Nāsadīya*) found in the *Ṛg-veda,* states:

> There was neither non-existence nor existence then;
> there was neither the realm of space nor the sky which is beyond.
> What stirred? Where? In whose protection?
> Was there water there, bottomlessly deep?
>
> There was neither death nor immortality then.
> There was no distinguishing sign of night nor of day.
> That one breathed, windless, by its own impulse.
> Other than that there was nothing beyond.
>
> Darkness was hidden by darkness in the beginning;
> with no distinguishing sign, all this was water.
> The life force that was covered with emptiness,
> that one arose through the power of heat.[1]

How are such ideas of "existence" and "non-existence" related to each other ontologically? Non-existence is a great problem even in Western philosophy, but there it has been considered in most cases as a deficiency of existence, as a malice, or a flaw. Ontology, to its bitter end, is based upon existence as a positive value. Even when nihilism came to the fore, the basis for its ontology was no different. In the history of philosophy in the West, ontology and realism were necessarily destined to meet with and to confront various kinds of nihilism. However, even in those systems of nihilism, it can be said that the strong tendency towards existence was not overcome, especially when their claims of nihilism are compared with the Eastern idea of 'non-existence' or the Buddhist thought of *śūnyatā*.

That being the case, it is highly questionable whether Buddhism that expounds *anātman* (non-self) and *śūnyatā* (emptiness) can be considered to deal with ontology? On the other hand, however, given the import of ontology, it cannot begin and end with realism; it must include nihilism within its fold. Furthermore, it must make the Eastern thoughts of 'non-being' and 'emptiness' its object of investigation. According to E. Conze:

> In Aristotelian metaphysics the principle of contradiction governs all that is (*to on*). Quite different is the supreme and unchallenged principle of Buddhist ontology, which is common to all schools and has been formulated on many occasions. It states that the truth "lies in the middle" between "it is" and "it is not." Not approaching either of these dead ends, the Truth-finder teaches Dharma by the middle way.[2]

In view of this statement, it is evident that Buddhism cannot be gauged directly on the basis of Aristotelian ontology or can such an ontology be found therein. However, if one is to deal with Buddhist ontology, it is not difficult to find various ontological expressions and explications in the sūtras and treatises. There is a cosmological theory that was formulated on the basis of the mythical Mt. Sumeru; also there are world views of the cosmos in which the world is divided into three levels, or in which various kinds of aeons are systematized into the categories of the three times. There are other thoughts, such as the dharma-realm (*dharma-dhātu*), suchness (*tathatā*) emptiness (*śūnyatā*), and so forth that are akin to the ideas of the absolute and true reality. On the basis of the theory of dharmas, in which all existences (*dharma*) are divided into the two groups of the conditioned (*saṃskṛta*) and the unconditioned (*asaṃskṛta*), even a metaphysical study is developed in Sino-Japanese Buddhism under the name "reality characteristic theory" (実相論). However, this form of ontology is not an ontology that positively gives credit to existence; on the contrary, it is an ontology that gives credit to non-being and the empty as the positive principle. Because such an ontology refers to the middle path that is beyond the extremes of existence and non-existence, Conze refers to this as "the new ontology."[3] When Conze says, the new ontology, he is probably referring to "new" in contrast to the Hīnayānic ontology, but it can be said equally in regard to ontology in Western philosophy that focuses on the existent.

When viewed from a standpoint of ontology in Western philosophy, Buddhism can be seen as providing new and unique materials. In contrast, however, when viewed from a Buddhistic standpoint, there still remain the problem of whether an ontology can be truly established within Buddhism, because ontology is not at all the primary aim of Buddhism, nor did Buddhism try to establish a theoretical philosophy. The question of whether

Buddhism is a religion or a philosophy is a problem discussed by scholars after Buddhism was introduced to the Western world. Religion and philosophy are the brainchild of Western thinking and are assumed to be in opposition to each other. Ideas that concur exactly with them cannot be found in India, China, or Japan. Rather, in India, philosophy and religion are bound as one, and it is difficult to think of Buddhism as one or the other. Also, it is generally thought that Buddhism does not conflict with philosophy or science and is on intimate terms with them. Buddhism is, indeed, to a high degree intellectual and philosophical. However, the thoughts and ideas that form the nuclei of Buddhism are the products of intuitive insight that are highly religious in character rather than philosophical. In any event, Buddhism cannot be synchronized with Western philosophical ideas directly and it is also somewhat distanced from the ways of Western religions. Simply stated, Buddhism is a religion that is strongly colored by philosophy.

That Buddhism has the two aspects of philosophy and religion can be known from the fact that *wisdom* and *expedient actions* or *wisdom* and *practice* exhibit the kernel of Buddhist teachings. What symbolizes Buddhism more than anything else is liberation and nirvāṇa, and also the traversing of the path that leads one to those objectives. The former ones refer to the realization of Buddha's Wisdom, the wisdom that is characterized as non-discriminative; in accomplishing the traversing of the path, the Buddhistic practices become established. The completion of a moral life on the worldly level and the observance of ethical codes of conduct are included in these methods of Buddhist practices but central to them are yoga and meditation (*dhyāna*). Compared to other philosophies and religions throughout the world, the position that this yogic practice of contemplation and meditation occupies is relatively more important in Indian thought and Buddhist thought. In every case, proper wisdom implies and presupposes this yogic practice; it is the product of meditation. Scattered knowledge, disordered knowledge, that is not involved in meditation is neither true knowledge nor Buddha-Wisdom. True wisdom is different not only from the ordinary empirical knowledge of perception but also from the knowledge that pursues reason and rationality. Thus, it is clear that ontology that is accepted by most in such a sense has no place within Buddhism.

But, it is also true that Buddhist ontology, an ontology of the middle path that transcends the two extremes of existence and non-existence, cannot be totally negated within Buddhism. Seeing that a Buddhist ontology flows out of Buddha-Wisdom, it must rise high above the conventional world on the one hand, and on the other hand, it must have the quality of actualization (or realization) that results from the practice of yoga by which that height is reached. That ontology should be established in a milieu where human reason, though rooted in humanity, converts itself crosswise into Buddha's wisdom through yogic meditation (*dhyāna*). It can be called "practical philosophy," but it has nothing to do with theories of defending theology or with discussions of moral practice. The word practical here refers to the application of Yogic-practice, or the practice of the Middle Path that results from the practice of dhyāna. The fact that the Buddhists understand this as a "Middle Path" and not simply the "Middle" gives this practical philosophy its meaning. Thus, a Buddhist ontology, if ever there is to be one, must be established on the basis that it is the object of "wisdom" and, at the same time, the contents of meditative "practice." In such an ontology, various problems will arise. There will arise questions such as: "Of what kind of structure is our world of existence—that is, the world of bewilderment—wherein the dichotomy of subject/object always prevails?" or "How is this world of bewilderment related to and linked to the world of enlightenment?"and so on.

If it should be acceptable to understand Buddhist ontology in the manner stated above, one can anticipate many difficult problems in regard to it. To deal with those problems and to clarify them is no simple matter. In the discussion to follow, however, I will investigate various ontological topics from a Mahāyānic standpoint, while keeping in mind Buddhist ontology as discussed above.

II The Problem of Subjectivity and Objectivity

Owing to some circumstances I exist and the world exists. I am internal; the world is external. The general rule in Buddhism is that the "I" is referred to by the terms "ātman" (self) or "sattva" (sentient being), while the world that is external to the self is referred to by the term "dharma." To state it another way, I am "subject" insofar as I am what knows; the world is "object" insofar as it is what is known. When these two are referred to, respectively, as the "sentient-being-world" (*sattva-loka*) and the "receptacle-world" (*bhājana-loka*), the "I" as a sentient being is what exists within a receptacle, the outer world, and the "receptacle-world" is the environment that surrounds the "I." This means that a sentient being who dwells in the material environment is nothing more than a constituent part of the world. Or again, when these two are known as "self" and "what is possessed by the self" respectively, the "I", that is, a sentient being, occupies the central position of the world and the peripheral outer world is what belongs to that sentient being, that is, something owned by the sentient being. Thus, the contraposition of the "I" and the "world" is viewed from various perspectives in Buddhism.

In his book *Shukyō to wa Nanika* (What is Religion?), Keiji Nishitani provides two ontological queries. In the first one he asks, "What is the significance of each and every existence to me?" In the second one, he asks the very opposite question, "For what purpose do I exist?"[4] To ask what significance or purpose each and every existence has for me is a cultural question, as with respect to things cultural one can ask such a question. But a religious question differs from this. To ask, "What purpose does religion have for me?" is not a religious question, but a cultural one. Religion is what begins from earnestly questioning, "How is it that I exist?" or "From whence do I come and to where do I go?" or "For what purpose do I exist?"

In that sense, religion has its beginnings when one's own existence is challenged with a great big question mark. This is not knowledge with regard to some object nor is it a concern that is outwardly directed. It is a question that comes from within with regard to one's own subjectivity. When primitive Buddhism took anātman (non-self) as its foundation on the basis of questioning the ātman (self), there must have been such a religious, humanistic demand and aspiration lurking within its depth. This anātman (non-self) doctrine has a very strong theoretical and philosophical flavor. However, the fact that it captured the fancy of so many people's minds and charmed them is not owing to the theoretical and philosophical flavor, but was because it was nourished by the breath of religion.

Now, we shall turn for a moment to the ambience of opinions that surrounded Buddhism at the time of its establishment. The world of Indian thought that was advanced by great Upanishadic scholars had reached the height of discussing brahman and ātman. The doctrine of 'karman' was also firmly rooted there, and it was accepted by almost all thinkers as the fundamental way of thinking. Moreover, people thought that the practice of yoga was necessary for all kinds of refined thoughts. Here one finds sentiments that praised asceticism or its opposite, hedonism; sentiments that were closely intertwined with the lives of the people and that sought after property and sensuous pleasures or their opposite, seclusion. There were the extremes of materialism and complete negation of morality or ethics alongside spiritualism in which one devoted one's life to yogic meditation. One could find there all kinds of theoretical as well as practical philosophies. What stand did the Buddha take when he confronted these various thoughts? In regard to theoretical and philosophical thinking, he seemed to have attacked them at times with sharp criticisms. However, with regard to the matters of the practical life of the people, he seemed to have accepted them widely and even made compromises. He must have thought that, rather than negating them flatly from the beginning, it was better to elevate them to higher levels.

✓ *Brahman* (prayer), as the principle underlying the universe, had its origin in the religious prayers of the Vedas and was theorized as the first principle of all existences. There was not one intellectual of the time that questioned that principle. Brahman was purity itself, was sacred, was the prayer that came from the depth of people's hearts, was the principle that created the world and me, was the absolute principle to which gods and men submitted and paid honour. Irregardless of how people may have thought of its mystical quality, it cannot be denied that the Brahman was representative of the truth and was the name of everything truly true.

In its footsteps, followed the term ātman (self). Usually, ātman is understood to have meant, originally, ''breath,'' but gradually it took on the quality of individual existence or ''soul'' as the genesis of life. Although the ātman is the cognizing subject, it is never cognized nor objectified; it is the absolute subject, the absolute self. In contrast to brahman, which was a notion signifying the essence of the macrocosm and was deemed the primal source for the universe, ātman signified concrete microcosm within which that macrocosm was wholly reflected. As the microcosm overlaps with the macrocosm, both can be called the ''universe.'' When the ātman takes the macrocosmic brahman as its own and is united and becomes one with it, there is the final liberation for humanity. This is known through the statement, ''brahman and ātman are one'' and ātman becomes fulfilled in being united with brahman. It can be said that the philosophy and religion of the Upanishads reached their summit in this unity expressed in the statement, ''brahman and ātman are one.'' What must be noted here is this: in contrast to brahman, which is cosmical, objectified, and ontological, the ātman is subjective, epistemological, and practical. While keeping the abstract quality of brahman within itself, the ātman appeared on the scene as a more definite and concrete principle. It was the absolute existence that resembled the existence of god or Īśvara (lord, the Supreme being).

This means that the notion of ātman was accepted by the intellects of the time as having, along with brahman, dominating authority or as even surpassing the authority of the latter. The search for ātman, or the search for the self, was the first maxim to be observed by all people. The existence of this ātman that underlies all cognition and behavior as their subject was beyond questioning. Nevertheless, it was Buddha's message of ātman that negated the existence of such an ātman (self). This was encountered by the people of the time as an earth shaking, astounding event that went against tradition.

It cannot be determined whether this anātman doctrine attributed to the Buddha was indeed taught by him or, even if he should be credited with such a doctrine, it cannot be determined with what intention he might have taught such a doctrine. There are some scholars who claim that Buddha did not expound anātman, but merely stated, "this is not ātman." However, there is no evidence that the Buddha taught an ātman theory either. If this is not ātman and that is not ātman and everything else is not ātman, then it follows that ātman can be found nowhere within our world. In any event, the doctrine of anātman, has been claimed by the Buddha's disciples as one of the dharma-seals of Buddhism. The source for that must go back to the Buddha himself, because it is unreasonable to think that Buddha's disciples credited him with a doctrine of anātman that could not be traced back to him. Now then, with what intention did he explain such a doctrine?

In all probabilities, the Buddha explained, on many occasions, the religious and moral significance of rejecting attachment to the self and of overcoming egoism, because these activities, more than anything else, can give peace of mind in human life. Buddha's personality and behavior also must have been seen by his disciples as unselfish and not avaricious. What charmed his disciples was, indeed, the Buddha's personality of having abolished selfishness. The doctrine of anātman must have been recollected, first of all, through the memory of this quality. However, the doctrine of anātman is directly related to ontology, because the term ātman has been accepted as a concept expressing reality. Consequently, to claim "non-self" or "unselfishness" is not only to negate self and what is possessed by the self, but is also to negate a subjective entity such as a "soul," and it is thus linked to the negation of a substantive state of reality.

As pointed out above, ātman is tied closely to the idea of a substantive state of reality and it is likely that the ontological aspect of that substantive reality was also of concern to the disciples of the Buddha. There are many ways to connote a "self" and, in Buddhism, too, many terms (such as *puruṣa, pudgala, pṛthagjana, ārya,* etc.) are widely used to connote the ordinary, everyday personality or the personality of religious practitioners. However, as the term ātman was a special target of criticism, the Buddhist gave various definitions to that term. Among them, the definitions "being permanent," "one," and "almighty" are the most widely employed ones. That is to say, ātman is a permanent or eternal being; ātman is one and unique or one whole; ātman rules over others, is not controlled by others, is not dependent on others, and is self-dependent and almighty. Such definitions of the ātman reminds us of the almighty god or Īśvara as the absolute existence. In our daily life, we stealthily conceal within our "self" (*ātman*) a similar arrogance of absolutism, that is, an arrogance of permanence, oneness, and sovereignty over others. The teaching of anātman is there to point out that the self could not and should not be such a thing.

The doctrine of the five psycho-physical constituents (*pañca-skandha*) is one of the theories that leads one to the negation of the self. The five psycho-physical constituents of color/form, feeling, perception, volitional effort, and cognition tentatively constitutes an individual existence and it is not as though there exists a nucleus of a self therein. The reality of the first noble truth, that all is pain, is also closely related to this idea of anātman. If it were the case that a permanent, one, almighty ātman existed, then there could be no pain. Similarly, impermanence (i.e., not permanent) also expresses a negation of the ātman, because impermanence is defined as "whatever is composite will become extinguished" or is understood as "all things momentarily come into existence and become extinct." If the "momentariness" (*kṣaṇikatva*), the synonym for impermanence, was realized even with regard to rocks and other stable matter, we must admit that the intellectual climate of that time was highly intuitive in order to achieve such a realization. Also we see therein a penetrating insight by which the total negation of the substantive reality was realized. Like the doctrine of anātman, interdependent origination (*pratītya-samutpāda*), which is considered to be at the foundation of Buddha's teaching, is also a doctrine that negates the concept of a substantive reality insofar as it is a doctrine of mutual dependence and mutual cooperation. Interdependent co-origination does not simply signify a causal chain of movement from a cause to an effect.

These are the doctrines in which the logical side of the Buddha's teachings were systematized. However, what actually manifested anātman was Buddha's life and his activities. They not only proclaimed a theoretical negation of ātman, but they also manifested, in practice, the "agentlessness" or negation of an acting-subject and the nonclinging to the self. Here, like the incomparable clear moon, there shines through the breaks in the clouds a real subjectivity that is totally free and not captured by the ghost of egoism. The negation of self that comprised the absolute freedom of the Buddha's subjectivity is what charmed the people the most. That the ātman, which was accepted by everyone since the beginning of the Upanishads, was negated must have created quite a stir, still the charm it held was the force that drove everyone to Buddhism. They must have celebrated this negation of ātman, established by a mere monk, this which was so different and which was against a tradition governed by the Brahmans and the Kṣatriyas.

III Abhidharmic Philosophy

That which followed after the teaching of anātman, the teaching that comprised the intellectual experience that reverberated with life, was its theorization. At least, some generations of the disciples put forth their efforts toward this goal. Already, the canonical works known as the "āgama" were strongly characterized by an intention of transmitting rather than conveying the religious experience. It cannot be denied, however, that so long as this doctrinal theorizing advanced, damage was done to the rich religious contents. Abhidharmic philosophy, an analytical philosophy in regard to the characteristics of dharmas, did not escape from that trend. This abhidharmic philosophy, especially its analysis of the dharma-characteristics represented by teachers of the Vaibhaṣika and the Sarvāstivāda, a philosophy called "dharma-theory" (as put forth by Otto Rosenberg) was clearly full of ontological tendencies. The phrase, "self is empty but things (*dharmas*) exist" conveys its standpoint. It can be said that, at the expense of establishing the negation of ātman, so to speak, a tendency towards the affirmation of realism arose.

The explanation of anātman is, first of all, based on the logic of the five *skandhas* (five psycho-physical constituents) stated above. According to it, ātman that is assumed to be something like a "soul" does not exist; what exists is simply the five skandhas made up of psychological and physical elements. It is nothing but an aggregate or bundle of these elements that is fancied as an entity and is called provisionally the "ātman" or "I." The ātman as such, although it may be thought to be a substantive entity, is nothing more than an attachment to a fabricated misrepresentation. What really exists is not the ātman, but these elements. The theory of the five skandhas explains that every individual being exists as a "bundle" of elements, a dynamic flow, in which are included even the elements of epistemological processes such as the twelve *āyatana* (spheres of cognition) and the eighteen *dhātu* (bases of cognition). Here, the common expression, "I see something" is replaced by the expression, "something is seen by means of a cognitive organ called 'eye' "; thus, the subject "I" is negated and made unnecessary. Each one of the five skandhas is called "dharma."

The term dharma is packed with meanings—it can mean the teaching of Buddha; it can refer to Buddhism itself; or it can refer to the laws governing or causes of worldly things. However, in the abhidharmic dharma theory, dharma is defined as something that "keeps hold of its own essential qualities" (*sva-lakṣaṇa-dhāraṇatva*)—something governed by such laws. Such a dharma, thought of as "elemental being" or "categorical being," can be translated simply as "existence." By analyzing things and by selecting out the elemental qualities of them, many dharmas were established as existences. There are mental dharmas and material dharmas and dharmas not related to either. They are all the "conditioned" (*saṃskṛta*) dharmas—existences that are compounded and destined to change. Apart from these, there are the "unconditioned" (*a-saṃskṛta*) dharmas, unchanging and immovable. While the conditioned dharmas are limited, being controlled by the cause and effect relationship, the unconditioned dharmas are not limited at all.

With regard to the material dharmas, there is the analysis of the elements into various kinds such as into the categories of earth and so on, and there is also the recognition of atoms (*paramāṇu*). But the analysis of the mental dharmas, their characteristics, and their function occupies far greater space. Perhaps this is owing to the fact that great importance was placed upon the mental functions in reference to yoga praxis. Sensation, memory, and so forth, were thought to be individual, independent dharmas, as were faith, nonbelief, anger, hatred, remorse, volition and so forth thought to be dharmas as elemental existences. Moreover, acquisition and nonacquisition, birth and death, and so forth that did not belong to either the material or mental dharmas were also considered to be independent dharmas. These various dharmas were classified, at times, into a group of seventy-five dharmas and, at other times, into a group of one hundred dharmas.

In this dharma-theory it is remarkable that things are analyzed from the standpoint of psycho-epistemology, or functionalism as stated above. Dharmas represent the laws of universal order, as it were, but not those of the divine order. Further, the dharma-theory can be characterized as truly realistic as well as pluralistic. Each and every dharma is seen as real, substantive, and existent; not only the conditioned dharmas, but also the nonconditioned dharmas such as annihilation (*nirodha* equals *nirvāṇa*) are regarded as existent in reality.

The name of the Sarvāstivāda (literally the school that claims "all exists") originates from this tendency towards realism, and within this school, the dharma was claimed to exist throughout the three periods of time, past, present, and future. However, this claim contained many subtle problems and it was the object of many criticisms levied against it from other schools ever since those days. The Sarvāstivāda's claim that something existed throughout the three periods of time was none other than a way of fusing the idea of time, abstracted and notional, to the idea of real existence found in the dharmas. Here, we see a kind of idealism in that something notional or conceptual is thought to exist in reality. Together with the notions of "acquisition," "birth," and so forth set up as dharmas and regarded as real existences, the realism, "existence throughout three periods of time," can be called an "idealistic realism." Opposing this Sarvāstivāda idealistic realism, the Sautrāntika claimed that reality is found only in the present and not in past or in the future; however, the Sautrāntika itself can be seen as a realist school.

The teaching of anātman was a negation of the substantive view of existence as explained above. The doctrine that things "became extinguished at the very moment of birth"—that is, impermance (*anityatā*)—is at the very foundation of the Sarvāstivāda teaching; it probably follows the tenet of *anātman,* the negation of substantive reality. But, seen in its totality, this dharma-theory is a kind of pluralistic realism and one may well wonder whether it can be in agreement with the anātman ideal. If it is the case that acquisition, birth, or life can be established as dharmas having real existence idealistically, then it would necessarily follow that the ātman is also, idealistically, an independent dharma. Was not the establishment of a kind of subject (*pudgala*) by the Vātsīputrīya also depended upon such circumstances? Although the five skandhas were thought of as dharmas having real existences in order to prove anātman, was it not more likely that they contributed to the collapse of the very standpoint of anātman? In any event, is it not for these reasons that the Mahāyānic view "self (*ātman* or *pudgala*) as well as dharmas exist" rather than the view "Self is empty but dharmas exist" came to the fore?

IV Śūnyatā in Mahāyāna Scripture

True ontology can be said to have begun with the advent of Mahāyāna or with the appearance of Nāgārjuna. However, that ontology was not an ontology that affirmed existence, but was an ontology that had negation as its principle.

It has been said that Mahāyāna has its roots in the Prajñā-pāramitā-sūtras. In summary, the Prajñā-pāramitā-sūtras expound śūnyatā (emptiness) and praise the wisdom of prajñā by which emptiness is seen. More than anything else, śūnyatā refers to non-existence or no-thing and is a negation; however, it is not that it lacks the meaning of affirmation. In the later period of Chinese Buddhism, there is an expression, "truly empty, [hence] unfathomable existence" (真空妙有). It conveys the meaning of negation and affirmation simultaneously, or thereby that negation is itself affirmation or emptiness (*śūnyatā*) is itself existence. However, as this affirmation is affirmation that acknowledges negation or is established by passing through negation, it cannot be a direct affirmation. At the same time, because it is an affirmation that acknowledges negation, it signifies that it can be an absolute affirmation. Such being the case, emptiness (*śūnyatā*) is strongly charged with the quality of negation, more than anything else. It is this form of negation that is expounded in the Prajñāpāramitā-sūtra and that is at the foundation of Mahāyānic thought.

How did the spirit of negation, that is, the Mahāyānic spirit, arise around the turn of the Christian era? The background for this can be thought about in various ways. For one thing, one can think about the social condition of the community (*saṅgha*) of the time and its deterioration. The deterioration of the saṅgha does not necessarily result from the evil customs dating back several centuries, but it could occur at any time once a community was formed. In the sūtras, the lives of several delinquent monks (*śramaṇas*) are explained. We find, for example, fewer truly genuine śramaṇas than the many who dress like a śramaṇa, who put on an outer airs of a śramaṇa and fool the people, or who become a śramaṇa merely for the purpose of seeking fame and gain (*Kāśyapa-parivarta,* §121 *f.*). In an older text, we find examples of bhikṣus, who are addicted to the pleasures of life, who ornamented themselves with trinkets, who slept in luxurious, extravagant beds, who hoarded their money earned by fortunetelling, or who committed robbery, and murder, and even swindled (*Sāmañña-phala-sutta* §45). Those people who were sincere must have felt a desperate feeling of nihility when they saw such circumstances. The fact that such corruptions have been recorded in the Buddhist scriptures indicates, on the one hand, that such incidents did occur, and on the other hand, the deep reflections on the part of the compilers of the texts as well as their counterattack against these evil doers. Even among the direct disciples of the Buddha, there were the group of six Bhikṣus, who were always reprimanded for daring to do inappropriate actions. There are also records of those disciples who were overjoyed with the thought that they were no longer bound to Śākyamuni's instructions upon hearing about the teacher's death. The lives of such feeble spirited ones and fools can be found in every period of human history.

In spite of these fools, the *Vinayas* or rules of the monk's community were generally upheld by its members, although the rules for the deportment of bhikṣus were already suffering from formality, a kind of mannerism. However, beyond that, the mannerism with respect to the doctrine was probably something very difficult to endure by sharp witted monks. That mannerism was seen particularly in the Abhidharmic dharma-theory. Therein, side by side with the formality and fixing of the Vinaya rules, each word and sentence of the Buddha's teachings was fixed and settled. This tendency of fixing and settling was innate to the dharma-theory from its beginning.

As stated earlier, the realistic dharma-theory, that was devised for the sake of proving anātman, had within it a sense of setting back the anātman doctrine. The fixing and settling of teachings such as the five *skandhas,* the twelve *āyatanas* (spheres of cognition), the eighteen *dhātus* (bases of cognition), and *pratītya-samutpāda* (dependent co-origination) with its twelve limbs as an interpretation of *saṃsāra,* literally and according to the words, must have consolidated the teachings in an exact way. However, when the doctrines were fixed into something like creeds or articles of faith, freedom of thought was crushed. To establish the pluralistic dharmas as existence meant that the people's aspirations for the monastic ultimately became tangled and caught in the net of dogma.

What was the significance behind the Buddha's teachings of impermanence (*anitya*), non-self (*anātman*), and suffering (*duḥkha*), which were expressed by words that moved everyone deeply? Was it for the sake of establishing a system of an intertwining "net of dogma" as an unchangeable creed? Was not the true spirit of non-self and impermanence to be found elsewhere? Such questions, probably, arose in the context of the fixation of dogma and mannerism stated above. One must look for the true intention of the Buddha by breaking through the dharma-theory to its depth. This break-through is what developed into the Mahāyāna movement. However, on the other hand, if the corruption of the professional bhikṣu was unendurable even to ordinary eyes, then it can be assumed that this Mahāyāna movement was augmented by the ideas of ordinary people, although such a fact is not clearly evident in the scriptures. The ordinary lay persons never lost touch with their respect for the bhikṣus, but at the same time, they were aware that the truth was no longer to be found in the teachings and practices of the mannerisms of those professional bhikṣus.

Central to the Mahāyāna movement was a spirit of negation that broke through the dharma-theory according to which the term "emptiness" was selected.

The representative texts in which the term śūnyatā can be found is the genre of Buddhist literature known as the Prajñā-pāramitā, wherein one finds the expression, "Matter is emptiness and the very emptiness is matter" (*rūpaṃ śūnyatā śūnyataiva rūpaṃ*)." Although this expression may seem to indicate, on the surface, that "things in particular are empty and are negated," what is basically negated is none other than one's clinging to the physical material existence (*rūpa*) as a substantive entity (*dharma*) by virtue of becoming fixed on the concept of rūpa (color/form), expounded, for instance, in the theory of pañca-skandha. However, the emptiness that is expounded in the Prajñāpārmitā literature is not always expressed by the term śūnya. In the *Vajracchedikā-prajñāpāramitā-sūtra,* the term "śūnya" is not to be found; however, we do encounter sentences such as:

> . . . The Lord replied: Here, Subhuti, someone who has set out in the Bodhisattva-vehicle should produce a thought in this manner: "all beings I must lead to Nirvana, into that Realm of Nirvana which leaves nothing behind; and yet, after beings have thus been led to Nirvana, no being at all has been led to Nirvana."[5]

The negation that appears in the phrase, ". . . no being at all has been led to Nirvana," is the sense in which *śūnyatā* is expressed here. Moreover, we also find the following statements:[6]

> Great, O Lord, great, O Well-Gone, would that heap of merit be! And why? Because the Tathagata spoke of the "heap of merit" as a non-heap. That is how the Tathagata speaks of "heap of merit."

and also,

> . . . the Tathagata has taught that the dharmas special to the Buddhas are just not a Buddha's special dharmas. That is why they are called "the dharmas special to the Buddhas."

Here, we find that the textual style is to expound first, for example, the heap of merits or the special dharmas, then to negate them, and then to affirm them once more on the basis of the negation. The same textual style is used repeatedly in the discussions on the Buddha-bodies, the Thirty-two Marks of a Buddha, the ornaments of the Buddha Lands, the Characteristics of Reality, or the Perfections. These are all negated strongly first and then affirmed through the process of negation. This is not typical of the *Vajracchedikā* alone; it is a form commonly found in all of the Prajñā-pāramitā literature.

The negation that transpires through this process of emptiness (*śūnya*) has been considered variously. For example, śūnya has been considered to be seen in samādhi or to be the object of visualization in the practice of dhyāna. Śūnyatā, together with the "signless" (*animitta*) and the "wishless" (*apraṇihita*), are said to be three doors of deliverance. When these are expounded in the sūtras, animitta is explained as a non-existent sign, apraṇihita as a negated wish, and śūnyatā as a negation of existence. Because the sūtras are what reflect directly the mystical experience, that emptiness is also thought to be intuitive and mystical. When it is stated that "there is a sign through the signless," or likewise, "there is existence through emptiness," that emptiness seems to be much akin to mystical nothingness. Or śūnyatā may have been understood by comparing it to "tranquility." The bhikśus were advised to practice meditation (*dhyāna*) in a quiet spot such as in the forest. Or again, even though the word may differ, śūnyatā may have been considered in relationship to open-space (*ākāśa*), because open-space, that contains the multitude of things in its vacuity and that is left unmarked by the flight of a bird through it, bears the meaning of infinity and absoluteness. However, here, in the context of the various possible meanings of śūnyatā, the term will be considered from the point of negation in view of two aspects. That is, śūnyatā will be considered first from the aspect of the negation of substance and secondly from the aspect of the negation of attachments.

Originally, the teaching of anātman was an expression of the negation of substance. Śūnyatā is actually a revival of the teaching of anātman, an expression of its true meaning. The meaning of ātman, originally based on the view of an individual characterized by egoism and self-interest, as explained above, was expanded to include the reality of a fundamental and universal ātman. Consequently, the anātman is the negation of the fundamental ātman that includes the spirit of ethical non-selfishness and impartial self-denial. In each one of these cases, especially in the case of the universal-self, the ātman refers to a substantive existence. Substantive existence in this context refers to what is negated by *pratītya-samutpāda* (inter-dependent origination) and is, in that sense, what is absolute existence. It is the "substance" or "essence" of whatever exists. Anātman, consequently, refers to the non-existence of both "self" and "substance." These are understood in the same manner even in the context of śūnyatā. That is, the formula is not "self (*ātman*) is empty but things (*dharmas*) exist" (p. 164), but is "self and things are both empty" or "the emptiness of both person (*pudgala*) and things." The phrase, "the emptiness of both person and things" (an idiom found mainly and usually in Chinese Buddhism) is expressed in the Sanskrit texts by phrase, "the selflessness of person and things" (*pudgala-dharma-nairātmya*). Here we see that the term "nairātmya," as the negation of substantive existence, is substituted (by the Chinese Masters) for the term śūnyatā. In this manner, the anātman was first an expression of the negation of a self and then by going through the stage of the anātman of the universal-self, it became an expression of the emptiness of whole world; hence, the expression "matter is emptiness."

However, in the Prajñāpāramitā-sūtras, not only do we find the expression "matter is emptiness," but we also find the expression "emptiness is matter." The expression emptiness is matter is not merely the reverse of the expression matter is emptiness. The expression matter is emptiness is negatively oriented, whereas the expression emptiness is matter is positively oriented. In this context, we should understand that the two orientations, negative and positive, are combined into one in a fashion of a paradox. In one sense, the negatively oriented expression, matter is emptiness involves a paradox, but the positive oriented expression, "the very non-existent emptiness exists as matter" is more paradoxical than the former. Further, these two paradoxical viewpoints are paradoxically linked to each other. Such a contradictory and paradoxical preposition is spelled out in the Prajñāpāramitā-sūtras as originating from their author's direct yogic and intuitive insights. For example, the *Vajracchedikā* quoted above, the statement, "dharmas special to the Buddhas are not dharmas special to the Buddhas . . ." is a negatively oriented expression, while the statement, "That is why they are called, 'dharmas special to the Buddhas' " is a positively oriented expression. In this manner, a negation always includes within it an affirmation. The statement, "truly empty, [hence] unfathomable existence," (p. 166) can also be understood in this context as moving through negation to affirmation. Just as in the case where both the negative and positive orientations are expressed, so too in the case when only the negative orientation is expressed, it should be understood that therein the positive orientation is also included. Even if that be the case, negation and affirmation do not move from one to the other, in an alternative way, and thus, it does not mean that when something is negated there follows something that is affirmed (the so-called relative negation, *paryudāsa-pratiṣedha*). Therefore, when it is said that the multitude of things is empty and at the same time, emptiness is the multitude of things, this means that emptiness is beyond or transcends both negation and affirmation.

"To go beyond" or "to transcend" does not mean to transcend and to go out externally only; it also means to transcend and to go in internally. By this I mean śūnyatā is both transcendent and immanent at the same time; it negates outwardly, but affirms inwardly. It is as the domain of the bodhisattva explained in the *Vimalakīrtinirdeśa-sūtra:*

> Not the domain of the ordinary individual and not the domain of the saint, such is the domain of the bodhisattva. The domain of the world yet not the domain of the passions, such is the domain of the bodhisattva. Where one realizes nirvāṇa, yet does not enter final and complete nirvāṇa, there is the domain of the bodhisattva.[7]

The domain of the bodhisattva does not lie somewhere halfway between the ordinary individual and the saint nor does it not lie somewhere between saṃsāra and nirvāṇa; it is beyond these. Because it is transcendent, it is immanent therein. In contrast to the negative orientation of śūnyatā, there is, herein, also a positive, affirmative orientation.

The negative orientation of śūnyatā is not, however, merely an existential negation; its actual contents is the negation of attachments held by ordinary individuals. In this sense, the negation of substance is no other than the negation of attachments to substance. It would be appropriate, in this connection, to quote a passage from the Chinese translation of the *Vajracchedikā-sūtra:*

> Without dwelling anywhere, the mind should be produced.

However, the Sanskrit text reads:

> A great bodhisattva should produce a mind freed from attachments.[8]

and this passage is followed by:

> That is, he should not produce a mind attached to something.

The Chinese term, "chu" (住) means not only "to live," "to dwell," and "to abide," but also means "to stick to," "to adhere to" because the word chu is given as a definition for the word "cho" (著) which means "clinging." On the other hand, the Sanskrit term *pratiṣṭhita* (cognate to *pratisthā*), as an adjective, means "standing," "abiding," "fixed," "established," and so forth, and the dictionaries do not explicitly give the meanings of "clinging," "adhering." However, as is evident from the Chinese translation above, we can assume that pratiṣṭhita also has the meaning "clinging" implicitly. Therefore, I translated its negative form, a-pratiṣṭhita, as "freed from attachments." Conze translates this a-pratiṣṭhita as "unsupported" (and as "not established," elsewhere), but he, on the other hand, suggests as many as twenty possible meanings for it and in enumerating those meanings, he gives "not fixed on," "not rest on," "not abide in," "not attached to," "not cling to," and others. Thus, the meaning "attachment" for pratiṣṭhita is also admitted by him.

However, so long as the mind is produced, it is directed to some object, dwells in that object, and naturally adheres to what it has grasped. The mind is always clinging to something. Therefore, to state: "The mind should be produced without clinging (i.e., without dwelling anywhere)" is itself a contradiction. It is equal to saying, "One should think without thinking." But this is the paradox that is emphasized in the Prajñāpāramitā-sūtras. The statement, "to think without the affliction of clinging" is not meant to be understood in an ethical sense. It reflects a movement from mind to no-mind and no-mind to mind, and thereby transcends both mind and no-mind. This is the very essence of śūnyatā that can be reached by virtue of eliminating clinging.

The term "apratiṣṭhita" reminds one of the term "apratiṣṭhita-nirvāṇa," non-dwelling nirvāṇa. The domain of the bodhisattva—that is, ". . . does not enter final and complete nirvāṇa . . ." of the *Vimalakīrtinirdeśa* mentioned above—is none other than "non-dwelling nirvāṇa." A bodhisattva does not dwell in the world of saṃsāra owing to his wisdom and does not remain in nirvāṇa owing to his compassion. The term non-dwelling nirvāṇa does not mean only that one does not enter and remain in nirvāṇa but it also means that one is not attached to nirvāṇa, and that is because nirvāṇa originates in śūnyatā. Nirvāṇa or cessation (*nirodha*), as one of the noncomposite dharmas, was made into a concrete substantive reality according to the Sarvāstivādin's realism. However, even that nirvāṇa is śūnyatā.

There are many other ways of understanding the meaning of śūnyatā than those discussed above, and they have had a strong influence on the lives of the practitioners. For example, combined with the view of impermanence, it educated the practitioner in the futility and emptiness of life. Or again, having realized that all things mundane—honor and fame, wealth and happiness, love and hate, pleasure and pain—are śūnya (empty), the practitioner is unmoved by them. In realizing śūnyatā, the practitioner obtains tranquility of mind. This heightened state of the mental tranquility comes forth from the basic principle of śūnyatā that is none other than the negation of substantive existence. Because everything is *śūnya,* there is no thing that can serve as a basis. This is to say, one stands in a bottomless void; śūnyatā is based on the baseless. To this extent, the above-mentioned apratiṣṭhita means "not dwelling anywhere" or "no abode in which to dwell."

V Nāgārjuna's Madhyamaka Philosophy.

It was Nāgārjuna who consolidated such ideas of śūnyatā found in the sutras into a philosophical system. Nāgārjuna who lived around the second or third C.E., was a great philosopher and a monk-scholar second only to the Buddha. It was owing to him that Mahāyāna Buddhism got a firm philosophical foundation and almost all forms of Mahāyāna schools of later times regard and accept him as their founder.

Taking its stand on the negation of śūnyatā, Nāgārjuna's philosophy contributed to an unique Buddhistic development that came to be known as the "Mādhyamika school." This school, enforcing the Mahāyānic idea, exerted its influence not only on Buddhism but also on all of the Indian systems in various ways. Even from the viewpoint of the world's history of ideas, Nāgārjuna's unique contribution should not go unnoticed in that the underlying principle of his philosophy was a thoroughgoing negativism. At times, his philosophy was rejected by outsiders as a form of nihilism. Nihilism in the Indian context, however, referred to the negation of a future life as the fruition of ethical and religious good acts. Its counterposition was the so-called realist position that affirmed a future life. Both are ethical oriented and have little ontological significance.

Nāgārjuna linked this idea of śūnyatā to the idea of dependent origination (*pratītya-samutpāda*) that had been the core of Buddhism since its beginning, and on account of that, his philosophy of negation did not end up being a nihilism that negated the religious efforts of humankind nor did it deviate from Buddhism. Moreover, in so far as it established the system of the two truths (*satya-dvaya*), it was successful in expounding its philosophical structure and its delicate minutiae. Its exposition is very logical, but on account of its logicality of thoroughgoing negation, it has a tendency even to negate logic itself. (In fact, the Mādhyamika school is later divided into two schools: the Svātantrika that affirmed logical reasoning and the Prāsaṅgika that negated it.) However, in actuality, Nāgārjuna's system of negation was directed mainly to the realist view of the Abhidharma philosophy.

At the beginning of his work, the *Mūlamadhyamakakārikā* (Fundamental Verses on the Middle), Nāgārjuna expounds on the eightfold negation thus:

> I pay homage to the perfectly enlightened one, the best among all teachers,
> Who expounded the dependent origination that is beyond frivolous talk and is tranquil and blissful [as having the characteristics of]
> Neither extinct nor arising; neither having end nor eternal;
> Neither one nor many; neither coming nor going.[9]

Here, Nāgārjuna has taken up the old idea of pratītya-samutpāda and has described it to have the eight-fold negation as its characteristic. As this eight-fold negation eventually came to signify śūnya, it essentially referred to "dependent origination as qualified by emptiness."

The same idea appears at the end of Nāgārjuna's *Vigrahavyāvartanī* (Averting the Controversy):

> I pay respect to that Incomparable Buddha who taught emptiness, dependent origination, and the middle path as synonymous.[10]

From this, it can be known that not only are emptiness and dependent origination treated as synonyms, but even the middle path is treated the same.

The term "dependent origination" (*pratītya-samutpāda*), as pointed out above, refers to the fundamental thought of the Buddha. As the words "originate through dependency" indicate, and also as the definition—that is, the four-fold phrase beginning with "This being that exists . . ." shows, "dependent origination" makes manifest the relative and conditional status regarding all existing things. The fact that everything is relative to every other thing, be it in regard to cognition or to how things exist, means that there is nothing "absolute" anywhere. Nāgārjuna has expressed this fact by the term "niḥsvabhāva" (no self-nature), that is, things have no nature of their own.

The term "self-nature" (*svabhāva*) is defined by Nāgārjuna as "that which cannot be artificially produced (*akṛtrima*) or that which is not dependent (*nirapekṣa*) on others."[11] Self-nature, therefore, refers to the inherent essence of a thing, to what exists in and of itself, or to a substantive being, unchanging and immovable. In other words, it is an "absolute existence." To accept such a self-nature is to go against the idea of dependent origination. In view of the above-mentioned phrase, "This being that exists . . . ," the fact of "that exists" is dependent upon and conditioned by the fact of "this being"; it is not owing to the fact that "that" has its own self-nature, an inherent, substantive nature of its own. Or again, when it is stated that "this" or "that" are relative to each other, it does not mean that first there are a substantive "this" and a substantive "that," and thereafter, the two are mutually "relative" to each other. If this and that are taken as substantive existences and then they are combined as being relative to each other, then this is none other than a realist's claim. Although it speaks of "relatedness" of substantive existences, this relationship can not be a "universal relativity" or an "absolute relativity." Universal relativity manifested by dependent origination always points to the non-substantiveness of all things. Or to state it another way, emptiness of śūnyatā of everything simply means that all entities have "no self-nature" and accordingly, are relative and dependently originating. True reality is, fundamentally, relative relationship itself. When this pure relationship is "clung to" or "grasped" in daily life as a "this" or a "that," then it is concretized and not seen for what-it-is. This means that one becomes attached to reality in the belief that "this is real" or "that is real." No self-nature exists originally; what one believes to be a self-nature comes into existence only as object of one's attachment.

As a rule, śūnyatā (emptiness) means "niḥsvabhāva" (no self-nature). Emptiness is usually expressed as "no self-nature, hence emptiness." Accordingly, dependent origination, which means "no self-nature" is itself equal to emptiness. This is why Nāgārjuna has described pratītya-samutpāda as emptiness in his *Mūlamadhyamakakārikā* by means of the eight-fold negation and made emptiness, dependent origination, and the middle path synonymous in his *Vigahavyāvartanī* quoted above. Furthermore, because that dependent origination is equivalent to emptiness, it is "blissful and beyond frivolous talk"; it is beyond speculation. And yet, the Buddha expounded in various manner the principle of interdependent origination that was beyond speculation; thus, he was considered to be "the best among the teachers." Nāgārjuna skillfully gave expression to the paradoxical view of the Prajñāpāramitā-sūtra that linked negation (i.e., emptiness) to affirmation (i.e., Buddha's teaching) when, in his salutation to the Buddha, he states that even though dependent origination is beyond all concepts and all categories and is itself emptiness, the Buddha has dared to take the trouble of expounding it.

Since early times, the idea of dependent origination, has been organized into a twelve limbed chain of causation. Beginning with ignorance and ending with a mass of pains such as birth, old age, death, the twelve limbs have been understood as a system of causation that explains the actuality of the present human world, a world of confusion. It explains the actuality called "saṃsāra" in which one goes from one life to the next one through a cycle of births and deaths. Nāgārjuna also adopted this kind of interpretation of dependent origination. There is a term "idaṃpratyayatā" that means "a state of having this as its cause or condition" (for convenience sake, I shall refer to it simply as "conditionedness") and which, having almost the same meaning as dependent origination, appears as the first part of a compound, the other term often being pratītya-samutpāda.[12] In the pre-Mahāyāna sūtras, the term "conditionedness" appears as an interpretation of the twelve limbs of dependent origination, but, in the Mahāyāna treatises, it seems to be related more to the aforementioned phrase beginning with "This being that exists . . ." and to convey the meaning of "universal relativity" discussed above. In the terms "dependent origination" and "conditionedness," Nāgārjuna detected the meanings not only of the saṃsāric status of humankind (and liberation from it), but also of the more fundamental principle of universal relativity and, through it, the negation of the absolute. He combined this kind of dependent origination with the idea of śūnyatā and inserted niḥsvabhāva (no self-nature) between them as a medium. Dependently originating things have "no self-nature," hence they are empty.

However, at the same time, it cannot be denied that dependent origination has an "exists" aspect, and the fact that dependent origination was explained by the twelve limbs to show the human situation of saṃsāra clearly manifests that. In contrast, śūnyatā tends more towards "negativity" and "non-existence" and refers to none other than the world of enlightenment as seen through the eyes of a yogin's experience. When it is stated that "dependent origination is itself emptiness," it means that such existence and such non-existence, or confusion and enlightenment, are tied together directly as being one and the same. The statement "dependent origination is itself emptiness," which expresses Nāgārjuna's basic standpoint, points to enlightenment or the realization in which one sees no self-nature—that is, emptiness in the midst of a world which exists as originating dependently. Consequently, it can be said that the principle underlying the statement, "dependent origination is itself emptiness" is the model and principle for maxims such as "bewilderment/affliction is itself the awakened state" or "birth-and-death (*saṃsāra*) is identical to nirvāṇa." The same ideas are expressed in the *Vimalakīrtinirdeśa-sūtra* as ". . . released in liberation without abandoning afflictions . . ."[13] or "when the bodhisattva follows the wrong way, he follows the way to attain the qualities of the Buddha."[14] However, the fact that affliction is liberation or that birth-and-death is identical to nirvāṇa is not so clearly evident to us. Expressions like these that link together opposites seem to be illogical and meaningless or seem even to speak blasphemous of the superiority of nirvāṇa and enlightenment. At best, they might be accepted as particular expressions of mystical intuition.

Nāgārjuna attempted to give these maxims a logical foundation on the basis of his realization of emptiness in dependent origination. Dependent origination is the fundamental principle of the Buddha's teachings and, at the same time, it is a theory that explains the real aspects of the world of bewilderment and afflictions. Emptiness, on the other hand, is the principle of negation (negating both affliction and liberation) that affirms the middle path through negation. These two, dependent origination and emptiness, are linked and mediated by no self-nature. That emptiness affirms the middle path, that is, enlightenment, means that both saṃsāra and nirvāṇa are empty, and as discussed earlier in the context of "not dwelling in nirvāṇa," one becomes freed from attachments to both saṃsāra and nirvāṇa by realizing this. Both saṃsāra and nirvāṇa, referred to in the maxim "saṃsāra is identical to nirvāṇa," are empty, because both have no self-nature. They are identical only because they are mediated by no self-nature. The term "identical" in the maxim does not mean that two opposite and contradictory things are directly, intuitively, or immediately (without intermediary) identical. It means that they are identical because their essential nature is the same in that both are characterized as having "no self-nature." In the realization that saṃsāra is empty and that nirvāṇa is also empty, the two become identical. In other words, in order to be identical, no self-nature must intervene—that is, the logic of śūnyatā must function as their mediator. Therefore, the maxim "saṃsāra is identical to nirvāṇa" is modeled after the statement, "dependent origination is emptiness." The term "identical" indicates the realization of emptiness as detected in the context of dependent origination.

However, it is also true that bewilderment is, in every respect, bewilderment and not enlightenment and that enlightenment is never bewilderment. Bewilderment and enlightenment are absolutely worlds apart. It would be wrong to force theses two into one. In relationship to this idea, Nāgārjuna and later Mādhyamikas in particular have discussed a theory known as the Twofold truth. The two truths refer to the conventional truth and the ultimate truth. Conventional truth refers to ordinary truth established by the logic and concept common in the mundane and public world. Ultimate truth refers to truth that is revealed when the logic and concept of the ordinary, common, mundane, and public world has been transcended. It is truth that is "inexpressible" through ordinary language and that is "inconceivable" by ordinary logic. Conventional truth is truth no doubt, but seen from the perspective of this ultimate truth, it is a truth with limitations, a truth of a lower degree, and in the final analysis, it must be said to be false. To that degree, the ultimate truth negates ordinary concepts and logic and is closely aligned to emptiness. Conventional truth, in contrast, belongs to the world of existence that is at the basis of bewilderment and affliction. However, the Twofold truth was established not as an ontological theory in which existence was classified as belonging to the conventional truth and emptiness, its negation, to the ultimate truth; it is traditionally understood to be established with regard to elucidating the Buddha's teaching. Therefore, we can understand the Twofold truth as being more logical than ontological.

The unique characteristic of the two truths is not only that they are opposite to each other as perverted and correct, false and true, but also that conventional truth can never become the ultimate truth and that the ultimate truth always transcends the conventional truth. In our earlier discussion on dependent origination and emptiness, we observed that, in spite of the fact that an opposition of affirmation and negation was implied between them, dependent origination was itself seen as emptiness ("dependently originating hence emptiness"); their relationship was understood in terms of continuity. In contrast, in the context of the two truths, no matter how high conventional truth may ascend, it can never become the ultimate truth; there is no continuity between them and they are completely severed from each other. Although we can infer logically and conceptually what the enlightenment of the Buddha was, we cannot reach its true essence from such an inference. Whatever it may be that is grasped and conceptualized as the real, it remains always within the boundary of the conventional and the ultimate truth is always one step removed. The terms, "unattainable," "inconceivable," and so forth show a kind of agnosticism in denoting the ultimate truth in such a manner. The fact that Vimalakīrti held a "noble silence" without speaking a word in regard to the ultimate truth is understandable when viewed from the standpoint of the Twofold truth. In other words, no matter how much we may stack up or elevate our conventional world or our samsaric and cyclic existence, it will never reach the world of the ultimate truth. The motive for setting up the Twofold truth seems to have been mainly to emphasize this absolute separation and noncontinuity.

The result of this is that it is not possible to claim "birth-and-death is identical to nirvāṇa." It was owing to the direct perception of the yoga practitioner that the enlightenment that "birth-and-death is identical nirvāṇa" was uncovered; however, in so far as that enlightenment is drawn back into our own logical thinking, birth-and-death cannot be, at once, nirvāṇa. Herein lies the complex problems of the relationship between logic and enlightenment and between our consciousness or will and the ultimate nirvāṇa. The theory of the Twofold truth reveals this absolute separation and suggest a response to how one might or might not overcome such a separation. Nāgārjuna's introduction of the logic of negation served to solve these problems. Emptiness,originally intuitively experienced, is formulated logically by him, and this can be called, in a broad sense, "the dialectic of emptiness."

Nāgārjuna clarified the logic of *niḥsvabhāva* (no self-nature) of all things that functioned in the previous discussion as a mediator for making opposites "identical." The process of his reasoning is exemplified by the so-called catuṣkoṭi (*tetralemma,* four alternative propositions), by which he directed his negation to the earlier Abhidharmic realism. Catuṣkoṭi consists of any four alternative propositions such as, for example, "exists," "does not exist," "both exists and does not exist," and "neither exists nor does not exist." It is observed that the existence of all things is summed up and represented by these four propositions and that, dialectically speaking, there is no other possibility. Nāgārjuna's argument consists of probing into whether each proposition can stand on its own. Through this examination, he attempts to point out that if a proposition is stated with a belief in a "self-nature," that is, if it is based on a substantive realistic view, it necessarily falls into a contradiction of antinomy and cannot stand on its own. Therefore he concludes that if a proposition is to be established, it must have "no self-nature," that is, it must be empty.

"Origination" is a quality of existence. In the first chapter of the *Mūlamadhyamaka-kārikā,* Nāgārjuna points out by means of the tetralemma that "origination" cannot be established if one takes the standpoint of realism. That is, "to originate" means that something originates from itself, or from something other, or from both itself and other, or without a cause. This can be understood from the view that the cause and its result are either the same or different. In brief, if it is claimed that something originates from "itself," this would result in a contradiction of antinomy, because when something originates from itself, there would be no need for it to originate as it already exists; or otherwise, a thing would be continuously originating without end. If something is said to originate from "something other," then something different like fire would originate from something other like water; or otherwise, all things would arise from all other things.

If something originates from "both itself and something other," then the difficulties involved in the above cases would only be compounded. If something originates "without a cause," then everything would originate at all times and everywhere. Thus, it can be seen that the origination of a thing cannot be established on the basis of any one of the four propositions.

Thus, in the manner mentioned above, the realistic way of thinking was negated by Nāgārjuna. What is negated here, however, is not the fact of origination, but the fact that, so long as "origination" is claimed as a reality having its own "self-nature," it cannot originate from itself or from something other. Instead, when it has "no self-nature," that is, when the belief in a substantive "self" is negated and all is empty—then every instance of origination is established just-as-it-is.

The reason that Nāgārjuna fully employed such a logic was to lead us to the horizon of our world as empty. However, preceding this logic and hidden deep within it are his direct perception and experience of emptiness. It is not that emptiness could be reached through logic. Rather, on the contrary, logic flowed out from that emptiness. Consequently, the logic that leads one to emptiness, be it the tetralemma or for that matter any other form, must be empty; the logic of emptiness is not to be grasped as a reality having a nature of its own. Logic belongs to the domain of conventions and the ultimate reality is always beyond that. Although Nāgārjuna argues freely using the tetralemma and other forms of logic, he does not take his stand on logic, but his logic is one that melts and dissolves into emptiness. In his *Vigrahavyāvartanī,* Nāgārjuna clearly states: "I have no position."[15] He does not attempt to assert, claim, or prove something by means of logical propositions. For those who are versed in realism and in logic, this may seem strange; however, in the Mādhyamika where everything including logic is seen as empty one cannot make a case for the substantiation of a logical claim. Logic is empty and only in so far as it is empty can it be established. The Mādhyamika position, if one may speak of such, can be understood as a position only in so far as even the assertion of emptiness vanishes. It is a position of no position that has wiped out all basis and that transcends both logic and notions.

But it is owing to such a position on emptiness and it is only within such a context that language can be revived and become truly logical. This is said to be the recovery of the conventional. Recovery of the conventional means that, through the realization of emptiness and the ultimate truth, the conventional is revived and becomes meaningful just-as-it-is. Although Nāgārjuna, for the most part, directs his discussion in the *Mūlamadhyamakakārikā* to the negation of the conventional he addresses the recovery of the conventional particularly in chapter XXIV when, in response to his opponents criticism that "if everything is empty, then logic, teaching, and practice would become meaningless,'' he answers that logic, teaching, and practice are truly possible because they are empty.

Śūnya (empty) is not simply a refutation or negation; through it the conventional finds it raison d'être in its manner of existence, its meaning, and its function. This is why it is said ''truly empty, [hence] unfathomable existence.'' Even the Buddha's teachings such as the five psycho-physical constituents (*pañca-skandha*), the four noble truths, and so forth cannot constitute a true teaching so long as they are thought to have a nature of their own and to be realistic. The same can be said of the path of practice. In the negation of the path as a path, the path becomes truly practiced for the first time. Although in the context of the Twofold truth, the ultimate truth was absolutely separate from the conventional and was transcendent, it was for that very reason that the conventional could remain as the conventional. In the later Mādhyamika school, the term ''saṃvṛti-mātra'' (convention only or nothing but convention) came to be used, probably because of Yogācāra vijñapti-mātra influence. The deeper one's realization that only the ultimate truth is the highest, unique reality, the more one becomes aware that the world that remains is ''nothing but convention.'' One realizes that it is ''a world full of deception and nothing but falsehood.'' On the one hand, the Twofold truth theory points to the severance from and the noncontinuity with the ultimate truth, but on the other hand, it is the horizon on which the conventional is recovered, admitted, and given a place in its own right.

VI The Three-Nature Theory of the Yogācāra School

It was the Yogācāra-Vijñānavāda School that advanced this recovery of the conventional (or the tendency towards *saṃvṛti-mātra* of the Madhyamaka) even further. This School inherited Nāgārjuna's Madhyamaka thought and reached its peak around the fourth to fifth centuries with the advent of Asaṅga and Vasubandhu. This did not mean simply that the thoughts of this school were heightened but it also meant that the philosophy of Mahāyāna Buddhism was brought to completion.

It seems that, as they attached special importance to Buddhist praxis, they gained the name Yogācāra. In contrast to praxis, however, they also had a highly developed system of theoretical investigation and they maintained two theories—namely, the cognition theory and the three-nature theory. It is from the perspective of the first theory that, by elaborating the theory of cognition, the principle of ''representation-only'' (*vijñapti-mātra*) is established and consequently this school is also called the ''Cognition School'' (*vijñāna-vāda*). When the question of ontology is at issue, it may seem that the central theme of this school would be the theory of representation-only (or cognition-only) wherein only cognition exists and the external world is non-existent, but such an ontological idea belongs rather to a little later period. As the foundation for the theory of cognition, this school has the three-nature theory that is much closer to ontological thought and which, though original to this school, has carried on the tradition of the śūnyatā thought of the earlier period. Consequently, the discussion to follow will focus on the three-nature theory rather than on the theory of cognition.

The three-nature theory, however, does not represent only a purely ontological theory, for it is intertwined with a theory of cognition or perception on the one hand, and on the other, it is the object of contemplation, that is, the theory of yogic praxis. This is just like the case of śūnyatā in which śūnyatā was, on the one hand, the object of mediation and, on the other, a principle of logic developed by Nāgārjuna.

The three-nature theory demonstrates that the world has three natures (*tri-svabhāva*) or three aspects or three characteristics. The three natures refer to the "imagined or conceptualized" (*parikalpita*) nature, the "other dependent" (*paratantra*) nature, and the "consummated" (*parinișpanna*) nature. These three do not represent three distinct territories of the world. They refer to the fact that the world is characterized as being completely "imagined" at one time, as an "other-dependent" existence at another time, and as a "consummated" world at still another time. The former situation constitutes the world of bewilderment/affliction, the latter one, the world of enlightenment, and there is the world of the "other-dependent" that mediates between the two.

When the world is described as "(falsely) imagined," this description is made from an epistemological standpoint, because it is a prescription based on human knowledge or recognition that always contain an element of error. The world of bewilderment/affliction is a world filled with ignorance and error in regard to the recognition of the truth. Understood from this perspective, it is natural that this school showed great interest in the investigation and accomplishment of a theory of cognition. This theory of cognition became the object of yogic introspection for a yogin when he contemplated on his mind and consciousness.

The consummated world, in contrast, refers to a "world that becomes manifest" as a result of a yogin's perfection of his yoga praxis. It is not that the consummated world lies dormant somewhere from the beginning, but the world is something that is to be consummated by praxis. A beautifully blooming flower may be misunderstood and falsely imagined in many ways by the ordinary person, but when seen by a sage, that very same flower materializes in a world of a consummated flower. This consummation is the objective for which Buddhism aims and since it is perfected through yoga praxis it is said to be very "practical."

In contrast to these two—the cognitive world and the practical—the "other-dependent" is said to be "ontological," because things exist solely by virtue of "depending on others" and not substantively. This other-dependent world signifies none other than the world of dependent origination taught by the Buddha. Just as dependent origination is the logical foundation for Buddha's teaching, so too, the other-dependent is central to and at the foundation of the three-nature theory. The world as the imagined and the consummated are two worlds that come into view on the basis of the "other-dependent." With the other-dependent as the basis, an imagined world of bewilderment/affliction makes its appearance on the one hand and on the other hand, it converts into the world of enlightenment.

"Cognition" (*vijñāna*) explained in the theory of cognition, has the nature of being other-dependent and it represents a "dependently originating" world. Here, everything, the seer and the seen, exist in an "dependently originating" way. However, human's cognitive functions do not remain long on the peak of a purely dependently originating world, but, just as a carriage on the peak of a hill will naturally roll down, so, too, the cognitive functions are inclined to fall astray in that they have a tendency to attribute the quality of the absolute upon themselves. That is, the *seeing* self attributes the quality of the absolute upon itself and the *thing* seen is seen as something absolute. Here the imagined world makes its appearance. Thus, by virtue of clinging to what is imagined as the substantive real, the imagined world, that is a falsified world, becomes established with the genuine dependently originating world as its basis. If this belief of taking the world as substantively real were wiped out, and the other-dependent were revived in its pure "other-dependent" state, then it would be a pure world. That is, the consummated world would be revealed.

In this manner, the convertibility from bewilderment/affliction to an awakened state becomes actualized on the basis of the "other-dependent." That bewilderment cannot become an awakened state immediately and directly is akin to the case that affliction cannot become *bodhi* immediately and directly as stated above. In spite of that, a conversion to the awakened state has to exist in some way or another. Indeed, it exists, and it is possible for ordinary beings to obtain it. The conversion becomes possible because the other-dependent nature intervenes and functions as its mediator. The imagined and bewildered world came into being originally when the other-dependent world, the foundation for the imagined world, was colored by false imagination. When the coloring is wiped away, the other-dependent world is recovered and this recovery is at once the establishment of the consummated world. Because it was the other-dependent nature that functioned as a mediator, the conversion from the other-dependent to the imagined reflects, at the same time, a conversion from the other-dependent to the consummated. The conversion of bewilderment/affliction to the awakened state is none other than the conversion of the other-dependent to the consummated. In this manner, the other-dependent mediates between bewilderment/affliction and the awakened state and it is the place in which the meaning of identical in the phrase "bewilderment/affliction is itself the awakened state" can be established.

This structure of the three-nature theory will be considered in relation to vijñāna, cognition or consciousness. Cognition, as stated above, essentially is of the nature of the "other-dependent." When the entire world is regarded to be represented by this vijñāna, it can be said that "the triple worlds are consciousness-only." Consciousness, however, is inclined always to turn into false imagination, just like the other-dependent nature has a tendency to fall down into the imagined nature. The possibility for removing the cognition of the imagined nature and for the presence of the fundamental nondiscriminative wisdom (*nirvikalpa-jñāna*) of the Buddha, that is, the cognition of the "consummated" nature, lies in the fact that cognition has the structure of the other-dependent nature and that everything is "consciousness-only."

Nondiscriminative wisdom, however, does not act; it is immovable. The wisdom that functions as the Buddha's activity—Buddha's wisdom that functions in this world—is the "wisdom acquired subsequently" (*pṛṣṭha-labdha-jñāna*). This wisdom is a discriminative but genuine (or pure) wisdom that is acquired subsequently to nondiscriminative knowledge and that can be characterized as the other-dependent but not as the consummated *or* as the imagined. This fact exhibits a case of a different kind of conversion, that is, the conversion in which the consummated converts back to the other-dependent. It is in this revival of the other-dependent—that is, in the wisdom acquired subsequently—that "consciousness-only" is truly established in terms of "representation-only" (*vijñapti-mātratā*). The "consciousness-only" referred to above, is not yet the ultimate truth. The ultimate truth of representation-only does not become manifest simply by eliminating false imagination, because it is not unusual that the other-dependent becomes an object of even the imagining cognition of ordinary people and the other-dependent cannot be truly the other-dependent without penetrating into the consummate and returning from it. Likewise, without penetrating into nondiscriminative wisdom, consciousness-only also cannot become the ultimate truth of representation-only.

However, there is a difference between the significance of the Buddha's wisdom and the three-nature theory. The other-dependent nature is the basis for all the three natures, and accordingly, for the entire world. But this does not mean that the Buddha's wisdom that is acquired subsequently to non-discriminative wisdom is likewise the basis for all things in the world, because the Buddha's wisdom is no longer oriented towards the imagined world. In contrast, *vijñāna,* as a cognitive function of human beings, is of the nature of other-dependent and serves as the foundation for both delusion and enlightenment; consequently, it serves as a mediator between bewilderment and the awakened state. This is what the three-nature theory explicates.

From the discussion above, it should now be clear that in order for the theory of cognition to be completed it is necessary for it to be supported by the three-nature theory. That the three-nature theory had the other-dependent at its center and that this referred to the Buddha's teaching of "dependent origination" have been expressed repeatedly. Nāgārjuna started out from this teaching of dependent-origination and saw "emptiness" (*śūnyatā*) therein. In contrast, it may seem as if the three-nature theory is closely aligned with "existence" rather than with emptiness. However, the three-nature theory has the theory of "three non-natures" in its immediate background and it is therein that emptiness can be seen.

The three-nature theory goes on to explain each one of the three natures in terms of "non-nature." The term "non-nature" is a translation for the term, *niḥ-svabhāva,* that appeared in the previous discussion on Nāgārjuna and that was translated "no self-nature" in that context. First, with regard to the "imagined" nature, there is "non-nature in reference to marks" (*lakṣaṇa-niḥsvabhāva*). Marks, forms, characteristics, and so forth are discriminated there, but, because they are products of imagination, they are said to have "no self-nature" and to be empty and nonexistent. Secondly, with regard to the "other-dependent" nature, there is "non-nature in reference to origination" (*utpatti-niḥsvabhāva*). This means that all is empty, because, as everything is dependent upon every other thing, nothing can originate on its own accord nor exist in and of itself. Lastly, with regard to the "consummated" nature, there is "non-nature in an ultimate sense" (*paramārtha-niḥsvabhāva*). This means that by negating the imagined world, emptiness which is ever present manifests itself. Schematically speaking, Nāgārjuna's statement, "dependent-origination is identical to emptiness" corresponds to what is meant by "non-nature in reference to origination" in the three-nature theory that can be paraphrased as the other dependent is empty in respect to its origination.

The three natures are not only affirmative and existential, but are also negative and empty. At the beginning of the *Madhyāntavibhāga* (I.1), it is explained that emptiness is seen in the context of cognition and that in emptiness, the same cognition is revived and seen; this same logic can be applied to the structure of the three-nature theory. The text goes on to explain the viewpoint of existence and nonexistence as follows:

> The ''imagined nature'' is always non-existent. The ''other-dependent'' is existent, but not as real reality. The ''consummated'' is both existent and non-existent in an ultimate sense.[16]

Seen in this light, the three-nature theory can be said to be an ontological theory. This is a very advanced ontological theory that combines both the dharma-theory of the Abhidharmic philosophy and the Mādhyamika philosophy of emptiness. This ontology is not promulgated from an interest in ontology per se, but is an ontology that brings about the perfection of yogic practices. It is an ontology for the sake of actualizing the awakened state. Motivated mainly by the three-nature theory, the Yogācāra school shed new light on and gave new meaning to problems of perennial principles such as dependent origination and the theory of cause and effect or to problems of yogic praxis such as the three learnings of morality, concentration, and wisdom. By the same principle, discussions concerning nirvāna and liberation, systematic explications on the Buddha-bodies, and other kinds of investigations were carried out by this school. Thus, the three-nature theory had the role of providing a logical basis for theoretical developments on the one hand, and on the other, it served as the object of meditation for the yoga practitioner. Consequently, the three-nature theory is a theory of ontology only in the sense expressed above.

The special characteristic of this ontology is that the three natures comprise a triadic system. In contrast, a bi-polar system is seen in Nāgārjuna's theory wherein ontology was established from the perspective of a tension between the two poles of dependent origination and emptiness. To that degree, dependent origination or the other-dependent nature in the three-nature theory may be slightly different from dependent origination expressed as one of the poles in Nāgārjuna's thought, because for Nāgārjuna the two poles are bewilderment/affliction and enlightenment (which roughly stand for dependent origination and emptiness, respectively), while in the three-nature theory, what corresponds to them are the ''imagined'' and the ''consummated'' natures and dependent origination, which can be equated to emptiness, intervenes between the two as the ''other-dependent'' nature. In this other-dependent nature, the tension between dependent origination and emptiness continues and is regarded as an axis around which the imagined world and the consummated world revolve and develop. Together with the other dependent that functions as their axis, the imagined and the consummated formulate a ''triadic system.'' The fact that the other-dependent possesses the two aspects (*dvaya-aṃśa*) of defilement and purity also shows that, as the third factor in the triad, the other dependent mediates between the two and becomes a basis for them.

With the passing of the Asaṅga-Vasubandhu era, the organic structure of this three-nature theory as well as the principle of convertibility between the three natures seemed to be soon forgotten though their concepts remained and became synonyms for delusion and the awakened state. Later Vijñānavādins put their efforts into explaining the theory of cognition rather than explicating the three-nature theory. The result of this was a much more reinforced ontological theory whose claim was that "Only cognition exists; external reality does not exist." An expression similar to that can be found in the earlier Yogācāra treatises, but its contents is understood differently by the earlier Yogācāras and the later Vijñānavādins. The Yogācāras were hardly concerned with the problem of whether an external world existed or not in so far as they considered the question of an external reality to be a problem of the realist's ontology. When, as an object of passion, the outer world obstructed yogic practice, only then did the Yogācāras show their concern regarding it and deal with it. In other words, the outer world was taken into consideration as a problem only when it obstructed yogic practices; the Yogācāras did not show an interest in it as an object of ontological or metaphysical investigation. Therefore, the phrase, "The triple world is representation only (vijñapti-mātra)," is a phrase that describes one's attitude in interacting with the world; it is not a phrase that intends to prove or to determine objectively an absolute and ultimate existence.

In later times, however, in accordance with the change in scholarly interest and in the demands of the time, the Vijñānavādins endeavored mainly to develop their cognition theory and to maintain an ontological view that claimed that only cognition is the unique and ultimate existence. It cannot be denied that scholarly achievements in epistemology, ontology, polemics, and logic, were greatly advanced by their efforts; but, is it not the case that such a realism of mind-only that annihilates all other things is a derailment from the Buddhist standpoint?

A negation of the outer world stands in sharp contrast to the Abhidharmic realism of the dharmas. By transcending both negation and realism, Nāgārjuna was able to reach the new horizon of śūnyatā. This horizon reached by Nāgārjuna was accepted by the Yogācāras and thereby they took their stand on the middle path, but this did not mean that they simply struck a balance between the "existence" of cognition and the "non-existence" of the outer world. It would seem, therefore, that if an ontology of a Buddhist kind is to be considered seriously, then it would have to be based, not on an ontology of 'being'—that is, not in an ontic sense, but on transcending both existence and non-existence—that is, in the movement toward śūnyatā. In other words, ontology in a Buddhism context is not an ontology of 'being,' but that of śūnyatā.

Chapter 13

From Mādhyamika to Yogācāra: An Analysis of *MMK*, XXIV.18 and *MV*, I.1–2

In the Sino-Japanese Buddhist tradition, the Mādhyamika and Yogācāra-Vijñānavāda tenets have been understood to be both parallel and opposite to each other. The San-lun-tsung, the Chinese version of the Mādhyamika, was regarded as nihilistic or as Emptiness School, and the Fa-hsiang-tsung, the Vijñānavāda, was regarded as realistic or an Existence School. While the former was characterized as Mahāyāna due to its doctrine of emptiness, the latter was considered to be semi-Mahāyāna for three basic reasons: (1) the Vijñānavāda remained realistic like the Abhidharma School; (2) it elucidated the three yānas side by side without being confined to the Bodhisattvayāna; and (3) it did not emphasize the doctrine of Buddha-nature. These traditional but erroneous views have now been revised by modern scholars. Presently, the Madhyamaka philosophy, which began with Nāgārjuna, is believed to be wholly inherited by Maitreyanātha, Asaṅga, and other Yogācāras. The Prajñāpāramitā sūtras are equally revered as authentic by both schools, and further, the doctrine of emptiness occupies an important position even in the Yogācāra school.

While, in the history of Western philosophy, it was deemed necessary for a newcomer to negate and transcend previous philosophies through criticism, the situation in Buddhism, especially Yogācāra Buddhism, was such that it developed its doctrines in a fairly different pattern from that of Western philosophy. The Yogācāras developed their doctrines by inheriting the entire body of thought of their former masters. Of course, even though a faithful transmission of a teaching without any changes was intended, in so far as there was a development, this development necessarily involved a degree of change. Therefore, although both schools advocated the doctrines of 'śūnyatā,' the manner in which they interpreted the meaning of this term has been different. In accordance with the divergent views held by the schools as they grew in India and in China, there has been a difference in how they worded the doctrine and in how they logically developed it.

The verse XXIV.18 of Nāgārjuna's *Mūlamadhyamaka-kārikā* (hereafter, *MMK*)[1] has been famous in the Sino-Japanese tradition since the T'ien-t'ai school elaborated the doctrine called "Threefold Truth" and took this verse as one of its bases. The verse concludes with the term "madhyamā pratipat" (Middle Path), and hence the treatise was named "*Madhyamaka-kārikā*." On the other hand, there is a treatise of the Yogācāras named "*Madhyāntavibhāga*" (hereafter, *MV*). The root verses of this text have been ascribed to Maitreyanātha or Asaṅga and the prose commentary (*bhāṣya*) has been attributed to Vasubandhu. The features of the first two verses, *MV,* I.1–2,[2] closely resemble those in verse XXIV.18 of *MMK*. In this paper, I would like to examine all three verses in the hope that I can trace an aspect of the development of Buddhist philosophy from Mādhyamika to Yogācāra.

It seems that T. R. V. Murti was also aware of this similarity.[3] After pointing out that the Abhidharmic systems interpreted *pratītya-samutpāda* (originating co-dependently) incorrectly and arguing that the Mādhyamika system was a reinterpretation of it as *śūnyatā,* he refers to *MMK,* XXIV.18. He then explains the Vijñānavāda position by saying, "In the Vijñānavāda, *śūnyatā* is accepted, but with a modification," and quotes *MV.* I.1 as the Vijñānavāda formula. He should, however, have included *MV,* I.2 in the formula, because the two verses together not only represent the basic tenet contained in the first chapter of *MV,* but also the fundamental point of view that the treatise is attempting to express.

At the outset, let us examine in detail *MMK,* XXIV.18. The verse in Sanskrit is as follows:

> yaḥ pratītyasamutpādaḥ śūnyataṃ tāṃ pracakṣmahe /
> sa prajñaptir upādāya pratipat saiva madhyamā / /

This can be rendered in English as follows:

> What is originating co-dependently, we call emptiness.
> It is a designation based upon (some material). Only this
> is the Middle Path.[4]

In this verse we see four key terms: "pratītya-samutpāda" (originating co-dependently), "śūnyatā" (emptiness), "upādāya-prajñapti" (designation based on some material), and "madhyamā pratipat" (Middle Path). Generally, these four are associated with each other and in some way considered equal. According to Candrakīrti's explanation, śūnyatā, upādāya-prajñapti and madhyamā-pratipad are considered to be "different names" (*viśeṣa-saṃjñā*, synonyms)[5] of pratītya-samutpāda. Of these four terms, however, the last three (omitting the first, *pratītya-samutpāda*), were taken by the T'ien-t'ai school to constitute the so-called Threefold Truth: the truth of the empty (*k'ung*) the provisional (*chia*), and the middle (*chung*).[6]

As the context of the verse and Candrakīrti's "viśeṣa-saṃjñā" suggest, these three or four terms are regarded as reciprocally identical and simultaneous, but not in chronological sequence. Especially in the T'ien-t'ai doctrine, the ultimate and perfect identity of the three is emphasized. It is true that there is no chronological sequence of the four terms, but neither is it permitted to rearrange them and state them in reverse order; there must be something that led the author to select the four terms and mention them in this particular sequence. I believe this something can be called the author's "logic," and consequently the four terms are in logical order, being linked to each other through a process of reasoning.

Now, to begin with, all interpretations are in agreement with the fact that what is originating co-dependently is empty, or nonexistent. In other words, codependent origination is characterized by emptiness. This is, as Murti puts it, a reinterpretation of *pratītya-samutpāda* in contradistinction to the Abhidharmic interpretation, which understands it from a realistic viewpoint, taking it to be existent. This reinterpretation is revolutionary, because pratītya-samutpāda, which had been conceived of in terms of something real, existent and affirmative is now declared to be empty, nonexistent, and negative. In order to give a logical rationale for this process, Candrakīrti (as well as Buddhapālita and Bhāvaviveka) introduced the phrase: "Because it is devoid of self-being (*niḥsvabhāva*) it is empty."[7] Here, existence and nonexistence or affirmation and negation are combined into one. This indicates the dynamism or paradox spoken about in Mahāyāna texts. It differs from the static idea of the Abhidharmic systems and corresponds to what the Prajñāpāramitā-sūtras expounded in the formula: "rūpam eva śūnyatā" (this very matter is the essence of emptiness).

Next, the verse states that śūnyatā in this context is "upādāya-prajñapti," or "a designation based upon (some material)." Although the compound upādāya-prajñapti is problematic, and scholars have interpreted it differently,[8] it is safe to assume that it can be interpreted as: "upādānam upādāya prajñapti."[9] In this case, upādāna means: "material as cause"; upādāya (an absolutive) literally means: "having taken to one-self," "appropriating" and therefore, I have translated it "based upon," which is an interpretation also substantiated by the Tibetan translation *brten nas* (depending on). Prajñapti (Tib. *gdags pa*) or "designation" is of a worldly or conventional character, being opposite to paramārtha, which is supramundane, and beyond any conceptualizations. Thus, the phrase as a whole means: "a designation based upon (some material)."

Jaques May translates the compound upādāya-prajñapti as "désignation métaphorique" (he seems to prefer this translation to L. de La Vallée Poussin's "désignation en raison de"), and, after equating "śūnyatā equals upādāya-prajñapti," he gives the following explanation: "La śūnyatā est désignation métaphorique de la réalité absolue." And also equating "śūnyatā equals madhyamā-pratipad" in regard to the fourth pada, he gives a similar interpretation: "Madhyamā pratipad est aussi une désignation métaphorique de la réalité absolue. . . ."[10]

His interpretations would indicate that absolute reality manifests itself on the level of conventional truth, metaphorically taking the names śūnyatā or madhyamā-pratipad. If this be the case, these explanations seem not to coincide with the two equations mentioned by him, and also seem to disregard the positive role played by upādāya-prajñapti as the third key term. As he explains, any concepts, names or designations, are conventional; they are not on the level of ultimate truth and cannot represent the ultimate reality, which remains silent (*tūṣṇīṃ-bhāva*), beyond all grasping (*anupalabdhi, anabhilāpya*). This is the truth revealed by Nārārjuna in terms of the Twofold Truth (*satya-dvaya*), the conventional and the ultimate. But, I believe, the present verse is not intended to discuss the Twofold Truth; rather it expresses a logical process starting from the Buddha's pratītya-samutpāda and concluding with the Buddha's Middle Path. In this process, upādāya-prajñapti occupies an important stage.

Venkata Ramanan translates upādāya-prajñapti as "derived name," although he does not clarify how and from what the name is derived. He states, however, "the [meaning of] relativity, conditionedness (partītya-samutpāda) . . . is also conveyed by upādāya-prajñapti, derived name."[11]

It is my contention that upādāya-prajñapti is another name for pratītya-samutpāda. In a passage, Candrakīrti states: "[Those foolish people] do not see the truth of *pratītya-samutpāda* which has the most profound meaning, being free from [the wrong views of] eternalism and nihilism, and being given the name *upādāya-prajñapti*."[12] This indicates that upādāya-prajñapti and pratītya-samutpāda are synonymous.

According to Avalokitavrata's explanation of the phrase upādānam upādāya prajñaptiḥ,[13] the word *upādāna* (material cause) means "hetu-pratyaya" (cause and condition): a sprout is so named based upon a seed, its upādāna; Tathāgata is so designated based upon the virtues such as the ten powers, the four convictions, and as His upādāna. Being thus designated as based upon causes and conditions, not only the sprout but also Tathāgata is empty, devoid of self-being. It is clear that Avalokitravrata interprets upādāya-prajñapti with the meaning of pratītya-samutpāda.

However, the compound upādāya-prajñapti, although similar to pratītya-samutpāda of the first pada, should still be different from it for the reason that, in the second pada, pratītya-samutpāda has been negated and declared as śūnyatā. In the third pada, in contrast to this, upādāya-prajñapti is pratītya-samutpāda revived from within śūnyatā after having been once negated. In other words, the world of pratītya-samutpāda, in so far as it has been negated or has a negative aspect (first and second padas), is śūnyatā. But, in spite of this negation, in so far as the ultimate reality does not cease to manifest itself as upādāya-prajñapti (third pada), pratītya-samutpāda is operative and functioning in the saṃsāric world, and therefore, still alive. Without this aliveness or the revival from śūnyatā, even madhyamā pratipat could not be established. The Middle Path *is* a dynamic path and not a mere cessation or extinction as expressed by the "Hīnayānic" nirvāṇa (of course, I do not intend "Hīnayānic" to refer to Theravāda). One of the meanings of "Mahāyānic" nirvāṇa is the Bodhisattva's *apratiṣṭhita-nirvāṇa* (not dwelling in nirvāṇa).

Such a revived pratītya-samutpāda is a "designation" (*prajñapti*) for it appropriates, depends upon, or bases itself upon (*upādāya*) something else, or some kind of material (*upādāna*). In this sense, it is synonymous with *saṃketa* (conventional symbol) and *loka-vyavahāra* (common practice), terminologies used to designate conventional truth. Thus upādāya-prajñapti means "a designation based upon some material." Because it comes after the negation of śūnyatā, it is a knowledge gained by a sort of bodhi enlightenment. It can also involve the Buddha's *laukika-pṛṣṭhalabdha-jñāna* (conventional knowledge functioning after nondiscriminative knowledge is obtained), to use the later Yogācāra terminology.

To recapitulate, pratītya-samutpāda is twofold:

1. the first order pratītya-samutpāda as expounded in the first pada of the verse, and
2. The second order pratītya-samutpāda (equals upādāya-prajñapti) as expounded in the third pada.

The first order pratītya-samutpāda is said to be "direct," because it has not yet been denied and represents the ordinary worldly life that is not yet negated as śūnyatā. In other words, people are living it without any awareness of its true nature as śūnyatā. This pratītya-samutpāda dies in the second pada. In spite of its death, or its negation, worldly life necessarily continues, but now it is accompanied by a kind of śūnya consciousness. The third pada represents this stage, in which the second order pratītya-samutpāda is revived.

This second order or revived pratītya-samutpāda is said to be "indirect," because it has come through śūnyatā and consequently was not derived directly from the first order. In contrast to the first order, which must be negated, and which corresponds to the word rūpa of "rūpam eva śūnyatā," the second order is a reaffirmed pratītya-samutpāda that corresponds to the word rūpa of "śūnyataiva rūpam" (this very essence of emptiness is matter). Although the first order pratītya-samutpāda must be negated, there still is a need for "a life" in which people can strive to live a moral life or can make every effort to exert themselves in religious practices.

Finally, the fourth pada states: "Only this is the Middle Path." The Middle is always revealed by being freed from two extremes, such as existence and nonexistence, or affirmation and negation. The dynamic movement from the first order pratītya-samutpāda of the first pada, to its negation (*śūnyatā*) in the second pada, and further to its revival as the second order pratītya-samutpāda (equals upādāya-prajñapti) in the third pada is the Middle Path (*madhyamā-pratipad*). It is dialectical, moving from affirmation to negation and again to affirmation. The Middle is not a point between two extremes and cannot be found at a certain point, because the path is a total process, dynamic, and dialectical. (The Middle can be found even in the extremes in so far as affirmation is negation and negation is affirmation.)

To conclude this section, the four terms explained above can be equated in a straight line:

pratītya-samutpāda = śūnyatā
= upādāya-prajñapti
= madhyamā-pratipad

But from the above discussion and from the dialectical character of the whole process, I would rather equate them in the following way:

pratītya-samutpāda (affirmative) = *śūnyatā* (negative)

[*śūnyatā* =] *upādāya-prajñapti* (*affirmative*)

= *madhyamā-pratipad*

The equation of pratītya-samutpāda equals śūnyatā is the most basic: all others are derived from it. Any one of these terms can be equated with madhyamā-pratipad, but only through the whole process of negation and affirmation as discussed above.

Having examined *MMK,* XXIV.18, we are now in a position to analyze the two verses of *MV* that elucidate the notions of abhūta-parikalpa, śūnyatā, and madhyamā-pratipad. In Sanskrit, verses I.1–2 read as follows:

> abhūtaparikalpo 'sti, dvayaṃ tatra na vidyate /
> śūnyatā vidyate tv atra, tasyām api sa vidyate / I.1 /
> na śūnyaṃ nāpi cāśūnyaṃ tasmāt sarvaṃ vidhīyate /
> sattvād asattvāt sattvāc ca, madhyamā pratipac ca sā / I.2 /

This can be rendered in English as follows:

> There exists unreal imagination; duality does not exist therein
> Emptiness, however, exists in it, and also the former exists in the later. (I.1)
> Therefore it is stated that all entities are neither empty nor non-empty
> Because of existence, because of non-existence, and again because of existence. And this is the Middle Path. (I.2)[14]

The word "imagination" (*parikalpa*) generally refers to cognitive functions or consciousness (*vijñāna*), which in turn is characterized by the Yogācāras as "dependent-on-other" (*paratantra*), that is, *pratītya-samutpāda.* Basically speaking, the cognitive functions or thought of ordinary people is always stained by ignorance, hence the word "unreal" (*abhūta*). The phrase "there exists unreal imagination" (the first pada), however, does not mean that existence (of the imagination) is proclaimed or insisted in a metaphysical or ontological sense. It simply describes the fact that all the common features of daily life are constituted by cognitive functions. Thus, the fact that "unreal imagination exists" is the beginning point of the Yogācāra's Weltanschauung. "Duality" (*dvaya*) means the duality of subject and object. Although, on the one hand, cognition necessarily implies a dichotomy, on the other hand, from the viewpoint of ultimate truth, neither the object grasped nor the grasping subject has substantive existence. Therefore, "duality does not exist therein" (the second pada), that is, duality does not exist as substantial reality to be found in unreal imagination. This negation of duality, or the absence of cognition with regard to duality, is restated in the third pada, employing the term śūnyatā: "Emptiness, however, exists in it (i.e., in unreal imagination).'' Because śūnyatā is found in unreal imagination, unreal imagination is negated and, therefore, equal to śūnyatā itself. Thus far, the verse conveys a meaning similar to the equation pratītya-samutpāda equals śūnyatā in the *MMK*. In the fourth pada, however, the opposite is also true: ''the former [unreal imagination] exists in the latter [in emptiness].'' The phrase is important in that it means the revival of unreal imagination (or pratītya-samutpāda) and corresponds to upādāya-prajñapti of the *MMK*.

Next, in accordance with the above statement, verse I.2 reads: ''Therefore . . . all entities are neither empty nor nonempty.'' The reason for this is explained by three phrases beginning with ''because of.'' According to Vasubandhu's *Bhāṣya*, the first phrase, ''because of existence'' means ''because unreal imagination exists,'' and refers to the statement, ''neither empty.'' The second phrase, ''because of non-existence,'' meaning ''because duality does not exist,'' refers to the statement, ''nor non-empty.'' The third phrase, ''again because of existence,'' meaning ''because emptiness exists in unreal imagination and unreal imagination exists in emptiness,'' refers to the statement, ''neither empty.''

The verse concludes with the statement, ''This is the Middle Path.'' In this sense, the two verses clearly indicate that the *MV*, whose title was originally ''*Madhya-vibhāga'' (instead of Madhyānta-vibhāga*),[15] was originally written to elucidate the Middle Path and to exemplify that very fact by discussing the emptiness of unreal imagination.

When one compares verse XXIV.18 of the *MMK* with these two verse of *MV*, the similarity between them should now become obvious. The reason why Murti should have given both verses as the Yogācāra formula should also be clear. As stated previously, these two verses of *MV* are key verses of this text and convey the fundamental idea of the Yogācāra school. And one can see that the Yogācāras, indeed, inherited the ideas of emptiness and the Middle Path from Nāgārjuna. It is almost as if Maitreya-nātha or Asaṅga imitated, elaborated and expanded Nāgārjuna's verse. An analysis of these two verses will not only help us to understand Buddhist thought, but will also demonstrate how these ideas progressed in the development of Buddhist thought from Mādhyamika to Yogācāra.

Now that we have discussed the MMK verse and the two verses of *MV* individually, I would like to devote the remainder of this paper to a comparative study of the similarities and differences between the *MMK* verse and the two verses of *MV*. The corresponding padas of these verses and the relationship of them can be diagrammed as follows (the four padas are indicated by the letters: a, b, c, and d, respectively):

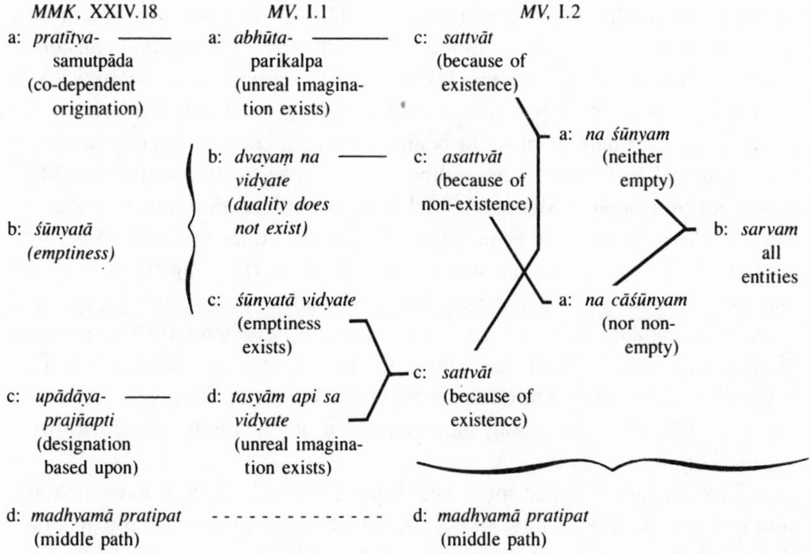

As the figure suggests, the point of departure for the two schools differs. *MMK,* XXIV.18a begins its discussion with *pratītya-samutpāda,* whereas *MV,* I.1a begins its discussion with *abhūtaparikalpa.* The different topics with which the two texts begin reflect the fact that, while the discussions found in the *MMK* are always metaphysical and abstract, dealing with such notions as *pratītya-samutpāda, utpatti* (arising), *gamana* (going) and so on, the author of *MV* replaced these notions with ones such as *citta* (mind), *vijñāna* (consciousness), and *abhūtaparikalpa* (unreal imagination), which are more concrete, practical, and related to everyday life situations. But, abhūtaparikalpa, which is essentially vijñāna, is not contextually different from pratītya-samutpāda, because it also has the nature of paratantra (dependent-on-other), as stated before. Therefore, even though abhūtaparikalpa is a term deeply associated with a monk's yogic practices, in so far as it is of paratantra nature and is taken as the starting point or the primary object of investigation, abhūtaparikalpa does not differ from pratītya-samutpāda, where the Mādhyamikas begin their investigation.

Whereas *MMK,* XXIV.18b simply and directly informs us that pratītya-samutpāda is śūnyatā, without elaborating its logical process, *MV,* I.1 gives a fuller explanation and develops its view round a more complicated logical process. Here śūnyatā is discussed from two points of view: non-existence (of duality) and existence (of śūnyatā). The discussion extends its logical argument into *MV,* I.2 as the diagram indicates. At first, the śūnyatā established by negating the "duality" of subject and object may seem far removed from the "emptiness" of the *MMK*. When one considers, however, that the author of the *MV* wanted to demonstrate the śūnyatā of abhūtaparikalpa, which is characterized as "pratītya-samutpāda" and is the most logical and natural place to begin one's reflection in yogic practice, it is not unusual to find that the author of *MV* chose to negate the "duality" of subject and object. Moreover, it should be noticed that not only the object but also the subject is negated. The later Vijñānavāda is sometimes referred to as a school in which the outer world (object) is negated (*bāhyārthābhāva*) and only the existence of inner consciousness (subject) is maintained (*vijñānamātra*).[16] But this is not the case here. By the negation of both subject and object the śūnyatā of the whole world is intended. This is parallel to the statement often found in the Mahāyāna sūtras, "all entities are empty," and to the Mādhyamika equation of the whole world (*pratītya-samutpāda*) with śūnyatā.

This śūnyatā is not a mere negation; it transcends both existence and nonexistence. Consequently, *MMK* (XXII.11) states: "one should not proclaim something as empty, nor non-empty." *MV,* I.2, however, gives us a more elaborate explanation. It first states that "all entities are neither empty nor non-empty" and then continues to explain this statement on the basis of three reasons: existence, nonexistence, and existence. On the foundation of such a paradoxical statement, the *MV* finally develops its thought into the Middle Path.

Undoubtedly, the three reasons beginning with "because of existence" are reasons expounding different levels. The first two, "because of existence" and "because of non-existence" that are obviously paradoxical and on the same level represent affirmation and negation respectively. The third reason, "again because of existence," must be understood to transcend the former two and, therefore, to be different from the first, in spite of the fact that the first and the third reasons are worded in the same way. The meaning of existence in the third reason is twofold: (1) it includes the existence of śūnyatā and (2) the existence of unreal imagination.

Śūnyatā was originally characterized by negation and nonbeing. Therefore the "existence of śūnyatā" is itself a contradiction and this has been the focus of attack by Bhāvaviveka, the Madhyamaka polemicist. The Yogācāra teachers, however, aware of this contradiction, dared to define śūnyatā as "non-existence of the duality and existence of [that] non-existence" (*MV,* I.13). Śūnyatā is thus simultaneously nonexistent as well as existent.

As for the "existence of unreal imagination," it corresponds to the second order pratītya-samutpāda. As I have shown in my previous discussion, pratītya-samutpāda is once negated as śūnyatā, but revived again in the term upādāya-prajñapti (*MMK,* XXIV. 18c). But *MV* does not stop with the statement that emptiness exists in unreal imagination; it goes on further to say that unreal imagination exists in emptiness: "also the former exists in the latter" (*tasyām api sa vidyate*). That is to say, abhūta-parikalpa (as paratantra is equal to pratītya-samutpāda) is revived in the midst of emptiness, as the second order abhūtaparikalpa, so to speak, after its duality is negated. It is in a sense a redeemed and justified abhūtaparikalpa. This revived abhūtaparikalpa is to be understood as contextually the same as "designation based upon (some material)" (*upādāya-prajñapti*).

In conclusion then, it is now clear that the zigzagging logic found in the *MMK*, XXIV.18, which develops its thought through the steps of affirmation (*pratītya-samutpāda*) to negation (*śūnyatā*) and further to affirmation again (*upādāya-prajñapti*) is followed exactly by the author of the *MV*, with the exception that the latter, using a little different wording, adds the logical basis for this dynamic process with statements such as "because of existence," and so on. By zigzagging logic I mean a paradoxical and dialectical logical process that evidences a dynamism continually moving from being to non-being and again to being, in which the former two are transcended. Both texts agree with each other in so far as they arrive ultimately at the same Middle Path through that vital and dialectical process.

Although I have attempted to show that these texts are similar in their schemes of developing the Middle path, very subtle problems remain. It may be true that the Yogācāras inherited in general the Mādhyamika thought concerning śūnyatā. But, is it proper to speak of the logical process involved in establishing śūnyatā as the same in both schools? Isn't it that, although the name śūnyatā is shared by both, what is intended by this name is entirely different in the two schools? For one thing, their points of departure differ: the Mādhyamika starts from pratītya-samutpāda, while the Yogācāra starts from abhūta-parikalpa. Another remarkable difference is that the Yogācāra speaks of the "existence of non-existence" when defining śūnyatā. We must also pay attention to the fact that, although both the Mādhyamikas and the Yogācāras are thought to base their idea of śūnyatā on the Prajñāpāramitā-sūtras, the Yogācāras also place importance on the *Cūḷasuññata-sutta* of the Majjihima-nikāya. (For details about this point, readers are referred to my discussion in another paper.)[17] Due to these differences, one can assume that there is, or could be, a considerable difference between the two schools concerning their idea of śūnyatā.

Even if there is such a difference, however, is it due to natural development during the course of time, or to the different tenets particular to the schools, or to the differences in texts upon which they establish themselves? Or, rather are we to say that in spite of these questions, the difference, if any, is negligible when contrasted to the vast universality and ultimacy of ideas such as śūnyatā, the Middle Path, and co-dependent origination?

Chapter 14

Ascent and Descent Two-Directional Activity in Buddhist Thought

It is an honor and a privilege to have been selected as President of the Sixth Conference of the International Association of Buddhist Studies and to be invited to address you on this auspicious occasion.

At the first Conference, held at Columbia University in 1978, I discussed several topics relating to Buddhist studies. Of course, many more topics remain to be discussed. Today, however, I would like to consider, with your kind permission, an idea that I cherish in my own study of Buddhist thought.

Buddhists have formulated doctrines around various key terms such as *pratītya-samutpāda, anātman, śūnyatā,* and *tathatā,* all of them conveying the fundamental standpoint of Buddhism. It will be found upon examination, however, that most of these doctrines contain within them two opposite tendencies, or directions, or activities. By this I mean that in the structure of Buddhist thought as well as in the way that it is expounded are found two activities or movements, one of ''going forth'' or ''going upward,'' the other of ''coming back,'' or ''coming down.'' The two activities for the sake of convenience can be named simply ''ascent'' and ''descent.''

Ascent can be understood as an activity or movement from this world to the world yonder, or from this human personal existence to the impersonal *dharmadhātu,* the world of *dharmatā.* Descent is the reverse; it is revival and affirmation of humanity, or personality in human existence. These two activities function in opposite directions, so they tend to be paradoxical, at times illogical, even contradictory. But, in fact, it is this two directional activity, frequently encountered in Mahāyānic ideas, that constitutes the characteristic feature of the Mahāyāna. Paradoxes, such as ''being and yet non-being,'' ''purified and yet not purified,'' commonly encountered in the Prajñāpāramitā and other Mahāyāna sūtras, are polar opposites.

But the two-directional activity differs from ordinary paradox. It is through it that the dynamic movement of Mahāyāna thought reveals itself.

While the ideas of ascent and descent are to be found throughout Mahāyāna Buddhism, it was a text of Pure Land School that influenced me most in formulating the idea. T'an luan (476–542), in his commentary on Vasubandhu's *Upadeśa of Sukhāvatī-vyuha,* designated the two-directional activity with the terms "aspect of going forth" (往相) and "aspect of coming back" (還相). According to him, a follower of the Pure land teaching transfers the merit he has obtained in two ways: first, he transfers his merits toward his birth in the Pure Land; this is called the "merit-transference in the aspect of going forth." Second he transfers his merits towards his return to this world of suffering for the purpose of benefiting others; this is the "merit-transference in the aspect of coming-back." Being born in or going forth to the Pure Land refers to ascent, because it is by ascending to the Pure Land that one obtains the great enlightenment, while coming back from the Pure Land refers to descent, because it is by descending once again to this world that one fulfills his act of benefiting others.

The idea of including the coming back into this world within the context of fulfilling one's purpose is a unique one. The search for paradise is a concept common to all religious quests. But the concept of seeking earnestly to return to one's original abode of suffering is rarely seen, and T'an-luan's case is perhaps one of the few exceptions. He established this unique idea of two-directional activity as early as the sixth century.

I know of no Sanskrit term that corresponds to the idea of the two-directional activity as it is found in the later Chinese text, but, as we shall see, the basic connotation was already developed rather elaborately in Indian Mahāyāna.

The notion of ascent and descent is found also in Christianity. There, however, it seems that the aspect of descent comes prior to the aspect of ascent. As the incarnation of God, or as Son of God, Jesus Christ descends from Heaven to earth and brings his Father's message. After the crucifixion and resurrection, his earthly life ends and he ascends to Heaven.

The Buddhist notion of ascent and descent is the reverse of this. Gautama Siddhārtha, after living as a human being on the earth, ascends to the throne of *mahābodhi,* and thereafter, as a Buddha, descends to the world to engage in missionary work. He enters *parinirvāṇa* at the end of his life, but according to Mahāyānic belief, his activities on earth as a Buddha continue forever, even after the parinirvāṇa. The general pattern of two-directional activity in Buddhism is this: the ascent to enlightenment comes first and from there, the message comes down.

Nirvāṇa is the highest virtue to which a Buddhist aspires; there is no difference in this regard between the earlier and later forms of Buddhism.

The attainment of nirvāṇa is the result of the activities directed toward ascent. Thus, knowledge or wisdom (*prajñā*) also belongs to the same line of ascent, because nirvāṇa is realized only through the elimination of avidyā, ignorance of non-knowing, the fundamental defilement (*kleśa*). All practices and learnings likewise belong to the category.

Another virtue, however, to which a Buddhist aspires, is Compassion (*karuṇā*). It is, for a bodhisattva, no less important than wisdom. Compassion is an activity directed toward descent, because benefiting others is the bodhisattva's primal concern. Owing to his deep compassion, a bodhisattva refrains from entering nirvāṇa so long as his fellow beings are not saved. Rejecting even the exquisite pleasure of nirvāṇa, he devotes himself to the works of benefiting others.

Wisdom and Compassion, thus representing opposite directions, stand side by side as the two cardinal Buddhist virtues, the indispensable constituents of enlightenment. They are compared to the two wheels of a cart or the two wings of a bird.

Now, it goes without saying that the sūtras and śāstras are filled with examples that teach, encourage, urge, or admonish people to ascend to their final aims. But which are doctrines that represent the direction of descent?

In addition to the doctrine of Compassion just mentioned, there is the doctrine of 'apratiṣṭhita-nirvāṇa,' which means "not dwelling in nirvāṇa," that is, rejecting entry into nirvāṇa. Another term that indicates the direction of descent more positively than this is saṃcintyabhavopapatti, which means "willingly to take rebirth in this world." However, as I have discussed these doctrines elsewhere,[1] I shall refrain from going into them in detail here.

In consideration of these two directions, naturally it follows that there exists a summit where the ascent ends and from which the descent begins. What is the characteristic of this summit?

Such a summit can be seen in the career of Gautama Buddha. When he advanced to *vajrāsana* and realized *mahābodhi* at Bodhgaya, he reached nirvāṇa. This great event marks a summit in his life. The thirty-five years previous to this event belong to the ascent, while the forty-five years of his mission that followed represent the direction of descent. We are apt to consider the eighty years of his life as a single, continuous ascent to parinirvāṇa. But his life is better seen as consisting of two periods, divided by the summit that constitutes the pivotal point where ascent turns to descent and where the life of acquiring self-benefit becomes a life of benefiting others.

The pivotal point or summit has a double character of being simultaneously negative and affirmative. This double character is due to and corresponds to the two directions of ascent and descent.

The ascent implies a negative movement, because to aspire to something higher implies a negation of the present state of existence in anticipation of a higher one in the future. Ascent is always nihilistic in character—through self-negating practice, a practitioner finally reaches the summit of negation, which may be called "śūnyatā," "negated-ness" or "zero-ness."

Descent, on the other hand, naturally implies an affirmative movement. As stated before, a bodhisattva's primary concern is the practice of benefiting others. He must once deny the saṃsāric world; but if it should then be totally forsaken, there would be no place for a bodhisattva to fulfill his obligation of helping others. It is in this sense that the world is affirmed in the process of the descent.

The structure of two-directional activity with its summit is clearly seen in the Yogācāra theory of the three knowledges. The three knowledges are: (1) knowledge held in the stage of preparatory practice (*prāyogika-jñāna*), (2) non-discriminative knowledge (*nirvikalpa-jñāna*), and (3) knowledge acquired subsequently (*tat-pṛṣṭhalabdha-jñāna*). Of these, nondiscriminative knowledge is knowledge in which every form of duality of subject and object has been abolished; hence, it is non-dual and non-discriminative and represents the ultimate enlightenment in this school. It is realized on the path of intuitive sight (*darśana-mārga*) through arduous practice, and it occupies the position of the summit in the sense stated above. Knowledge belonging to the preparatory stage of practice (*prāyogika-jñāna*), is itself discriminative but aims for nondiscriminative knowledge. It is knowledge practiced in the direction of ascent. Knowledge acquired subsequently (tat-pṛṣṭhalabdha-jñāna), is obtained and arises from the nondiscriminative knowledge. It is discriminative and worldly but differs from the first kind of knowledge in that its activity is directed in the direction of descent. It is a pure form of knowledge because it flows out from nondiscriminative knowledge.

This kind of knowledge might seem superfluous, and one might question the need for it; because once the ultimate enlightenment—nondiscriminative knowledge—is obtained there would be no need for it. But it is this knowledge that an enlightened one must employ as he descends from the dharmadhātu to work in this world. As activity in the direction of descent, that is, in the direction of compassion, it differs from ordinary, human knowledge belonging to the preparatory state; it differs also from the nirvāṇic silence that is essentially nondiscriminative knowledge. The formulation of the system of three knowledges by adding the third stage was one of the great achievements accomplished by the Yogācāras.

The two-directional activity is observable also in various other cases. Two words, āgama and adhigama, with gam or "to go" as their common root, are often contrasted. The term "āgama" literally means "coming hither'' and is widely used to denote doctrines, precepts, and sacred works, including Buddhist canonical texts; hence, it indicates the movement ''coming down from above,'' that is, descent. In opposition to this, ''adhigama'' means ''acquisition,'' and, especially in Buddhism, ''spiritual realization,'' which implies an upward movement or ascent. Thus, the two terms connote salvation from above and self-realization from below.

The two-direction activity can be observed even in a single term. The term tathāgata, for instance, has two meanings of ''thus-gone'' (*tathā-gata*) and ''thus-come'' (*tathā-āgata*). Interpreting these two meanings in accordance with the scheme stated above, it is possible to interpret thus-gone as representing the Buddha's wisdom that denotes ascent, while thus-come can be interpreted as Buddha's compassion that denotes descent. In the same way, the term bodhisattva also can be understood in two ways: (1) ''a sattva who aspires for bodhi'' (ascent) and (2) ''a sattva who has incarnated from bodhi'' (descent).

The *Mūlamadhyamaka-kārikā,* XXIV.18, presents a zigzagging logic, in which dependent co-origination (*pratītya-samutpāda*) is identified with the three notions of emptiness (*śūnyatā*), designation based upon some material (*upādāya-prajñapti*), and the middle path (*madhyamā-pratipad*). It is zigzagging because what exists is identified with what does not exist, which is them identified with what exists. This zigzagging logic defies straightforward reasoning and understanding, but if we apply the idea of the two-directional activity, the logic will be understood easily. The identification of dependent co-orgination with śūnyatā is the activity in the direction of ascent, and the identification of śūnyatā with designation based upon some material (which designation, I think, is another name for dependent co-origination) is the activity in the direction of descent; śūnyata occupies the position of summit as stated above. The final situation, called the ''middle path,'' synthesizes the two directions and is itself the summit between them; it is equated not only with śūnyatā, the summit, but also with dependent co-origination and designation, thereby fully synthesizing the two direction.[2]

These two directions, however, are further claimed to be one and the same activity, even as they are opposite and contradictory. That is to say, ascent is descent and descent is ascent. But, how is this identity of contrary directions possible?

If we properly understand the double character of the summit mentioned above, that is, the two meanings of śūnyatā, ''non-existence'' (*abhāva*) on the one hand, and ''existence of that non-existence'' (*abhāvasya bhāvaḥ*) on the other, as defined by the *Madhyāntavibhāga* (I.13)—such as identity will become comprehensible.

Further, such an identification can be illustrated by the English word "realization." The verb "to realize," meaning "to make real," has two different senses: (1) "to understand clearly," "to conceive vividly as real," and (2) "to bring into concrete existence," "to actualize." When we say "realization of truth," we mean that we are aware of the truth and, at the same time, we mean that the truth realizes itself, or actualizes itself, in our awareness. "To be aware" is *our* understanding—it belongs to ourselves; but if it is a *real* understanding, it is consummated only through the actualization of the truth itself. The former, the understanding constituting our "self-realization," denotes the direction of ascent, while the latter, the "self-realization" of the truth, denotes descent. Thus, in the single word realization both directions of ascent and descent have been combined and unified.

The two aspects of this realization, or enlightenment, are comparable to the two words adhigama and āgama referred to earlier. Within a religious context, adhigama, our understanding or realization, cannot be realized without āgama, the teaching, which always illuminates the path of adhigama from above. At the end of this path, there is a sphere or a field where adhigama and āgama become identical, become one and the same activity. That is to say, adhigama is deepened to the depth of āgama and āgama becomes our own adhigama.

Realization of such a sphere in which ascent is descent and descent is ascent is called "satori" or "enlightenment" in Zen Buddhism and "salvation" or "faith in Pure Land Buddhism." As Nishitani Keiji puts it: ". . . the actualization of the Buddha's Great Compassion and the witness of faith by sentient beings are seen to be really one, a single realization."[3] Here, "the actualization of the Buddha's great compassion" is in the direction of descent, and "the witness of faith" in the direction of ascent. They are "really one, a single realization." Through the witness of faith, one meets the Buddha and his great compassion; it is a realization even of the identity between the Buddha and ordinary beings.

So much for the identity of ascent and descent. However, it is equally true that ascent is not descent; descent is different from ascent. Śūnyatā is the meeting place where adhigama meets āgama and becomes identified with it. But śūnyatā is not a mere nihilism that engulfs all entities in its universal darkness, abolishing all differences and particularities. On the contrary, śūnyatā is the fountainhead from which the Buddha's compassionate activity flows out. Śūnyatā, the summit, is reached, but in the next moment, differentiation and discrimination occurs again, notwithstanding the identity accomplished by śūnyatā. Therefore, we can say that the two directions, ascent and descent, are simultaneously identical and not identical.

The emphasis is often placed on the upward direction alone, the "aspect of going forth" and "being born in the Pure Land." But, unless a religion contains the "aspect of return," it is still incomplete and imperfect. Unless concern is directed to the world once more, the ultimate goal of religion cannot be fulfilled. T'an-luan made a great contribution to Buddhist thought when he clarified the concept of return. It is my belief that the concept of two-directional activity is indispensable for judging the authenticity of a religious teaching. It should be used as a touchstone to aid us as we study and reexamine the various aspects of Buddhist doctrine.

Chapter 15

Emptiness

The phrase "all things are empty" means that everything is nonexistent, that all experienced phenomena are empty (*śūnya*) and vain, and thus that all objects and qualities are negated in both an ontological and ethical sense. But this negation is not mere nothingness. It rather indicates an affirmative absolute being, freed from objectifications and qualifications. The Chinese word *k'ung* 空 (hollow, hole, vacant, sky) took on this deeply philosophical meaning when it was used for the Sanskrit *śūnya* of Indian Buddhism. In India, the term śūnya appears quite early, in the period of Hīnayāna Buddhism, but Mahāyāna Buddhism, which arose later at about the time of Christ, made this notion of emptiness its fundamental standpoint. From that time on, almost all forms of Buddhism, including those transmitted into Tibet, China, Korea, and Japan, have taken emptiness as their most important basic idea.

I Etymology and Definition

The Sanskrit śūnya seems to derive from the root *śvi* "to swell," the connection apparently being that something which looks swollen from the outside is hollow inside.[1] Indian mathematicians called the zero, which they had invented, "śūnya," but "śūnya in this usage did not merely signify non-being. Likewise, while the Buddhist use of the term expresses strong negation, it has at the same time the positive connotation of ultimate reality, for it indicates immediate insight into an absolute through an affirmation that has passed through negation, a negation of relativity. Such an absolute was already recognized in the philosophy of the Upanishads in the negation expressed as "ṇeti, neti." This set the stage for the later Buddhist notion of emptiness. There are discussions on the meaning of emptiness even in early Hīnayānic texts such as the Pāli Nikāyas and Sanskrit Āgamas. One of them, the *Cūḷasuññata-sutta* (Lesser Discourse on Emptiness) reads:

> It is seen that when something does not exist somewhere, that place is empty with regard to the former. And yet it is to be understood that when something remains somewhere it does exist as reality.[2]

This teaches that emptiness signifies non-being and privation, but that at the same time an ultimate reality can be discovered within emptiness. This passage is often quoted in later Yogācāra texts as a true definition of emptiness. The character of emptiness as both negative and affirmative led some Chinese thinkers to equate it with the term *li* 理, principle, rather than with *k'ung*, empty. This same point is stressed when it is rendered into English as ''absolute'' rather than ''emptiness.''

II Emptiness as Seen in the Scriptures

But the primary negative meaning of the term emptiness is clear from its general usage. There are many source passages in the early texts where emptiness means simply nonexistence; that was its significance in the Abhidharma philosophies. For example, when the truth of suffering of the Fourfold Truths is interpreted in these early scriptures, suffering is usually defined using four words: ''impermanence, suffering, empty, and no-self.'' Empty here indicates the non-being of ''I'' and ''mine,'' a significance more or less synonymous with the fourth definition of no-self. Furthermore, the ''three doors of emptiness,'' emptiness (the non-being of beings), formlessness (the absence of images or symbols of beings), and desirelessness (freedom from desire), were conceived at an early date as a single path or door to liberation. Here in each case the basic connotation is clearly negative. But in each of these examples the purpose was not an ontological investigation, for as a Buddhist teaching, emptiness is a mediative object for the practitioner to aid him in the abandonment of desire and attachment.

In the first Mahāyāna texts, the Prajñāpāramitā scriptures, *prajñā* indicates wisdom, specifically the wisdom that gains insight into emptiness. In these scriptures, meditation on the above-mentioned three doors to liberation is heavily emphasized, with the first, meditation on emptiness, standing for all three. The phrase, ''all beings are empty'' (*rūpam eva śūnyatā*) is the basic theme of the Prajñāpāramitā scriptures, which go on to say that ''emptiness just as it is is being'' (*śūnyataiva rūpaṃ*). The notion of emptiness is not necessarily expressed only in terms of emptiness. Various Prajñāpāramitā-sūtras and texts such as the *Vimalakīrti Sūtra*, which are faithful to the Prajñāpāramitā teaching, express the meaning of emptiness through contradictory, paradoxical, and seemingly absurd expressions. In these texts we read, for example, that ''a bodhisattva is not a bodhisattva and that is why there is a bodhisattva." Here the first negation, "is not," corresponds to the emptiness of beings, while the second affirmation, "there is," indicates that emptiness just as it is is being. Since emptiness is always absolute negation, emptiness itself must be negated. The two themes of transcending the being of things through negation and of suggesting true reality in that transcendence, correspond to negation and the negation of negation, respectively.

In various scriptures, emptiness is examined from many aspects and classed into several varieties. The most fundamental classification offers a twofold division: the emptiness of individual subjectivity (of personhood, *pudgala*) and of external beings (*dharma*). In addition, schemas of three, four, six, seven, ten, eleven, and thirteen kinds of emptiness are found. Particularly famous are the schemas of sixteen, eighteen, and twenty kinds of emptiness. Such a variety comes about not from any difference in emptiness itself but from the difference of the objects that are to be negated as empty: there is no multiplicity in emptiness, because it is an absolute negation without limitation.

As it appears in the scriptures, emptiness is generally expressed in enigmatic, intuitive maxims, with hardly any logical analysis or systematic organization. The nameless religious sages, who compiled the Prajñāpāramitā and other Mahāyāna scriptures, acted boldly through their own experimental grasp of the emptiness of self and beings, but they apparently had no interest in rationalizing that experience.

But philosophical inquiry was a concern of the Mahāyāna scholar monks of Nāgārjuna and Āryadeva, who wrote in the second or third century, and Asaṅga and Vasubandhu, who wrote in the fifth. Mādhyamika thought developed through the efforts of Nāgārjuna and Āryadeva, while Yogācāra-Vijñaptimātra thought was created by Asaṅga and Vasubandhu. All subsequent Indian Mahāyāna philosophy developed in reference to these two schools of Buddhist thought.

III Emptiness in the Mādhyamika School

Nāgārjuna formulated the philosophy of emptiness upon the basis of the Prajñāpāramitā scriptures. In the *Stanzas on the Middle* (*Mūlamadhyamaka-kārikā*), his principal work, he bases his criticism of philosophical systems in the experience of emptiness, and develops together with it his dialectic focussed on disclosing the inevitability of logical error (*prasaṅga*). He states that "inasmuch as beings dependently co-arise they are said to be empty." and he explains co-arising as "neither passing away nor arising, neither terminated nor eternal, neither one nor many, neither coming or going.''[3] Dependent co-arising is the basic truth of Buddhism; it is the substance of Gautama Buddha's awakening. But it was Nāgārjuna who first related it directly to emptiness. Dependent co-arising, described as ''if this exists, then that exists; if this arises, then that arises,''[4] is the becoming of beings in dependence on others, the relativity of all beings to each other. For example, the notion of left depends on the notion of right; they are relative one to the other. Thus, they do not exist independently and are not realities with their own essences (*svabhāva*). The negation and absence of such essence (*niḥsvabhāva*) is identical with emptiness. These negations include not only the essence of beings, but also all descriptions of dependent co-arising, such as arising and passing away.

Philosophy in general begins from the premise that essence is self-evident. Nāgārjuna, however, explains essence (*svabhāva*) as absolute being, defining it as ''being neither created nor relative to others,''[5] that is, unchanging (no arising of being from non-being) and not dependent on others. Hence, the definition of essence by Candrakīrti as ''a nature inhering in itself'' (*svo bhāvaḥ*). Yet such essences are not particularly evident in our present world where everything exists in relation to something else and where everything changes. For example, a flame exists in dependence on a match and after being lit, goes out. All meanings expressed in words are real only in this sense and to assume essences in them is unreasonable, for they are not real entities. Thus, Nāgārjuna defines emptiness by stating that ''all things are empty because they have no essences.''

It is nevertheless true that in the deepest level of our consciousness we want to postulate some real ''existence''; and we find that fact reflected in terms such as ''dharmatā and dharma-dhātu,'' which seem to signify essence. But, although these terms indicate reality, they are equated at the same time with emptiness and are said to be beyond our cognition. Thus, another definition of emptiness that is widely accepted (especially in Chinese Buddhism) states that ''all things are empty because they exist beyond our cognition'' (literally, ''unobtainable [*anupalabdhi*], hence empty''), this in contrast to Nāgārjuna's ''absence of essence (*niḥsvabhāva*), hence empty.''

Although the Mādhyamika masters negated words and ideas that they thought might presuppose the existence of essences, they themselves employed ordinary words and logic and developed a dialectical reasoning but they asserted it was solely for the purpose of awakening people to the truth of emptiness. It was partly for this reason that Nāgārjuna introduced the central teaching of the ''two truths,'' ultimate meaning (the highest truth, the content of the immediate insight of wisdom) and worldly convention (truth in the world). The ultimate truth or the truth of ultimate meaning, which always transcends conventional truth, is beyond thought and language. This is why the Buddha always remained in his "(noble) silence" when he was questioned on metaphysical matters, and why, although he preached for forty-five years, he could assert that during that time he had never preached a single syllable.

Yet the truth of ultimate meaning cannot be expressed unless it relies on conventional truth: it must be expressed in words. In this sense the preaching of Śākyamuni and the dialectical reasoning of Nāgārjuna are both conventional truth. The distinguishing characteristics of the twofold truth are "transcendence" and the fact that the conventional can never be the ultimate, while the notion of emptiness is a natural outcome of the notion of dependently co-arising. This notion of emptiness, which is not necessarily equated with the transcendent ultimate, holds valid for both the ultimate and conventional truths: in the conventional truth everything dependently co-arising is without essence and empty, and in the ultimate truth every duality is negated and empty.

The dialectic of Nāgārjuna is formulated in various ways, the most well-known being the tetralemma: being, non-being, both being and non-being, neither being nor non-being, a formulation meant to include all possible cases. Through analysis and critique of these four possibilities, all propositions are revealed to be inherently contradictory insofar as they are formulated in a context of essences. This deconstructive (*prāsaṅgika*) reasoning points to the emptiness of beings.

In the final analysis, the tetralemma can be reduced to a final dilemma of being or non-being. The Middle Path is manifested in the overcoming of such a dilemma. This is the sense in which emptiness, the absence of essence in dependently co-arising beings, is synonymous with the Middle Path preached by the Buddha. Nāgārjuna and his followers, the advocates of insight into emptiness (空觀学派 śūnyavāda), are thus called "Mādhyamika (中觀学派), teachers of the Middle Path," and Nāgārjuna's main work was titled *Stanzas on the Middle [Path]* 中論.

Deconstructive dialectics were applied to all relative relationships such as cause and result, motion and change, substance and properties, I and mine, whole and part. The notion of emptiness was applied not only to the Hīnayānic realism of the Abhidharma teachings on such themes as the five aggregates (*skandha*), but also to the highest principles of Buddhism, such as the *tathāgata* and *nirvāṇa*. It not only offered a critique of the Abhidharma pluralistic realism; it criticized metaphysics in general. It even leveled criticism against its own teaching. Therefore, in the eyes of the Mādhyamika thinkers, there was no Mādhyamika position. According to them a self-assertion of emptiness is "an (erroneous) view (*dṛṣṭi* 見) of emptiness"[6]; it cannot be "(true) insight 觀 into emptiness." According to Nāgārjuna, the dialectic of emptiness is presented simply to make beings aware of emptiness, which is originally present prior to theorizations, through the use of conventional language and reasoning. Since all reasoning involves conventional truth, and there is no reasoning specific to Mādhyamika or consequent upon its notion of emptiness, emptiness has no standpoint of its own; its standpoint is the standpoint of no standpoint, so to speak. Or rather, its standpoint is the middle path. Since being and non-being are transcended in the emptiness of the Middle Path, being as such is non-being. Likewise, since the life-death cycle is not an essential life-death cycle and cessation (*nirvāṇa*) is not an essential cessation, the life-death cycle is itself cessation (saṃsāra is nirvāṇa).

The height to which Nāgārjuna's philosophy developed the negative reasoning of emptiness is unparalleled in the history of philosophy. His intent, however, was not merely to construct a philosophical and metaphysical system, but to offer a model for religious practice. This concern is evident from his identification of emptiness with the Middle Path, the path of practitioners. The Prajñāpāramitā-sūtra itself teaches the purity of giving as the tripartite emptiness of giver, gift, and recipient of the gift. Emptiness, which in the Prajñāpāramitā scriptures is a matter of direct religious insight was systematically elaborated by Nāgārjuna as an object of meditation for the practitioner.

IV Emptiness in the Yogācāra School

As stated above, true "insight" into emptiness differs from "(erroneous) views about emptiness," which are merely mistaken clinging to emptiness. Even during the time of Nāgārjuna, Buddhist thinkers were aware of the danger inherent in emptiness, of people mistaking it for a nihilistic view (*nāsti-vāda*) that would negate all human work and effort. In a sūtra[7] it was proclaimed that "emptiness is severance and freedom from all views, but it is very difficult to save those who engender views about emptiness (cf. n. 6) and cling to them." Nāgārjuna himself warned that "a mistaken view of emptiness will destroy an unwise person, as surely as an ineptly handled poisonous snake."[8]

It is generally believed that the Yogācāra thinkers evolved their ideas in response (or in reaction) to this danger inherent in the doctrine of emptiness. Actually, they taught consciousness (*vijñāna*) as the sole ultimate existence (hence, they are also called "Vijñāna-vāda") and departed from the "no-essence" (*niḥsvabhāva*) theory of the Mādhyamika by advocating the theory of the "three natures" (*tri-svabhāva*) in which the nature, aspect, or characteristic of the world was explained as the imagined, other-dependent, and consummated. If Mādhyamika is to be called the school of emptiness or non-being, then Yogācāra-Vijñānavāda can be called the "school of being."

But Yogācāra does not merely advocate the realism of consciousness against the insight into emptiness. As their name would imply, the Yogācāra thinkers put central emphasis on the practice of yogic meditation, and, in that context, they were entirely faithful to the teaching of emptiness. They often attacked mistaken ideas about emptiness (*durgṛhīta-śūnyatā,* "wrongly-grasped emptiness") and put importance on a true understanding of emptiness (*sugṛhīta-śūnyatā,* "well-grasped emptiness") Early Yogācāras seem to have been aware that they were both a complement to and a development of the Mādhyamikas.

Nevertheless, the Yogācāra interpretation of emptiness is not entirely identical with that of Mādhyamika. The restoration of an affirmative aspect that has passed through negation or emptiness is present in Nāgārjuna. But the Yogācāra, as is evident especially in Maitreya's *Analysis of the Middle and Extremes* (*Madhyānta-vibhāga*) went a step further. Maitreya's text[9] begins with a consideration of the process of knowing (or everyday consciousness, *vijñāna*) in its dependently co-arising character, proceeds to deny the dichotomy of subject and object that always appears within that process, and then expresses the meaning of emptiness through this negation. Further it points out that in the midst of that emptiness, the activity of consciousness nevertheless undeniably exists. This whole process (from the affirmation of dependent co-arising to the negation of dichotomy and on to the recovering or reaffirmation of consciousness as reality) is called the "Middle Path." This interpretation given in the *Analysis of the Middle and Extremes* is close to Nāgārjuna's equation of dependent co-arising first with emptiness and then with the Middle Path. But it goes further and defines emptiness as "the non-being of subject and object and the being of that non-being."[10] This follows logically from the above explanation. The assertion that emptiness is not merely "non-being" but also the "being of non-being" became the salient feature of the Yogācāra school.

The insistence that emptiness has both negative and affirmative dimensions is related to the definition of emptiness quoted above from the *Cūḷasuññata-sutta,* a text never quoted in Madhyamaka. Yet this "being of non-being" was criticized by later Mādhyamika followers as a contradiction in terms and an erroneous interpretation of emptiness; together with the ideas of consciousness-only and the three-nature theory, it became an object of censure. But the Yogācāra teachers were fully aware of this contradiction, and insisted on the said interpretation of emptiness. They equated emptiness with notions such as suchness (*tathatā*), reality-limit (*bhūta-koṭi*), ultimate truth (*paramārtha*), and dharma-realm (*dharma-dhātu*), all affirmative expressions. In accordance with the usual differentiation between existence (*dharma*) and reality (*dharmatā*)—"things (*dharma*) are empty, and this is the real nature (*dharmatā*) of things"—they very likely distinguished between what is empty (*śūnya*) and emptiness (*śūnyatā*) itself, understanding the former as negative emptiness and the latter affirmatively as an absolute. This distinction does not seem to be clearly stated in the Prajñāpāramitā literature or in Nāgārjuna.

The notion of emptiness remained central in Indian Buddhism to its last days, but from about the seventh century it developed in the direction of Tantrism. After Buddhism was introduced into Tibet, the notion also played a central role in Tibetan Buddhism.

V China and Japan

In China, Indian Mādhyamika was represented by the San-lun (Three Treatise) school, while Yogācāra was in the main represented by the Fa-hsiang (Dharma-characteristics) school. Elucidation of the philosophy of emptiness was carried on chiefly by the San-lun school. But even in the Fa-hsiang school, which is more realistic than the Yogācāra, its counterpart in India, the themes of true or absolute emptiness (*chen-k'ung* 真空) and wondrous being (*miao-yu* 妙有) appear.

Since Prajñāpāramitā scriptures were translated into Chinese as early as the second or third century, many Chinese literati and monk-scholars were familiar with the notion of emptiness. But they tended to interpret this foreign concept in terms of "nothingness" (*wu* 無), a notion that was familiar to them from the native Taoist thought of Lao-tzu and Chuang-tzu. No less than six different interpretations of emptiness are said to have appeared in the early period of Chinese Buddhism. But all of them represented compromises with Taoist thought and did not reflect the true significance of the original Buddhist concept.

The introduction of authentic Indian Buddhism into China began with Kumārajīva (ca. 350–409) in the early fifth century. Kumārajīva came to China from the city of Kucha in Central Asia, having studied Mādhyamika both in his native city and in India. After arriving in Ch'ang-an, he translated many scriptures and commentaries, including the Prajñāpāramitā-sūtras (four different versions) and the "three treatises" of the San-lun school: Nāgārjuna's *Stanzas on the Middle* (*Mūla-madhyamaka-kārikā*) and *Treatise in Twelve Gates* (**Dvadaśa-dvāra*), and Āryadeva's *Treatise in a Hundred Stanzas* (**Śataka*), as well as the *Commentary on the Perfection of Wisdom* (**Mahā-prajñāpāramitā-upadeśa*). He had many learned disciples, whose teachings prospered and later formed the basis of the San-lun school.

Chih-i 智顗 (538–597) based the doctrines of his T'ien-t'ai school upon Nāgārjuna's *Stanzas on the Middle* (XXIV.18), equating dependent co-arising (called "provisional," *chia* 假, by Chih-i), Emptiness, and the Middle Path. Chih-i's contemporary Chi-ts'ang 吉藏 (549–623), who is regarded as the reviver of the San-lun school, attempted to consolidate all the teachings on emptiness that had appeared since Kumārajīva. In the San-lun school, the negation (*che-ch'ien* 遮遣) of emptiness is called "the refutation of falsehood" (*p'o-hsieh* 破邪), that is, the criticism of other teachings. This refutation of falsehood is in itself the "manifestation of truth" (*hsien-cheng* 顕正) or the elucidation of the true teaching.

In the Hua-yen school, regarded as the highest point in Chinese doctrinal development, the "insight into true emptiness" seems also to play a central doctrinal role in the key Hua-yen notion of the "Dharma-realm of Ultimate Truth" (*li-fa-chieh* 理法界). The same "insight" also seems to establish the notion of "identity" or "mutual interpenetration," which is at the core of the Hua-yen doctrine. It underlies the theme of the "Dharma-realm of the Interpenetration of the Ultimate and the Phenomenal" (the unity of basic principle, *li* 理, with phenomena, *shih* 事), and the theme of the "Dharma-realm of the Interpenetration between Phenomenon and Phenomenon" (the unified non-dual realm representing original truth).

In what was culturally the most Chinese school, Ch'an 禪, the early Prajñāpāramitā scriptures were revered. The Ch'an principle of "not relying upon words" can be seen as a Chinese development of emptiness.

In almost all the doctrines of the various Chinese Buddhist sects, including those of the Pure Land school and the idea that Buddhahood is found in all sentient beings, there is a philosophical interplay between what is empty and what is not empty. "True emptiness," which is said to surpass the Hīnayānic understanding of emptiness, is at the same time equalled with "wondrous being" on a higher level, again exceeding any mode of being found in the Hīnayāna.

The first Buddhism introduced into Japan was that of the Chinese San-lun school. Sanron (the Japanese pronunciation of San-lun) doctrine became the standard thought for Japanese students studying Buddhism. The notion of emptiness, together with the notion of dependent co-arising, was therefore held in special veneration from the very beginning of Japanese Buddhism.

A *waka* poem by the Dharma master Jitsu-i 実伊, included in *Further Collection of Waka Old and New* (*Shoku kokin wakashu*), reads: "We speak about mind, but there is no mind; when enlightenment comes, what is one enlightened to?" Not only is the mind declared to be nonexistent, awakening itself is said to be empty.

But the notion of emptiness does not seem to have undergone much philosophical or doctrinal development in Japan. It seems rather to have permeated the Japanese sensibility itself as a feeling of transience, and can be seen reflected in the native Japanese love of simplicity, and the aesthetic ideals of *wabi* and *sabi,* the taste for elegant simplicity. In literature, the abbreviated haiku form appeared. In painting, this same tendency to spareness is seen in the preference for simple India-ink drawings. The perception of reality in the vacant spaces between the black lines of a Zen painting also has its roots in the original notion of emptiness.

Chapter 16

Yogācāra—A Reappraisal

In the Sino-Japanese Buddhism of old, the Mādhyamika school, represented by San-lun-tsung, and the Vijñānavāda, represented by the Fa-hsiang-tsung, are assumed to be mutually antagonistic to each other in that the former advocates the teaching of non-being or *śūnyatā,* while the latter, the teaching of being or existence. Such an assumption is apparently a misunderstanding, or at least an oversimplification of the tenets of these two schools. I believe, however, these two schools, both representing the apex of Mahāyāna philosophy, are established on the foundation of the thought of *śūnyatā;* the Yogācāra-Vijñānavāda does not take a position opposed to the śūnyavāda.

Many religious geniuses, who cherished or experienced with devotion the Mahāyāna ideas, produced many texts and expounded in them various aspects of the Mahāyāna, its different themes, and topics such as the profound philosophy of śūnyatā in the Prajñāpāramitā-sūtra, the bodhisattva career in the *Daśabhūmika,* the one-vehicle and the idea of eternal Buddhahood in the *Saddharma-puṇḍarīka,* the fundamental bodhisattva vows and praxis in the *Avataṃsaka,* and the highest bliss of the Pure Land in the *Sukhāvatīvyūha.* There is also the highly dramatic and literary *Vimalakīrtinirdeśa,* in which both the idea of śūnyatā and the bodhisattva path are explicated. In this way, Mahāyāna Buddhism around the first to fifth century A.D. flourished and expanded its utmost brilliancy. During the course of several centuries, the Mahāyāna sūtras. including those mentioned above, developed and nourished various ideas that finally constituted many doctrines peculiar to the Mahāyāna.

The Mahāyāna developed in these sūtras was further adorned with Nāgārjuna's philosophy of śūnyatā. Although it is not certain whether Nāgārjuna was acquainted with all of these sūtras, it cannot be negated that he gave a firm foundation for the establishment of the Mahāyāna. He was, as the founder of the Mahāyāna philosophy, a great genius who, by synthesizing those Mahāyāna texts along with the *āgamas* and the *nikāyas,* formulated a Mahāyāna philosophy centering around śūnyatā, without which the

Mahāyāna could not have been founded. However, it seems that, although he established the philosophy of 'śūnyatā' for the first time in history as the fundamental principle of Mahāyāna, his works did not cover all of the details involved in Mahāyāna thought. He established the principle but whether he expounded clearly the application of that principle is another thing. Asaṅga and Vasubandhu, who followed about one or two centuries later, established this principle as a concrete praxis, so to speak. Inheriting the entire philosophy of śūnyatā, they accomplished the other phase of Mahāyāna about which Nāgārjuna did not seem to expound in detail. His philosophy had to be complemented by Asaṅga, Vasubandhu, and other Yogācāras who deepened it in various aspects and details. The Mahāyāna that was started by Nāgārjuna became fully accomplished by the Yogācāra-Vijñānavāda and this can be fully understood if we look into such terms as "apratiṣṭhita-nirvāṇa" and "nirvikalpa-jñāna" used in Yogācāra texts. But before doing that, I must clarify my view on two opposite directional tendencies of Buddhism.

It is my contention that we can find in Buddhism two opposite directional tendencies or movements or activities: one is "going upward" or "going thither," and the other is "coming down" or "coming hither." For the sake of convenience, I call these two "ascent" and "descent," respectively. The ascent refers to transcending this world and going yonder, and the descent means the reverse, the returning back to this world. For example, our aspiration to obtain liberation (*vimukti*) or enlightenment (*bodhi*) is in the ascending line, while the teachings taught by the Buddha in order to save sentient beings is in the descending line.

In the Mahāyāna Buddhist literature, the two-directional movements of ascent and descent are represented most properly by the terms "prajñā" (wisdom) and "karuṇā" (compassion). Liberation and enlightenment are attained by means of prajñā owing to its power to eliminate *avidyā* (ignorance); therefore prajñā belongs to the level of "ascent." The practices and learnings that support and nourish prajñā belong to this category also.

To benefit others is a bodhisattva's primal concern; therefore he "comes down" into the world of his fellow beings. Owing to his deep compassion, a bodhisattva refrains from entering into nirvāṇa or from obtaining liberation, so long as his fellow beings have not yet been saved. Rejecting even the exquisite pleasures of nirvāṇa, a bodhisattva devotes himself to the work of benefiting others. This activity of karuṇā, compassion, is an activity moving towards the "descent."

Thus, prajñā and karuṇā, representing two opposite directions, stand side by side to each other as the two cardinal virtues, the indispensable constituents of liberation and enlightenment. In the texts, they are compared to two wheels of a cart or the two wings of a bird.

The utmost end of ascent may be called a "summit" and the descent, naturally, begins from this point. In a bodhisattva's career, such a summit is "śūnyatā" or "dharmadhātu," because these are reached by the cultivation of prajñā. They represent the goal of prajñā, the summit, reached through the ascent movement and they belong to the supra-mundane world. The great compassion of the Buddhas, *mahākaruṇā,* flows out from the summit of śūnyatā and is directed towards the mundane world. It is a flowing down from dharmadhātu as a movement of descent. Thus, the summit, śūnyatā, simultaneously combines and divides as the locus for the ascent of prajñā and the descent of karuṇā.

The two-direction movement is not confined to the discussion on prajñā and karuṇā alone. If I am allowed to generalize the tendencies of the Mādhyamikas and the Yogācāras, then they can be assumed to be the movement of ascent and descent, respectively.

Propositions of the Mādhyamikas, for the most part, aim at the realization of śūnyatā—the summit, mentioned above—and are propositions supporting the direction of ascent. By dealing with rather abstract notions such as *pratyaya* (causes), *gamana* (movement), and so forth or metaphysical concepts such as *ātman* (soul), *svabhāva* (self-nature), and so forth, they elucidate a way of realizing ultimate reality.

In contrast to this, the Yogācāra focused on the problem of "mind" in terms of vijñāna (cognition), a problem that was of great concern to any practitioner. In fact, their name Yogācāra derives from their utmost attention directed deeply towards yoga-praxis as a means of realizing enlightenment. To this degree, compared to the Mādhyamikas, the Yogācāras were more in the direction of descent.

It was the Yogācāras that can be credited for having systematized a path of Buddhist practice, which was not sufficiently clarified by the Mādhyamikas. The Yogācāras were able to accomplish this by their methods of investigating what we, today, term the "subconscious" in the ordinary human mind; by establishing a systematic presentation of mind by their elaborate divisions of six cognitions (*pravṛtti-vijñāna*), *manas,* the seventh, *ādana-vijñāna* or *ālaya-vijñāna,* the eighth cognition; and by establishing a new world-view on the basis of their three-nature theory (*trisvabhāva*), a theory developed by applying the Mādhyamika śūnyatā to their Weltanschauung. That is, they analyzed and rearranged the practice of the *nirvedha-bhāgīya,* the six *pāramitās,* the ten *bhūmis,* and so on, and set up a path system, known as the "five mārgas," that included the path of accumulation (*sambhāra-mārga*) at the beginning and the path of perfection (*niṣṭhā-mārga*) or the Buddha-stage (*buddha-bhūmi*) at the end. These systems and analysis show that the Yogācāras tended towards the direction of "descent." Of course, one may assume the system of the five mārgas as of an ascending character, because it aims at the final Buddhahood. But the descending feature involved in it will be clarified later in this paper.

Although the two-direction movements of ascent and descent can be found throughout the many Yogācāra treatises, it is the perspective of descent found in the Yogācāra that complements the Mādhyamika. Of the various doctrines promulgated by the Yogācāras, two doctrines that specifically suggest the direction of descent will be mentioned. The two doctrines are the doctrine of "apratiṣṭhita-nirvāṇa" and "nirvikalpa-jñāna" together with "tat-pṛṣṭha-labdha-jñāna," two doctrines that are hardly seen in the Madhyamaka system.

Nirvāṇa is the ultimate goal to which everyone should aspire, and it is regarded as the highest virtue, common to both Hīnayāna and Mahāyāna. In the Yogācāra, however, nirvāṇa is divided into four. That is, to the usual Hīnayānic *nirvāṇas, sopadhiśeṣa,* and *nirupadhiśeṣa,* the Yogācāras added two others, the *prakṛti-viśuddha-nirvāṇa* and *apratiṣṭhita-nirvāṇa.* Prakṛti-viśuddha-nirvāṇa refers to the idea that "beings are in nirvāṇa originally pure" and this form is seen expounded in various Mahāyāna Sūtras. In contrast, apratiṣṭhita-nirvāṇa, which means "nirvāṇa that is not dwelled in" or simply "not dwelling in nirvāṇa," appears in, among other Yogācāra texts, Asaṅga's *Mahāyāna-saṃgraha* as the subject matter of its ninth chapter.

The ninth chapter of the *Mahāyāna-saṃgraha* is entitled, "phala-prahāṇa." "Elimination (*prahāṇa*) [of all defilements (*kleśa*)] as the fruit (*phala*) [of Buddhahood that results from the three learnings]." The elimination of defilements is generally equated with nirvāṇa (or with *vimukti* liberation). But, here, Asaṅga specifies nirvāṇa as apratiṣṭhita-nirvāṇa and this means that a bodhisattva does not enter into final nirvāṇa before all beings have been liberated from saṃsāra. In other words, a bodhisattva does not dwell in nirvāṇa but comes out of it and enters into the life of saṃsāra. The word, apratiṣṭhita appears also in the Prajñāpāramitā, and there, it seems to mean not only "not dwelling" but also "not clinging to." From this perspective, apratiṣṭhita-nirvāṇa means "not clinging to nirvāṇa" or "a nirvāṇa not clung to." Another expression, "apratiṣṭhita-saṃsāra-nirvāṇa" occurs in the commentary to the *Mahāyāna-sūtrālaṃkāra* (XVII.32), and this means a bodhisattva neither dwells in nor clings to either saṃsāra or nirvāṇa. In regard to this expression, the commentary states:

> Since he possesses compassion (*kāruṇikatva*), a bodhisattva does not become agitated by *saṃsāra* or does not feel weary of *saṃsāra;* therefore, he does not dwell in *nirvāṇa.* Again, since he possesses the highest wisdom, he is not bound by the faults of *saṃsāra;* therefore, he does not dwell in *saṃsāra.*

I shall refrain from explaining the term, apratiṣṭhita-nirvāṇa, further at this time, because I have already discussed it at length elsewhere together with the notion of 'saṃcintya-bhavopapatti' which means "to take birth willingly, volitionally, in the world of existence." In any event, these ideas show the direction of descent that embodies the sublime thought of returning to this world of existence for the purpose of benefiting others. It is noteworthy that, although the term apratiṣṭhita is found in the Prajñāpāramitās as mentioned above, the compound word consisting of both apratiṣṭhita and nirvāṇa is, in all probability, an innovation by the Yogācāras around the time of Asaṅga or by Asaṅga himself in his *Mahāyāna-saṃgraha.*

The second Yogācāra doctrine mentioned above was the doctrine of 'tat-pṛṣṭhalabdha-jñāna' that appears in the eighth chapter of the *Mahāyāna-saṃgraha.* Following the older pattern of the three learnings (*sīla, samādhi, paññā*), Asaṅga explains the third one, paññā, which he refers to as "adhiprajñā," as *nirvikalpa-jñāna* (non-discriminative wisdom).

Asaṅga divides this non-discriminative wisdom further into three kinds:

1. *prāyogika-jñāna,* knowledge held on the stage of preparatory practice,
2. *nirvikalpa-jñāna,* non-discriminative wisdom or knowledge that is often called "fundamental wisdom" in the Sino-Japanese Buddhist traditions, and
3. *tat-pṛṣṭhalabdha-jñāna,* knowledge acquired subsequent to that.

Of these, prāyogika-jñāna belongs to the preparatory stage of practice and to the mundane world; therefore, it is itself discriminatory and not non-discriminative. But, because it is a knowledge that aims for and is destined to obtain non-discriminative knowledge, that is, the fundamental wisdom, it is included in the category of non-discriminative wisdom.

Tat-pṛṣṭhalabdha-jñāna, the knowledge acquired subsequently, is obtained from and arises from non-discriminative knowledge. It is also referred to as "śuddha-laukika-jñāna," that is, purified mundane knowledge; therefore, it, too, is discriminative and belongs to this mundane world. It is included in the category of non-discriminative wisdom, because it is a pure form of knowledge that flows out of non-discriminative knowledge.

Although both knowledges, prāyogika and tat-pṛṣṭhalabdha, are discriminative, there is a difference between them. Knowledge (1), that is, preparatory knowledge is in the direction of "ascent" as it aims towards the fundamental wisdom. The latter knowledge, (3), that is, subsequent knowledge, is in the direction of "descent" as it results from the fundamental wisdom.

In contrast to these two, the truly non-discriminative knowledge is nirvikalpa-jñāna. It is a knowledge in which every form of the subject / object duality, the discrimination between being and non-being, and so on, have been abolished; therefore, it is non-dual and non-discriminative. It represents the ultimate enlightenment in the Yogācāra school.

The non-discriminative wisdom is realized on the path of intuitive insight (*darśana-mārga*) after going through arduous practice on the preparatory stages (*prayoga-mārga*); but, as it is instantaneous and momentary, the subsequent knowledge, (3), arises in the next moment. The term, "non-discriminative knowledge" poses a paradox, as it is self-contradictory, for knowledge originally implies a discrimination of some kind. However, the Yogācāras use this term to express the highest wisdom (*prajñā*) in which vijñāna (cognition), not jñāna (wisdom), is abolished. Consequently, its explanation ends up in paradoxical language such as the explanation, "[this wisdom] is no-knowledge and is not no-knowledge at the same time" or as the *Vimalakīrtinirdeśa* puts it, "it sees [tathāgata] without seeing."

This system of the three knowledges exhibits the pattern of "ascent" and "descent" with the "summit" in between. That is, non-discriminative wisdom results from the ascent of the preparatory knowledge and functions as the cause for the descent of the subsequent knowledge; consequently, it combines both knowledges in itself as the summit to which one ascends and from which one descends. The same pattern is visible in the system of the five paths, especially in the relationship between the *prayoga-mārga* (the preparatory stage) as the ascent, the *darśana-mārga* (the path of insight) as the summit (the *dharma-dhātu* being realized on the first *bhūmi*, and the *bhāvanā-mārga* (path of cultivation, second to tenth *bhūmi*) as the descent. Thus, the path of cultivation and the subsequent knowledge share the same direction of descent from the summit. Therefore, the knowledge that functions on the path of cultivation must be the knowledge that flows out subsequently from the fundamental wisdom.

What is of utmost importance here is the fact that the subsequent knowledge, which is a mundane discriminative knowledge, is established as a result of the non-discriminative wisdom. The knowledge that results from non-discriminative wisdom may seem superfluous and unnecessary, because once the ultimate enlightenment—non-discriminative wisdom—has been realized there would be no need for it. But it is exactly this knowledge that the Enlightened One must employ as the "descent" from the *dharmadhātu* and that is made to work in this world for the purpose of benefiting others. All of the Buddha's preaching is constituted of this knowledge. As an activity of compassion, that is as an activity in the direction of "descent," it differs from the ordinary human knowledge, which is discursive and belongs to the preparatory stages. It also differs from the nirvāṇic silence that is essentially non-discriminative wisdom.

As I state before, this process of the five mārgas might be regarded as operating in the direction of ascent. It is true that the system of the five mārgas ends with *niṣṭha-mārga,* the highest stage. However, it should now be clear from the above discussion that the path of cultivation, coming after the path of insight, is in the descending direction, where the subsequent knowledge functions. The final goal is reached at the end of the path of cultivation through the subsequent knowledge, but it must be different from the mere realization of śūnyatā or dharma-dhātu acquired on the path of insight, which precedes the path of cultivation. In this final goal, the Buddha stage, because prajñā and karuṇā are conjoined into the one taste of enlightenment, there is no difference between the ascent and the descent. Ascent is descent, and descent is ascent. In accord with this fact of the Buddha bhūmi, even on the path of cultivation, to descend means to ascend to the final goal. This means that by descending to this world with karuṇā and by perfecting the benefits for others (*parārtha*), the true Buddhahood is accomplished.

Ordinary human thinking, languages, concepts, logic, are negated, in Buddhism, from the viewpoint of ultimate reality; consequently, we encounter the negation of discrimination by terms such as "akalpa," "avikalpa," "nirvikalpa," and so on found throughout Buddhist literature. However, the compound in which the term "nirvikalpa" is combined directly with the term "jñāna" is generally scarcely seen except in the Yogācāra texts. This seems to indicate, again, that the term "nirvikalpa-jñāna," notwithstanding the apparent contradiction involved, was a term innovated by the Yogācāras around the time of Asaṅga.

In any case, the formulation of the system of the three (non-discriminative) knowledges by adding the third state, subsequent knowledge, was another great achievement accomplished by the Yogācāras.[1] By adding the third, subsequent knowledge, human languages, concepts, that were once negated by non-discriminative knowledge, or by the Mādhyamika śūnyatā, could be revived in their own rights and could become the constituents of the activities of the Buddhas and bodhisattvas. In this sense, too, the Yogācāras can be said to have complemented the Mādhyamika's general tenets, and thereby brought the Mahāyāna thought to its full scope and completion.

Appendix

Sources of Essays

For the sources of the essays, the following journals or books are to be acknowledged. Furthermore, the following people are to be credited for the English translations:

1. "Buddhist Subjectivity," trans. by D. Kanzaki and M. Hattori, in *Religious Studies in Japan,* ed. by the Japanese Association for Religious Studies (Tokyo: Maruzen, 1959), pp. 257–262. A translation of the Japanese original which appeared in *Journal of Indian and Buddhist Studies,* vol. 1 no. 1, July 1952. Edited and revised by L. S. Kawamura.

2. Y. Fujitani trans. "An Interpretation of the term "Saṃvṛti" (Convention) in Buddhism." First appeared (in English) in *Silver Jubilee Volume of the Zinbun-Kagaku-Kenkyusyo* (Kyoto: Kyoto University, 1954), pp. 550–61. Translated into Japanese by S. Katsura for inclusion in *Chūkan to Yuishiki.* Edited and revised by L. S. Kawamura.

3. "The Bodhisattva Returns to this World" in *The Bodhisattva Doctrine in Buddhism.* L. S. Kawamura, ed. *SR Supplements:* 10 (Waterloo: Wilfrid Laurier University Press, 1981), pp. 61–79.

4. Y. Fujitani trans. "The Silence of the Buddha and its Madhyamic Interpretation" in *Studies in Indology and Buddhology. Presented in Honour of Professor Susumu Yamaguchi on the Occasion of his Sixtieth Birthday.* G. M. Nagao and J. Nozawa eds. (Kyoto: Hōzōkan, 1955), pp. 137–151. A translation of the Japanese original which appeared in *Tetsugaku-kenkyū* (*Journal of Philosophical Studies*), 430. vol. 37, no. 8, 1955.

5. "What Remains in Śūnyatā" in *Mahāyāna Buddhist Meditation.* In Memory of Richard H. Robinson, ed. by M. Kiyota (Honolulu: University of Hawaii Press, 1978), pp. 66–82. Translated into Japanese by S. Katsura for inclusion in *Chūkan to Yuishiki.* This article resulted as an enlargement and revision of the Japanese work "Amareru mono" (given the English subtitle, "The Term 'aviśiṣṭa' in Yogācāra Philosophy"), *Journal of Indian and Buddhist Studies,* vol. 16 no. 2 March, 1968, pp. 497–501.

6. "The Buddhist World-View as Elucidated in the Three-Nature Theory and Its Simile," *The Eastern Buddhist,* new series, vol. 16, no. 1. Spring 1983,

pp. 1–18. First appeared in *Tōhō Gakuhō* (Kyoto), vol. 11, no. 4. 1941. English translation delivered as a lecture at the University of Calgary, Canada, in November 1982.

7. "Connotations of the Word Āśraya (Basis) in the Mahāyāna-sūtrālaṃkāra." First appeared in *Sino-Indian Studies*, vol. 5, nos. 3–4, 1958 (Liebenthal Festschrift), ed. by K. Roy, pp. 147–155. Translated into Japanese by S. Katsura for inclusion in *Chūkan to Yuishiki*.

8. "Usage and Meaning of Pariṇāmanā," L. S. Kawamura trans. Presented at the First Conference of the International Association of Shin Buddhist Studies, held in Kyoto, 1983.

9. "The Tranquil Flow of Mind: An Interpretation of Upekṣā." First appeared in Publications de l'Institut Orientaliste de Louvain, no. 23. *Indianisme et Bouddhisme. Mélanges offerts à Mgr Étienne Lamotte*. Louvain-la-neuve: Institut Orientaliste, 1980, pp. 245–258. Ms. Michele Martin and L. S. Kawamura's advice and help in rendering this paper into English is gratefully acknowledged.

10. "On the Theory of Buddha-Body (Buddha-*kāya*)," Ms. U. Hirano trans. In *The Eastern Buddhist*, new series. vol. 6, no. 1, May 1973. pp. 25–53. A translation of the Japanese original which appeared in *Tetsugaku-kenkyū* (*Journal of Philosophical Studies*), 521 (vol. 45, no. 3), 1971. Revised by L. S. Kawamura.

11. "The Logic of Convertibility." L. S. Kawamura, trans. Japanese original first appeared in *Tetsugaku Kenkyū* (*Journal of Philosophical Studies*), 405 (vol. 35, no.7), 1952, under the title, "Tenkan no Ronri." Reprinted in *Chūkan to Yuishiki* (Tokyo: Iwanami Shoten, 1978). pp. 237–265.

12. "Buddhist Ontology." L. S. Kawamura, trans. First appeared in M. Saigusa ed., *Kōza Bukkyō Shisō*, vol. 1 (Tokyo: Risōsha, 1974), pp. 55–94. This paper was meant neither for general readers nor for academic specialists; it was written for the "general intellectuals" of Japan, specifically from the perspective of applying the western or modern philosophical ideas of ontology to Buddhism.

13. "From Mādhyamika to Yogācāra, An Analysis of MMK, XXIV.18 and MV, I.1–2." This paper first appeared in *The Journal of the International Association of Buddhist Studies*, vol. 2. no. 1, 1979, pp. 29–43. Translation into English was assisted by Ms. Michele Martin and L. S. Kawamura.

14. "Ascent and Descent: Two-Directional Activity in Buddhist Thought." L. S. Kawamura, trans. Given as a Presidential Address for the Sixth Conference of the International Association of Buddhist Studies (IABS) held in Tokyo, Japan, September, 1983. Published in *The Journal of the International Association of Buddhist Studies*, vol. 7. no. 1. 1984, pp. 176–183.

15. "Emptiness." John Keenan, trans. First appeared in Japanese in *Buritanika Kokusai Dai Hyakka-jiten* (*Britannica International Encyclopedia*) vol. 6. March, 1973. Included in the author's *Chūkan to Yuishiki*. Revised by Norman Waddell and G. M. Nagao.

16. Yogācāra—A Reappraisal. This paper was first read at the Annual Meeting of the American Academy of Religion held in Atlanta, Georgia (November 21–25, 1986) and is based upon the paper, "Ascent and Descent: Two-Directional Activity in Buddhist Thought" given as the Presidential Address for the Sixth Conference of IABS.

Notes

Chapter 1: Buddhist Subjectivity

1. Hajime Nakamura, *Tetsugaku-teki Shisaku no Indo-teki Tenkai* (Development of Philosophical Thinking in India) (Tokyo: 1949). The second article.

2. Editor's note: The ideas of "ascent" and "descent" are ideas that appear in the author's (Professor Nagao's) more recent writings. See the chapter, "The Bodhisattva Returns to This World" in this book.

3. Susumu Yamaguchi: "Trisvabhāvanirdeśa of Vasubandhu, Skt. text and Japanese translation with annotation," *Journal of Religious Studies*, New Series no. 8, 1931, pp. 121–130, 186–207. Reprinted in *Yamaguchi Susumu Bukkyogaku Bunshu* (Tokyo: Shunjusha, 1972). Louis de la Vallée Poussin: "Le petit traite de Vasubandhu-Nāgārjuna sur les trois natures," *Mélanges chinois et bouddhiques*, 2e vol., 1932–33, pp. 147–161. Thomas A. Kochumuttom, *A Buddhist Doctrine of Experience* (Delhi: Motilal Banarsidass, 1982). For a study of the text, see pp. 90–126 and for a translation into English, see pp. 247–259. Stephen Anaker, *Seven Works of Vasubandhu—The Buddhist Psychological Doctor.* Religion of Asia Series, no. 4. L. R. Lancaster and J. L. Shastri eds. (Delhi: Motilal Banarsidass, 1984). pp. 287–297. Editor's note: The last two books mentioned here were not available to the author when he wrote this paper.

4. *Trisvabhāva,* kk. 2–3:

> yat khyāti paratantro 'asau yathā khyāti sa kalpitaḥ /
> pratyayādhīna-vṛttitvāt kalpanā-mātra-bhāvataḥ / / 2 / /
> tasya khyātur yathākhyānaṃ yāsadā 'vidyamānatā /
> jñeyaḥ sa pariniṣpannaḥ svabhāvo 'nanyathātvataḥ / / 3 / /

See also G. M. Nagao's Japanese translation in *Seshin Ronshū* (*Works of Vasubandhu*) in series *Daijō Butten* [Mahāyāna Scriptures] (Tokyo: Chūō Kōron Sha 1976), vol. 15 p. 194. Editor's note: This note has been added anew.

5. That the subjective expression "appearer" corresponds to the other-dependent nature is clear also from verse twenty three of the *Trisvabhāva-nirdeśa,* where the imagined nature and the other-dependent nature are respectively called

"transacting itself" (*vyavahāra-ātman*) and "transactor" (*vyavahartṛ-ātmaka*), and the consummated nature is explained as the "cutting off of transacting from transactor" (*vyavahāra-samuccheda*).

Chapter 2: An Interpretation of the Term "Saṃvṛti"

1. G. M. Nagao, "The Fundamental Standpoint of the Mādhyamika Philosophy" (in Japanese), *Tetsugaku Kenkyū* (Journal of Philosophical Studies, nos. 366–371, Kyoto, 1947–1948. Reproduced in *Chūkan to Yuishiki*. (Tokyo: Iwanami Shoten, 1978).

2. *Wogihara Unrai Bunshū* (Collected Works of Dr. U. Wogihara) (Tokyo: 1938), p. 784; F. Edgerton, *Buddhist Hybrid Sanskrit Dictionary* (New Haven: 1953), p. 541.

3. R. C. Childers, *Pāli-English Dictionary* (London: 1875), p. 436

4. U. Wogihara, op. cit., maintains that *saṃ*-√man is the proper and correct root for "convention," and that the meaning "covering (or concealing)" (to be discussed later) is derived from another root, *saṃ*√vṛ.

5. F. Edgerton, *Buddhist Hybrid Sanskrit Dictionary.*

6. S. Yamaguchi, ed., *Sthiramati, Madhyāntavibhāga-ṭīkā* (hereafter, *Sthiramati*. Nagoya: Libraire Hajinkaku, 1934. Reprint Tokyo, 1966).

7. Other examples of variations in spelling are: *satva* for *sattva, upāyya* for *upāya*.

8. Sir M. Monier-Williams, *Sanskrit-English Dictionary* (Oxford: 1899), p. 1116.

9. Louis de la Vallée Poussin, *Mūlamadhyamaka-kārikās* (St.-Pétersbourg: 1913. Bibliotheca Buddhica, IV), p. 492, lines 10–12.

10. Theodere Stcherbatsky, *The Conception of Buddhist Nirvāṇa* (Leningrad: 1927), pp. 134, 232.

11. The word *saṃvṛti* in the Mahāyāna-sūtrālaṃkāra, chap. XVI, 41, is translated into Tibetan by 'khor-ba (= saṃsāra) and not by the usual *kun-rdzob*. This usage is also adopted in Sthiramati's *Commentary* (Peking edition Mdo-'grel, vol. XLVII, Tsi, fol. 36a–b. Reprint. ed., vol 109. p. 16). The word nirvṛti, which also appears in this verse, had already been equated with *nirvāṇa* not only in Buddhist writings but also in pure Sanskrit. Therefore, the equation of *nirvṛti* and *nirvāṇa* here is not unusual, but this apparently is claimed as a precedent, and *saṃvṛti* is here equated with saṃsāra and used in its stead.

12. C. Bendall, ed., *Śikṣāsamuccaya* (St.-Pétersbourg: 1897–1902. Bibilotheca Buddhica. I), p. 257, lines 7–8: *saṃvṛti = nāmadheya, saṃketa, prajñapti.*

13. U. Wogihara, ed., *Bodhisattvabhūmi* (Tokyo: 1930), p. 49, lines 3–5. (See also note 12).

14. Louis de la Vallée Poussin, *Madhyamakāvatāra par Candrakīrti* (St-Pétersbourg: 1912. Bibliotheca Buddhica IX), pp. 107 and 102.

15. Louis de la Vallée Poussin, ed. *Bodhicaryāvatāra of Śāntideva* (Calcutta: 1901) (Bibliotheca Indica, N. S. no. 983), pp. 353, 361.

16. S. Yamaguchi, *Sthiramati*, pp. 123–125.

17. = *parikalpita* (imaginary assumption = imagined), *paratantra* (depending on others = other-dependent), and *parinispanna* (complete and perfect = consummated).

18. *Saṃvṛtti-satya* is here almost equal to the Absolute. Yamaguchi, *Sthiramati*, p. 124, lines 24–25; *udbhāvanā-saṃvṛttyā parinispannaḥ saṃvṛtti-satyam*.

19. On this point, there appears to be a controversy even within the circle of Mādhyamika philosophy between Bhāvaviveka as Svātantrika and Candrakīrti as Prāsaṅgika. In the system of the latter, who claims *saṃvṛti* strictly as "covering" or "hindrance," there is doubt as to why *saṃvṛti* has the right to be said to "manifest" the truth. Furthermore, if *saṃvṛti* can approach the Absolute of *paramārtha* by virtue of being "manifested," then there is likely to take place a misleading confusion of the Twofold Truth. Bhāvaviveka, on the other hand, may be rather closer to the Vijñāna-vādins, especially in his view of *tathya-saṃvṛti*, that is, the "true convention."

20. Yamaguchi, *Sthiramati*, p. 125, line 1: *avasara-saṃgraha-vyavasthānam*, literally, [(1) and (3) are] established from the viewpoint of variable situations.

21. The meaning here is this: Even when a *vikalpa* functions with the utmost logical precision, using accurate syllogism (*tarka*), and so on, it is still "false" and "untrue" insofar as it remains a *vikalpa* and is contrasted with paramārtha [editor's note].

22. This reminds us of the fact that *paramārtha* is equated with *tūṣṇīṃbhāva* (being silent). This means that *paramārtha* is *atarkagocara* beyond logical reasoning) or beyond *vikalpa*, an expression found often, especially in the Mādhyamika tradition.

23. 義淨撰、南海寄歸内法傳、四巻、, Taishō, vol. LIV, p. 228b; J. Takakusu, *A Record of the Buddhist Religion by I-tsing* (Oxford: 1896), p. 168.

24. Dharmapāla (Hu-fa 護法 530–61) was the ācārya at Nālanda in the middle of the sixth century and is revered by the Hossō (Fa-hsiang) Sect as its highest authority. His original work, the *Vijñaptimātratā-siddhi*, is not extant, but it is claimed that Hsüan-tsang translated it into Chinese. It is this translation that Tz'u-ên claims as his authority.

25. 窺基撰、大乘法苑義林章、七巻、二諦章、 *Taishō*, vol. XLV, p. 287c.

26. 窺基撰、成唯識論述記、二十巻、 *Taishō*, vol. XLIII, p. 243c.

27. This curious method of translating a Sanskrit word using two or more characters and then analyzing them separately as if it were a compound in the original is not unusual in Chinese Buddhist scholarship, but why Tz'u-ên, who was the foremost disciple of Hsüan-tsang and thus probably well-versed in the Sanskrit language, should have adopted such a method is quite puzzling.

28. 冠導阿毘達磨倶舍論 ed., Rev. Kyokuga Saeki (佐伯旭雅), vol. 22, p. 10b; Louis de la Vallée Poussin, *L'Abhidharmakośa de Vasubandhu* (Paris: 1925), VI, p. 139–40; U. Wogihara, ed., *Yaśomitra: Sphuṭārthā* (Tokyo: 1934), p. 524; P. Pradhan, *Abhidharma-koshabhāṣya of Vasubandhu* (Patna: 1967), p. 334.

29. *Mahāvyutpatti*, ed., R. Sakaki, 3061: *lujyata iti lokaḥ, 'jig-pas na 'jig-rten*. The expression is found in Wogihara. *Yaśomitra*. p. 23, line 6 and in P. Pradhan, *Abhidharma-koshabhāṣya of Vasubandhu* (Patna: 1967), p. 5, line 16. See also *Wogihara Bunshū*, p. 801, where the word is elucidated as follows: *loka* is originally *u-loka:* this is later understood from Pāli *loga* (Skt. *roga*), that is, "breaking up," the root of which is √*luj* (Skt. √*ruj*).

30. See note 32 below.

31. As Nāgārjuna also declares in his *Mūlamadhyamaka-kārikā*, chap. XXIV, 10: "Without recourse to verbal designations (of *saṃvṛti*), *paramārtha* is ineffable."

32. *Prākṛtako lokaḥ*, that is, the vulgar world, as expressed in *Bodhicaryāvatāra-pañjikā*, p. 368–369.

33. Asaṅga, *Mahāyānasaṃgraha*, chap. on *Jñeyalakṣaṇa*.

34. The term *saṃvṛti-mātra* (*kun-rdzob-tsam*) appears in Candrakīrti's *Madhyamakāvatāra*, p. 108 (ad VI, 28). See my article "Fundamental Standpoint of Mādhyamika Philosophy," *Tetsugaku Kenkyū*, no. 370, p. 34 ff. (*Chūkan to Yuishiki*. pp. 104, 106). Tsong-kha-pa quotes this passage in his *Lam-rim chen-mo*, fol. 263a, 318a (Peking popular edition).

35. Another suggestion may be added here. We have the term "*sāmvṛta*" by Candrakīrti, which means "covered," that is, *saṃvriyate etad iti sāmvṛtaḥ*. "Being covered" is nothing other than the "Truth." In this case, *sāṃvṛta*, that is, "being *saṃvṛti*" is, according to Stcherbatsky, almost equated with *pratītya-samutpāda, śūnyatā*, and *paramārtha*. Cf. Theodere Stcherbatsky, *Nirvāṇa*, pp. 90, 154, 156.

Chapter 3: The Bodhisattva Returns to this World

1. Har Dayal, *The Bodhisattva Doctrine in Buddhist Sanskrit Literature* (Delhi: Motilal Banarsidass, 1970 Reprint), p. 2.

2. Ibid., p. 3.

3. *Ch'êng wei shi lun*. Shindō Edition (Nara: Shōsōgaku Seiten kankōkai, 1930) *chüan* 10, p. 9. The four kinds of nirvāṇa are mentioned, probably for the first time in Chinese texts, by Paramārtha in his translation of Vasubandhu's commentary on the *Mahāyānasaṃgraha*.

4. Éteinne Lamotte, *La somme du grand véhicule d'Asaṅga* (*Mahāyāna-saṃgraha*) Tome II (Louvain: Bureaux du Muséon, 1938) p. 47*.

5. Th. Stcherbatsky, *The Conception of Buddhist Nirvāṇa* (Leningrad: The Academy of Sciences of the USSR, 1927, pp. 185, 204.

6. E. Obermiller, "The Sublime Science of the Great Vehicle to Salvation," *Acta Orientalia*, 9 (1931), pp. 162, 174.

7. J. Takasaki, *A Study on the Ratnagotravibhāga* (*Uttaratantra*), Serie Orientale Roma, XXXIII (Roma: Istituto Italiano per il Medio ed Estremo Oriente, 1966), pp. 84, 204.

8. F. Edgerton, *Buddhist Hybrid Sanskrit Grammar and Dictionary*, vol. II (New Haven: Yale University Press, 1953), p. 48.

9. Edward Conze, *Vajracchedikā Prajñāpāramitā* Serie Orientale Roma, XIII, 2nd. ed. (Roma: Istituto Italiano per il Medio ed Estremo Oriente, 1974), p. 95.

10. See n. 12 below.

11. See n. 18 below.

12. Sylvain Lévi, *Asaṅga, Mahāyāna-sūtrālaṃkāra, exposé de la doctrine du grand véhicule, selon le système yogācāra* (Hereafter *MSA*). vol. 1, (Paris: 1907), XVII.42:

karuṇāniḥsaṅgatāyāṃ ślokaḥ /

āviṣṭānāṃ kṛpayā na tiṣṭhati manaḥ śame kṛpālūnāṃ /
kuta eva lokasaukhye svajīvite vā bhavet snehaḥ / / 42 / /

sarvasya hi lokasya laukike saukhye svajīvite ca snehaḥ / tatrāpi ca niḥsnehānāṃ śrāvakapratyekabuddhānāṃ sarvaduḥkhopaśame nirvāṇe pratiṣṭhitaṃ manaḥ / bodhisattvānāṃ tu karuṇāviṣṭatvān nirvāṇe 'pi mano na pratiṣṭhitaṃ / kuta eva tayoḥ sneho bhaviṣyati /

See also Sthiramati's commentary on it. D. T. Suzuki, ed., *Tibetan Tripitaka, Peking edition* (hereafter *TTP*), vol. 109 (Tokyo-Kyoto: Tripitaka Research Institute, 1957), pp. 34.5.6–35.1.1:

. . . 'phags pa nyan thos dang rang sangs rgyas rnams 'jig rten gyi bde ba dang srog la chags pa med kyang sdug bsngal thams cad spangs pa'i mya ngan las 'das pa la chags pas mya ngan las 'das pa la gnas pa'o / / byang chub sems dpa' rnams ni nyan thos dang rang sangs rgyas rnams kyi zhi ba phyogs gcig pa'i mya ngan las 'das pa 'jig rten gyi bya ba thams cad kyi phul du phyin pa de la yang ma chags mi gnas te / 'dis ni mya ngan las 'das pa la mi gnas pa bstan to / /

13. *MSA*. XVII, 32:

apratiṣṭhitasaṃsāranirvāṇatve ślokaḥ /

vijñāya saṃsāragataṃ samagraṃ duḥkhātmakaṃ caiva nirātmakaṃ ca /
nodvegam āyāti na cāpi doṣaiḥ prabadhyate kāruṇiko 'grabuddhiḥ / / 32 / /

sarvaṃ saṃsāraṃ yathābhūtaṃ parijñāya bodhisattvo nodvegam āyāti kāruṇikatvāt / na doṣair bādhyate 'grabuddhitvāt / evaṃ [na] nirvāṇe pratiṣṭhito bhavati na saṃsāre yathākramaṃ /

14. G. M. Nagao, *Madhyāntavibhāga-Bhāṣya: A Buddhist Philosophical Treatise, edited for the first time from a Sanskrit Manuscript* (hereafter *MV*. Tokyo: Suzuki Research Foundation, 1964), p. 74–75:

avaikalyāpratikṣepo 'vikṣepaś ca prapūraṇā /
samutpādo nirūḍhiś ca karmaṇyatvāpratiṣṭhitā /
nirāvaraṇatā tasyā 'prasrabdhisamudāgamaḥ / / 29 / /

. . . saṃsāranirvāṇāpratiṣṭhatā avinivartanīyabhūmivyākaraṇalābhasamudāgamaḥ / saṃsāranirvāṇābhyām avinivartanāt / /

15. S. Yamaguchi, ed., *Sthiramati: Madhyāntavibhāgaṭīkā* (Nagoya: Libraire Hajinkaku, 1934; reprint, Tokyo, 1966), p. 257.

16. *MSA*. XIX, 61–62:

Mahāyānasaṃgrahavibhāge dvau ślokau /
gotraṃ dharmādhimuktiś ca cittasyotpādanā tathā /
dānādipratipattiś ca nyāmāvakrāntir eva ca / / 61 / /
satvānāṃ paripākaś ca kṣetrasya ca viśodhanā /
apratiṣṭhitanirvāṇaṃ bodhiḥ śreṣṭhā ca darśanā / / 62 / /

17. *MSA*, XIX, 62 commentary: kṣetrapariśodhanam apratiṣṭhitanirvāṇāṃ cāvinivartanīyāyāṃ bhūmau trividhāyāṃ /

18. *MSA*. IX, 14:

pravṛttir udvṛttir avṛttir aśrayo nivṛttir āvṛttir atho dvayādvayā /
samā viśiṣṭā api sarvagātmikā tathāgatānāṃ parivṛttir iṣyate / / 14 / /

. . . abhisaṃbodhiparinirvāṇadarśanavṛttyā dvayā vṛttiḥ / saṃsāranirvāṇāpratiṣṭhitatvāt saṃskṛtāsaṃskṛtatvenādvayā vṛttiḥ / . . .

19. *MSA*, XIX, 62 Commentary: śreṣṭhā bodhir buddhabhūmau / tatraiva cābhisaṃbodhimahāparinirvāṇasaṃdarśanāveditavyā / . . .

20. MSA, IX, 70:

sattveṣu samatājñānaṃ bhāvanaśuddhito mataṃ /
apratiṣṭhasamāviṣṭaṃ samatājñānam iṣyate / / 70 / /

yad bodhisatvenābhisamayakāle sattveṣu samatĵñānaṃ pratilabdhaṃ tad bhāvanāśuddhito bodhiprāptasyāpratiṣṭhitanirvāṇe niviṣṭaṃ samatājñānam iṣyate /

21. *TTP* vol. 108, p. 263.2.1–2:

. . . sangs rgyas kyi sar mi gnas pa'i mya ngan las 'das par zhugs nas / 'khor ba dang mya ngan las 'das pa gnyis ka la tha dad pa med cing ro gcig par dmigs pa ni mnyam pa nyid kyi ye shes yin par 'dod do zhes bya ba'i don to / / de bas na sangs rgyas kyi sa'i mdo las kyang / . . .

22. É. Lamotte, *The Teaching of Vimalakīrti* (Vimalakīrtinirdeśa) translated by Sara Boin (London: Routledge & Kegan Paul, 1976), p. 182 v. 13.

23. E. Conze, *Materials for a Dictionary of the Prajñāpāramitā Literature* (Tokyo: Suzuki Research Foundation, 1967), p. 395.

24. Unrai Wogihara, ed., *Abhisamayālaṃkār'ālokā Prajñāpāramitāvyākhyā* (Tokyo: Toyo Bunko, 1932–35), p. 103.

25. E. H. Johnston, ed., *Ratnagotravibhāga Mahāyānottaratantra-śāstra* (Patna: Bihar Research Society, 1950), p. 47.

26. U. Wogihara, ed., *Bodhisattvabhūmi* (Tokyo: 1930–36; Reprinted Tokyo: Sankibo Buddhist Book Store, 1971), p. 226:

saṃcintya caṇḍāla 'ntānām ā śūnām arthaṃ kartukāma upadravaṃ saṃśamitukāmo vinayitukāma, ā caṇḍālānām ā śūnāṃ sabhāgatāyām upapadyate /

27. *MSA*, IV, 24–25:

cittāvyāvṛttau ślokau /
māyopamānvīkṣya sa sarvadharmān udyānayātrām iva copapattiḥ /
kleśāc ca duḥkhāc ca bibheti nāsau saṃpattikāle 'tha vipatti-kāle / / 24 / /
svakā guṇāḥ satvahitāc ca modaḥ saṃcintyajanma rddhivikurvitaṃ ca /
vibhūṣaṇaṃ bhojanam agrabhūmiḥ krīḍāratir nitya kṛpātmakānāṃ / / 25 / /
. . . saṃcintyopapattir udyānabhūmiḥ / . . .

28. MSA, XI, 30, commentary:

. . . nirmāṇopamāḥ saṃcintyabhavopapattiparigrahe 'saṃkliṣṭasarvakriyāprayogatvāt /

29. MSA, XX-XXI, 8:

upapattivibhāge ślokaḥ /
karmaṇaś cādhipatyena praṇidhānasya cāparā /
samādheś ca vibhutvasya cotpattir dhīmatāṃ matā / / 8 / /
caturvidhā bodhisatvānām upapattiḥ karmādhipatyena yādhimukticaryābhūmi sthitānāṃ karmavaśenābhipretasthānopapattiḥ / praṇidhānavaśena yā bhūmipraviṣṭānāṃ sarvasatvaparipācanārthaṃ triyagādihīnasthānopapattiḥ / samādhyādhipatyena yā dhyānāni vyāvartya kāmadhātāv upapattiḥ / vibhutvādhipatyena yā nirmāṇais tuṣitabhavanādyupapattisaṃdarśanāt /

30. *MSA, XVIII, 19–21:*

dhṛtivibhāge sapta ślokaḥ . . . /
vineyadurvinayatve kāyācintye jinasaya ca /
duṣkareṣu vicitreṣu saṃsārātyāga eva ca / / 20 / /
niḥsaṃkleśe ca tatraiva dhṛtir dhīrasya jāyate /
. . .

ebhis tribhiḥ ślokair dhṛtiprabhedaṃ darśayati / . . . / punar duṣkaracaryātaḥ / saṃcintyabhavopattitaḥ / tadasaṃkleśato 'pi prabhedaḥ /

31. *MSA*, XVIII, 44, commentary:

katham utpattitaḥ, saṃcintyabhavopapattau cakravartyādibhūtasya viśiṣṭakāya-vedanādi saṃpattau tadasaṃkleśataḥ /

32. *MSA*, XX–XXI, 12:

upapattau ca saṃcintya saṃkleśasyānurakṣaṇā /
. . . / / 12 / /

. . . saṣṭhyāṃ [bhūmau] pratītyasamutpādabahulavihāritayā saṃcintya-bhavopapattau tatra saṃkleśasyānurakṣanā / . . .

33. *TTP*, vol. 109, p. 114.3.8–4.2: dran pa dang shes bzhin ma nyams par gang nas gang du skye ba de dang der / 'di dang 'dir skye bar bya'o zhes shes bzhin du skye bas na / bsams bzhin du skye ba na yang rten cing 'brel te 'byung ba bsgom pa na mang du gnas pas nyon mongs pas mi gos pa'i phyir kun nas nyong mongs pa rjes su srung ba zhes bya'o / /

34. *Ch'êng wei shih lun*, Shindō Edition, chüan 9, p. 31, line 10.

35. MV, I, 13:

dvayābhāvo hy abhāvasya bhāvaḥ śūnyasya lakṣaṇaṃ / / 13 a,b / /

dvayagrāhyagrāhakasyābhāvaḥ / tasya cābhāvasya bhāvaḥ śūnyatāyā lakṣaṇam ity abhāvasvabhāvalakṣaṇatvaṃ śūnyatāyāḥ paridīpitaṃ bhavati /

36. See Toshihiko Izutsu, trans. *Rūmī Goroku*, Islam Classics, no. 2 (Tokyo: Iwanami Shoten, 1978). This is a Japanese translation of the *Kitāb Fī-hi Mā Fī-hi* of Jalal al-Dīn Rūmī. In his Introduction, the translator, Izutsu, discusses (pp. 427–35) such Sūfī ideas as fanā' (passing away) and baqā' (continuously remaining) and su'ūd (ascending) and nuzūl (descending). He compares and equates them with such Buddhist concepts as "going-thither" and "coming hither," "returning to the origin and arising from it," and "ascending and descending."

Chapter 4: Silence of the Buddha and its Madhyamic Interpretation

1. H. Beckh, *Buddhismus* (Sammlung Göschen), I, S. 113–4.

2. For instance, cf. *Saddharmapuṇḍarīka*, *Pūrvayoga-parivarta*, where we find frequent reference to *tūṣṇīṃbhāvenādhivāsayati sma*.

3. Troy Wilson Organ, "The Silence of the Buddha," *Philosophy East and West* (Honolulu: 1954), IV, 2, July, p. 129.

4. *Udāna*, I, p. 11.

5. *Dīgha-N.*, I, p. 179 (*Poṭṭhapāda-s*).

6. These words actually defy translation. The following may suggest their subtle flavor: solitude, retirement, voluntary exile from the world, patina, poverty, liking, and predilection.

7. The following may be mentioned among others: *Pāli-tipiṭaka, Vinaya, Mahāvagga;* Chinese translations, *Taishō* no. 189 (*Taishō,* vol. III, p. 642), no. 290 (p. 805), no. 191 (p. 953), no. 187 (p. 603); the Sanskrit original of the latter,*Lalitavistara,* ed., by S. Lefmann, 1902, p. 392. About Pāli texts, cf. G. J. Jennings, *The Vedāntic Buddhism of the Buddha* (London: 1948), pp. 36–38.

8. E. J. Thomas, *Early Buddhist Scriptures,* 1935, p. 23.

9. Ibid., p. 24.

10. Ibid., p. 25.

11. Cf. Jennings, op. cit., pp. 550–556; §§ "Unanswered Questions," "Metaphysics repudiated; Realism."

12. These questions are enumerated in several suttas, e.g.: *Dīgha-N.,* ix (*Poṭṭhapāda*), xxix (*Pāsādika*); *Majjhima-N.,* sutta 63 (*Māluṅkyāputta*), sutta 72 (*Vacchagotta*); *Saṃyutta-N.,* XXXIII, 1, etc.

13. Organ, op. cit.

14. Ibid., p. 139.

15. Tetsurō Watsuji, *Genshi Bukkyō no Jissen-tetsugaku* (Practical Philosophy of Primitive Buddhism) (Tokyo: 1927), pp. 133–4. Author's translation.

16. *Saṃyutta-N.,* IV, p. 400 *ff.* Cf. Organ, p. 129.

17. Cf. Jennings, op. cit., p. 556, "Rationalism."

18. *Aṅguttara-N,* III, 65, 3 (I, p. 189), *Majjhima-N.,* sutta 38 (I. p. 265), as quoted in S. Radhakrishnan, *The Dhammapada* (London: 1950), p. 10.

19. Radhakrishnan, ibid, quotes the gāthā *Jñānasārasamuccaya,* 31. (see S. Yamaguchi, "*Jñānasārasamuccaya,*" Otani Gakuho, XIX, 4, p. 66). The same gāthā is also quoted in S. Mookerjee, *The Buddhist Philosophy of Universal Flux* (Calcutta: 1935) p. xl, from *Tattvasaṃgraha-pañjikā* (Gaekwad Oriental series ed.), p. 12. In the *Tattvasaṃgraha* (Bauddha Bharati series ed.), it is k. 3537.

20. *Taishō,* vol. XVI, p. 692c; É. Lamotte, ed. and tr. *Saṃdhinirmocana-sūtra* (Louvain: 1935), p. 186–7.

21. *Taishō,* vol. XIV, p. 551c; cf. Organ, p. 137–8.

22. *Taishō,* vol. XXXII, p. 576a.

23. *Hua-yen Wu-chiao-chang, Taishō,* vol. XLV, p. 477a.

24. *Mūlamadhyamaka-kārikās* (*Mādhyamikasūtras*) *de Nāgārjuna, avec la Prasannapadā Commentaire de Crandrakīrti,* publiée par Louis de La Vallée Poussin (Bibliotheca Buddhica, IV, St-Pétersbourg, 1913), p. 372 (chap. XVIII *Ātma-parīkṣā,* k. 9). (Hereafter, *Prasannapadā*). See also J. W. de Jong, *Cinq chapitres de la Prasannapadā* (Paris: 1949), p. 29.

25. *Prasannapadā,* p. 491.

26. Ibid., p. 538; Theodore Stcherbatsky, *The Conception of Buddhist Nirvāṇa* (Leningrad: 1927), p. 208.

27. *Prasannapadā,* p. 57, lines 7–8; Stcherbatsky, op. cit., p. 138.

28. See note 44.

29. *Prasannapadā,* p. 444.

30. Ibid., p. 534.

31. Ibid., p. 475.

32. Ibid., p. 505–6. The chap. XXV (Nirvāṇa), k. 1 and 2 stand in a similar relation of question and answer; see ibid, pp. 519, 521, and Stcherbatsky, op. cit., pp. 183 and 186.

33. "Vigrahavyāvartanī," ed. by E. H. Johnston and A. Kunst, *Mélanges chinois et bouddhiques*, vol. IX, 1951. Translation of text into French by S. Yamaguchi (*JA*, 1929), into English by G. Tucci (*Pre-Diṅnāga Buddhist texts on Logic*, Baroda, 1929), and into Japanese by Yamaguchi (*Mikkyō Bunka* 1949–50, incomplete).

34. *Taishō*, vol. XXXII, p. 576a.

35. A similar analogy, but with a slight difference in meaning, is read also in the *Vigrahavyāvartanī*, k. 3 and k. 25, where Nāgārjuna claims that both voices, prohibitive and prohibited, are altogether without substance.

36. *Prasannapadā*, p. 500.

37. Ibid., p. 503. In the T'ien-t'ai school it is called 三諦偈 or the "verse of Threefold Truth."

38. Vigrahavyāvartanī, p. 151: svayam adhigantavyā anayā diśā kiṃcic chakyaṃ vacenopadeṣṭum iti /

39. The purport of the words "discriminating between the Twofold Truth" appears in Nāgārjuna's own gāthā (the *Mūlamadhyamakakārikā*, XXIV.9) for which see *Prasannapadā*, p. 494 and for Candrakīrti's restatement of it, see ibid, p. 69 line 1, and p. 495 line 9.

40. Gadjin M. Nagao, "Chūkan-tetsugaku no Komponteki Tachiba," *Tetsugaku-kenkyū*, no. 370, pp. 22 *ff*. Reprinted in *Chūkan to Yuishiki* pp. 92 *ff*. See also Nagao, *A Study of Tibetan Buddhism* (Tokyo: 1954), p. 158.

41. Nagao, "An Interpretation of the Term "Saṃvṛti" (Convention) in Buddhism." First appeared in *Silver Jubilee Volume of the Zinbun-Kagaku-Kenkyūsyo* (Kyoto: Kyoto University, 1954), pp. 550–561. Revised and reprinted in the present volume.

42. *Prasannapadā*, p. 492 (XXIV, 8).

43. Ibid., p. 2–3; . . . advayajñānālaṃkṛtaṃ mahākaruṇopāyapuraḥsaraṃ prathamacittotpādaṃ tathāgatajñānotpattihetum ādiṃ kṛtvā yāvād ācāryārya-nāgārjunasya viditāviparītaprajñāpāramitānīteḥ . . . karuṇayā parāvabodhārthaṃ śastrapraṇayanaṃ . . .

44. For instance, *Vigrahavyāvartanī*, k. 29–30; *Nyāya-ṣaṣṭika*, k. 50. (As for the Yamaguchi's Japanese version of the latter, see his *Chūkan Bukkyō Ronkō* or *Mādhyamika Buddhism Miscellanies* (Tokyo: 1944), p. 100. The same phraseology by Āryadeva, Candrakīrti, et al, are found in Nagao, *A Study of Tibetan Buddhism*, pp. 235, 264.

45. See note 43.

46. Nagao, *A Study of Tibetan Buddhism*, p. 279 *ff*., where *Prasannapadā*, pp. 34–36 and others are interpreted. See also Prasannapadā, pp. 57, line 9, 74, line 1.

47. *Prasannapadā*, p. 24, line 7: tathā cācāryo bhūyasā prasaṅgāpatti-mukhenaiva parapakṣaṃ nirākaroti sma.

48. Ibid., p, 23, line 3: prasaṅgaviparītena cārthena parasyaiva saṃbandho, nāsmākaṃ, svapratijñāyā abhāvāt.

49. See, for instance, *Taishō*, vol. III, p. 953a; p. 604c.

50. T. W. Rhys Davids, *Buddhism* [Non-Christian Religious Systems] (London: 1887), pp. 39–42.

Chapter 5: What Remains in *Śūnyatā*

1. Richard Robinson, *The Buddhist Religion* (California: Dickenson, 1970), p. 53.

2. Sylvain Lévi, ed., *Mahāyānasūtrālaṃkāra* (Paris: H. Champion, 1907), p. 76, XI, 77; Étienne Lamotte, ed. and trans., *La somme du grand véhicule d'Asaṅga* (*Mahāyānasaṃgraha*) (Louvain: Bureaux du Muséon, 1938), vol. II. pp. 115–18; Dignāga, *Prajñāpāramitāpiṇḍārthasaṃgraha,* vv. 19–54, in E. Frauwallner, ed., "Dignāga, sein Werk und seine Entwicklung," *Wiener Zeitscrift für die Kunde Süd-und Ostasiens* III (1959), pp. 141–43.

3. Gadjin M. Nagao, ed., *Madhyāntavibhāga-bhāṣya* (hereafter, *MV.*). (Tokyo: Suzuki Research Foundation, 1964), pp. 24–26; Frauwallner, "Dignāga," p. 141, vv. 8–18.

4. *Majjhima Nikāya,* sutta no. 121. See I. B. Horner, *Middle Length Sayings,* vol. III, pp. 147 *ff.* The translation of quotations from this sutta as it appears in this essay is the author's.

5. . . . imam eva kāyaṃ paṭicca saḷāyatanikaṃ jīvitapaccayā.

6. Iti yaṃ hi kho tattha na hoti, tena taṃ suññaṃ samanupassati; yaṃ pana tattha avasiṭṭhaṃ hoti, taṃ santaṃ idam atthīti pajānāti

7. *The Cūḷasuññata sutta* (*Majjhimanikāya,* sutta no. 121) is discussed by Ruegg in connection with the idea of the *tathāgatagarbha.* See David Seyfort Reugg, *La théorie du Tathāgatagarbha et du gotra* (Paris: École française d'extrême-orient, 1969), pp. 319 *ff.* Some of the texts to be discussed later are also referred to extensively in this study.

8. Other editions of the *Madhyāntavibhāga* besides the author's (note 3) are: Susumu Yamaguchi, *Sthiramati: Madhyāntavibhāgaṭīkā* (Nagoya: Librairie Hajinkaku, 1934; reprinted Tokyo, 1966); V. Bhattacharya and G. Tucci *Madhyāntavibhāgasūtrabhāṣyaṭīkā of Sthiramati,* Part I (London: Luzac, Calcutta Oriental Series no. 24, 1932); and R. C. Pandeya, *Madhyāntavibhāga-śāstra* (Delhi: Motilal Banarsidass, 1971). English Translations have been published by F. T. Stcherbatsky, "*Madhyāntavibhāgasūtra,*" Bibliotheca Buddhica XXX (1936); and by D. L. Friedmann, *Sthiramati, Madhyāntavibhāga-ṭīkā, Analysis of the Middle Path and the Extremes* (Utrecht: 1937).

9. *Madhyāntavibhāga* I.1: abhūtaparikalpo 'sti, dvayaṃ tatra na vidyate / śūnyatā vidyate tv atra, tasyām api sa vidyate / cf Reugg, *La théorie,* pp. 323 *ff.*

10. *Madhyāntavibhāga* I.2: na śūnyaṃ nāpi cāśūnyaṃ tasmāt sarvam vidhīyate / sattvād asattvāt sattvāc ca, madhyamā pratipac ca sā /

11. evaṃ "yad yatra nāsti tat tena śūnyam iti yathābhutaṃ samanupaśyati yat punar atrāvaśiṣṭam bhavati tat sad ihāstīti yathābhūtaṃ prajānātī" ty aviparītaṃ śūnyatālakṣaṇam udbhāvitam bhavati.

12. The translation from the *Madhyāntavibhāga* is the author's. Compare the Sanskrit original with the Pāli text.

13. There must have existed a version of the *Cūḷasuññāta-sutta* in Sanskrit, of which the author of the *Laṅkāvatāra-sūtra* had knowledge. The *Laṅkāvatāra-sūtra,* edited by B. Nanjio (Kyoto: Otani University Press, 1923), p. 75, expounds *itaretara-śūnyatā* (mutual emptiness) as follows:

itaretara-śūnyatā punar mahāmate katamā, yad uta yad yatra nāsti tat tena śūnyaṃ'' ity ucyate . . . aśūnyaṃ ca bhikṣubhir iti bhāṣitaṃ mayā, sa (=prāsāda) ca taiḥ / (= hastigavaiḍakādi) / śūnya ity ucyate . . .

This passage seems to include some quotations from the *Cūḷasuññata-sutta;* at least the sentence enclosed within single quotation marks is the same as the first part of the passage quoted in the *Madhyāntavibhāga.* The *Laṅkāvatāra-sūtra,* which expounds the doctrines of both the Yogācāra and the *tathāgata-garbha,* declares the śūnyatā taught in the *Cūḷasuññata-sutta* (or the *itaretara-śūnyatā,* as the *Laṅkāvatāra-sūtra* calls it) to be of inferior character, while the Yogācāras evaluate it as an ''unperverted'' interpretation. Also cf. Ruegg, *La théorie,* pp. 321, 325.

14. dvayābhāvo hy abhāvasya bhāvaḥ śūnyasya lakṣaṇam.

15. For instance, Bhāvaviveka's attack is found in his *Madhyamaka-hṛdaya,* chapter V, vv. 10–16 (Peking reprint edition, vol. 96, pp. 11–13). Cf. Susumu Yamaguchi, *Bukkyō ni okeru Mu to U tono Tairon* (*Controversy between the Theories of Nonbeing and Being in Buddhism*) (Tokyo-Kyoto: Kōbundō-shobō, 1941), pp. 178–210 and Appendix, pp. 6–8.

16. Edward Conze, *Buddhist Wisdom Books* (London: George Allen and Unwin, 1958), p. 81: rūpaṃ śūnyatā, śūnyataiva rūpaṃ.

17. In quoting Candrakīrti's *Prasannapadā,* Tsong-kha-pa argues to this effect in his *Lam-rim chen-mo* (Peking reprint edition, vol. 152, no. 6001), p 133–2. Cf. author's Japanese translation, *Chibetto Bukkyō Kenkyū* (Tokyo: Iwanami, 1954), pp. 124 *ff.*

18. As for the term *upādāya prajñaptiḥ,* see Jacques May, *Candrakīrti, Prasannapadā Madhyamakavṛtti* (Paris: Adrien Maisonneuve, 1959), p. 161, n. 494; pp. 237–38, n. 840; etc.

19. *Mahāyānasūtrālaṃkāra* XIV.34; *Madhyāntavibhāgabhāṣya* III.3, III.7.

20. For instance, Candrakīrti criticizes the notion of *paratantra* in his *Madhyamakāvatāra,* (VI. 72–83), Louis de La Vallée Poussin, ed., (St.-Pétersbourg: Biblioteca Buddhica IX, 1912), 166–181.

21. U. Wogihara, ed., *Bodhisattvabhūmi* (Tokyo: Seigo Kenkyukai, 1930–1936), pp. 47–48; N. Dutt, ed., *Bodhisattvabhūmi* (Patna: K. P. Jayaswal Institute, Tibetan Sanscrit Works Series vol. VII, 1966), p. 32. Cf. Ruegg, *La théorie,* pp. 322 *ff.*

22. yataś ca ''yad yatra na bhavati. tat tena śūnyam iti samanupaśyati. yat punar atrāvaśiṣṭaṃ bhavati. tat sad ihāstīti yathābhūtaṃ prajānāti.'' iyam ucyate śūnyatāvakrāntir yathābhūtā aviparītā. For the Tibetan translation, see note 24.

23. Chinese versions: *Taishō* no. 1605, vol. XXXI, p. 675a, line 21; no. 1606, vol. 31, p. 720c, line 17. Tibetan versions: Peking reprint edition no. 5550, vol. 112, p. 252–3–1; no. 5555, vol. 113, p. 172–1–6. In Sanskrit, V. V. Gokhale, ''Fragments from the *Abhidharmasamuccaya* of Asaṃga,'' Journal of the Bombay Branch, Royal Asiatic Society. N. S., 23 (1947); Pralhad Pradhan, ed., *Abhidharma Samuccaya of Asanga* (Santiniketan: Visva-Bharati, 1950), p. 40. Cf. Ruegg, *La théorie,* pp. 321 *f.*

24. As this portion is lacking in the original Sanskrit published by Gokhale, Pradhan tried in his book to fill in the lacunae by his "retranslation." But because of his misunderstanding of the passage, and also his ignorance about the relationship between the texts mentioned earlier, the passage in question appears here with entirely different features and must be revised thoroughly. The Tibetan versions are as follows:

(Bodhisattvabhūmi) gang gi phyir "gang la gang med pa de ni des stong par yang dag par mthong la / 'di la lhag ma gang yin pa de ni 'di na yang dag par yod do zhes yang dag pa ji lta ba bzhin du rab tu shes pa" de ni stong pa nyid la yang dag pa ji lta ba bzhin du phyin ci ma log par zhugs pa zhes bya ste /

(Abhidharmascamuccaya) "gang la gang med pa de ni des stong par yang dag par rjes su mthong ba ste / 'di la lhag ma gang yin pa de ni 'dir yod pa'o / / zhes yang dag pa ji lta ba bzhin du rab tu shes so" / / 'di ni stong pa nyid la 'jug pa yang dag pa ji lta ba ste / phyin ci ma log pa zhes bya'o /

25. *Taishō* no. 1602, vol. XXXI, p. 553b.

26. G. Tucci, *Minor Buddhist Texts,* Serie Orientale Roma IX, part I (Roma: Istituto Italiano per il Medio ed Estremo Oriente, 1956), pp. 53 *ff.*

27. For example, sarvābhāvād, abhāvasya sadbhāvān . . . (v. 11). Also see v. 46 and the commentary on v. 15 (*Taishō* no. 1513, vol. XXV, p. 877a).

28. So called in the *Vimalakīrtinirdeśa;* cf. Étienne Lamotte, *L'Enseignement de Vimalakīrti* (Louvain: Bibliothéque du Muséon, vol. 51, 1962), p. 34.

29. See Edward Conze, ed. and trans., *Vajracchedikā Prajñāpāramitā,* Serie Orientale Roma XIII (Roma: Istituto Italiano per il Medio ed Estremo Oriente, 1957), p. 70 (8).

30. Ibid., p. 76 (14a).

31. The passage that includes "what remains" also appears in the *Madhyamakāvatāra* (Louis de la Vallée Poussin, p. 139, ad VI.57), but this is introduced by Candrakīrti to demonstrate the position of the rival Vijñāna school. This passage is close to one found in the *Bodhisattvabhūmi*. Jayānanda comments on this passage as follows (Peking reprint edition, vol. 99, p. 147–5):

> yatra [in something whatsoever] means "in the paratantra;" yan nāsti [what does not exist] means "the duality of subject and object does not;" tat means "the paratantra;" tena śūnyam means "is śūnya with regard to duality;" avaśiṣṭaṃ bhavati [what remains] means "knowledge which is śūnya with regard to duality" (gzung ba dang 'dzin pas stong pa'i shes pa).

Jayanada also comments that the passage is used to introduce the testimony of the Āgamas (suttas). We can notice in this commentary that the interpretation is fairly different from that of the treatises mentioned above; that the opponent here attacked by Candrakīrti is the later Vijñānavāda (as distinguished from the earlier Yogācāras), probably the sākāra-vāda, which holds a view of "Idealistic Realism," that is, the Realism of *vijñāna* (knowing) or of *paratantra*.

32. For one thing, the authorship is ascribed to Maitreyanātha, the founder of the Yogācāra school, in the Tibetan tradition.

33. E. H. Johnston, ed., *The Ratnagotravibhāga Mahāyānottaratantraśāstra* (Patna: Bihar Research Society, 1950), p. 76. Jikido Takasaki, *A Study on the Ratnagotravibhāga,* Serie Orientale Roma, XXXIII (Roma: Istituto Italiano per il Medio ed Estremo Oriente, 1966), pp. 300–302. Cf. Ruegg, *La théorie,* pp. 319 *ff.*

34. *Taishō* no. 353, vol. XII, p. 221c; no. 310 (48), vol. XI, p. 677a. Kenryū Tsukinowa, *Zōkanwa Sanyaku Gappeki Shōmankyō Hōgatsudōji-shomon-kyō* (Hōdōkai, 1940) p. 132. Jikidō Takasaki, *Nyoraikei Kyōten* (Tokyo: Chūō-kōronsha, 1975) p. 110. Alex Wayman and Hideko Wayman trans. *The Lion's Roar of Queen Śrīmālā,* (New York and London: Columbia University Press, 1974), p. 99.

35. . . . evaṃ "yad yatra nāsti tat tena śūnyam iti samanupaśyati / yat punar atrāvaśiṣṭaṃ bhavati tat sad ihāstīti yathābhūtam prajānāti" /

36. The *tathāgatagarbha* seems to me to occupy a supreme position—a position akin to that of Brahman or Ātman, or other "Absolute Being," in Brahmanical philosophy. If this is the case, it is difficult for the *tathāgatagarbha* to include within itself elements of contamination as entities to be negated, or to possess the "double structure" of *abhūta*-entities to be negated, or to possess the "double structure" of *abhūta-parikalpa* = śūnyatā.

37. The "itaretara-śūnyatā" of the *Laṅkāvatāra-sūtra* (note 13 above) and the idea of "gzhan-stong" in the Jo-nang-pa school have been studied minutely by Ruegg, *La théorie,* pp. 325 *ff.*, 337. Though I am not quite sure of these ideas, what I have tried to suggest with the phrase "arithmetical subtraction" seems to be applicable to these ideas.

38. Johnston, *Ratnagotravibhāga,* p. 35, line 3 . . . paramārthataḥ saṃsāra eva nirvāṇam ity uktam.

39. *Madhyāntavibhāga* I.22.

Chapter 6: The Buddhist World View as Elucidate in the Three-nature Theory and Its Similes

1. The term "three-nature" is sometimes replaced by "three-characteristic" (*trilakṣaṇa*); the implication remains virtually the same. Main sources for the theory are: *Saṃdhinirmocanasūtra,* chapters VI–VII; *Yogācārabhūmi-viniścaya-saṃgrahaṇī* (*Taishō* XXX, p. 703a *ff.*); *Mahāyānasūtrālaṃkāra,* XI.13, 38–41, etc.; *Madhyāntavibhāga* (hereafter *MV.*), chapter III; *Tri-svabhāva; Triṃśikā,* kk. 20–24; *Ch'êng-wei-shih-lun, chüan* 8–9.

2. "Willows are green and flowers are red" is a popular Zen saying which denotes the Zen enlightenment or *Satori.* The willows and flowers in this saying are not those belonging to the imagined world, but those viewed by the enlightened ones, that is, those of the consummated nature. While there is a difference of dimension between the ordinary, mundane level, and the supramundane, still willows remain willows, flowers remain flowers.

3. In this sense, it is not strictly identical with the world dealt with by a scientist; it is realized only upon realization of the consummated world. See n. 13 below.

4. É. Lamotte, ed., *Mahāyānasaṃgraha*, IX.1:
de la 'khor ba ni gzhan gyi dbang gi ngo bo nyid de kun nas nyon mongs pa'i char gtogs pa'o / / mya ngan las 'das pa ni de nyid rnam par byang ba'i char gtogs pa'o / / gnas ni de nyid gnyi ga'i char gtogs pa ste / gzhan gyi dbang gi ngo bo nyid do /

> Saṃsāra refers to the other-dependent nature in its aspect of defilement. Nirvāṇa refers to the same in its aspect of purity. The basis refers to the twofold aspect of the same, the other-dependent nature.

With regard to the "twofold aspect (=two division) of the other-dependent nature," see n. 9 below for the locus of its first appearance.

5. "Convertibility" is the author's translation; a Sanskrit equivalent is not readily available. Convertibility may include various notions, "change, transformation" (*vikāra, pariṇāma, anyathābhāva*), "turnabout, transmutation" (*parāvṛtti*), and so forth. Special attention may be drawn to the term *paryāya* which, originally meaning "turning round, revolution; way, manner; opportunity, occasion," and so on, is generally used in the meaning of "synonym," "convertible term." *Mahāyānasaṃgraha*, II.17 reads:

> gzhan gyi dbang gi ngo bo nyid ni rnam grangs kyis na (=paryāyeṇa) gzhan gyi dbang ngo / / rnam grangs kyis na (=paryāyeṇa) de nyid kun brtags pa'o / / rnam grangs kyis na (=paryāyeṇa) de nyid yongs su grub pa'o / /

"The other-dependent nature is on occasion the other-dependent; on occasion the same is the imagined; and on occasion the same is the consummated."

Here, the term *paryāyeṇa* ("on occasion") indicates simply what the author has called "convertibility." For more details, see the author's article, "Logic of Convertibility."

6. "Medium" "mediator," and the like are also notions obtained by extending the function of the "basis." It is not a translation of a Sanskrit term.

7. With regard to the notion of crossing over to the consummated world indirectly via the other-dependent world, and the notion of "recovery," see below.

8. *Mahāyānasaṃgraha*, III.8 (*Taishō*, XXXI, p. 143a). The first two factors in the simile, snake and rope, are often used as a simile for delusion in other schools such as the Mādhyamika, but the third factor, hemp, and the rest, are peculiar to this simile.

9. *Mahāyānasaṃgraha*, II.29 (*Taishō*, XXXI, p. 140c), where the simile is introduced to illustrate the famous theory of "the other-dependent nature having two divisions (=twofold aspect)." The simile appears by name in *Mvy* 7650.

10. While the term non-discriminative or non-dichotomizing wisdom rarely appears in the Mādhyamika texts, it is, together with its counterpart "the mundane (discriminative) wisdom obtained after [the non-discriminative wisdom is accomplished]" (*pṛṣṭhalabdha-laukikajñāna*), one of the most important notions of the Yogācāra school.

11. The simile of *māyā* is widely used not only in the Yogācāra but also in other schools for the purpose of illustrating the delusive character of the world. For the simile's special association with the three-nature theory, see: *Mahāyānasūtrālaṃkāra,* XI.18–29; *Trisvabhāva,* kk. 26–30.

12. *Triṃśikā,* k. 21cd; niṣpannas tasya purveṇa sadā rahitatā tu yā. The English is a free translation. Although a short treatise of only thirty verses, the *Triṃśikā* of Vasubandhu is one of the fundamental texts of the Yogācāra-vijñānavāda.

13. *Triṃśikā,* k. 22d; nādṛṣṭe 'smin sa dṛśyate.

14. The opposite direction, from the consummated to the other-dependent, also suggests remarkable Buddhist features such as: a bodhisattva's return from the nirvāṇic world to the saṃsāric world, descending from Buddhahood to bodhisattvahood, from the non-discriminative wisdom to the mundane discriminative but pure wisdom.

15. Cf. *Mahāyānasaṃgraha,* II.17; *Trisvabhāva,* kk. 18–21; *Triṃśikā,* k. 22ab.

16. The term "cognition-only" (*vijñāna-mātra,*) or more properly, "presentation-only" (*vijñapti-mātra*), is referred to variously as "mind-only" (*citta-mātra*), "discrimination-only" (*vikalpa-mātra*), and so on, but for convenience, the term "cognition-only" will be used here.

17. *MV.*, I.3; artha-sattvātma-vijñapti-pratibhāsam prajāyate / vijñānam. . . .

18. It seems that there are different types of "cognition-only" according to the situations under which it is expounded. *Dharmadharmatā-vibhāga,* IX.7 (section number given by S. Yamaguchi; ed. J. Nozawa, p. 17.7–10) reads:

> Having acquired [the illusiveness of the conceptual discrimination], one realizes the acquisition of the cognition-only. Having acquired the cognition-only, one realizes the non-acquisition of all objects. From the non-acquisition of all objects, one realizes the non-acquisition of even cognition-only. From the non-acquisition of that, one realizes the acquisition of the non-distinction of the two, the objects and the subject. (Author's translation)

This is the so-called 'means for entering into the characteristic of non-existence' (*asallakṣaṇānupraveśopāya*) or the 'aid for penetration' (*nirvedhabhāgīya*), and expositions similar to the one quoted here are found in: *Mahāyānasūtrālaṃkāra,* VI.7–8; *MV.*, I.6–7; *Trisvabhāva,* kk. 35–37, and so forth. In these expositions, the "cognition-only" is once established as a realization of truth of a sort, but it is negated the next moment to lead one to a higher position, which is expressed in the above quotation as 'the acquisition of the non-distinction of the two, the objects and the subject,' that is, the acquisition of non-duality. "Cognition-only" established once but negated can be said to belong to a lower level. Apart from this, with regard to the higher level "cognition-only," Asaṅga declares in his *Mahāyānasaṃgraha,* chapter III, that to realize cognition-only means the realization of the three natures, the ultimate truth. Further, in his *Triṃśikā,* kk. 25d and following, Vasubandhu defines the consummated nature as the state of cognition-only. In these texts, cognition-only is never negated, itself being the highest reality. It is likely that the cognition-only of the lower level is referred to by terms such as "*vijñaptimātra*" or "*cittamātra,*" while the cognition-only of the higher and ultimate level is named always "*vijñaptimātratā,*" *with a* "*-tā*" affixed.

19. *Saṃdhinirmocana-sūtra,* VI.8 (ed, É. Lamotte, pp. 61–62; *Taishō,* vol. XVI, p. 693b).

Chapter 7: Connotation of the Word Āśraya (Basis) in the *Mahāyāna-sūtrālamkāra*

1. *MSA.*, edited by Sylvain Lévi, Paris, 1907. The author refers in this paper to the number of chapters in Roman symbols and verses in Arabic numbers.

2. See author's paper "The Terminologies of the *Mahāyāna-sūtrālaṃkāra*" (in Japanese), which appeared in the *Journal of Indian and Buddhist Studies,* vol. 4, 2 (Tokyo 1956).

3. U. Wogihara, *Sanskrit-Japanese Dictionary* (Tokyo: 1940–1948; completed and reprinted in 1979), p. 216.

4. F. Edgerton, *Buddhist Hybrid Sanskrit Grammar and Dictionary,* vol. 2, (New Haven: 1953), p. 110.

5. A. Bareau, "Index of *Viṃśatikā* & *Triṃśikā* of Vasubandhu", *Vak* no. 3 (Poona: 1953), p. 108.

6. Sir M. Monier-Williams, *A Sanskrit-English Dictionary,* p. 158.

7. This simile (text, p. 152, line 15) is analogous to the relationship between the sense organs (= support, seat) and the vijñānas or ideation that depend upon the former. This simile serves to prove and to establish the "momentariness" of the world. The sense organs as the āśraya will be discussed under (6). I am, however, inclined to think that through this passage the notion of the Budhist *pratītyasamutpāda* (dependent origination) was to be elucidated in terms of, and in relation between, the *āśraya* (the basis) and the *āśrita* (the dependent).

8. Sthiramati's commentary to the *MSA,* the *Mdo sde rgyan gyi 'grel bshad* (*Sūtrālaṃkāra-vṛtti-bhāṣya*), Tanjur, Peking ed., vol. Mi, 176a. Reprinted Peking edition, no. 5531, vol. 108, p. 270. Derge Tanjur, Tokyo University edition, vol. Sems tsams 3, p. 79 (Mi, 157b).

9. Other passages which belong to the same category are: *MSA*. I.12, III.4, XX–XXI.29, 47.

10. This group of eight terms is found elsewhere, in *MSA* XVII.5 and 9, where, however, the meaning of *āśraya* seems to be different. The Buddha is meant to be the *āśraya* of *pūjanā* in one place, and the ten sorts of virtuous men are enumerated as the *āśraya* of *sevanā* in another place. And in both cases, these *āśrayas* seem to be the object, not the subject, of *pūjanā* or *sevanā*.

11. The seven terms, *āśraya* to *kṣetra,* signify seven (excluding the vocative) syntactic cases, the nominative to locative, respectively. The last term *niśraya* means "resource" of liberality in three kinds: *adhimukti, manaskāra,* and *samādhi.*

12. Sthiramati's commentary to the *MSA,* the *Mdo sde rgyan gyi 'grel bshad* (*Sūtrālaṃkāra-vṛtti-bhāṣya*), Tanjur, Peking ed., vol. Mi, 107b. Reprinted Peking

edition, no. 5531, vol. 108, p. 243. Derge Tanjur, Tokyo University edition, vol. Sems tsams 3, p. 47 (Mi, 94b).

13. Ibid., Peking ed., vol. Mi, 109a. Reprinted Peking edition, no. 5531, vol. 108, p. 243. Derge Tanjur, Tokyo University edition, vol. Sems tsams 3, p. 47 (Mi, 96a).

14. Other examples are: *MSA*. VIII.12, XX–XXI.50.

15. Dehaḥ sendriyam śarīram, Sthiramati, *Madhyāntavibhāgaṭīkā* (ed. S. Yamaguchi), p. 161. Sthiramati's commentary on the *Triṃśikā* (ed., Sylvain Lévi), p. 19 gives a similar expression: āśraya ātmabhāvaḥ sādhiṣṭhānam indriya-rūpaṃ nāma ca.

16. The expression "*āśraya-parāvṛtti*" is considered separately under the ninth definition given in *MSA*.

17. A similar equating of *amala-āśraya* (or *amala-pada*, undefiled base) to *anāsrava-dhātu* (*dhātu* without any impurity), which actually means the *dharma-dhātu*, will be seen in *MSA*. IX.47, 48, 77.

18. The interpretations by both Vasubandhu and Sthiramati run roughly as above, but another one may be possible here. That the *dharmadhātu* is the basis not only of the *bodhisattvas*, but also of the hīnayānists, that is, *śrāvakas* and *pratyeka-buddhas*, suggests that the so-called *Tathāgatagarbha* (the matrix of the Buddha) is thought of. The Buddha is the matrix, from which all worldly things, mean and defiled, emanate. Concerning this idea see, for instance, the *Ratna-gotra-vibhāga*, ed. E. H. Johnston, I.56–57, where *citta-viśuddhi*, the mind in purity, is proclaimed to be the basis of all defilements, false discrimination and so on.

19. Besides those which will be enumerated below, we have examples of this expression in the commentaries on the following verses: *MSA*. VI.9, IX.12, XI.11, 33, 42, and XVI.67. Of these, a noteworthy explanation of this term is found in *MSA*. IX.12–17.

20. See the quotation from the *Triṃśikā* in note 15.

21. É. Lamotte, ed., *Mahāyānasaṃgraha* IX.1.

22. Ibid., X.3, 4, 5.

23. *Triṃśikā*, p. 19: upādāna = upagamana = ekayogakṣematva.

24. G. M. Nagao, ed., *Madhyāntavibhāgabhāṣya* I.1.

25. "Abode" here means "bhājana-loka" or receptacle-world, that is, the outer world surrounding human beings. "Object" and "body" refer to six sense-objects and six sense-organs, respectively.

26. *Manas* (the mind or minding), *udgraha* (perception or taking up), and *vikalpa* (imagination, discrimination, or thought construct) refer to the seventh "*manas*," the five cognitions, and the sixth cognition (*mano-vijñāna*), respectively. These three represent the noetic aspect (*grāhaka*) of the *ālayavijñāna*, while the afore-mentioned three, "abode" and so forth represent the noematic aspect (*grāhya*). The ultimate enlightenment, thus, consists of the *anāsrava-dhātu*, the revolving of *grāhya*, and the *vaśitā* or mastery, the revolving of *grāhaka*.

27. In the translations and commentaries of Chen-ti or Paramārtha.

Chapter 8: Usages and Meanings of *Pariṇāmanā*

1. U. Wogihara ed., *Aṣṭasāhasrikā*, pp. 328–9: evam anumodya "anumodanāsahagataṃ puṇyakriyāvastu anuttarāyāṃ samyaksambodhau pariṇāmayāmi"—iti vācaṃ bhāṣeta "anuttarāyāḥ samyaksambodher āhārakaṃ bhavatav" iti / Translation by Edward Conze.

2. J. Radher, ed., *Daśabhūmika-sūtra*, p. 20, (1 VV), [sa bodhisattvaḥ] . . . tāni ca kuśalamūlāny anuttarāyāṃ samyaksambodhau pariṇāmayati /

3. G. M. Nagao, ed., *Madhyāntavibhāgabhāṣya*, p. 32: [bodhiprāptukāmena . . . bodhisattvena . . . prahīṇāvaraṇena sarvāṇi kuśalamūlāni anuttarāyāṃ samyaksaṃbodhau pariṇāmayitavyāni /

4. J. Radher, op. cit., p. 58.18–19: sarvā bodhisattvācaryāpagatakleśakalmāṣā bodhipariṇāmanādhipatyena pratyetavyā(ḥ). Translation by Franklin Edgerton, *Buddhist Hybrid-Sanskrit Dictionary*, p. 323, right column.

5. *TTP*, XXV, 286–1–2: . . . byang chub sems dpa'i spyod pa thams cad byang chub yongs su bsngos pa'i dbang gis nyon mongs pa'i rnyog pa dang bral bar . . . yid ches par bya ste /

6. Both editions of *Daśabhūmika*, Rahder and Ryūkō Kondō (p. 119.4), have *pratyetavyā* that Edgerton wrongly emends and reads as *pratyetavyāḥ*.

7. *Mahāyānasūtrālaṃkāra* XX–XXI.11, *Vyākhyā:* caturthyāṃ bodhipakṣabahulavihāriṇo 'pi bodhipakṣāṇāṃ saṃsāre pariṇāmanā /

8. *Mahāyānasūtrālaṃkāra* XX–XXI.11: tau ca labdhāryamārgasya bhaveṣu pariṇāmanāt / acintyapariṇāmikyā upapattyā samanvitau / /

9. *Vyākhyā* on the above: acintyo hi tasyāryamārgasya pariṇāma upapattau, tasmād acintyapariṇāmikī.

Chapter 9: Tranquil Flow of Mind: An Interpretation of *Upeksā*

1. Kōgen Mizuno, *Pali Bukkyō o Chūshin toshita Bukkyō no Shinshiki-ron* (Mind and Mental Factors in Buddhist Philosophy, on the basis of Pāli Buddhism) (Tokyo: Sankibō Busshorin, 1964), pp. 630–31.

2. Ibid., p. 632.

3. See Abbreviations.

4. *Triṃśikā*, p. 27.29–28.6: upekṣā cittasamatā cittapraśaṭhatā cittānābhogatā / ebhis tribhiḥ padair upekṣāyā ādimadhyāvasānāvasthā dyotitā / tatra laya auddhatyaṃ vā cetaso vaiṣamyaṃ / tasyābhāvād ādau cittasamatā / tato 'nabhisaṃskāreṇāprayatnena samāhitacetaso yathā[bhi]yogaṃ samasyaiva yā pravṛttiḥ sā cittapraśaṭhatā / sā punar avasthā layauddhatyaśaṅkānugatācirabhāvitvāt / tato bhāvanāprakarṣagamanāt tadvipakṣadūrībhāvāt tacchaṅkābhāve layauddhatyapratipakṣanimitteṣv ābhogam akurvato 'nābhogāvasthā cittasyānābhogatā / iyaṃ ca sarvakleśopakleśānavakāśasaṃniśrayadānakarmikā /

5. É. Lamotte, *Saṃdhinirmocana Sūtra, L'explication des mystères* (Louvain-Paris, 1935), VIII.18, p. 97; *Taishō* 676, vol. XVI, p. 699b.

6. Unrai Wogihara ed., *Bodhisattvabhūmi* (Tokyo: Taishō Daigaku, 1930–36), p. 83.7–9 and p. 205.15–18. Nalinaksha Dutt, ed., Tibetan Sanskrit Works series VII (Patna: K. P. Jayaswal Research Institute, 1966), p. 59.1–2 and p. 141.23–25.

7. See Abbreviations.

8. *TTP*, vol. 108, p. 319–1–5 *f.*, vol. 109, p. 53–5–4 *f.*, p. 55–1–5 *f.*, p. 61–2–1 *f.*

9. Sylvain Lévi, *Matériaux pour l'étude du systēme Vijñaptimātra* (Paris: 1932), p. 89, n. 1.

10. Herman Jacobi, *Triṃśikāvijñapti des Vasubandhu, mit Bhāṣya des Ācārya Sthiramati* (Stuttgart: Verlag von W. Kohlhammer, 1932), S. 31.

11. Walpola Rahula, *Le compendium de la super-doctrine (philosophie)* (*Abhidharmasamuccaya*) *d'Asaṅga* (Paris: École Française d'extrême-orient, 1971), p. 9.

12. Once Wogihara suggested a relationship between *praśaṭha* and *praśānta* on the basis of its Tibetan equivalents in his *Bukkyō Jiten* [= *Mvy*] (Tokyo: Heigo Shuppansha, rev. ed., 1929), p. 22, n. 109.19. Later, however, he simply says "meaning uncertain" in his dictionary *Bon-wa Dai-jiten* (Tokyo: Suzuki Research Foundation, 1965), p. 875.

13. *MV.* p. 52.8: tasya layauddhatyasyopaśāntau satyāṃ praśaṭha-vāhitā cittasyopekṣā.

14. *Visuddhimagga*, p. 466 *f.* (as quoted by Mizuno, op. cit., p. 638).

15. Daisetz T. Suzuki, *Zen and Japanese Culture*, Bollingen series LXIV (Princeton: Princeton University Press, 1971), p. 97.

16. Ibid., p. 107.

17. *MSA*, XVIII.61:

> upekṣayā yathākāmaṃ sarvatra viharaty asau /
> pṛṣṭhalabdhāvikalpena vihāreṇa sadottamaḥ /

18. Suzuki, op. cit. pp. 146, 147.

19. *Ch'êng-wei-shih-lun* (*Taishō* 1585, vol. XXXI, pp. 30b. 31a.) emphasizes a nominal, temporary existence of *upekṣā*. It states that *upekṣā* is an entity provisionally named as such based upon the four substantial entities (*dharmas*): *alobha, adveṣa, amoha,* and *vīrya*. The substance and function of *upekṣā* are reduced to and only seen in these four dharmas. *Upekṣā* is no other than a name given to an aspect or special state of *alobha* and the others and does not exist apart from these four. This theory of "provisional existence" of *upekṣā* seems to originate from the *Viniścaya-saṃgrahaṇī* section of *Yogācārabhūmi* (*Taishō* 1579, vol. XXX, p. 602b; *TTP* 5539, vol. 110, p. 259–4), where it is stated that the last three members of the eleven good mental factors—*apramāda, upekṣā,* and *ahiṃsā*—are "*saṃvṛti-sat*" (conventional, provisional existence). It ensues that the other eight mental factors are "*dravya-sat*" (substantial, real existence). The author is not sure how to understand this *saṃvṛti-sat*, but he believes that on the basis of these four mental factors combined, a higher mental state such as *upekṣā* is established on a new horizon; it is a state that cannot be expressed by *alobha* and the other three alone.

20. When the author had almost finished writing this paper, an article by H. B. Aronson discussing *upekṣā* arrived (A. K. Narain and L. Zwilling ed., *Studies in Pāli and Budhism,* Delhi: B. R. Publishing Corporation, 1979, pp. 1–18). Unfortunately it reached him too late for use in this paper. However, since the structure and basis of his argument are quite different from those of the author, it did not seem out of place to publish this paper as well.

Chapter 10: On the Theory of Buddha-body (*Buddha-kāya*)

1. *Dīghanikāya,* xvi (*Mahāparinibbāna-sutta*), 2, 26, (vol. 2, p. 100); 6. I (do. p. 154).

2. *Majjhima-nikāya* (Sutta 28), vol. 1, pp. 190–1.

3. *Saṃyutta-nikāya* (Samyutta 22, 87), vol. 3, p. 120.

4. Besides the *dharma-kāya* in this sense, there is one called "*pañca-dharmakāya*" of Sarvāstivāda, which says that the Buddha, or *dharma-kāya,* has the five attributes of moral conditions (*śīla*), meditation (*samādhi*), wisdom (*prajñā*), emancipation (*vimukti*), and the awareness of emancipation (*vimukti-jñāna-darśana*). The same idea can be seen in such works as the *abhidharmakośaśāstra,* the *Satyasiddhiśāstra, Milindapañha,* and *Visuddhimagga.* Nāgārjuna has also referred to this idea (N. Dutt, *Aspects of Mahāyāna Buddhism,* p. 108). However, as for the five attributes, which afford various interpretations, the general view is that they are the actualized stages of self-cultivation. Moreover, this *dharma-kāya* can be interpreted as a gathering of the *dharma;* therefore, it is doubtful whether it can be regarded as being directly identical with *dharma-kāya* as a way of manifesting the Buddha. Also see fn. 8.

5. Shan-tao of T'ang China clearly designated Amida-Buddha as Reward-Body (or Assumed-Body). Cf. *Kuan Wu-liang-shou ching shu* (觀無量壽經疏), *chüan I* (*Taishō,* vol. XXXVII, p. 250b).

6. In the Chinese translations there are various names given for the three bodies. This variety is largely due to the different terms used in different texts and to the different translations given to them by different translators. Among the various systems of enumerating the three bodies, the most popular are the following two:

(1) a set consisting of Dharma-body (法身), Reward-body (報身), and Assumed-body (應身);

(2) a set consisting of Dharma-body, Assumed-body and Apparitional-body (化身).

Again, in a system that appeared a little later, the following three bodies are given: Essence-body (*svābhāvika-kāya* 自性身), Enjoyment-body (*sāṃbhogika-kāya* 受用身), and Transformation-body (*nairmāṇika-kāya* 變化身). They will be explained in the following section. Although some subtle differences in ideas can be seen between these groups, which probably underwent historical development, as far as the three bodies are grouped into a doctrinal system, the content is not as disparate as it first appears to be.

7. *Mūlamadhyamakakārikās,* XXII; *Ratnāvalī,* III. 13. Also cf. *Prajñāpāramitopadeśa* (大智度論), *Taishō,* vol. XXV, p. 121c (Étienne Lamotte, *Le Traité,* p. 513), p. 278a.

8. The *kāya* (身) of *buddha-kāya* is generally understood vaguely to designate the 'body'. In the Yogācāra-vijñāna school studies were made on the meaning of the word kāya. The *Ch'êng-wei-shih-lun* (成唯識論 , *chüan* 10, Shindo ed., p. 253), following the view of the *Buddhabhūmy-upadeśa* (佛地經論) by Bandhuprabha and others (*Taishō,* vol.XXVI, p. 325b), says: "The meanings, 'substance' (體), 'dependence' (依), and 'assemblage' (聚), combine to make the word *kāya* (身)." These three meanings are further annotated to mean respectively, "essential nature" (體性), "basis" (依止 , probably "foundation" for Buddha's virtues), and "accumulation of merits" (衆德聚). Thus, we can surmise various meanings such as "body" (not only physical body but also essential body), "totality," "collection," "group," and so forth, in the word *kāya.* With the exception of "dependence" or "basis," most of these meanings can be traced in a dictionary. (cf. Edgerton, *Buddhist Hybrid Sanskrit Dictionary,* pp. 177–8).

9. However, there are delicate differences in nuance in the manner of description in śāstras; consequently, *dharma-kāya* is not necessarily identical with *svābhāvika-kāya* in all instances. That is, in the śāstras the concept of the old '*rūpa-kāya*' (Physical-body) hardly became an issue; all Buddha-bodies were, on the one hand, emancipated bodies (*vimukti-kāya*), free from "the barrier of delusions," and on the other hand, *dharma-kāyas,* rid of "the barrier of the known." In this *dharma-kāya* can be recognized the three Buddha-bodies of *svābhāvika-kāya, sāṃbhogika-kāya,* and *nairmāṇika-kāya.* Of these, the *svābhāvika-kāya,* especially, corresponds to the *dharma-kāya,* (*dharmatā-kāya*). Books in which the word *dharma-kāya* seems to have been used both in the broad and the narrow senses as here described are the *Mahāyānasaṃgraha, Abhisamayālaṃkāra, Ch'êng-wei-shih-lun,* and so forth.

10. The *Mahāyānasūtrālaṃkāra* (hereafter referred to as *MSA*) expounds the significance of the purification of the *Dharma-dhātu* in chapter IX (56–59), and in its last section named "The Meaning of its Arising" (*vṛtty-artha*) it treats of the *trikāya.* Similarly, in the *Ratnagotra-vibhāga,* various meanings of the word "āśraya-parivṛtti" (轉依 revolving of the basis) are given (II. 1–2), and as "The Meaning of its Revolution," the *trikāya* is explained in detail (II. 38–61). That the *dharma-dhātu,* which is essentially immovable, starts revolving and manifests itself in some way has something in common with the concept of "the absolute in the phenomenal relativity" (眞如隨緣) in later ages.

11. The original word for the Reward-body (報身) was generally understood to be the *sāṃbhogika-kāya,* which will be interpreted to mean "to enjoy (*saṃbhoga*) the result as a reward for the vow which is its source" (因願報酬). However, as explained in the following note 17, there is an example in which the word "*niṣyanda*" (等流 , literally, flowing down) has been translated as 報 (reward). Again, the word *vipāka* or *vaipākika* (異熟 , literally, ripening, fruition) has also been considered as the original for the Reward-body. (Cf. Yamaguchi Susumu and others, 佛教學序說 , *An Introduction to Buddhist Studies,* p. 216).

12. It has been traditionally interpreted that the physical body of the Buddha preached to *śrāvakas* or his disciples, and the *sāṃbhogika-kāya* preached to *bodhisattvas*. In the Mahāyāna sūtras, however, it is told that both *śrāvakas* and *bodhisattvas* joined the same asembly and listened to the same sermons. Gautama Buddha actually preached at Benares and then at various places for forty-five long years. But, at the same time, those sermons by Gautama (*nairmāṇika-kāya*) were totally annihilated in the *Prajñāpāramitā sūtras*. Was there no bodhisattva listening to Guatama's preaching? If both the *śrāvakas* and *bodhisattvas* were admitted to have attended the same assembly, in which capacity, the *sāṃbhogika* or the *nairmāṇika-kāya*, did the Buddha teach? In such a case, who and where were the *śrāvakas* and *bodhisattvas*? Was Queen Vaidehī in the *Amitāyur-dhyāna Sūtra* really an ordinary sinful woman, not a *bodhisattva*? Although these questions are not easily answered, investigations into them might offer suggetions with regard to what true sermons should be. In a later period, there also appeared sūtras that advocated sermons by the *dharma-kāya*.

13. The thirty-two physical marks are said to belong exclusively to either a *cakravartin* (a king who has conquered the whole world) or the Buddha. It is clear that they were thought in reference to the physical body so long as they were characteristics possessed by a worldly king; however, later this idea was elevated to the point that even the *rūpa-kāya* was understood as the *sāṃbhogika-kāya* and these characteristics were said to be visible only to the bodhisattvas. All Buddha's biographies record the incident of Asita, an ascetic, who, holding the baby Gautama in his arms, noticed the thirty-two marks and predicted that the child would become a Buddha, but who, at the same time, shed tears because he was too old to be able to hear the Buddha's sermons.

14. *Mahāyāna-saṃgraha-bhāṣya* (攝大乘論釋), *Taishō*, vol. XXXI, 374c.

15. Yamaguchi, Susumu, *Sthiramati: Madhyāntavibhāgaṭīkā*, p. 191 line 11: "svābhāviko yasmiṃ kāye vyavasthite 'bhisambudhyate . . . sa sāṃbhogikaḥ kāyaḥ" Tib.: "ngo bo nyid kyi sku ste / sku gang la bzhugs nas mngon par rdzogs par byang chub ste / . . . de ni longs spyod rdzogs pa'i sku'o." Japanese translation, p. 304.

16. The words, "original enlightenment" (本覚) and "initial awakening" (始覚), are borrowed from examples in the *Mahāyāna-śraddhotpāda śāstra* and others. The former is the enlightenment as one's Buddha-nature found amidst defilement, while the latter is the enlightenment realized when the defilement is removed.

17. The word "*niṣyanda-kāya*" can be seen in the *Mahāyāna-saṃgraha* (*Taishō*, vol. XXXI, p. 151c line 26). In the *Laṅkāvatāra Sūtra* we find the words, *niṣyanda-buddha, dharmatā-niṣyanda-buddha* (Nanjio, ed., *Laṅkāvatāra Sūtra*, pp. 56–7; cf. the index), which are translated into Chinese variously as follows: 報佛、法佛報佛、法性所流佛. The word 報 (result or reward) in these translations may be connected with the idea of the Reward-body. The *Ratnagotra-vibhāga* (II.49) explains *sāṃbhogika-kāya* as "the outflow of the great compassion" (*karuṇā . . . niṣyanda*).

18. A. K. Chatterjee, *The Yogācāra Idealism* (Varanasi: Motilal, 1962), p. 226: "Though He (=*Tathāgata*) is in phenomena and is Himself but phenomenal,

he yet knows that true nature of phenomena and therefore transcends it at the same time.'' In connection with these two aspects, the same author quotes from the *MSA*, XVIII.38. This gāthā expounds the two kinds of *saṃbhāra* (equipment): ''The equipment of merits'' promises an existence in this world like that of a god or of a *cakravartin* (Emperor as a conqueror); ''the equipment of knowledge'' signifies that in spite of the above, there is transcendence of it. This can be regarded as describing the two aspects of, as it were, 'the non-abiding in *nirvāṇa*' (不住涅槃) and 'the non-abiding in *saṃsāra*' (不住生死). See below, pp. 113–14.

19. As has been described in note 6, between the Reward-body and the Assumed-body, there is some conceptual indistinctness in their spheres. In order to set up a system of the three bodies and clarify the distinctions between them, some people adopted a method called 開眞合應 : the True body (眞身) is divided (unfolded) into the Dharma-body and the Reward-body; to these two, the Assumed-body (應身) is added to form the three bodies. Some others, conversely, adopted the method of 開應合眞 : first the Assumed-body (應身) is divided into the Assumed-body and the Apparitional-body (化身): to these the True body is added. (Cf. Hui-yuan, *Ta-ch'eng-i-chang, chüan* 19, *Taishō*, vol. XLIV, pp. 839a–840c). According to the former, the Reward-body is different from the Assumed-body, but according to the latter, the said Assumed-body is almost the same as the Reward-body of the former in content. But, in short, these ways of thinking only figured out the three Buddha-bodies by dividing either the True body (眞身) or the Assumed-body (應身): therefore, they precisely took the position, in principle, of the two-body theory composed of the True body and the Assumed-body, because underlying them were the principles of ''augmenting'' (合) and ''unfolding'' (開). On the other hand, it seems that in Indian *śāstras*, the system of the triangular concept of the three Buddha-bodies has been established by instituting the *sāṃbhogika-kāya*. The interpretation through the Chinese terms ''augmenting'' (合) and ''unfolding'' (開) adds to the ambiguity regarding the meaning of the triangular concept that differs in principle from the meaning of the two-body theory that simply treats of diametric bodies. But at the same time it may be said that this ambiguity is what serves to manifest the significance and the double character of the *sāṃbhogika-kāya* or the Reward-body.

20. A. K. Coomaraswamy, *Buddha and the Gospel of Buddhism* (Bombay: 1956), p. 239.

21. A. K. Chatterjee, op. cit., p. 230 *ff*.

22. Various śāstras can be referred to with regard to the idea of ''non-abiding in *nirvāṇa*.'' Among them, however, special mention may be made of S. Yamaguchi ed., *Sthiramati Madhyāntavibhāgaṭīkā*, p. 68, lines 12–17 (in Tib.) = p. 267 lines 12–16 (in Skt. restored); p. 187 lines 14–22, and so forth, (Japanese trans. pp. 105, 299–300), where we can clearly see ideas related to the three Buddha-bodies.

23. The word ''saṃcintya-bhavopapatti'' (literally, taking birth at will, 故意受生 or 故思受生 in Chinese) appears in various *Prajñāpāramitā-sūtras*, and is expounded in the *Mahāyānasūtrālaṃkāra* (XI.30, XVIII.44, XX–XXI.12), the *Mahāyāna-saṃgraha* (*Taishō*, vol. XXXI, p. 140b line 29), the *Bodhisattvabhūmi* (p. 414; *Taishō*, vol. XXX, p. 576b), and so forth. In the

Bodhisattvabhūmi (p. 226; *Taishō* vol. XXX p. 532b), the *bodhisattva* is said "to let himself be born even among the caṇḍāla (outcasts), or as far down as among dogs," for the purpose of benefiting others. In the *Ch'êng-wei-shih-lun,* the following phrases, probably conveying the same meaning, are found: 故意方行 ("one acts just intentionally," Shindō ed., *chüan* 9, p. 29 line 5), and 留煩惱障助願受生 (detaining the obstacles of defilement, one takes birth in accordance with his vow," ibid., p. 31 line 10).

24. The *Ta-ch'êng-i-chang* (大乘義章), *chüan* 19 (*Taishō,* vol. XLIV, no. 670, p. 841b). In mentioning these four Buddhas, Hui-yüan seems to refer to the 'Four *chüan Laṅkāvatāra*' (四巻楞伽), translated by Guṇabhadra of the Liu-Sung dynasty (*Taishō,* vol. XVI, no. 670, p. 481b lines 8–9 and p. 482b lines 17–19). In this sūtra, however, the Merit Buddha, the third of the four Buddhas mentioned by Hui-yüan, does not appear; instead, the names "Reward Buddha" (報佛) or "Rewardingly-born Buddha" (報生佛) can be seen. Since the *sāṃbhogika-kāya* is especially the source of the Buddha's merits, Hui-yüan must have called it the "Merit Buddha." These passages correspond respectively to the gāthās II.49 and II.95 in the Skt. original (B. Nanjio, *Laṅkāvatāra Sūtra,* pp. 28, 34). According to this, the Incarnation Buddha (the fourth) reads *nairmāṇika* (buddha), and the Merit Buddha (the third) reads *vipākaja* or *vipākastha,* which corresponds exactly to the Chinese translation 報生佛 (Buddha born as a result or as a reward). The Wisdom Buddha (the second) and the Suchness Buddha (the first), taken together, correspond to the one word *tathatājñāna-buddha* (Suchness-wisdom Buddha), which is translated in other Chinese versions of the *Laṅkāvatāra* into 如智佛 or 真如智慧佛. Judging from these points, it is questionable whether this one word can be divided into two to make a total four Buddhas, because it might be that the sūtra originally gave only three, not four, Buddhas or Bodies, namely, the Incarnation Buddha, the Reward Buddha, and the Suchness-wisdom Buddha. This last one, the *tathatājñāna-buddha,* is probably equal to the *dharma-kāya* or *svābhāvika-kāya,* but at the same time, it reminds us of the name *jñāna-dharma-kāya* (Wisdom-dharma Body) which appears in the *Abhisamaya-ālaṃkārāloka* (see note 28). It should be noted that "*sāṃbhogika-kāya*" has been scarcely use in the *Laṅkāvatāra.* Again, Hui-yüan gives here many four-body theories other than the one described above. His book was, in fact, originally devoted to the enumeration of almost all the Buddha-body theories, ranging from a theory of one body to that of ten bodies. I shall not go into detail here, however.

25. *Buddhabhūmy-upadeśa* (佛地経論), *chüan* 7 (*Taishō,* vol. XXVI, p. 326a). *Ch'êng-wei-shih-lun* (成唯識論), *chüan* 10, Shindō, pp. 15 *ff.*

26. Cf. U. Wogihara (ed.), *Abhisamayālaṃkārālokā-prajñāpāramitāvyākhyā* (Tokyo: 1935), p. 21 (I. 17), p. 914 *ff.* (VIII.1 *ff*). However, both in the gāthās I.17 and VIII.1 of the *Abhisamayālaṃkāra,* the four-body theory is not necessarily clear. The commentator Haribhadra also states that there are different views, some advocating the threefold body and some the fourfold body. He himself seems to favour the theory of fourfold body (the *svābhāvika-kāya, dharma-kāya, sāṃbhogika-kāya,* and the *nairmāṇika-kāya*). Among these four *kāyas,* the second one, *dharma-kāya,* is specified and called "*jñāna-dharma-kāya*" (Wisdom-dharma Body) in the *Hor chos 'byung* (*The Buddhist History of Mongolia,* written by Āyurvardhana or Jigme

Rigpi-dorje). The tradition of this specification was probably created in Tibet and has been widely accepted in Tibetan Buddhism.

27. It seems to be quite late in history that the mutual relationship between the eight *vijñānas* (*ālaya-vijñāna, kliṣṭa-manas, mano-vijñāna,* the five primary *vijñānas*), the four wisdoms (*ādarśa-jñāna, samatā-jñāna, pratyavekṣā-jñāna, kṛtyānuṣṭhāna-jñāna*), and the threefold body (*dharma-kāya, sāṃbhogika-kāya, nairmāṇika-kāya*) came to be clearly recognized and consolidated, though views on it are not necessarily the same. It is Sthiramati's commentary on the *Mahāyānasūtrālaṃkāra* (*MSA*), IX.60 (Tibetan Tripiṭaka, Peking reprint ed., vol. 108, p. 261–1 to –2) that describes at a single place the relationship between the above three, which can be graphed as follows:

Trikāya		**Four Wisdoms**		**Eight *Vijñānas***
dharma-kāya	=	*ādarśa-jñāna* (mirror wisdom)	←———	Revolving of the *ālaya-vijñāna*
sāṃbhogika-kāya	=	*samatā-jñāna* (equality-wisdom)	←———	Revolving of the defiled *manas*
		pratyavekṣā-jñāna wisdom of intellectual mastery)	←———	Revolving of the *mano-vijñāna*
nairmāṇika-kāya	=	*kṛtyānuṣṭhana-jñāna* (wisdom of duty-fulfillment)	←———	Revolving of the five primary *vijñānas*

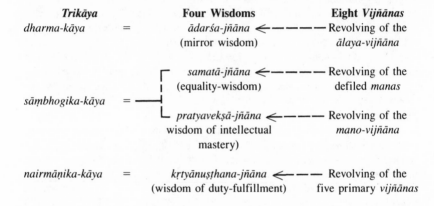

Of these, as for the relationship of the eight *vijñānas* and the four wisdoms, views same as the above can also be seen in the general explanation of *āśrayaparāvṛtti* in Sthiramati's commentary on *MSA*, IX.12 (Peking ed., ibid., p. 251–3; the same can also be seen in the commentary by Asvabhāva on the *Mahāyāna-saṃgraha,* translated by Hsüan-chuang (*Taishō* vol. XXXI, p. 438A). (Its Tibetan translation differs from it.) In the Chinese translation of the *MSA*, IX.67–74, there exist a number of phrases that are not contained in the Sanskrit text, but refer to the relationship between the eight *vijñānas,* the four wisdoms and the *trikāya.* According to them the relationship between the eight *vijñānas* and the four wisdoms is the same with Sthiramati's interpretation given above, but the relationship between the four wisdoms and the *trikāya* is different: the *ādarśa-jñāna* and the *samatā-jñāna* are apportioned to the *svābhāvika-kāya;* the *pratyavekṣa-jñāna* to the *sāṃbhogika-kāya;* and the *kṛtyānuṣṭhāna-jñāna* to the *nairmāṇika-kāya.* The *Ch'êng-wei-shih-lun* has adopted this Chinese translation of the *MSA* as it is, relating to the eight *vijñānas* and the four wisdoms (Shindō ed., 10, p. 15), and for the relationship with the *trikāya,* it gives a view close to Sthiramati's interpretation (Shindō ed., 10, p. 26). Obermiller introduces what is called "Candragomin's theory," whose description, however, includes indistinct points (E. Obermiller, *The Sublime Science of the Great Vehicle-to Salvation*, p. 101).

28. Theories on the Buddha-body, mostly following the three-body system, are expounded in the *Ratnagotra*, I.149–152 and II.38–41, but the limits between the three bodies are not clearly shown so far as the virtues attributed to them are concerned. Similarly in II.61 and II.68, there is a tendency rather to pull back the concept of the three-fold body to that of the twofold body. In III.1 and the rest, especially, discussions are carried on in the form of a mutual confrontation involving the twofold body, such as the Body of Ultimate Truth and the Body of Conventional Truth.

29. In this regard the idea is somewhat closer to Hinduism. See note 21 above.

30. *MSA*, III.7, especially in its Sthiramati's commentary.

31. Ibid., III.11.

32. Takasaki Jikidō, *A Study on the Ratnagotra-vibhāga* (*Uttaratantra*), Serie Orientale Roma, XXXIII (Roma: Instituto Italiano Per Il Medio Ed Estremo Oriente, 1966). The author has many other treatises, among which see "Āśrayaparivṛtti and Āṣrayaparāvṛtti" (*Nippon Bukkyō Gakkai Nempō*, 25, 1960); in the above book see III "Keypoint in the Discourse" of the Introduction.

33. *Taishō*, vol. XXXI, p. 139b, É. Lamotte, *La somme du grand véhicule* (Louvain: Bureau du Muséon, 1938), tome II, p. 110 (II.17).

34. *MSA*, IX.37.

35. *Madhyāntavibhāga*, I.22c.

Chapter 11: Logic of Convertibility

1. By this I mean that Asaṅga and Vasubandhu did not intend to establish a new school in opposition to the Madhyamaka idea. However, it is also a well-known fact that after the Mādhyamika and the Yogācāra were established as two independent schools, severe debates took place between them.

2. See G. M. Nagao, "The Fundamental Standpoint of the Madhyamaka Philosophy" (in Japanese), *Tetsugaku Kenkyū*, vols. 366–371 (1947–1948). Reprinted in *Chūkan to Yuishiki* (Mādhyamika and Vijñānavāda), (Tokyo: Iwanami Shoten, 1978).

3. In this school, all doctrinal statements are divided into three categories: object (*viṣaya*, a practitioner's object of learning), practice (*pratipatti*), and fruit (*phala*). *Vijñānas* and the three natures are the two main theories of this school and correspond to the first category, the object of learning. Of these two theories, we see, in Vasubandhu's *Triṃśikā*, a kind of "sequence of exposition" in that the theory of *vijñānas* is first expounded extensively and then the three-nature theory is explained briefly. The same sequence can be found also in Asaṅga's *Mahāyana-saṃgraha*. Even in Vasubandhu's *Trisvabhāva-nirdeśa*, which takes the three-nature theory as its main theme, the sequence of exposition is the same.

4. Sthiramati, *Triṃśikā-bhāṣya*, S. Lévi's ed., p. 16.1 and p.36.11.

5. The confrontation with the Sāṃkhya is a great concern not only in the Vijñāna-vāda but also in Buddhism in general. See Yaśomitra's commentary on the *Abhidharma-kośa,* Wogihara edition, p. 148.3, where the terms "*saṃtāna,*" "*pariṇāma,*" and so on are discussed.

6. *Triṃśikā-bhāṣya,* Sylvain Lévi ed., p. 16.1. Sthiramati does not mention here the dichotomy of subject and object. However, as it seems that as the dichotomy is essential in cognition, his discussion is focused on simply the nature of "evolving."

7. The "twofold evolving" is discussed also in the *Ch'êng-wei-shih-lun,* but its explanation seems to be fairly different from that of Sthiramati. See note 8.

8. There is a tendency in the Fa-hsiang school to understand the word "cognition" in terms of "cognizer" which is contrasted to the term "cognizable." Such an understanding seems to be largely influenced by the special liking (commonly found in China) to apply notions of *neng* (能 active; doer) and *so* (所 passive; done) to many verbal stems (forms). Hsüan-tsang's translation of *pariṇāma* (evolving) as *neng-pien* (能変 evolver) is on the same line. See below and note 9.

9. The "twofold evolving" in the *Ch'êng-wei-shih-lun* is translated by Hsüan-tsang as *yin-neng-pien* (因能変 *hetu-pariṇāma*) and *kuo-neng-pien* (果能変 *phala-pariṇāma*). It is rather 'two-fold evolver," as *neng-pien* means evolver. Of these *kuo-neng-pien,* "evolver as phala," appears as if it connotes "evolving" in a reverse direction. It is possible to interpret Hsüan-tsang's translation in that way. But, the general understanding of the "two-fold evolver" in the Fa-hsiang school is as follows. *Yin* (*hetu*) refers to seed; it is an "evolver" because from the seed all eight cognitions evolve and come into being. *Kuo* (*phala*) refers to these eight cognitions that are the fruits of the seed; they are also referred to as "evolvers" in that they evolve into the two divisions of subject and object. They thereby represent all phenomenal appearances. In such an interpretation, however, we see only the one-directional movement from cause to effect; not the reverse direction.

10. *Triṃśikā-kārikā.* kk.20,21 are summarized.

11. See author's paper, "On the word Paryāya" (1940), reprinted in *Chūkan to Yuishiki* (1978), pp. 406–412.

12. Sthiramati, *Triṃśikā-bhāṣya,* Sylvain Lévi ed., p.46.3 and 49.19.

13. *Mahāvyutpatti,* R. Sakaki edition, nos. 204, 206.

14. See also *Abhidharmakośa-bhāṣya,* Pradhan ed., p. 421 (Hsüan-tsang's translation, *Taishō* vol. XXIX, no. 1558) and Yaśomitra's commentary on it, Wogihara ed. p. 654. Yaśomitra, on the same page, also explains the term "*paryāya*" in the meanings of *viśeṣa* and *krama.*

15. In the *Mahāyāna-sūtrālaṃkāra,* ad XI.35 (Sylvain Lévi ed., pp 63–64), we see the term *paryāyeṇa* used in the following manner: "It is really mind that appears in various ways as greed, hatred, and so on, according to the occasion (*paryāyeṇa*); at the same time, it also appears in various modes (*citrākāram*) such as faith, and so on."

16. É. Lamotte, *La Somme du Grand Véhicule,* tome I, p. 32; G. M. Nagao, ed., text appended to his Japanese translation of the *Mahāyāna-saṃgraha,* (vol. 1) P. 76. English translation is the author's.

17. See É. Lamotte, *La Somme du Grand Véhicule*, tome I, p. 36; G. M. Nagao, (vol. 1) p. 83:

> / gal te rnam grangs kyis gzhan gyi dbang gi ngo bo nyid ngo bo nyid gsum du zin na / 'o na ji ltar ngo bo nyid gsum bye brag med par mi 'gyur zhe na / rnam grangs gang gis gzhan gyi dbang yin pa des kun brtags pa ma yin / yongs su grub pa ma yin no / / rnam grangs gang gis kun [tu] brtags pa yin pa des gzhan gyi dbang ma yin / yongs su grub pa ma yin no / / rnam grangs gang gis yongs su grub pa yin pa des gzhan gyi dbang ma yin / kun brtags pa ma yin no / /

18. *Triṃśikā-bhāṣya*, Sylvain Lévi ed., p. 16.16.

19. For an extensive treatment of *abhūta-parikalpa*, see, especially S. Yamaguchi ed., Sthiramati's *Madhyānta-vibhāga-ṭīka*, p. 13 *f*. The *Mahāyāna-saṃgraha* also equates cognition with *abhūta-parikalpa* which, though other-dependent in nature, is the basis for the "unreal" appearances (II.2); it goes on to say that the other-dependent establishes itself neither as defilement nor as purity, that is, it differs from both the imagined and the consummated (II.18).

20. É. Lamotte, *La Somme du Grand Véhicle*, tome I, p.32; Nagao (vol.1) p. 75.

21. The author's interpretation of the passage discussed above differs greatly from that of Dr. H. Ui seen in his *Studies of the Mahȳāna-saṃgraha* (Tokyo: Iwanami Shoten, 1935), p. 426 f. The term translated here as "some specific form" (*ākāra*) corresponds to Hsüan-tsang's translation, 相 *hsiang*. As it is likely that Gupta has translated it as 因縁 *yin-yüan* and Paramārtha as 因 *yin*, the Sanskrit might have been *nimitta* rather than *ākāra*, but on the basis of Tibetan *rnam pa* and Vasubandhu's commentary, the author has adopted *ākāra*. Étienne Lamotte also gives *ākāra* here. It is further explained to mean "in some such form" (*yathā*). Instead of *yathā*, Étienne Lamotte understands it to be *katham* (*ji ltar na*), which, however, does not agree with 如 *ju* in the three Chinese translations.

22. Lévi ed., p.39.27: niṣpannas tasya pūrveṇa sadā rahitatā tu yā.

23. For this and the following statement by Sthiramati, see, ibid., p. 40.4–5 and 40.7 respectively:

> [40.4–5] tena grāhya-grāhakeṇa paratantrasya sadā sarvakālaṃ atyanta-rahitatā yā sa pariniṣpanna-svabhāvaḥ.
>
> [40.7] rahitatā ca dharmatā.

24. Étienne Lamotte, *La Somme du Grand Véhicule*, tome I, p.37; Nagao, (vol. 1) p. 86: sangs rgyas bcom ldan 'das rnams kyis / theg pa chen po shin tu rgyas pa bstan pa gang yin pa'i bstan pa der kun brtags pa'i ngo bo nyid ji ltar rig par bya zhe na / med pa'i rnam grangs bstan pas rig par bya'o /

25. With regard to the notion of the "consummated" (parinṣpanna), it should be noticed that it is closely related to "practice." By this I mean that the "consummated" means to be perfected and accomplished only through practice. It does not

signify an absolute being, existing, unrelated to and prior to practice. It is to be established each and every time and consummated by everyone through practice alone.

26. *Dhātu* means esentially "element" although it is also widely used in the meanings of "sphere, region, or world" as in the case of *lokadhātu*. Very often in Buddhist texts, it is defined as *hetu* "cause," probably from the meaning "element."

27. Étienne Lamotte, *La Somme du Grande Véhicule*, tome I, p. 81 d; Nagao (vol.2) p. 101: gnas ni de nyid gnyi ga'i char gtogs pa ste / gzhan gyi dbang gi ngo bo nyid do.

28. Étienne Lamotte, *La Somme du Grande Véhicule*, tome I, p. 25; Nagao, (vol 1) p. 59; yod pa ma yin pa dang / nor ba'i don snang ba'i gnas (=asadbhrānty-artha-pratibhāsa-āśraya) gang yin pa 'di ni gzhan gyi dbang gi mtshan nyid do.

29. Étienne Lamotte, *La Somme du Grande Véhicule*, tome I, p.81; Nagao, (vol.2) p. 101: gzhan gyur pa ni gang gzhan gyi dbang gi ngo bo nyid de nyid kyi gnyen po skyes na gang kun nas nyon mongs pa'i cha ldog cing rnam par byang ba'i char gyur pa'o.

30. Sylvain Lévi, *Triṃśikā-bhāṣya*, p.44 7–13 the contents of which are here summarized.

31. The term "*anādikāliko dhātuḥ*" (*dhātu* from time immemorial) is found in a verse quoted in the *Mahāyāna-saṃgraha* (I.1) from the *Abhidharma-mahāyāna-sūtra* and is explained as a synonym of *ālaya-vijñāna* and as the basis/cause for both *saṃsāra* and *nirvāṇa*. The same term, however, is understood to mean the *tathāgata-garbha* in the *Ratnagotravibhāga* (Johnston ed., p. 72) that quotes the same verse.

32. *Madhyānta-vibhāga*, I.6–7. The "means" (*upāya*) here refers to the means for acquiring "realization" (*abhisamaya*), which is equal to entering the path of insight (*darśana-mārga*) or the first *bhūmi*.

33. For the specific meaning of the term "consummated" as closely related to "practice," see note 25.

34. The word *pariṇāma* or *pariṇāmanā* is translated into Tibetan, usually, as 'gyur, bsgyur, and so forth that have the meaning "evolving." But, when the Sanskrit term is used in the meaning of "transference," the Tibetans have translated it as *bsngo-ba*, *yongs-su-bsngo-ba*, and so forth.

35. S. Yamaguchi, *Sthiramati, Madhyānta-vibhāga-ṭīkā*, p. 81.9–10 and pp. 86–87.

36. The merit-transference is explicated in *Madhyānta-vibhāga* II.10, II.13, V.3, V.6, and in *Mahāyāna-sūtrālaṃkāra* V.9, XI.56, XVI.52, XX–XXI.11.

37. This Sanskrit form is taken from the *Mahāyāna-sūtrālaṃkāra*. The phrase also appears in other texts such as the *Śrīmālādevī* and the *Laṅkāvatāra* with some modifications. According to the Sanskrit text of the latter, it appears in various forms: *acintya-pariṇāma-cyuti*, °*pariṇāminī-cyuti*, °*pariṇati-cyuti*, and so forth. All of them give *cyuti* (death) instead of *upapatti* (birth), but the meaning does not change on account of that. The Tibetan translation of the Śrīmālādevī suggests that the same Sanskrit form as that in the *Laṅkāvatāra* has been used in it.

38. The word *manomaya-kāya* is an old term that appears in the Āgamas and Nikāyas. Both Kenryū Tsukinowa (in his edition of the *Śrīmālādevī,* p. 81, notes 1 and 2) and Louis de la Vallée Poussin (in his *Siddhi,* p. 503 ff.) comment on this word extensively. They understand it in accordance with the Chinese *pien-i,* "transformation." However, what is the motive of that production or "transformation" in the phrase, "body produced by mind?" It is natural that a body is produced or created by previous *karman,* the essence of which is *cetanā,* the will of mind. However, such a body is not be specified as "inconceivable." The phrase "by mind" must suggest a special intention, the intention to be born with a body into the samsaric world, and this intention or motive is none other than *pariṇāmanā,* to transfer merit. Therefore, it is not satisfactory to understand *manomaya-kāya* simply through the interpretation of *pariṇāmikī* as *pien-i,* "transformation," instead of as "merit-transference."

39. Sylvain Lévi, *Mahāyāna-sūtrālaṃkāra,* p. 69.

40. For Asvabhāva's commentary, see *Tibetan Tripiṭaka,* Peking edition (Tokyo–Kyoto: reprint edition), vol 108, p. 162.4 and for Sthiramati's commentary, ibid., p. 288.5.

41. For a discussion on the Bodhisattva's practice of "not abiding in nirvāṇa" and "taking birth in this world willingly," refer to the author's paper, "The Bodhisattva Returns to This World" included in this volume.

Chapter 12: Ontology in Mahāyāna Buddhism

1. Wendy Doniger O'Flaherty trans., *Hindu Myths.* (New York: Penguin Books. First translated 1981. Reprinted 1983). p. 25. See also, Louis Renou ed., *Hinduism.* (New York: Washington Square Press, 1961). p. 47 for an earlier translation of this verse.

2. E. Conze, *Buddhist Thought in India* (Woking and London: George Allen & Unwin Ltd, 1962). p. 219.

3. Ibid., p. 219.

4. Keiji Nishitani, *Shūkyō to wa Nanika* (What is Religion?) (Tokyo: Sōbunsha, 1956). p. 4–5.

5. See, E. Conze, *Buddhist Wisdom Books,* p. 57.

6. Ibid., p. 39, and p. 40 for the following statement.

7. Robert A. F. Thurman, *The Holy Teaching of Vimalakīrti* (Pennsylvania: Pennsylvania State University Press, 1981), p. 47–48. The author has modified the last sentence of Thurman's translation.

8. E. Conze, *Vajracchedikā Prajñāpāramitā* (Roma: IsMEO, 1974), pp. 35–36; . . . bodhisattvena mahāsattvenaivam apratiṣṭhitaṃ cittam utpādayitavyaṃ yan na kvacit-pratiṣṭhitaṃ cittam utpādayitavyam. . . . The translation above is the author's. Conze's translation reads: . . . the Bodhisattva, the great being, should thus produce an unsupported thought, that is, he should produce a thought which is nowhere supported by form.

9. Louis de la Vallée Poussin, *Mūlamadhyamakakārikās de Nāgārjuna*, p. 3 and p. 11: anirodham anutpādam anucchedam aśāśvataṃ / anekārtham anānārtham anāgamam anirgamaṃ / / yaḥ pratītyasamutpādaṃ prapañcopaśamaṃ śivaṃ / deśayaṁ āsa saṃbuddhas taṃ vande vadatāṃ varaṃ /

10. E. H. Johnston and Arnold Kunst, "The Vigrahavyāvartanī of Nāgārjuna with the author's Commentary," *Mélanges chinois et bouddhiques*, Neuvième volume: 1948–1951, p. 151: yaḥ śūnyatāṃ pratītyasamutpādaṃ madhyamāṃ pratipadaṃ ca / ekārthaṃ nijagāda praṇamāmi tam apratimabuddham / / See also, K. Bhattacharya, *The Dialectical Method of Nāgārjuna* (*Vigrahavyāvartanī*) (Delhi: Motilal Banarsidass, 1978), p. 48 (English translation) and p. 53 (Sanskrit text).

11. *Mūlamadhyamaka-kārikā*. XV.2.

12. U. Wogihara, *Bodhisattva-bhūmi*, p. 303.22: tathāgata-bhāṣitāḥ sūtrāntāḥ. . . . śūnyatā pratisaṃyuktāḥ idaṃpratyayatā-pratītyasamutpādānulomāḥ /

13. Thurman, p. 24.

14. Ibid, p. 64.

15. *Vigrahavyāvartanī*, K. 29: nāsti ca mama pratijñā; its auto-commentary: na mama kācid asti pratijñā. See also Bhattacharya, op. cit., p.23 (English translation) and p. 29 (Sanskrit text).

16. *Madhyāntavibhāga*, III.3. Here the text is paraphrased.

Chapter 13: From Mādhyamika to Yogācāra An Analysis of *MMK*, XXIV.18 and *MV*, I.1–2

1. Louis de la Vallée Poussin, *Mūlamadhyamakakārikās* (*mādhyamikasūtras*) *de Nāgārjuna, avec la Prasannapadā Commentaire de Candrikīrti*, Bibliotheca Buddhica IV (St. Pétersbourg: 1903–13), p. 503.

2. Gadjin M. Nagao ed., *Madhyāntavibhāga-bhāṣya, A Buddhist Philosophical Treatise Edited for the First Time from a Sanskrit Manuscript* (Tokyo: Suzuki Research Foundation, 1964), pp. 17–18.

3. T. R. V. Murti, *The Central Philosophy of Buddhism* (London: George Allen and Unwin Ltd., 1955), pp. 7–8.

4. Other translations by modern scholars are available in: Jacques May, *Candrakīrti, Prasannapadā Madhyamakavṛtti* (Paris: Adrien-Maisonneuve, 1959), p. 237; Frederick J. Streng, *Emptiness: A Study in Religious Meaning* (Nashville & New York: Abingdon Press, 1967), p. 213; Kenneth K. Inada, *Nāgārjuna. A Translation of his Mūlamadhyamakakārikā with an Introductory Essay* (Tokyo: Hokuseido-shoten, 1970), p. 148.

5. Louis de la Vallée Poussin, *MMK*, p. 504.14.

6. Cf. J. Takausu, *The Essentials of Buddhist Philosophy* (Honolulu: Office Appliance Co., Third ed.). p. 129: "Therefore, objectively, we have the triple truth, and subjectively, we have the triple knowledge. Of the triple truth, the Void is at the same time the temporary, the temporary is at the same time the middle, which is at the same time the Void."

7. Louis de la Vallée Poussin, *MMK*, p. 500.15.

8. F. Edgerton, *Buddhist Hybrid Sanskrit Dictionary* (New Haven: Yale University Press, 1953), p. 145 (s.v. *Upādāya*); May, Candrakīrti, p. 161, n. 494; p. 237, n. 840.

9. Bhāvaviveka interprets *upādāya-prajñapti* as "*nye bar len pa dag la brten nas gdags pa*" in his *Prajñāpradīpa-mūlamadhyamakavṛtti*. The Tibetan Tripiṭaka (Peking edition), ed. D. T. Suzuki, 95, p. 247–1–2.

10. May, p. 238, n. 840.6.

11. K. Venkata Ramanan, *Nagarjuna's Philosophy* (Delhi: Motilal Banarasidass, 1975), p. 339a.

12. Louis de la Vallée Poussin, p. 214–215.

13. Avalokitavrata, *Prajñā-pradīpa-ṭīkā*, Tibetan Tripiṭaka (Peking edition), 97, p. 227–3. The following is an abridged translation.

14. Cf. Th. Stcherbatsky, *Madhyānta-vibhanga*, Bibliotheca Buddhica XXX (Moscow: Academy of Sciences of USSR Press, 1936), pp. 16, 24.

15. The title, *Madhyāntavibhāga*, "Elucidation of the Middle and Extremes," is generally used, but the author himself states that the treatise was originally called *Madhya-vibhāga*, "Elucidation of the Middle." Therefore, it can be interpreted to be more a "Madhyamaka-śāstra" than that of Nāgārjuna. Actually, its discussion on the Middle appears initially in verses I.1–2 and then in verses V.23–24. See the author's article "On the Title *Madhyānta-vibhāga*" (in Japanese), in *Chūkan to Yuishiki* (Mādhyamika and Vijñānavāda: A Collection of papers on the Mahāyāna Philosophy) (Tokyo: Iwanami Shoten, 1978), pp. 443–454.

16. In the earlier Yogācāra, too, we can find the affirmation of the non-being of outer things and being of cognition-only. But at the same time it is stated that perceiving the truth of cognition-only, the non-being of outer things is perceived, and when an outer object is not perceived, the perceiving subject likewise is not perceived (*MV*, I.6). After the realization of such *śūnyatā*, the cognition-only that is different from the first one and equal to *tathatā* (suchness), or *parinișpanna-svabhāva* (consummated nature), and in which impressions of both subject and object (*grāha-dvyavāsanā*) are extinguished, is re-attained.

17. G. M. Nagao, "What Remains in Śūnyatā" in *Mahāyāna Buddhist Meditation*, ed., Minoru Kiyota (Honolulu: The University Press of Hawaii, 1978), pp. 66–82; reprinted in the present volume.

Chapter 14: Ascent and Descent Two-Directional Activity in Buddhist Thought

1. "The Bodhisattva Returns to This World." Reproduced in the present volume.

2. For these discussions, please refer to the author's article: "From Mādhyamika to Yogācāra; An Analysis of *MMK*, XXIV.18 and *MV.*, I.1–2" reproduced in the present volume.

3. Keiji Nishitani, *Religion and Nothingness*, trans. by Jan Van Bragt (Berkeley: University of California Press, 1982), p. 27.

Chapter 15: Emptiness

1. Edward Conze, *Buddhism* (New York: Philosophical Library. n.d.), p.130.
2. *Majjhima Nikāya*, sutta no. 121.
3. Phrases in the invocational salutation stanzas of the *Stanzas on the Middle*.
4. This idiomatic phrase that expresses the essence of dependent co-arising is often followed by the formula of the twelve members dependently co-arising.
5. *Stanzas on the Middle, MMK*. xv.2.
6. See *Stanzas on the Middle, MMK*. xiii.8: *śūnyatā-dṛṣṭi*.
7. *Kaśyapa-parivarta*, section 65.
8. *Stanzas on the Middle, MMK*. xxiv.11.
9. *Analysis of the Middle and Extremes, MV.* I.1–2.
10. *Analysis of the Middle and Extremes, MV.* I.13.

Chapter 16: Yogācāra—A Reappraisal

1. I once heard a lecture in which knowledge was divided into three kinds: (1) knowledge through the senses, (2) knowledge through reason, and (3) knowledge through intuition. This division is probably a commonly accepted one. The third one, knowledge through intuition, is concerned especially with religious realization and corresponds to "non-discriminative wisdom"in Buddhism. The other two, represent the ordinary way of thinking and they can be seen as corresponding to *pratyakṣa* (direct perception) and to *anumāna* (reasoning), respectively. However, in that lecture, there was no mention of a knowledge that corresponds to the "knowledge acquired subsequently," which is characterized as being both discriminative and non-discriminative or as the unity of reason and intuition. Moreover, there was no explanation of how knowledge through intuition worked upon the world. Intuition was mentioned, but we wonder how it functions in the next moment. That is, the three kinds of knowledges explained by the lecturer do not account for the direction of "descent" that follows from the summit of non-discriminative intuitive knowledge. Herein lies the difference between the three kinds of non-discriminative knowledge (of the *Mahāyāna-saṃgraha*) and the three kinds of knowledges explained by the lecturer.

Bibliography

A. Books

Anaker, Stephen. *Seven Works of Vasubandhu—The Buddhist Psychological Doctor.* Religion of Asia Series. no.4. Lancaster, L. R. and Shastri, J. L. ed. Delhi: Motilal Banarsidass, 1984.

Beckh, H. *Buddhismus.* Sammlung Göschen. I, S.

Bendall, C., ed. *Śikṣāsamuccaya.* Biblotheca Buddhica, I. St.-Pétersbourg: 1897–1902.

Bhattacharya, K. *The Dialectical Method of Nāgārjuna (Vigrahavyāvartanī).* Delhi: Motilal Banarsidass, 1978.

Bhattacharya, V and Tucci, G. *Madhyāntavibhāgasūtrabhāṣyaṭīkā of Sthiramati,* Part I. Calcutta Oriental Series no. 24. London: Luzac, 1932.

Boin, Sara, trans. Lamotte, Étienne, *The Teaching of Vimalakīrti (Vimalakīrtinirdeśa).* London: Routledge & Kegan Paul, 1976.

Chatterjee, A. K. *The Yogācāra Idealism.* Varanasi: Motilal, 1962.

Childers, R. C. *Pāli-English Dictionary.* London: Pali Text Society, 1875.

Conze, Edward. *Buddhism.* New York: Philosophical Library. n.d.

——— *Buddhist Thought in India.* Woking and London: George Allen & Unwin Ltd, 1962.

——— *Buddhist Wisdom Books.* London: George Allen and Unwin, 1958.

——— *Materials for a Dictionary of the Prajñāpāramitā Literature.* Tokyo: Suzuki Research Foundation, 1967.

——— ed. and trans. *Vajracchedikā Prajñāpāramitā.* Serie Orientale Roma XIII. Roma: Istituto Italiano per il Medio ed Estremo Oriente, 1957.

Coomaraswamy, A. K. *Buddha and the Gospel of Buddhism.* Bombay: 1956.

Dayal, Har. *The Bodhisattva Doctrine in Buddhist Sanskrit Literature.* Delhi: Motilal Banarsidass, 1970 Reprint.

Dutt, N. *Aspects of Mahāyāna Buddhism*. London: 1930.

——— ed. *Bodhisattvabhūmi*. Tibetan Sanscrit Works Series vol. VII. Patna: K. P. Jayaswal Institute, 1966.

de Jong, J. W. *Cinq chapitres de la Prasannapadā*. Paris: 1949.

Edgerton, Franklin. *Buddhist Hybrid Sanskrit Grammar and Dictionary*. 2 vols. New Haven: Yale University, 1953.

Friedmann, D. L. *Sthiramati, Madhyāntavibhāgaṭīkā, Analysis of the Middle Path and the Extremes*. Utrecht: 1937.

Horner, I. B. *The Collection of Middle Length Sayings*. vol. 3. London: 1959.

Inada, Kenneth K. *Nāgārjuna. A Translation of his Mūlamadhyamakakārikā with an Introductory Essay*. Tokyo: Hokuseido-shoten, 1970.

Izutsu, Toshihiko., trans. *Rūmī Goroku*, Islam Classics, No. 2. Tokyo: Iwanami Shoten, 1978.

Jacobi, Herman. *Triṃśikāvijñapti des Vasubandhu, mit Bhāṣya des Ācārya Sthiramati*. Stuttgart: Verlag von W. Kohlhammer, 1932.

Jennings, G. J. *The Vedāntic Buddhism of the Buddha*. London: 1948.

Johnston, E. H., ed. *The Ratnagotravibhāga Mahāyānottaratantra-śāstra*. Patna: Bihar Research Society, 1950.

Kiyota, Minoru, ed. *Mahāyāna Buddhist Meditation*. Honolulu: The University Press of Hawaii, 1978.

Kochumuttom, Thomas A. *A Buddhist Doctrine of Experience*, Delhi: Motilal Banarsidass, 1982.

Kondō, Ryūkō, ed. *Daśabhūmīśvaro Nāma Mahāyānasūtraṃ*. Tokyo: Daijyō Bukkyō Kenyō-kai, 1936. Reprint Tokyo: Nakayama Shobō, 1962.

Lamotte, Ėṭienne. *L'Enseignement de Vimalakīrti*. Louvain: Bibliothéque du Muséon. 1962.

——— ed. and trans. *La somme du grand véhicule d'Asaṅga* (*Mahāyānasaṃgraha*). Louvain: Bureaux du Muséon, 1938. vols. I and II.

——— *The Teaching of Vimalakīrti* (*Vimalakīrtinirdeśa*). Boin, Sara. trans. London: Routledge & Kegan Paul, 1976.

——— *Le Traité de la Grande Vertu de Sagesse de Nāgārjuna* (*Mahāprajñāpāramitāśāstra*). Louvain: Institute Orientaliste, 1949. Reprint 1966. Three volumes.

——— *Saṃdhinirmocana Sūtra, L'explication des mystères*. Paris: University de Louvain, 1935.

La Vallée Poussin, Louis de, ed. *Bodhicaryāvatāra of Śāntideva*. Bibliotheca Indica, N.S. no. 983. Calcutta: 1901.

——— ed. *Madhyamakāvatāra par Candrakīrti*. Biblioteca Buddhica IX. St. Pétersbourg: 1912.

——— *Mūlamadhyamakakārikās (mādhyamikasūtras) de Nāgārjuna, avec la Prasannapadā Commentaire de Candrakīrti*. Bibliotheca Buddhica IV. St.-Pétersbourg: 1903–13.

——— ed. and trans. *Vijñaptimātratāsiddhi—La Siddhi de Hiuan-Tsang*. 2 vols. Paris: Librairie Orientaliste Paul Geuthner, 1928.

Lévi, Sylvain. *Asaṅga, Mahāyāna-sūtrālaṃkāra,* Exposé de la Doctrine du Grand Véhicule, Selon le Système Yogācāra. 2 vols. Paris: 1907.

——— ed. *Mahāyānasūtrālaṃkāra*. Paris: H. Champion, 1907.

——— *Matériaux pour l'étude du système Vijñaptimātra*. Paris: 1925.

May, Jacques. *Candrakīrti, Prasannapadā Madhyamakavṛtti*. Paris: Adrien Maisonneuve, 1959.

Mizuno, Kōgen. *Pali Bukkyō o Chūshin toshita Bukkyō no Shinshiki-ron* (*Mind and Mental Factors in Buddhist Philosophy, on the basis of Pāli Buddhism*). Tokyo: Sankibō Busshorin, 1964.

Mookerjee, S. *The Buddhist Philosophy of Universal Flux*, Calcutta: University of Calcutta, 1935.

Monier-Williams, Sir M. *A Sanskrit-English Dictionary*. Oxford: 1899.

Murti, T. R. V. *The Central Philosophy of Buddhism*. London: George Allen and Unwin Ltd., 1955.

Nagao Gadjin, M. *Chūkan to Yuishiki*. Tokyo: Iwanami Shoten, 1978.

——— *Chibetto Bukkyō Kenkyū* (*A Study of Tibetan Buddhism*). Tokyo: Iwanami Shoten, 1954.

——— *Madhyāntavibhāga-bhāṣya: A Buddhist Philosophical Treatise*, edited for the first time from a Sanskrit Manuscript. Tokyo: Suzuki Research Foundation, 1964.

——— *Seshin Ronshū* (*Works of Vasubandhu*) in series *Daijō Butten* (*Mahāyāna Scriptures*), vol. 15. (Tokyo: Chūō Kōron Sha 1976).

Nakamura Hajime, *Tetsugaku-teki Shishaku no Indo-teki Tenkai* (*Development of Philosophical Thinking in India*). Tokyo: 1949.

Nanjio, Bunyo. *Laṅkāvatāra-sūtra*. Kyoto: Otani University Press, 1923.

Narain, A. K. and Zwilling L., eds. *Studies in Pāli and Buddhism*. Delhi: B. R. Publishing Corporation, 1979.

Nishio, Kyō, *A Tibetan Index to the Mahāvyutpatti—With Its Sanskrit Equivalents.* Kyoto: Isseido Publishing Co, 1941.

Nishitani, Keiji. *Shūkyō to wa Nanika* (*What is Religion?*). Tokyo: Sōbunsha, 1956.

——— *Religion and Nothingness.* Van Bragt, Jan. trans. Berkeley: University of California Press, 1982.

Obermiller, E. *The Sublime Science of the Great Vehicle to Salvation. Acta Orientalia,* 9. 1931.

O'Flaherty, Wendy Doniger, trans. *Hindu Myths.* New York: Penguin Books. First translated 1981. Reprinted 1983.

Pandeya, R. C. *Madhyāntavibhāga-śāstra.* Delhi: Motilal Banarsidass, 1971.

Pradhan, Pralhad, ed. *Abhidharma Samuccaya of Asanga.* Santiniketan: Visva-Bharati, 1950.

——— ed. *Abhidharma-koshabhāṣya of Vasubandhu.* Patna: K. P. Jayaswal Research Institute, 1967.

Radhakrishnan, S. *The Dhammapada.* London: 1950.

Radher, J., ed. *Daśabhūmika-sūtra.* Paris: Paul Geuthner. Louvain: J. B. Istas, 1926.

Rahula, Walpola. *Le compendium de la super-doctrine (philosophie) (Abhidharmasamuccaya) d'Asaṅga.* Paris: École française d'extrême-orient, 1971.

Ramanan, K. Venkata. *Nagarjuna's Philosophy.* Delhi: Motilal Banarasidass, 1975.

Renou, Louis, ed. *Hinduism.* New York: Washington Square Press, 1961.

Rhys Davids, T. W. *Buddhism* (Non-Christian Religious Systems). London: 1887.

Robinson, Richard. *The Buddhist Religion.* California: Dickenson, 1970.

Ruegg, David Seyfort. *La théorie du Tathāgatagarbha et du gotra.* Paris: École française d'extrême-orient, 1969.

Sakaki, Ryozaburo, *Honyaku Myogi Daishu* (*Mahāvyutpatti*). Kyoto: Shingonshu Kyoto Daigaku, 1915.

Stcherbatsky, T. F. *The Conception of Buddhist Nirvāṇa.* Leningrad: The Academy of Sciences of the USSR, 1927.

——— "Madhyāntavibhāgasūtra." *Bibliotheca Buddhica* XXX. Moscow: Academy of Sciences of USSR Press, 1936.

Streng, Frederick J. *Emptiness: A Study in Religious Meaning.* Nashville & New York: Abingdon Press, 1967.

Suzuki, Daisetz T. *Zen and Japanese Culture.* Bollingen series LXIV. Princeton: Princeton University Press, 1971.

Takakusu, J. *A Record of the Buddhist Religion by I-tsing*. Oxford: 1896.

——— *The Essentials of Buddhist Philosophy*. Honolulu: Office Appliance Co., Third ed. 1956.

Takasaki, Jikido. *A Study on the Ratnagotrivibhāga*. Serie Orientale Roma, XXXIII. Roma: Istituto Italiano per il Medio ed Estremo Oriente, 1966.

——— *Nyoraikei Kyōten*. Tokyo: Chūō-kōronsha, 1975.

Thomas, E. J. *Early Buddhist Scriptures*. 1935.

Thurman, Robert, A. F. *The Holy Teaching of Vimalakīrti*. Pennsylvania: Pennsylvania State University Press, 1981.

Tsukinowa, Kenryū. *Zōkanwa Sanyaku Gappeki Shōmankyō Hōgatsudōji-shomonkyō*, Hōdōkai, 1940.

Tucci, G. *Minor Buddhist Texts*, Serie Orientale Roma IX, Part I. Roma: Istituto Italiano per il Medio ed Estremo Oriente, 1956.

——— *Pre-Diṅnāga Buddhist Texts on Logic*. Baroda: 1929.

Ui, Hakuju. *Shodaijoron Kenkyu* (*Studies of the Mahāyāna-saṃgraha*). Tokyo: Iwanami Shoten, 1935.

Van Bragt, Jan. trans. Keiji Nishitani. *Religion and Nothingness*. Berkeley: University of California Press, 1982.

Watsuji, Tetsurō. *Genshi Bukkyō no Jissen-tetsugaku* (*Practical Philosophy of Primitive Buddhism*). Tokyo: 1927.

Wayman, Alex and Hideko trans. *The Lion's Roar of Queen Śrīmālā*. New York and London: Columbia University Press, 1974.

Wogihara, Unrai, ed. *Abhisamayālaṃkār'ālokā Prajñāpāramitāvyākhyā*. Tokyo: Toyo Bunko, 1932–35.

——— ed. *Bodhisattvabhūmi*. Tokyo: Seigo Kenkyukai, 1930–1936. Reprinted Tokyo: Sankibo Buddhist Book Store, 1971.

——— *Bon-wa Dai-jiten* (*Sanskrit-Japanese Dictionary*). Tokyo: 1940–1948; Tokyo: Suzuki Research Foundation, reprint 1965. Expanded and reprinted in 1979.

——— *Bukkyō Jiten* [= *Mvy*]. Tokyo: Heigo Shuppansha, rev. ed., 1929.

——— ed. *Spuṭārthā Abhidharma-kośa-vyākyā*. Two Parts. Tokyo: Sankibo Buddhist Book Store, 1971. First published in 1936.

Wogihara Unrai Bunshū (*Collected Works of Dr. U. Wogihara*). Tokyo: 1938.

Yamaguchi, Susumu. *Bukkyo-gaka Josetsu* (*An Introduction to Buddhist Studies*). Kyoto: Heirakuji Shoten, 1961.

——— *Bukkyō ni okeru Mu to U tono Tairon* (*Controversy between the Theories of Nonbeing and Being in Buddhism*). Tokyo–Kyoto: Kōbundō-shobō, 1941.

——— *Chūkan Bukkyō Ronkō* (*Mādhyamika Buddhism Miscellanies*). Tokyo: 1944.

——— ed. Sthiramati, *Madhyāntavibhāga-ṭīkā*. Nagoya: Libraire Hajinkaku, 1934. Reprint Tokyo, 1966.

——— "Trisvabhāvanirdeśa of Vasubandhu, Skt. text and Japanese translation with annotation," *Journal of Religious Studies*, new series No. 8, 1931, pp. 121–130, 186–207. Reprinted in *Yamaguchi Susumu Bukkyogaku Bunshu* (Tokyo: Shunjusha, 1972).

——— *Yamaguchi Susumu Bukkyogaku Bunshu*. Tokyo: Sunjusha, 1972.

B. Journal Articles

Bareau, A. "Index of *Viṃśatikā* & *Triṃśikā* of Vasubandhu." *Vak* no. 3. Poona: 1953.

Frauwallner, E., ed. "Dignāga, sein Werk und seine Entwicklung." *Weiner Zeitscrift für die Kunde Süd-und Ostasiens* III. 1959.

Gokhale, V. V. "Fragments from the Abhidharmasamuccaya of Asaṃga." *Journal of the Bombay Branch, Royal Asiatic Society*. N.S., 23. 1947.

Johnston, E. H. and Kunst, A eds. "The Vigrahavyāvartanī of Nāgārjuna with the author's Commentary." *Mélanges chinois et bouddhiques*, Neuvième volume 1948–1951.

La Vallée Poussin, Louis de. "Le petit traite de Vasubandhu-Nāgārjuna sur les trois natures." *Mélanges chinois et bouddhiques*, 2e vol., 1932–33, pp. 147–161.

Nagao, Gadjin, M. For a complete list of articles used in the publication of this book, consult "Appendix—Sources of Essays" on page 227.

——— "Chūkan-tetsugaku no Komponteki Tachiba (The Fundamental Standpoint of the Mādhyamika Philosophy)." *Tetsugaku* (Journal of Philosophical Studies), nos. 366–371. Kyoto: 1947–1948. Reprinted in *Chūkan to Yuishiki*. John Keenan trans. *Fundamental Standpoint of Mādhyamika Philosophy*. New York: SUNY Press, 1989.

——— "An Interpretation of the Term "Saṃvṛti" (Convention) in Buddhism." *Silver Jubilee Volume of the Zinbun-Kagaku-Kenkyūsyo*. Kyoto: Kyoto University, 1954.

——— "The Terminologies of the Mahāyāna-sūtrālaṃkāra" (in Japanese). *Journal of Indian and Buddhist Studies*, vol. 4, 2. Tokyo: 1956.

Organ, Troy Wilson. "The Silence of the Buddha." *Philosophy East and West,* IV, 2. July. Honolulu: University of Hawaii. 1954.

Obermiller, E. "The Sublime Science of the Great Vehicle to Salvation." *Acta Orientalia,* 9. 1931.

Takazaki, Jikiko. "Āśrayaparivṛtti and Āśrayaparāvṛtti." *Nippon Bukkyō Gakkai Nempō,* 25. 1960.

Yamaguchi, Susumu. "Jñānasārasamuccaya." *Otani Gakuho,* XIX, 4.

——— "Vigrahavyāvartanī." French translation. *JA,* 1929.

C. Chinese / Pāli / Sanskrit / Tibetan Texts

Abhidharmakośa-bhāṣya of Vasubandhu, Pradhan, Prahlad ed. Patna: 1967. See also, *Taishō* vol. XXIX, no. 1558.

Abhidharma-kośa-vyākyā. Wogihara, Unrai, ed. Two Parts. Tokyo: Sankibo Buddhist Book Store, 1971. First published in 1936.

Abhidharma Samuccaya of Asanga. Pradhan, Pralhad, ed. Santiniketan: Visva-Bharati, 1950.

Abhisamayālaṃkārālokā Prajñāpāramitāvyākhyā. Wogihara, Unrai, ed. Tokyo: Toyo Bunko, 1932–35.

Aṅguttara Nikāya, iii, 65, 3.

Aṣṭasāhasrikā. Unrai Wogihara, ed.

Bodhicaryāvatārapañjikā, Prajñākaramati's Commentary to the Bodhicaryāvatāra of Śāntideva. La Vallée Poussin, Louis de., ed. Bibliotheca Indica, N.S. no. 983. Calcutta: 1901–1914.

Bodhisattvabhūmi. Dutt, Nalinaksa, ed. Patna: K. P. Jayaswal Institute, Tibetan Sanscrit Works Series, vol. VII. 1966.

Bodhisattvabhūmi. Wogihara, U., ed. Tokyo: Seigo Kenkyukai, 1930–1936.

Bodhisattvabhūmi. Taishō, vol. XXX.

Buddhabhūmyupadeśa. Taishō, vol. XXVI.

Ch'êng wei shi lun. Shindō Edition. Nara: Shōsōgaku Seiten Kankōkai, 1930. See also, *Taishō* no. 1585, vol. XXXI.

Cūḷasuññata sutta. Majjhimanikāya, sutta no. 121.

Daśabhūmika-sūtra. Radher, J., ed. See also, Kondō, Ryūkō, ed.

Derge Tanjur, Tokyo University edition.

Dīgha-Nikāya, ix (Poṭṭhapāda-sutta); xvi (mahāparinibbāna-sutta); xxix (pāsādika).

Hua-yen Wu-chiao-chang. *Taishō*, vol. XLV, no. 1867.

Hor chos 'byung (*The Buddhist History of Mongolia*). Written by Āyurvardhana or Jigme Rigpi-dorje.

Kāśyapa-parivarta a Mahāyānasūtra of the Ratnakūṭa Class. von Staël-Holstein, Baron A. Shanghai: Commercial Press, 1926.

Kuan Wu-liang-shou ching shu. *Taishō*, vol. XXXVII.

Lalitavistara. Lefmann, S., ed. Halle A. S. 1902–08. See also, *Taishō* vol. III, nos. 186, 187.

Lam-rim chen-mo. Tsong-kha-pa. *TTP.* vol. 152, no. 6001.

Laṅkāvatāra-sūtra. Nanjio, B., ed. Kyoto: Otani University Press, 1923.

——— *Four chüan Laṅkāvatāra*. *Taishō*, vol. XVI. no. 670.

Madhyamakāvatāra. La Vallée Poussin, Louis de, ed. St.-Pétersbourg: 1912.

Madhyamaka-hṛdaya. *TTP.* vol. 96.

Madhyāntavibhāga-bhāṣya. Nagao, Gadjin M., ed. Tokyo: Suzuki Research Foundation, 1964.

Madhyāntavibhāga-śāstra. Pandeya, R. C., ed. Delhi: Motilal Banarsidass, 1971.

Madhyāntavibhāgasūtrabhāṣyaṭīkā of Sthiramati. Part I. Bhattacharya, V. and Tucci, G. eds. Calcutta Oriental Series no. 24. London: Luzac, 1932.

Madhyāntavibhāgaṭīkā. Yamaguchi, S., ed. Nagoya: Librairie Hajinkaku, 1934; reprinted Tokyo, 1966.

Mahāparinibbāna-sutta.

Mahāvagga.

Mahāvyutpatti. R. Sakaki. Kyoto: Shingonshu Kyoto Daigaku, 1916. K. Nishio. *A Tibetan Index to the Mahāvyutpatti*. Kyoto: Isseido Publishing Co., 1941.

Mahāyānasaṃgraha in E. Lammote, ed. *La somme du grand véhicule*. Louvain: Bureau du Muséon, 1938.

Mahāyāna-saṃgraha-bhāṣya. *Taishō*, vol. XXXI.

Mahāyānasūtrālaṃkāra. Sylvain Lévi, ed. Paris: H. Champion, 1907.

Majjhima-nikāya, sutta 28; sutta 38; sutta 63 (Māluṅkyāputta); sutta 72 (Vacchagotta): sutta 121.

Mdo sde rgyan gyi 'grel bshad (*Sūtrālaṃkāra-vṛtti-bhāṣya*). Tanjur, Peking edition. vol. Mi. Reprinted Peking edition. no. 5531, vol. 108. *Derge Tanjur.* Tokyo University edition. vol. Sems tsams 3.

Mūlamadhyamakakārikās (mādhyamikasūtras) de Nāgārjuna, avec la Prasannapadā Commentaire de Candrakīrti. La Vallée Poussin, Louis de, ed. Bibliotheca Buddhica IV. St.-Pétersbourg, 1903–13.

Nyāya-ṣaṣṭika. Yamaguchi's Japanese translation in *Chūkan bukkyō Ronkō* (*Mādhyamika Buddhism Miscellanies*). Tokyo: 1944.

Pāli-tipiṭaka.

Prajñā-pradīpa-mūlamadhyamaka-vṛtti. TTP.

Prajñā-pradīpa-ṭīkā. TTP.

Prajñāpāramitā-piṇḍārtha-saṃgraha in E. Frauwallner, ed. "Dignāga, sein Werk und seine Entwicklung," *Wiener Zeitscrift für die Kunde Süd-und Ostasiens* III. 1959.

Prajñā-pāramitopadeśa. Taishō, vol. XXV.

Prasannapadā. See *Mūlamadhyamakakārikās* above.

Ratnāvalī.

Ratnagotravibhāga Mahāyānottaratantra-śāstra. Johnston E. H., ed. Patna: Bihar Research Society, 1950.

Saddharmapuṇḍarīka. Pūrvayoga-parivarta.

Saṃdhinirmocana Sūtra in Lamotte, É., ed. *Saṃdhinirmocana Sūtra, L'explication des mystères.* Louvain-Paris: 1935.

Saṃyutta-nikāya. iv; xxii; xxxiii; lxxxvii.

Śikṣāsamuccaya. Bendall, C., ed. Bibilotheca Buddhica, I. St.-Pétersbourg: 1897–1902.

Sphuṭārthā Abhidharmakośavyākhyā. Yaśomitra. Wogihara, Unrai, ed. Tokyo: Sankibo Buddhist Book Store, 1971 reprint. First published in 1936.

Ta-ch'eng-i-chang. Taishō. vol. XLIV.

Taishō Shinshu Daizokyo. Takakusu, J. and Watanabe, K. eds. Tokyo: Taisho Issaikyo Kanko Kwai, 1927.

Tattvasaṃgraha-pañjikā. Gaekwad Oriental series edition and Bauddha Bharati series edition.

Triṃśikā in *Matériaux pour l'étude du système Vijñaptimātra.* Lévi, Sylvain, ed. Paris: 1932.

Trisvabhāvanirdeśa in Yamaguchi Susumu, "Trisvabhāvanirdeśa of Vasubandhu, Skt. text and Japanese translation with annotation." *Journal of Religious Studies*, new series no. 8, 1931, pp. 121–130, 186–207. See also La Vallée

Poussin, Louis de. ''Le petit traite de Vasubandhu-Nāgārjuna sur les trois natures.' *Mélanges chinois et bouddhiques*, 2e vol., 1932–33, pp. 147–161.

Udāna I.

Vajracchedikā Prajñāpāramitā. Conze, E., ed. Roma: IsMEO, 1974.

Vigrahavyāvartanī in Johnston, E. H. and Kunst, Arnold. eds. ''Vigrahavyāvartanī of Nāgārjuna with the author's Commentary.'' *Mélanges chinois et bouddhiques*, vol. IX, 1948–1951. S Yamaguchi. French translation. *JA*, 1929. G. Tucci. English translation *Pre-Diṅnāga Buddhist texts on Logic*. Baroda: 1929. S. Yamaguchi. Japanese translation (incomplete). *Mikkyō Bunka:* 1949–50. See also, Bhattacharya, K. *The Dialectical Method of Nāgārjuna* (*Vigrahavyāvartanī*). Delhi: Motilal Banarsidass, 1978.

Vijñaptimātratāsiddhi in La Vallée Poussin, Louis de, ed. and trans. *Vijñaptimātratāsiddhi—La Siddhi de Hiuan-Tsang*. Paris: Librairie Orientaliste Paul Geuthner, 1928. See also *Ch'êng wei shi lun*. Shindō Edition. Nara: Shōsōgaku Seiten Kankōkai, 1930. *Taishō* no. 1585, vol. XXXI.

Viniścaya-saṃgrahanī—Yogācārabhūmi. *Taishō* no. 1579, vol. XXX; *TTP* no. 5539, vol. 110.

Visuddhimagga.

Index of Terms

A

abandon moral precepts, 91
Abhidharma: philosophy, 20, 55, 56, 174; pluralistic realism, critique of, 213
Abhidharmic: dharma-theory, 167; philosophy, 163, 164, 186; realism, 179, 187
absolute: as universal subject, 10; emptiness, 45, 113, 216; emptiness (chen-k'ung) and wondrous being (miao-yu), 216; negation, 41, 73, 211; Reality, 15, 17, 156, 192
abyss of depravity, 21
acceptance: general (popular), 13
adventitious defilement (āgantuka-kleśa), 117
affliction: is itself enlightenment, 147; is itself bodhi (enlightenment), 142
affirmation: of this world, 33
agent: nouns, 10; as subject in the act of knowing, 11
aid for penetration: (nirvedhabhāgīya), 244
all entities, 53, 93, 175; are empty, 209, 212
all-seed-conscience: (sarva-bījaka), 39
almsgiving, 77
annihilation: of the basis, 80; of defilements, 59; of this world, 35
American Academy of Religion, 228
apparition, 69, 71
appearance: as khyāna, 141, 142; as occurrence, 43, 44; imagined nature as, 10, 73; of Buddha's threefold body, 106; of bewilderment/affliction, 183; of magical creations, 70, 72
appearance-only, 72, 73
appearer: 10–12; as the "transactor of linguistic conventions", 11; functions as the mediator, 11
Arhatship, 9, 23, 52
arithmetical remainder, 59
Aristotelian metaphysics: the principle of contradiction, 157
ascending: a Bodhisattva as a Buddha to be, 32–34; as aspiration to maintain liberation, 220; as merit transfer, 152; Hinayanic Arhat's aim, 9; in terms of five mārgas, 222, 236; to the Pure Land, 202
ascent: and descent, 201–06; and descent are the one and same, 32–34, 205; as a way to interpret the teaching, xii; as one of two directional tendencies, 220–25; āśraya-parāvṛtti as, 118, 120; from world of convention and language, 4, 5, 21; motivating power of, 33; notion of ascent and descent found also in Christianity, 202
attached: to the absolute, 64
attachment: being free of, 71; to the world, 70
attachment-action, 17
attainment: of Buddhahood, 9, 113; of fruit, 27
ātman-theory, 9
atoms: (paramāṇu), 165
austerity, 31
awakening: initial, 251; the thought of enlightenment, 85
awareness of self, 7, 8, 195, 196, 198, 206
awakened one, 103

B

bag-a', 34
basic principle: of Buddhism, 64
basic: āśraya, 64, 76, 121, 145, 243, 245–47, 250; ālaya-vijñāna as, 79–80; as

C

cognition-only: as mind-only, 117; as representation-only (vijñapti), 182, 244, 245; established once but negated, 244; theory of, 66, 72, 147
cognitive functions: thoughts of ordinary people, 195
commandments: of the Buddha, 48
coming down, 20, 32, 201, 205, 220
coming-hither, 32
common: as ordinary or vulgar, 13; man, 7, 39; meeting ground, of Buddhas and sattvas, 21; sense, 13, 22, 143
compassion: descends to saṃsāra, 32, 34, 172, 203–06, 220–22; of bodhisattva, 22, 26–30, 87, 88, 114, 151–52; karuṇā, *see also* upekṣa, 92; of buddha, 46–49, 110, 224; one of the four brahma-vihāras, 92, 102
compounded, 28, 164, 180
concentration: of a mind that is signless (animittaṃ cetosamādhiṃ), 52
conditioned: (saṃskṛta) dharmas, 164
conditionedness, 176
Confucianism, 7
consciousness-only, xi, 184, 215
consummated nature (pariniṣpanna-svabhāva), 10–12, 55, 59, 62, 67–74, 130–38, 140–48, 184–86, 214, 242, 257; defined, 244; denotes the world of enlightened ones, 229–30
consummated world, 63–66, 68, 70, 116, 120, 142, 146, 182–83, 242, 243
contaminated world, 63
contaminations or defilements, 58
contingent existence: (upādāya-prajñapti), 45
contradictory expressions: (vyatyasta-pada), 56
continuity of existence: i.e., corporeal, material existence of sentient beings, 125
continuity-series, 130
convention: to be concealed, 4, 13–16, 18–20, 181, 193, 212, 231, 238; to cover universally, 212
conventional: existence, 20; terminology, 15; recovery of, 180
conventional truth: definition of, 178; refers to ordinary truth, 178
conversion: (parāvṛtti) as convertibility, 65; as a turn-about, 4; from being to non-being, 130; from cause to effect, 126; from contamination to purity, 80; of one's whole existence, 115; of the world, 131; of the imagined nature of the world into the consummated nature, 131, 137, 140–48; of the other-dependent to the other-dependent, 134; of the other-dependent into the consummated, 137, 140–48, 184; of the other-dependent to the imagined, 140–48; of the world through non-discriminative wisdom, 69; similes of, 68–73; procedure of, 139; to an awakened state, 183; to the Mahāyāna of the persons of the two vehicles, 151
convertibility: as evolving of cognition, xi, 68, 124, 125, 131–32, 135, 136, 152, 243; as sequence of exposition, 125; as translation of prayāya, 243; as the turning around of the basis, 152; between kāraṇa and kārya, 128, 130; found in the three-nature system, 132; from bewilderment/affliction to an awakened state, 183; idea of, 65; includes various notions, 243; indicated by expression paryāyeṇa, 135; illustrated by similes, 72–74; of the other-dependent, 134; logic of, xi, 1, 4, 123–53, 147–48, 152; principle of, 146; of three natures, 68, 138–42, 187; *see also* vijñāna-pariṇāma, āśraya-parāvṛtti, parināmakī (merit-transfer); structure of, 150
converting cognition (vijñāna): into wisdom (jñāna), 125
corporeal: being, 52, 58; body, 79
correctness and straightness: of mind, 97
Cosmical Body: of the Buddha, 76, 79
Cosmological theory: of Buddhism, 157
covered truth, 18
covering: the Absolute, 14; the truth, 19
covering-manifesting, 21, 22
Creation Hymn: (Nāsadīya) of *Ṛg-veda*, 156
crossing over, 65, 66, 243; from this shore to the other shore, 65
crucifixion and resurrection, 202
crystal: (sphaṭika) simile of, 72

D

deception, 69, 181
deep compassion, 29, 32, 203, 220
defilement: (kleśa), 11, 24, 30, 59, 60, 66, 102; as obstacle of (kleśāvaraṇa), 32; accidental or adventitious (āgantuka-kleśa),

E

K

karman, 10, 30, 38, 112, 114, 130, 160, 259
keeping the defilement, 31
kenosis, 114
knowledge, 252, 260: acquired subsequently, 204, 223; analytical, 73; consummate nature as, 71; conventional, 193; disordered, 158; equipment (saṃbhāra) of, 252; highest (abhiñña), 38; human, 182; in the stage of preparatory practice, 204; non-discriminating, 101–02; non-discriminative, 184, 204, 224–25; of absolute, 42; religious, 160; transformed, 144; sambodhi, 41
Kusinãra, 28

L

Lamaism: in Mongolia, 2
languor or torpor: *see also* styāna, 94
last refuge or shelter, 76
liberation: (vimukti), 91, 220
life-death cycle: is itself cessation (saṃsāra is nirvāṇa), 214
lineage: (gotra) of the Buddha, 119
living beings: attaining Buddhahood, 115
locus: (āśraya), 55
logic: of identity, 148; of Love, 46, 48; of metaphysics, 155; of niḥsvabhāva (no self-nature), 179; of the mundane world, 47; of the Yogācāra School different from Madhyamaka School, 123
logical fallacies, 47
Lord Bhagavān, 52
love: towards humanity, 49
lowly beings, 30
lucidity: of mind, 60
lust and hate, 36

M

Madhyamaka, xi, xii, 2–4, 123, 124, 173, 181, 190, 198, 211, 216, 222, 240, 255, 261; philosophy, xi, 2, 173, 255, 261
Madhyamic: logic, 46; philosophy, 40, 41, 47–49
Mādhyamika, 1–5, 8, 9, 11, 13, 18, 19, 33, 34, 41, 46, 106, 123, 124, 173, 174, 180, 181, 186, 189, 190, 196, 198, 199, 211–16, 219, 221, 222, 225, 230–32, 238, 243, 255, 260, 261
magic show, 61, 67, 69–74; simile of, 71, 72, 74
magical creation: (nirmāṇa), 30
magically created: elephant, 70; form, 61, 69
magician, 61, 69–71
Mahāyāna, xi, xii, xiii, 1, 2, 4, 9, 13, 21–24, 28, 32, 33, 35, 38, 39, 40, 48, 51, 52, 61, 66, 74, 75, 83, 84, 87, 88, 95, 97, 99, 104–06, 109, 113–15, 119, 124, 127, 133, 134, 137, 139, 141, 142, 144, 147, 148, 151, 155, 166, 168, 173, 176, 181, 189, 191, 198, 201, 202, 209, 210, 211, 219, 220, 222, 223, 225, 229–30, 232, 233, 242, 245, 249, 251, 252, 254–59, 261
making service: to others, 29
manic depression, 94
manifestation: of the Perfect, 22; of truth (hsien-cheng), 217
mark: of pragraha (uplifting), 95; of śamatha, 95; of upekṣā, 95
marklessness: (nirnimittatā, nirnimittavihāra), 100
mastership, 79
matter: is emptiness, 170; emptiness is matter, 168
matrix; of the tathāgata, 57
maturation, 79, 84, 114, 144
meditation, 51, 52, 58, 92, 94, 158–60, 169, 182, 186, 210, 214, 215, 249, 261
meditational exercise: (bhāvanā), 95
medium or mediator: other-dependent nature as, 65
mental: depression, 92, 93, 95, 99, 101; dharmas, analysis of, 165; exaltation (auddhatya), 92–95; factors, 91–93, 97, 102, 147, 247, 248; inactivity, 93
Merit Buddha: as one of four Buddhas of *Laṅkāvatāra*, 114, 253
merit-transference, 83, 86, 148–52, 202, 258, 259; in an ascending direction, 152; in the aspect of going forth, 202
merits and virtues, 85
metaphysical: questions, 38, 43; speculation was "without profit (attha)", 38; topics, 38
metaphysics, 155
middle: always revealed by being freed from two extremes, 194

O

P

R

S

U

V

Index of Tibetan Terms

Index of Chinese and [J]apanese Terms

Index of Chinese and Japanese Terms

Index of Sanskrit Terms

A

akarmaṇyatā, 93; lack of agility or dexterity, 144
acintya, 15, 89
acintyatā, 40
acintya-pariṇāmikī: as what is transferred inconceivably, 89
  acintya-pariṇāmikī-upapatti, 88; "birth of inconceivable merit-transference" *MSA* XI.56 (Chin.), 151
ajñāna: not knowing, 14
atyantābhāvata: absolutely free [of sense-object], 141
advaya, 28, 29
  advayā vṛttiḥ, 28
adhigama, 206; as one aspect of "realization" or enlightenment, 206; definition of, 205
adhiprajñā: prajñā which is nirvikalpa-jñāna, 223
adhimukticaryā-bhūmi, 30
anabhilāpya, 15; ultimate reality beyond grasping, 192
  anabhilāpyatva, 40
anabhisaṃskāra, 96, 99, 100
anātmakatva, 56
anātman: as a teaching in which the belief that existence has an inherent nature is negated, 7, 166, 168; as negation of fundamental ātman, 170; as non-self, 168; explanation of, 164; foundation for Primitive Buddhism's questioning ātman, 160; manifested through Buddha's life and his activities, 163; one of the dharma-seals of Buddhism, 162
anābhoga: effortlessness, 100
anābhoga: effortlessness, 100
  anābhogatā, 93, 99; *see* also upekṣā, 92
anāsrava-bīja, 145
  anāsrava-dhātu: sphere of purity, 80
animitta: non-existent sign, one of three doors of deliverance, 169
  animittaṃ cetosamādhiṃ: as concentration of mind that is signless, 52
  animitta-sasaṃskāra, 100
  animitta-anabhisaṃskāra, 100
anityatā: as foundation of Sarvāstivāda teaching, 166
anityā: impermanence, 130, 168
aniyata-gotra: those not yet settled as śrāvakas, 88
  aniyata-gotra-śrāvaka, 85
anuttarāyai samyaksaṃbodhaye, 85
anupalabdhi: in the sense of "beyond our cognition", 212; ultimate reality beyond grasping, 192
  anupalabdhi-śūnya: non-perceptibility, 41
anumāna, 46: actual form of reasoning or syllogism, 46
anyathātva: as definition of pariṇāma, 125
anyonya-samāśrayeṇa: with one depending upon another, 15
aparapratyaya, 41
apraṇihita: negated wish, one of three doors of deliverance, 169
apratiṣṭhita, 24, 25, 27, 28; various English translations of, 172
  — nirvāna, 23–27, 29, 32, 33, 172, 203, 222; abides not in Nirvana, 22; as expression of āśraya-parāvṛtti, 143; Mahāyānic nirvāṇa, 222; not entering nirvāṇa, 88; suggests direction of descent in Yogācāra, 222

Ā

KH

G

CA

J

T

prayoga: actual form of reasoning or syllogism, 46; logical syllogism, 67
prayoga-mārga: preparatory stage, 224
prayukta-jana, 78
pravṛtti: coming forth, 14
pravṛtti-vijñāna: seven functioning cognitions, 128; six cognitions, 221
praśaṭha, 97, 99; prakrit form of Skt.
praśratha, 97; tranquil flow, 98
praśaṭhatā, 93, 96, 99; *see* upekṣā, 92
praśaṭhatva, 99
praśaṭha-svarasa-vāhitā; as definition of upekṣā, 98
praśrabdhi: alleviatedness, 102
prasaṅga, 211
prāsaṅgika: deconstructive reasoning, 213; one of two Madhyamaka Schools, 46, 47, 231
prahāṇa-saṃskāra, 98
prāyogika-jñāna, 204; first division of nirvikalpa-jñāna, 223
prārthanā, 85, 89

PHA

phala: as Buddhahood that results from three learnings, 222
phala-jñāna, 24; as corresponding to Buddha's abhisaṃbodhi, 28
phala-pariṇāma: see twofold evolving, 127
phala-prahāṇa, 24; as corresponding to Buddha's parinirvāṇa, 28

B

bāhyārthābhāva
claim of Later Vijñāna-vāda, 198
bīja, 79; affliction as bīja (seed) for attainment of nirvāṇa, 148; ālaya-cognition as hetu, 127
bīja-parāvṛtti, 80
buddha-karman, 112
buddha-kāya, 10, 103; as goal of āśraya-parāvṛtti, 121
buddhatva, 57
buddha-dharma, 43
buddha-dharma-paripāka, 111
buddha-bhūmi, 79, 221
bodhi, 66, 91; as the ascent of the two-direction activity, 205
bodhicitta, 84
bodhicittotpāda: mind creative of Enlightenment, 76
bodhi-pariṇāmanā, 85
bodhisattva, 9, 78; description of, 119
bodhisattva-bhūmi: of *Yogācārabhūmi*, 55
bodhisattva-mārga, 21, 22, 32, 84, 86, 87, 99
bodhisattva-yāna, 189
bodhgaya: Gautama realized mahābodhi, 203
bodhyaṅga, 92, 101
brahma-vihāra, 92
brahmā, 31; creator god, 112
brahmātman, 8; in the Upanishads, 128
brahman, 64; as prayer, 161; essence of the universe, 161; the Absolute, 112

BH

bhava: existence, 89; world of existence, 88
bhavopapatti, 29
bhājana-loka, 143; "I" as a sentient being in outer world and the outer world, 159
bhāvana, 95
bhāvanā-mārga, 79, 100
bhāṣya, 190
bhikṣu, 36; who are addicted to pleasures, 167
bhūta-koṭi, 87; equated with śūnyatā, 215
bhūmi, 30, 84, 86, 99; the 4th stage, 87; the 8th stage, 100
bhrānteḥ saṃniśrayaḥ: *see* basis for confusion, 144

M

madhyamā pratipat, 190; in the context of *MMK*, XXIV.18, 205; signifies move from pratītyasamutpāda through śūnyatā to upādāya-prajñapti, 194, 123
manas, 9, 221; ātma-cogitation, 121
manasaḥ-parāvṛtti, 80
mano-vijñāna: mind-consciousness, 121; minding-cognition, the sixth cognition, 139, 145; refers to parikalpa (what discriminates), 139

vijñāṇa-vāda: Cognition School established on vijñapti-mātra, 181
vijñāna-saṃtāna: continuity-series of cognition, 130
vinaya, 104, 167
vipaśyanā: intuitive discernment, 95; (or pragraha) if applied wrongly is auddhatya as only correct vipaśyanā is remedy for laya, 96
vipaśyanā-nimitta, 95
vipāka, 79
vipāka-kāya: Result-maturation Body, 114
vibhāga, 46
vibhutva, 30; as āśraya-parāvṛtti, 143; mastership, 79; state of power, 80
vimukti: liberation, 80, 91, 220, 222
vimukti-kāya, 24, 113; emancipation body, 114
vimukha, 87
vimokṣa: as āśraya-parāvṛtti, 143
viśeṣa-saṃjñā, 191
vīrya, 77, 95; energy of right practice, 77; right effort, 77
vṛtti, 107
vedanā, 92
Vaibhaṣika, 164
vyañjana: sexual organ, 77
vyatyasta-pada, 56
vyavasthāna, 16
vyavahāra, 15, 16, 18, 45, 46
vyavahārtṛ: transactor of linguistic conventions, 11

Ś

śāṭhya: a mental factor, 97
śabda, 132
śama: = nirvāṇa, 29
śamatha, 94, 95: *see* three marks, 94
śamatha-nimitta, 94
śamatha-vipaśyanā: obstacles for equilibrium of upekṣā, 96; synthesis of, 96
śamatha-vipaśyanā-yuganaddha, 51
śāśvata-vāda, 39
śikṣā (trīṇi śikṣāṇi): (three) learnings, 24
śīla, 32
śūnya, 41, 43, 44, 45, 61, 89, 100; etymology and definition, 209; mathematic zero, 209; not simply a refutation or negation, 181; seen in *Samādhi,* 169; term not found in *Varjracchedika-prajñā-pāramitā-sūtra,* 168; world devoid of the absolute, 64
śūnyatā, xi, xii, 1, 3, 4, 8, 13, 29, 33, 34, 40–49, 51–60, 64, 73, 74, 84, 93, 100, 105, 107, 110, 113, 114, 117, 120, 123, 124, 149, 150, 156, 157, 166, 168–73, 175–77, 182, 185, 187, 190–99, 201, 204–06, 210, 215, 216, 219, 220, 221, 225, 232; absolute negation, 73; analyzed into three, 55; as non-substantiality, 41; based on the baseless, 173; Bhāvaviveka attack on *MV.* I.1c, 198; Buddha's real essence, 107; established by negating the "duality" of subject and object, 198; in the context of *MMK,* XXIV.18, 205; negation of existence, one of three doors of deliverance, 169; simultaneously non-existent as well as existent, 198; summit of prajña (ascent) and karuṇā (descent), 221; the place where adhigama and āgama meet, 206; true meaning of, 54
śūnyatā-paramārtha, 42
śūnyatā vidyate tv atra, tasyām api sa vidyate: (*MV.* I.1 c,d), 195
śūnyataiva rūpaṃ: emptiness just as it is is being, 210
śūnyavāda, 213
śraddhā-vīrya-smṛti-samādhi-prajñā: the five faculties, 51
śrāmaṇas, 167
śrāvaka, 78, 88
śrāvaka-yāna, 88
śvi: to swell; verb root for śūnya, 209

S

sa prajñaptir upādāya pratipat saiva madhyamā: see *MMK,* XXIV.18cd, 190
saṃvara: election, choice, 14
saṃvartate: to turn; to go towards, 14
saṃvṛti, 47; conceals and covers ultimate truth, 137; conventional world, 47
saṃvṛti-mātra, 22, 181

H